THE AUTHORS

GODFREY VESEY is Emeritus Professor of Philosophy at The Open University, and Fellow and Vice-Chairman of The Royal Institute of Philosophy. He is the author, co-author, or editor of some thirty philosophy books, including twelve volumes of Royal Institute of Philosophy Lectures.

After studying mathematics and philosophy at the University of Sydney, PAUL FOULKES came to London, where in 1957 he obtained a PhD in philosophy at University College. He then became a publisher's editor, and from 1957–59 collaborated with Bertrand Russell on *Wisdom of the West*. Since 1963, he has been a freelance editor and translator. In the early 1970s he published a number of articles on philosophical logic. His interests include certain fundamentals in Greek mathematics.

COLLINS
DICTIONARY OF
PHILOSOPHY

G. Vesey and P. Foulkes

COLLINS
London and Glasgow

First published 1990

© G. Vesey and P. Foulkes 1990

ISBN 0 00 434370 0

British Library Cataloguing in Publication Data
Vesey, Godfrey
Collins dictionary of philosophy. (Collins reference dictionaries)
1. Western philosophy
I. Title   II. Foulkes, Paul
190

Printed in Great Britain by Collins, Glasgow

FOREWORD

Very likely, wisdom can neither be learnt nor taught, and if it could, then not in alphabetical order. However, this arrangement is suitable for conveying information. Hence this small collection, a kind of 'Who is Who and What is What in Philosophy'.

There are already many books of reference in this field. Some of them aim to include everything. What we here present is different. So far as we are able, we have tried to deal with central figures and issues, hinting at the intellectual flavour of each thinker and at the wider importance of general problems. Also, a certain amount of philosophical vocabulary must be explained, especially where it differs from ordinary usage.

Given so small a space for so large a field, the list of headwords had to be selective. Others would no doubt have chosen differently, but we trust that the most vital items are included. As long as people read philosophy, Plato and Aristotle will survive, while lesser, local sages now in vogue will vanish without trace.

Our list is anglo-centric, but covers western thought as a whole. What is said about philosophies from other areas is sketchy but at least acknowledges that they exist. The treatment of each item is not exhaustive, nor do we give bibliographies for further reading.

The work bears the mark of two authors, rather than a whole team. Each of us has gone over the other's work, but doubtless the book would have been different had we changed roles, each writing the other's entries. Our philosophical backgrounds differ somewhat, going back more than forty years to Cambridge, England (G.V.) and to Sydney, Australia (P.F.). Such divergence leaves enough general agreement to make mutual comment profitable, even if in the end we agree to differ on some points. Entries on Ancient Philosophy have had critical comment, kindly provided by Professor Myles Burnyeat of Cambridge, though he is of course not answerable for the views finally expressed.

Where so much remains controversial, one should not wholly hide one's own point of view, even if this were possible. What our leanings are will be clear enough. Those who disagree can then rehearse their own reasons for taking another view. There are in any case many questions in this field whose answers, if they are ever found, lie a long way ahead.

This fits in with our foremost aim: to capture our readers' interest, in the hope that they will pursue their inquiries further in more detailed works. If that happens, we shall not have laboured in vain.

P.F.   G.V.

A NOTE TO THE READER

For an overview of the contents of this dictionary, the following core entries can be read first: **empiricism, rationalism, idealism, existentialism, scepticism, metaphysics, epistemology, logic, ethics philosophical analysis, mind,** and **matter**. Cross-references from these will then lead into related entries.

Another way to the same end is to start by reading the entries on some key figures such as **Plato, Aristotle, Aquinas, Descartes, Leibniz, Locke, Berkeley, Hume, Kant, Hegel, Russell** and **Wittgenstein**.

Entries are listed in alphabetic order. The entry word is shown in **bold**, followed by an abbreviation for the relevant part of speech, in *italics*. Cross-references are marked in SMALL CAPITAL LETTERS. The cross-referencing is not comprehensive, but aims to point to selected entries for further explanation. In any entry a given cross-reference figures only once, when the word first occurs.

A

Abelard, Peter (1079–1142) French SCHOLASTIC philosopher and theologian. In the controversy on UNIVERSALS (whether what is general really exists or is merely a matter of naming by us), he took up a critical position that differs both from the extreme NOMINALISM of his teacher Roscelin (for whom a universal is just a 'breath of the voice') and the equally extreme REALISM of William of Champeaux (who saw universals as being in each thing that comes under them). On the former, it looks as if the Holy Trinity breaks up into three separate GODS (the doctrine was condemned at the synod of Soissons in 1092) (see CHRISTIANITY); on the latter, it is difficult to see how things can be separate at all. Abelard pointed out that though all existing things were individual, what named a universal was a term with meaning or significance, which functions as a PREDICATE in a PROPOSITION. Different things were not just called by the same word but shared real features. In his ethical thought he stresses the vital role of intention in moral action. This tends to emphasize our own attitudes and turns away from the influence of GOD (though not excluding it, nor yet incompatible with it). As a result, Abelard repeatedly clashed with church authorities. Though acknowledging the place of faith, he insisted that we must make full use of the reason that God has given us. He was popular as a teacher and attracted great crowds of students. The story of his passion for Heloise is one of the great love stories of history.

absolute, *n*. (from Latin *absolutus* loosened from, hence complete, unconditioned, independent) the opposite of relative. It enters philosophic vocabulary in the late 18th century. The absolute, as figuring in the German idealists of the period, means that which is unconditioned and is variously taken as the identity of knower with known (Schelling), the rational totality of thought (HEGEL), or simply the whole.

abstraction, *n*. the process by which we arrive at general words. A general word, such as 'man', is one that can be used generally, to refer to any man; unlike 'George Bush', which refers to a particular man.

ABSTRACTION

Philosophers give different accounts of abstraction. ARISTOTLE held mathematical features, such as circularity, not to exist separately from the things we describe as circular. Nevertheless, they can be treated as separate. He called them 'abstractions', and described the process by which the mathematician arrives at them as one in which he 'strips off all the sensible qualities . . . and leaves only the quantitative and continuous' (1061 a 29). This is a metaphor. One can strip off clothes and paint, but not the SENSIBLE qualities Aristotle mentions, such as weight and hardness. Elsewhere Aristotle says that it is 'possible to familiarize the pupil with even the so-called mathematical abstractions only through induction' (81 b 1). INDUCTION is the process whereby, from sense-perception of particulars, someone acquires an intuitive knowledge of UNIVERSALS. Perhaps Aristotle used the phrase '*so-called* mathematical abstractions' to convey that the reality behind talk of 'abstraction' is induction. However, he gives no plain account of induction. He says 'it is like a rout in battle stopped by first one making a stand and then another' (100 a 11).

For subsequent developments of ABSTRACTIONISM what matters in Aristotle is rather what he says about sense-perception. Although the FORM, circular, does not exist objectively apart from circular things, such as hoops, it can do so subjectively. When someone perceives a hoop the form of the hoop, circular, enters his soul, but not the MATTER of the hoop, the wood of which it is made. The form, as it exists in the soul, is what the word 'circular' directly symbolizes (16 a 3). Thus, if there is a process of abstracting at all, it is performed by the sense organs. Aristotle does not draw this inference, but several medieval philosophers do. Besides, we find in medieval philosophy the notions that different things resemble one another and that the mind can consider just the resemblance; and that what is in the mind is just as particular as the thing perceived but can serve as an image for all things similar to it.

Of modern philosophers who use the word 'abstraction' the best known is LOCKE. He assumes that words have MEANING by being signs of IDEAS, so that there must be general ideas for general words to signify. General ideas are got by separating ideas 'from the circumstances of time and place and any other ideas that may determine them to this or that particular existence' (*Essay*, III iii 6). They are 'the workmanship of the understanding'. The work is tricky: the general idea of a triangle 'must be neither oblique nor rectangle, neither equilateral, equicrural, nor scalenon; but all and none of these at once'

(*Essay*, IV vii 9). 'One has reason to suspect that such ideas are marks of our imperfection.' Perhaps Locke means that if we were perfect we could think and communicate directly in language without the mediation of general ideas. Not so BERKELEY: he holds that though we are not perfect we can think without abstract ideas. He ridicules the view 'that a couple of children cannot prate together of their sugar-plums, and rattles, and the rest of their little trinkets, till they have first tacked together numberless inconsistencies and so framed in their minds abstract general ideas' (*Principles*, Introduction 14).

The assumption that words have meaning by being signs of ideas has been disputed by WITTGENSTEIN, who holds that words have meaning by virtue of their use (see MEANING). It is a mistake to look for the use of a sign 'as though it were an object *co-existing* with the sign' (*The Blue and Brown Books*, Oxford, 1958, 5).

Following Wittgenstein, Peter Geach, who calls the doctrine that CONCEPTS are acquired by a process of abstraction 'abstractionism', says that the doctrine is 'wholly mistaken': 'no concept at all is acquired by the supposed process of abstraction' (*Mental Acts*, London, 1957, 18).

abstractionism, *n*. the doctrine that CONCEPTS are acquired by a process of ABSTRACTION.

academy, see GREEK ACADEMY.

accident, *n*. (from Latin *accidere* to happen) in Aristotelian LOGIC something that is irrelevant to the DEFINITION of an individual. It is essential to SOCRATES that he is of the species man, and genus animal, but an accident that he is white, or that he runs. ARISTOTLE called species and genera 'secondary SUBSTANCE' because they are the only PREDICATES that convey the ESSENCE of an individual being (or 'primary substance'). Hence the SCHOLASTICS distinguished between 'substantial FORMS' and 'accidents', the latter being thought of as not existing independently of the former.

action, *n*. both jogging and sweating are things people do, and one can ask both why someone goes jogging and why someone is sweating. Jogging is said to be an activity, or an action, but sweating is not. Why?

ARISTOTLE's treatment of MOTION (especially in *Physics*, Bk. 8, Ch. 5) suggests an answer. Someone has to do something, such as exercising or going to the Turkish Baths, to make himself sweat, but not to bring about his jogging. Furthermore he is not himself an intermediate link in an instrumental chain. Man is 'a movent that is not so in virtue of being moved by something else'.

3

DESCARTES has a different answer. To bring about jogging a man *does* have to do something: he has to perform an act, or acts, of will. These mental acts somehow produce the changes in the brain that cause the bodily movements the will aims at (see VOLITION).

Again, consider how we decide why someone goes jogging and why someone is sweating: people have *reasons* for jogging (see MOTIVE), and there are *causes* for their sweating. If someone is both jogging and sweating, the 'action description' of what he is doing answers to his interests, purposes and intentions.

In some way the person who acts is better able to say what he is up to than anyone else, but the action description he gives is not necessarily true. Even if he is not lying, he can be mistaken about causal matters, or about conventions, or about both. The jogger who, on being asked what he is doing, says 'keeping fit', may be wrong because he does not know that his over-activity is putting too much strain on his heart. A learner-driver who says he hand-signalled a right turn may be wrong because he does not know the difference between a turning-right signal and a slowing-down signal. The more basic an agent's action description of what he is doing, the less chance there is of his being wrong. Jogging is more basic than keeping fit, and sticking one's arm out is more basic than signalling. Some philosophers talk of a 'basic act', as though there were one action description in giving which an agent cannot be wrong. This is questionable. If an obedient patient who has lost sensation in one arm is asked to put the affected hand on top of his head while his eyes are closed, but his hand is held down, he will be very surprised on opening his eyes to find that the movement has not taken place. A Cartesian would say that at least he cannot be wrong about having willed the movement, but why should an 'act of will' be 'basic'? Others would say that the patient had not done anything, but merely thought he had. See FREEWILL AND DETERMINISM.

actuality and potentiality, in Aristotelian philosophy are related to FORM and MATTER. So far as the matter, brass, is concerned there is the potentiality of a candle-stick, a vase, a paper-weight. The actuality is the candle-stick, and so on. Matter without any form ('prime matter') has no actual existence; to exist it must have a form. So, in a sense, actuality is prior to potentiality. ARISTOTLE associates this with the doctrine that everything exists for the sake of an end.

aesthetics, *n*. (from Greek *aisthetikos* concerning perception) since A. J. Baumgarten (1714–62) the theory of the beautiful (see BEAUTY). Just as

ETHICS deals with questions of values in human actions, so aesthetics is concerned with values in works of art or in the appreciation of beauty in nature. Like ethics, aesthetics is a branch of practical philosophy, and subject to the same kind of difficulties. Amongst philosophers, it remains controversial whether there are objective aesthetic values at all, or whether beauty lies in the eye of the beholder. PLATO took the former view, although his treatment in terms of the THEORY OF FORMS ('it is by beauty that beautiful things are beautiful' *Phaedo*, 100d, cf. *Hippias Major*, 287c) does not tell us anything about beauty itself. At the opposite end of the range is the view that judgments concerning beauty are private, so that if I find something beautiful, nobody can gainsay: it is a matter of taste, and about that there can be no disputing. This second, subjective view is the normal position of the unreflective. At present, subjectivist theories seem to prevail. One current view links beauty with emotional attitudes. The extreme case is simply to dismiss aesthetic theory. Certainly it is difficult to talk sensibly about beauty.

An allied aesthetic concern has been to define art. This is a more specific question, since beauty is found also outside man's artistic creations, in nature. A general account of the whole range of artistic activities will not tell us much about any one part of it. The branch most widely discussed has been literature, which usually describes human situations and does not step outside the human sphere (descriptions of events in nature occurring only in so far as they impinge on a beholder). Literary theory begins with ARISTOTLE's *Poetics*, which largely sums up the practice of the great Athenian dramatists of the 5th century BC.

As for the 'fine arts' (drawings, painting, sculpture), if they are representative, whatever may be represented provides some criteria, though perhaps not all. If the works are abstract, it becomes less clear how to cope with them. Finally, music; the art of sound is a case apart. What is a beautiful tune? The music lover will no doubt recognize one when he hears it, but what can he say about it?

This last example brings out the general feature of attempts at aesthetic theory: what is there to say, and how are we to say it? The subjectivist simply leaves everybody to decide individually what is beautiful. A more subtle theory figures in Kant's *Critique of Judgment* (1790) (see KANT). He argues that aesthetic experience is a disinterested pleasure taken in some particular object; this pleasure is universally valid but not to be framed in general terms, and therefore not a matter of the understanding or of reason, but of 'judgment'. This still does not tell us much.

One who asserts that aesthetic values are OBJECTIVE must go on to tell us what specific features he is looking for, and at first blush the choice seems arbitrary: how can he defend what he chooses against what others choose? Still, that is not the main trouble: he could simply state that he was right and all the others wrong; that they might outnumber him no more makes their consensus right than the fact that at one time most people thought the earth was flat means that it was flat at that time. The difficulty is rather that the objectivist must give us some hints towards a definition, so that we have some rough notion where to look.

This may require a measure of training: the eye and the ear must be educated in order to perceive certain features, as must one's linguistic powers in order to assess literary worth. Such complications seem to be dispensable for the subjectivist, since he need merely attend to his feelings. Indeed, subjectivist theories have a certain egalitarian flavour—everyone can have his own view and it will be just as good as the next man's—which is one reason why they are so popular. By contrast, objectivism requires discrimination and rational judgment, and will therefore appeal at best to a minority (as does scientific theory in general).

The view that some appreciation of art has an important place in education goes back to Ancient Greece, where the practice of 'music' (that is, those arts presided over by the 'Muses') was regarded as vital in the moulding of young aristocrats. Since the 18th century ENLIGHTEN-MENT, a training in the elements of some at least of the arts has become widely accepted as a desirable part in any proper education. Thus children are taught to draw and paint, sing and play music, perhaps even to dance and write poetry. This is not meant to produce masterpieces, but to give pupils a feeling for these arts from within. One who has tried to draw simple shapes is better able to appreciate and understand the works of the great masters, and similarly for the other arts.

This raises an interesting question: is everybody amenable to this kind of aesthetic training? Different people certainly show more, or less, aptitude in this field, but do they all have at least some? The assumption seems to be that they have, just as we assume that everybody can be taught the elements of arithmetic. However, there seem to be a few who are tone-deaf, just as some are number-blind.

This can of course be made worse through bad teaching, but the condition is real enough.

These circumstances somewhat favour an objectivist approach: there is actually something there to be learnt and judged. It is the mark of the educated that they can perceive and appreciate such things. Education of course does not mean schooling, although schooling should aim at providing education. A sense for the beautiful is indeed often acquired by independent individual effort. Finally, aesthetics in the widest sense has to do with the setting in which we live and with the quality of the lives we lead. Without a sense of aesthetic appreciation we do indeed tend to spoil our own habitat.

a fortiori, *adv.* (*Latin* from the stronger) a term used in argument to show that a statement holds on stronger grounds than another already mentioned. Roughly equivalent to 'even more so'.

Keen eyesight is needed to become an engine driver, a fortiori it is needed to become an airline pilot.

agnosticism, *n.* (from Greek *a* not, *gnostikos* suitable for knowing) the view that our powers of knowing are bounded in certain regards, more particularly as to the ultimate reasons for things, and especially concerning the claims of religious dogma. The term 'agnostic' was coined by T. H. HUXLEY (1869) to distance himself from those who had set metaphysical views.

The notion that some things are unknowable is very old. ARISTOTLE's Prime Mover, needed to explain movement, cannot himself be known or explained (see FIRST MOVER). The *via negativa* in medieval theology is on similar ground in stating that we cannot know what GOD is, but only what he is not. A systematic account of the limitations of human knowledge is contained in the critical philosophy of KANT. In 19th century thought, this was further developed in critical work on METAPHYSICS and religion. In line with the romantic temper of the age, it was felt that such things lay beyond the reach of rational grasp, but might nevertheless be felt or experienced. Metaphysics and religion are thus taken to concern mood rather than reason. Today the term is mainly restricted to an attenuated denial of religious dogma: where ATHEISM rejects these outright, agnosticism remains non-committal about them. However, it can still be used to refer to a doubting attitude about certain basic theoretical views in science, such as those about the origin of life.

Albert the Great, St (*c.*1200–1280), a SCHOLASTIC philosopher and theologian who studied in Italy and taught in Paris, where Thomas

AQUINAS was his pupil, and at Cologne. He wrote commentaries on ARISTOTLE in the Neo-Platonist tradition. See NEO-PLATONISM.

Alexander, Samuel (1859–1938), Australian philosopher who became professor at Manchester, the main realist thinker (See REALISM) of his generation. He is best known for his *Space, Time and Deity* (1920) in which he worked out a metaphysic that enabled him to deal with the central problems of philosophy from a realist point of view (see META-PHYSICS, REALISM). He regards the world as set in space and time. From them develop organisms through various levels, evolving upwards to a higher one he calls 'deity'. A general notion of emergent evolutionary development had been put forward previously by Lloyd Morgan.

Within SPACE AND TIME everything that goes on is marked by a set of general features or CATEGORIES. Relations, too, are simply in space and time. As to COGNITION, knowing consists in one process being aware of another which is present to it: what knows (the mental act) is 'com-present' with what it knows (its OBJECTS), without at the same time looking at itself. Thus in knowing we do not 'know' ourselves (our minds) but other things, which exist in their own right.

Alexander rejects idealist speculation as handed down from the 19th century (see IDEALISM) and insists on things existing independently in one universal space–time. His views have influenced the work of John ANDERSON.

alienation, *n.* (from Latin *alienus* strange) estrangement, in philosophy, denotes the action (or its result) of estranging things or people from what is considered to be their proper state. The term was first used by HEGEL to describe what happens to 'absolute spirit' when it objectifies itself in the physical world of nature, a digression that is repaired when the spirit returns to itself in contemplating what we call the humanities (for him, and in German, 'sciences of the spirit'). Similarly for the individual who becomes alienated from himself when not living in the light of self-awareness, which is his task as part of the ABSOLUTE.

The notion of alienation was taken up by MARX, who sees in it the actions that deprive a man of the things he produces so that he becomes enslaved. He is then estranged from his true ESSENCE as a free man who works out his own destiny, and so becomes a mere object used by others. For Marx, this can be mended only by destroying the economic system that thus enslaves man.

This way of looking at the loss of free agency is likewise found in EXISTENTIALISM, when people lead inauthentic lives because they have made a wrong choice and are thenceforth divorced from their true selves (see BAD FAITH).

In a general way, sociologists use the term to refer to individuals or groups who have become disenchanted with their place in a community.

ambiguity, *n*. (from Latin *ambiguus* going both ways). **1**. the fact of several meanings (in particular two) attaching to a term, so that a sentence containing it has no determinate sense.

2. any statement that can be taken in more than one way. It is often the main point at which an argument breaks down.

analogy, *n*. (from Greek *ana* according to, *logos* proportion) a resemblance, in quality or structure, which enables us to pursue an argument in the same way as has already been done in another, resembling case. The original meaning of the term comes from Greek MATHEMATICS, where it denotes proportionality.

analysis, see PHILOSOPHICAL ANALYSIS.

analytic and synthetic (from Greek *analyo* put asunder, *syntithemi* put together) two terms introduced into philosophy by KANT, who classified PROPOSITIONS into analytic and synthetic. In the former, the SUBJECT is merely explicated by the PREDICATE, in which it is already contained. An analytic proposition does not convey new information but merely clarifies a term. In the synthetic case, the predicate adds something new and thus gives us additional KNOWLEDGE. This division cuts across a second one, also used by Kant, of propositions into A PRIORI and A POSTERIORI, according to their arising before or after EXPERIENCE respectively. Thus we have a four-fold classification: analytic *a priori* propositions are those that are true or false as a matter of LOGIC alone; synthetic *a posteriori* those that concern matters of empirical fact; analytic *a posteriori*, which are generally regarded not to exist, but might be taken to be those that arise when we frame new definitions in the light of experience; and synthetic *a priori*, which are preconditions of experience (hence *a priori*) and yet tell us something new, according to Kant. This last group is typical of his approach and remains highly controversial to this day: examples for him are all mathematical propositions, and the principle of causality (see CAUSE). There are many who would say that mathematical propositions are not synthetic and that the principle of causality is not *a priori*. As regards causality, Kant is right: our being able to experience anything at all presupposes causality. It follows that experience cannot show that causality ever breaks down, which in turn has important consequences in the way we must interpret certain scientific findings. As to MATHE-MATICS, opinions remain divided. There is the more general question whether any propositions are genuinely analytic: on this, too, thinkers are not unanimous. Kant argues that mathematical propositions are *a priori* and not empirical, because they carry necessity with them. However, they are not analytic, because they convey new information rather than just taking given CONCEPTS apart.

Kant regards a proposition as analytic if in denying it we are contradicting ourselves. An example might be the principle of IDENTITY, *A* is *A*, which cannot be denied without CONTRADICTION. Thus we may expect to find analytic propositions in the field of FORMAL logic, although these are clearly somewhat peculiar as propositions. Still, if one denies a synthetic proposition, *A* is *B*, one does not produce an immediate contradiction: it could well be that *A* is not *B*. All the same it is not entirely without consequence to suppose things to be different from what they are, because this may involve hidden contradictions. Arguing in this way can carry certain risks.

anarchism, *n.* (from Greek *an* not, *arche* rule) a condition in which there is no rule of any AUTHORITY. In political theory, this is described as a form of social arrangement in which people pursue their own affairs without impairing the scope of others. Whether this can be implemented on a large scale is very doubtful. In communist theory (see COMMUNISM), the political State will in the end wither away and leave humanity in an ungoverned or anarchic situation. See POLITICAL PHILOSOPHY.

Anaxagoras (*c*.500–*c*.428 BC) born at Clazomenae, near Smyrna in Ionia, Anaxagoras was the first philosopher to settle in Athens, where he spent much of his life. He wrote one book, copies of which could be made in Athens for one drachma in 399 BC. Fragments of it have survived. He was a close friend of the Athenian statesman Pericles, was prosecuted for impiety (holding the sun to be a red-hot mass of metal), and spent the last few years of his life in exile at Lampsacus, a colony of Miletus on the southern shore of the Hellespont. He died in the same year as PLATO was born.

Like the Milesians (see MILESIAN SCHOOL), Anaxagoras was concerned with the material of, and the moving force behind, the world. The following is a reconstruction of his thought, for which there is some evidence in the surviving fragments.

First, the material of the world. We can distinguish between *homoeomerous* things, like bone, the parts of which are the same (they are bone, also), and *non-homoeomerous* things, like arms, the parts of which are not the same (the parts of an arm are not further arms, but a hand, wrist, fore-arm, etc.). Non-homoeomerous things can be analysed into a variety of different homoeomerous things; e.g. an arm consists of, among other things, bone. Homoeomerous things are infinitely divisible into things of the same kind. But that is not the end of the story, for if the ultimate substance of the world were infinitesimal particles of all the different homoeomerous things it would not be possible to explain how things can appear to change into one another. Anaxagoras needed to explain how, in nutrition for example, food seems to change into the flesh of the person who eats it. His ingenious explanation was that a homoeomerous thing, such as bone, is apprehended as such because of the predominance of the quality of boniness in what has in fact, but in smaller proportions, all the other qualities (corresponding to all the different kinds of homoeomerous things). If, which is impossible, we could complete the infinite division of things into smaller and smaller pieces, the ultimate stuff of the universe would turn out to be of as many different kinds as there are different homoeomerous things, each distinguished by the predominance of one characteristic among as many characteristics as there are homoeomerous things. What appears to be change in substance—for example, from food to flesh—is really change in what quality predominates. In a sense the flesh is 'in' the food. What happens is that the flesh quality becomes predominant through a decrease in the proportion of the other qualities. The key idea is that of extraction.

Second, the moving force (the cause of movement or change). This is NOUS (Mind), the finest and purest of all things, with KNOWLEDGE about everything. Initially there was a motionless mixture of everything (v. ARISTOTLE, *Physics* 250 b 24). *Nous* caused this mixture to rotate; and this rotation mechanically caused the processes of extraction whereby things change as they do. Besides being the cause of the initial rotation of the mixture, there is a portion of *Nous* in living things.

Anaxagoras' originality lay both in what he said about the material of the world, and in what he said about the moving cause. He was criticised by Plato (*Phaedo* 97–98) and Aristotle (*Metaphysics* 985 a 18) for, as Aristotle put it, using reason as a *deus ex machina* and only dragging it in when he could not explain things otherwise. He did not use it, as they would have liked, as a FINAL CAUSE of everything. See PRE-SOCRATIC PHILOSOPHY.

ANAXIMANDER

Anaximander (*c*.610–*c*.547 BC), a pupil of THALES of Miletus. He led a colonizing expedition to Apollonia (on the Black Sea). He is said to have invented the gnomon (a vertical rod whose shadow indicates the sun's direction and height) to tell the time of day and time of year, to have constructed a spherical model of the universe with the earth remaining at rest at the centre simply because it was at the centre and so had no reason to move in one direction rather than another (the first use of the principle of SUFFICIENT REASON) and to have made a map of the known world (but of the sort which Herodotus, the first of the great Greek historians, later said made him smile).

Unlike Thales, Anaximander published a book. Theophrastus (a pupil of ARISTOTLE), and probably Aristotle himself, had knowledge of it. Simplicius, a 6th century Neo-Platonist, gave an account, largely derived from Theophrastus' writings, of Anaximander's theory about the *arche* (first principle) and ELEMENT of existing things. Thales had said it was water. Anaximander said it was neither water nor any other of the so-called elements, but 'a different substance which is *apeiron*' (usually translated as 'boundless' or 'unlimited'). This, together with a remark about things perishing into the things out of which they have their being, is the main indication we have of Anaximander's view.

Aristotle (*Physics* 204 b 24) suggests that Anaximander thought of the *arche* as qualitatively indefinite (neutral between the elements, the hot and the cold, the dry and the moist): if it were not, but were one of the elements, then, since the elements are opposed to one another, that element would 'annihilate' the others. By his remark about things perishing into the things out of which they have their being, Anaximander meant that, given that none of the elements are the real element, one element gives rise to its opposed element which in turn gives rise to the element out of which it has arisen, much as cold wet winter leads into hot dry summer, and vice versa. According to Theophrastus, Anaximander wrote of the opposed elements 'making recompense to one another for their injustice'. This is the first appearance of the idea of JUSTICE as a principle of COSMOLOGY, standing for law and regularity as against divine whim. See ANAXIMENES, MILESIAN SCHOOL, PRE-SOCRATIC PHILOSOPHY.

Anaximenes (*c*.587–*c*.527 BC), citizen of Miletus and pupil of ANAXIMANDER. He wrote a book that was known to Theophrastus (a pupil of ARISTOTLE).

Whereas THALES had held the first principle and element of existing things to be water, and Anaximander said that it was the boundless,

Anaximenes' view is summed up by Theophrastus as follows:

> Anaximenes, a companion of Anaximander, also says that the under-lying nature is one and infinite like him, but not undefined as Anaximander said but definite, for he identifies it as air; and it differs in its substantial nature by rarity and density. Being made finer it becomes fire, being made thicker it becomes wind, then cloud, then (when thickened still more) water, then earth, then stones; and the rest come into being from these.

With Anaximander the emphasis had been on 'the first principle' (starting point or originating cause); with Anaximenes it shifted to 'the element' and so to the explanation of how this element can change its appearance, by natural processes of rarefaction and condensation, from being fire, at one extreme, to stones, at the other. Though implausible today, it was an advance on Anaximander's explanations of change in terms of the give and take of the opposed elements, the hot and the cold, the dry and the moist. It invoked only one element, with a directly substantial name; it specified a non-metaphorical process of change (Anaximander, according to Theophrastus, had written of the opposites 'making reparation to one another for their injustice'); besides, the process was one that was quantifiable, and so amenable to mathematical treatment, though he himself was not aware of this.

From Anaximenes' point of view the choice of air as the element moreover explained what for Anaximander had been merely an assumption, namely that the first principle and element was in some sense alive, and so in a state of self-caused motion. The Ancient Greeks identified air (or breath) with life (cf. PLATO, *Phaedo*, 96b, and DESCARTES, who, in the *Second Meditation*, admitted to having once thought of his soul as 'something subtle like air or fire'). If the element of all existing things is air, then the desire, which may have been so general as not to be recognised as such, to think of the elemental matter of things as alive (HYLOZOISM) is satisfied. Thales, by making the first principle water had made a move in this direction, for moisture is life-giving. Anaximenes, by making it air, completed the move. See MILESIAN SCHOOL, PRE-SOCRATIC PHILOSOPHY.

Anderson, John (1893–1962), Scottish philosopher, professor at the University of Sydney (1927–1958), was the founder of what has since been called Australian Realism. He early reacted against the IDEALISM dominant in the Glasgow of his student days and was influenced by other anti-idealist thinkers such as William JAMES, the young Bertrand

RUSSELL and G. E. MOORE at Cambridge, the New Realists in North America and above all by Samuel ALEXANDER, who delivered his Gifford lectures (*Space, Time and Deity*) in Glasgow, 1916–1918.

Anderson's central position is that all events are complex states of affairs existing at one and the same level in SPACE AND TIME. Thus he rejects 'simples' and 'ultimates' of any kind: sense-data (see SENSE-DATUM), atomic facts (see ATOMISM), the absolute whole of the idealists, and the CLEAR and simple IDEAS of the rationalists (see RATIONALISM). We apprehend the world directly, without an intermediary level of items ('ideas') whose only function is to convey, for how could we apprehend these in turn? What we know are states of affairs existing independently of us in space and time, and our cognitive processes are likewise spatio-temporal. It is pointless to invent special entities for what we observe (such as substances to act as carriers of properties, in the way of ARISTOTLE), since these would have to exist on a separate level of their own and could never be known. All KNOWLEDGE comes from EXPERIENCE, under a set of categorial features (see CATEGORIES), which are common to all fields (in addition, there are of course more restricted features that characterise special fields). MATHEMATICS is just as much in the external world as other facts are. As for LOGIC, Anderson gave a comprehensive account of the logic of ordinary discourse, centring on the question of whether something is so or not so. His logical position informs his discussions on ETHICS, politics and AESTHETICS.

angst, *n.* (*German* fear), a term introduced into philosophy by existentialist thinkers (see EXISTENTIALISM). It denotes the state of mind produced when a person becomes aware of being finite in a world that is infinite. The source of this feeling of apprehension is ultimately the infinite nature of nothingness (or the void).

animism, or **panpsychism,** *n.* the theory that not only other human beings, and not only other animals, but also plants, and even things we do not ordinarily regard as living, have souls. In modern philosophy it is of interest mainly as a corollary of an even more speculative theory, PSYCHICAL MONISM. This is the theory that things which appear to us as material are 'in themselves' psychical. The theory was put forward as a pure speculation by Immanuel KANT (*Critique of Pure Reason*, 1781, A359). It may have been suggested to him by his reading of G. W. LEIBNIZ. The theory was taken up enthusiastically by G. T. Fechner in Germany (see William McDougall, *Body and Mind*, 1911, Ch. 11), by W. K. Clifford in England ('On the Nature of Things-in-Themselves',

Mind, 1878), and by C. A. Strong in America (*Why the Mind has a Body*, N.Y., 1903). Most present-day philosophers regard psychical monism as too metaphysical for serious consideration. Some do not regard physical monism ('physicalism' or 'MATERIALISM') in the same light.

Anselm, St (1033–1109), born at Aosta (Piedmont), entered the Benedictine order, becoming prior and later abbot in the Norman monastery of Bec. In 1093 he succeeded his former teacher, Lanfranc, as Archbishop of Canterbury. Anselm produced a version of what KANT later called 'the ONTOLOGICAL ARGUMENT' for the existence of GOD. Perhaps developing an idea for a DEFINITION of God he found in one of St AUGUSTINE's critical works on MANICHEISM, Anselm argued, in Chapters 2 and 4 of his *Proslogium*, as follows: (a) God can be thought, and is that than which a greater cannot be thought. (b) If something can be thought it is possible for it to exist. (c) Something which exists is greater than something which is merely thought. Therefore (d) God exists. (e) Something can be thought of as existing which cannot be thought of as not existing (f). This must be greater than something which can be thought of as not existing. Therefore (g) God cannot even be thought of as not existing. Therefore (h) someone who says there is no God cannot rightly understand what he is saying.

To follow this argument one would need to know what is meant by 'greater' in PROPOSITIONS (c) and (f). One may understand, say, 'Plato is a greater philosopher than Thales', without understanding 'Something is greater in virtue of existing'. Moreover, one can understand proposition (e) in FORMAL disciplines like MATHEMATICS and LOGIC. For example, the prime number between 3 and 7 can be thought of as existing, but not as not existing. What is meant by proposition (e) in connection with God?

A logical positivist is more likely to wonder about this than a Platonist (see LOGICAL POSITIVISM; PLATONISM). Anselm was familiar with Platonist thought through his reading of AUGUSTINE. In an earlier work, the *Monologion*, Anselm advances arguments for the existence of God which are clearly indebted to Plato's THEORY OF FORMS. The only element in these arguments not traceable to Plato's published works was the identification of God with the FORM of the Good. It may have been because Anselm wanted a proof of God's existence which was not obviously dependent on the acceptance of Platonist thinking that he progressed from the obviously Platonist arguments of the *Monologion* to the ontological argument in the *Proslogium*. Ostensibly the ontological argument is self-sufficient.

antinomy, *n*. (from Greek *anti* opposite, *nomos* law) in philosophy, contradictory conclusions apparently deduced correctly (see DEDUCTION). A series of these is set out in KANT's First Critique. For example, argument is exhibited to show both that the world must have a beginning, and that it cannot have. The premisses of these arguments are of course different.

a posteriori, see **a priori and a posteriori.**

appearance, *n*. (from Latin *apparentia* a becoming visible) constrasted with REALITY (from Latin *realitas* thinghood); philosophers traditionally consider how the two are related.

According to one use of the term 'appearance', the shape something appears to be to a given point of view is determined entirely by the laws of perspective. Thus a round object, seen from a point of view at a certain angle to its surface, will present an elliptical appearance. LEIBNIZ called this the 'optical' appearance.

To determine what optical appearance an object presents to a point of view it is not good enough to ask someone who occupies the point of view. He is almost certain to err on the side of the real shape he believes the object to be. Only if he erects a transparent screen at right angles to his line of vision of the object, and traces the object's outline on it, will he get its optical appearance right. In the case of an illusion, such as that given by the Müller–Lyer figure (Fig. 1), lines which are the same length in the original will be the same length in the tracing (i.e. in the optical appearance). In an ambiguous figure, such as the one which can be seen as a duck looking in one direction or a rabbit looking in the other (Fig. 2), the same ambiguity will appear in the tracing as in the original. In a quite different sense of 'appears', the lines in the Müller–Lyer figure will appear unequal in length, and the ambiguous figure will look to a perceiver either like a duck or like a rabbit.

The same philosopher often uses 'appearance' in both senses in the same context. REID, for example, remarks on the artist's need to acquire 'the habit of distinguishing the appearance of objects to the eye, from the judgments we form by sight, of their colour, distance, magnitude and figure' (*Inquiry into the Human Mind* VI 3). If we look at the sea from a cliff-top the 'judgment we form by sight' may be of a sea that is uniformly blue. To create this impression in the picture the artist must use a dark shade of blue for the near sea, a light shade for the far sea, and intermediate shades in between. To know what shade to use he must attend to the sea in a manner that must be learnt and may be described as attending to the optical appearance. However, Reid is not writing about the optical appearance when he says that the masters in painting 'know how to make the objects appear to be the same colour by making their picture really of different colours'; he is using the word 'appear' with the sense it has in the true proposition 'The person who draws the Müller–Lyer figure knows how to make lines of equal length appear to be unequal'. How things appear, in this sense, normally determines what people judge themselves to be looking at. We add 'normally' to provide for the exceptional cases in which a person has reason to think that things are not as they appear. This sense of 'appears' may thus be called the 'cognitive' ('pertaining to knowledge') appearance.

(a)

(b)

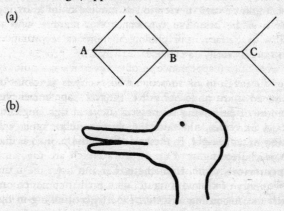

appearance (a) the Müller-Lyer figure, BC appears to be longer than AB.
(b) the duck/rabbit.

There are four related conceptual differences between cognitive and optical appearances. (a) Cognitive appearances are SUBJECTIVE, whereas optical appearances are OBJECTIVE. The optical appearance of an object to a point of view is a function of the object's real figure, colour, and spatial position, but of nothing else. There would still be optical appearances of objects to points of view even if all sentient life ceased to exist. Cognitive appearances of objects appear to sentient beings that can recognize them. (b) If something cognitively appears to somebody, he must know that it does; if optically, he need not. Psychological

17

experiments have shown that even if somebody is trying to attend to the optical appearance he may get it wrong. (c) Something can cognitively appear to somebody only if he possesses the appropriate CONCEPT (e.g. the duck-rabbit can look like a duck only to someone who knows what a duck looks like); not so for optical appearances. (d) Cognitive appearances are related to their objects by being true or false of them. For example, the lines in the Müller–Lyer figure look unequal in length, but this appearance is non-veridical; really they are equal. Nature has seen to it that we normally see things as they are, and so have occasion to say 'It appears to be . . .' only exceptionally. Optical appearances are not true or false of the objects of which they are appearances; no more than the size of one angle of a triangle is true (or false) of the other two angles, which determine its size.

For an understanding of sense-perception as our means of knowing about the world it is the cognitive appearance that matters. This is wholly in accord with the current psychological approach according to which PERCEPTION is really a HYPOTHESIS-making process. See SENSATION.

apperception, *n.* (from Latin *apperceptio*, *ad* to, *percipere* perceive) a CONCEPT introduced into philosophy by LEIBNIZ to denote the conscious awareness of perceiving something. Beyond this empirical apperception, KANT introduced the notion of transcendental apperception, the awareness of selfhood. J. F. Herbart (1776–1841) brought the term into use in psychology.

a priori and a posteriori, (*Latin* from the earlier and from the later) terms used in the theory of KNOWLEDGE to indicate what comes before and after EXPERIENCE. According to KANT, experience itself is possible only if we have certain prior notions of space, time (see SPACE AND TIME) and causality (see CAUSE) amongst others. Some but not all empiricists will deny this, holding that any such notions come from experience, and opinions on this point continue to differ. Likewise, PROPOSITIONS are called *a priori* or *a posteriori* according to how they are related to experience: the former if they come before it, the latter if they are conveyed by it. The most obvious case of *a priori* propositions are the principles of LOGIC, without which no rational activity can arise. The case of mathematical propositions is less clear. Kant regarded them, along with the principle of causality as *a priori* synthetic. Some thinkers deny the *a priori* synthetic and hold mathematics to be analytic. In general, the *a priori* conditions that make experience possible have the force of necessity. See ANALYTIC AND SYNTHETIC.

Aquinas, St Thomas (*c.*1224–1274), born at Roccasecca near Naples, Aquinas studied under the Benedictine monks at Monte Cassino, 1230–1239, then was a student of the liberal arts at the University of Naples from 1239 to 1244, when he entered the Dominican order. From 1245 to 1248 he studied the Dominican courses in philosophy and theology in Paris, then accompanied St ALBERT THE GREAT to Cologne. He returned to Paris in 1252 and continued to teach there until 1259, having been awarded the magistrate (doctorate) in theology in 1256. From 1259 to 1268 he taught at the papal Curia in Rome, and from 1269 to 1272 again in Paris. From 1272 he taught at the University of Naples, and died in 1274 on the way to the Second Council of Lyons. From 1252 to 1273 he wrote prolifically, his two best-known books being known under their Latin titles, the *Summa de Veritate Catholicae Fidei contra Gentiles* (or *Summa contra Gentiles* for short), and the *Summa Theologica.* His philosophy has been described as a Christianized Aristotelianism: just as St AUGUSTINE had looked to PLATO and the Platonists to provide a philosophy which could be married to the revealed truths of Christianity, so Aquinas looked to ARISTOTLE and the Aristotelians. However, this overlooks significant influences from STOICISM, NEO-PLATONISM, Augustine, BOETHIUS, and the Arabian commentators on Aristotle. Aquinas's philosophy (THOMISM) is especially highly regarded by Roman Catholics. Until recently the ecclesiastical law of the Catholic Church required students for the priesthood to study at least two years of philosophy and four of theology 'following the teaching of St Thomas'. We shall consider Aquinas's philosophy under the headings:

(a) 'Five Ways' of proving God's existence.
(b) Knowledge of God.
(c) Creation.
(d) The immortality of the soul.
(e) Ethics.

(a) *'Five Ways' of proving God's existence.* Each of these concludes with some such phrase as 'and this is what we all understand by GOD', although 'what we all understand by God' is identified with a different description in each way. In the first, it is 'some first mover which is not moved or changed by any other' (Aristotle's FIRST MOVER). This is part, but not all, of what Aquinas himself understands by God, for he holds God to be a genuine creator. The second way is an extention of the argument that there must be a first EFFICIENT CAUSE of the universe. The fifth way is an argument for the existence of a supreme designer, not very different from Plato's *demiurge* or divine craftsman. Central in Aquinas's conception of God are the ideas (i) that there is something that is necessary on its own account, and (ii) that there is something that is the fount of all goodness. The ways intended to establish the existence of a being answering these descriptions are the third and fourth ways respectively. The argument of the third way is as follows: We find there to be some things which are generated, survive for a while, but then suffer corruption and perish. Their eventual corruption and cessation of existence is natural to them (they are 'contingent'). If all things were of this sort a time would come when nothing existed. Since things come to exist only through things which already exist there would then be no things existing now. But there are. So in addition to contingent beings there must be necessary ones on which they are dependent. Every necessary being either has its necessity caused by another, or not. Not every necessary being can owe its necessity to another such being: the regress cannot be infinite. So there must be some being which has of itself its own necessity, and causes theirs in others. This is God.

In the fourth way Aquinas states that we can say that one thing is better than another only if there is a best, that the best in the relevant respect causes all the things that are less good in that respect, and that, being best, it is 'greatest as regards being'. 'Therefore there is some cause of existence and goodness and whatever other perfections are characteristic of things, and this we call God'.

Aquinas says that the first of the Five Ways is the most obvious. All of them seem to involve debatable assumptions and metaphysical principles (see METAPHYSICS).

(b) *Knowledge of God.* What can we know of the God whose existence is arrived at by the 'Five Ways'? Aquinas's answer is determined by his Aristotelian approach to questions of knowledge. Man's senses and cognitive abilities can give him direct knowledge of material things, but his knowledge of God is indirect. God can be described only in negative and analogical terms. Unlike man He is not corporeal, does not occupy space, is not composed of potentiality as well as actuality, and so on. If we describe Him as living, as powerful, as wise, these terms cannot mean the same as when we use them of beings whose existence is not necessary, beings created by God. Therefore our knowledge of God must be derivative and imperfect. But this does not mean that God's existence, goodness, etc., are derivative. As Aristotle said (72 a 1, 184 a 16, 1029 b 3), what to us seems prior is not prior in the order of being.

(c) *Creation*. With Plato and Aristotle, Aquinas held that everything has some intelligible meaning, some 'form'. (The exceptions to the principle were, for Plato, the 'invisible and formless being' which is made to partake of the intelligible by a divine craftsman (*Timaeus* 51a), and, for Aristotle, 'prime matter', which is in any case only an intellectual abstraction.) Plato held the FORMS to be self-existent: they exist independently both of the SENSIBLE things which exist by 'participating' in them, and of the divine craftsman who models things in their likeness. Aristotle denied that the forms are self-existent, and St Augustine held them to be ideas in God's mind. Aquinas agreed with Aristotle and Augustine.

Plato's divine craftsman is not really a creator; he works with pre-existing materials, the Forms and the 'invisible and formless being'. Similarly, Aristotle's PRIME MOVER is not really a creator; he moves, as FINAL CAUSE, what already exists. Aquinas's God is a true creator, an efficient (see EFFICIENT CAUSE) as well as a final cause. Plotinus, and sometimes Augustine, talk of the world as flowing, or emanating, from God, which implies that God does not exist independently of the world. According to Aquinas God does exist independently of the world. God freely creates the world in order to communicate, to share out, the perfection which is His goodness, a goodness which rational creatures are capable not only of manifesting but also of enjoying.

(d) *The immortality of the soul*. Plato held that SOUL and body are distinct, and that the soul is capable of passing 'into the realm of the pure and everlasting and immortal and changeless' (*Phaedo* 78d–79d). Aristotle held that the affections of soul—passion, gentleness, fear, pity, courage, joy, loving, hating—necessarily involve a body (403 a 16), but that the mind, or power to think, seems to differ from them, and so may be immortal (413 b 25). Aquinas, like Aristotle, held the soul to be the form of the body, but did not distinguish between an intellectual and a sensitive soul in man: there is only one rational soul, the FORMAL CAUSE of all human activities. Unlike the soul of a brute, the soul of man can know the nature of all bodies and reflect on itself. It must therefore be immaterial, and therefore immortal. Moreover, we have a natural taste for IMMORTALITY, as distinct from a mere distaste for death, and God would not have given us a natural appetite which was not satisfiable.

21

(e) *Ethics*. Greek ethics was naturalistic: questions of what men ought to do were treated as questions of what was in accordance with their nature. The debate was about man's true nature. Aristotle's ethics was, furthermore, teleological (see TELEOLOGY): questions about man's true nature were treated as questions of the end for which he was naturally fitted. Aristotle's ethics was also *eudaemonological*: the fulfilment of a man's true nature was identified with his happiness or well-being. In all these respects Aquinas's ethics was like Aristotle's. The difference arose from Aquinas's other-worldly conception of man's true nature. Being a creature of God, man must have his ultimate end in God. 'Ultimate beatitude consists in the vision of the divine essence, which is the very essence of goodness.' This perfect happiness is attainable only in the next life. Actions are right or wrong in so far as they tend to lead to the happiness that consists in the knowledge and love of God. In this lies man's perfection.

argument from design, also known as the teleological argument, one of the traditional arguments for the existence of GOD, which infers from the existence of design to that of a designer. Just as when we see a house we can infer that somebody must have built it, so the fact that the world has order in it allows us to conclude that somebody has ordered it. To this argument there are many objections. For a start, the ANALOGY is wrong: a house is a specific building in a given setting, but the world as a whole is not, being not even an OBJECT of which we can have any EXPERIENCE. Moreover, the argument issues in a REGRESS: who designed the designer? In structure the argument is the same as ARISTOTLE's COSMOLOGICAL ARGUMENT, inferring from motion to a prime mover: this, too, falls to the regress objection. We undeniably observe around us a world full of processes that are tuned to each other, or adapted. However, we cannot deduce therefrom that this realises some agency's plan or purpose, let alone that such an agency is the God affirmed by some particular religion.

Aristotle (384–322 BC), born in Stagira, Macedonia. He went to Athens and entered PLATO's Academy at 18. He remained there until Plato's death in about 347 BC, when he left Athens to live for five years at Assos in Asia Minor and at Mytilene on the island of Lesbos, working on philosophy and biology. In 342 BC he was invited to return to Macedonia to tutor the son of Philip II of Macedonia, the future Alexander the Great. This occupation lasted three or four years. After a further period at Stagira, Aristotle returned to Athens in about 335 BC and opened a philosophical school at the Lyceum or

Peripatos. On the death of Alexander the Great in 323 BC there was anti-Macedonian feeling in Athens. To avoid the fate of Socrates, Aristotle fled to Chalcis on the island of Euboea, leaving the school in the charge of his pupil Theophrastus. He died in 322 BC.

Aristotle's writings comprise works published by Aristotle but now lost, as well as works (perhaps lecture notes) not meant for publication, but which were collected, edited and arranged by others and first made generally available in about 60 BC, more than 250 years after he died. Hence there is much speculation about chronology and authenticity, some of which relates to the question of the rapidity and extent of the evolution of Aristotle's thought in an empiricist (see EMPIRICISM) direction away from that of Plato. Is it possible, for example, that his criticisms of Plato's THEORY OF FORMS in his *Metaphysics* were aired in the Academy, and that Plato's apparent self-criticisms of the theory in *Parmenides* were in fact suggested by his brilliant young pupil Aristotle? Firm evidence is lacking. We shall concentrate on the extant works and treat them as the philosophy of Aristotle. The main works may be grouped as follows:

Logical works: *Categories, On Interpretation, Prior Analytics, Posterior Analytics, Topics, On Sophistical Refutations.*

Physical works: *Physics, On the Heavens, On Generation and Corruption, Meteorology.*

Psychological works: *On the Soul, On Memory and Reminiscence, On Dreams, On Prophesying by Dreams.*

Biological works: *History of Animals, On the Parts of Animals, On the Progression of Animals, On the Generation of Animals.*

Other works: *Metaphysics, Nicomachean Ethics, Eudemian Ethics, Politics, Rhetoric, Poetics.*

Aristotle's works were edited by Bekker and others for the Berlin Academy between 1831 and 1870. Standard reference is now made to the page number, column and line of this Berlin edition. We shall pick out the following for brief discussion: causation, substance, scientific knowledge, the soul and the mind, the PRIME MOVER, and the good life.

Causation. A cause (in Greek, *aitia*), for Aristotle, helps to explain why a thing is as it is. He distinguishes four kinds: 'material cause', 'FINAL CAUSE', 'EFFICIENT CAUSE' and 'FORMAL CAUSE' (194 b 19, 983 a 26, 1013 a 24). The material CAUSE is the stuff of which a thing consists; for example, the cotton cloth of which a cotton dress is made, or the cotton threads of which the cloth is woven, or whatever goes to make up the threads. 'MATTER' is a relative term: the matter which, given a certain FORM, is a certain thing, has itself a form; hence one can ask of what more basic matter any matter is constituted. The REGRESS comes to an end in four different kinds of matter: earth, fire, air and water. These are the ELEMENTS (*stoicheia*) of the world, the bodies into which all other bodies may be analysed (302 a 16). The elements must have a form, and therefore a matter. However, this 'prime matter', as Aristotle calls it, exists only as a substrate. Matter could not exist without form, nor, excepting GOD, form without matter. Form and matter are not like a container and what it contains. They are more like two aspects of a thing: the matter, the cloth, of a dress, is potentially a table-cloth, curtains, bed linen, and so on; actually it is the dress, the form the cloth has in fact taken. Matter as such exists only potentially; to exist actually it must have a form. So actuality is, in a sense, prior to potentiality (see ACTUALITY AND POTENTIALITY). This goes with Aristotle's view that everything exists for the sake of an end (199 a 30, 1050 a 7). Earlier philosophers had ascribed the coming-to-be of things to necessity, but, Aristotle says, 'nature is a cause that operates for a purpose' (199 b 32). For example, the sharpness of front teeth is to be explained not in terms of sharp-teethed animals surviving because they could tear food with their sharp teeth (survival of the fittest) (see DARWINISM, EVOLUTION) but by reference to the end (*telos*, hence TELEOLOGY) of having sharp teeth (198 b 25). 'The process of evolution is for the sake of the thing finally evolved' (640 a 18). We no longer favour teleology, partly because understanding nature is now often subordinated to controlling or changing it. That a scientist might actually work to produce mutations would have been quite alien to Aristotle. For him each thing had its own essential nature, fixed for all time. The scientist's job was to discover it. The only change allowed for in his conceptual scheme was that produced by the 'efficient' or 'moving' cause; and this was the change from what is potentially a thing of a certain natural kind to what is actually a thing of that kind. It is the form of 'formal cause' that is important to the scientist. To have scientific knowledge is to know the formal cause and this is to know the DEFINITION of the ESSENCE of a thing (see below, *Scientific knowledge*).

Substance. In his many writings on substance Aristotle was evidently trying to satisfy a number of different criteria, three of which are (a) that, unlike Plato's Forms, substances should not be separate from things apprehended by the senses, (b) that, while remaining one and the same, substances should be capable of admitting contrary qualities, and (c) that, like Plato's Forms, substances should be definable. At first he seems to sacrifice the third CRITERION to the first, for one cannot define an individual, and Aristotle, distinguishing between 'primary substance' and 'secondary substance', says that primary substances 'are the entities which underlie everything else' (2 b 16), gives as examples of primary substance 'the individual man or the individual horse' (1 b 4). However, in applying the second criterion he gives priority to definability. It is done by distinguishing between quality-terms, like 'white', and species-terms, like 'man'. A man, while remaining a man, may take on a contrary colour (for example by painting his body), but a white object, while remaining white, cannot. Thus an individual man is a primary substance, an individual white object is not. It would be less misleading to describe these examples as 'the individual members of the species human or equine, in respect of being a member of one of those species'. All now turns on the meaning of the word 'species'. (Species, and the genera to which they belong, are Aristotle's 'secondary' substances.) Aristotle says that 'while some things are not substances, as many as are substances are formed in accordance with a nature of their own' (1041 b 28). What are these intrinsic 'natures'? They are the things, sometimes called 'essences' (1029 b 15), of which the scientist has knowledge when he is able to define them (2 b 30). Hence Aristotle's third criterion of substance turns out to be the one that matters. What, then, is scientific knowledge, and how is it attained?

Scientific knowledge. Plato, influenced by PYTHAGORAS, had supposed that JUSTICE, courage, BEAUTY, and so on, are definable as is, say mathematical circularity (Plato, *Letters* 342a–344b), that the definitions are true by nature, not convention (*Cratylus* 383a–384d), and that knowledge is of these supposed definitions (which combine the properties of being necessarily true, like the definitions of mathematical terms, and true 'by nature'). Plato further supposed, rather fancifully, that we were aware of these definitions in a previous non-bodily existence, but now need to be reminded of them. In some respects Aristotle's theory of KNOWLEDGE is like Plato's, in others not. He says that the sort of things that can be known scientifically are things that cannot be otherwise (71 b 15, 73 a 21), and that they are known only when they are seen to follow from premises which are necessary (73 a 24, 74 b 5) in the way in which definitions (72 b 24, 89 a 17) are necessary. A cognitive state is thus not one of knowledge unless it is arrived at by a process of demonstration, from premises which are themselves indemonstrable. These so-called 'basic' or 'primary' premises are known in another way, by intuition (100 b 11). However, intuition does not involve recollection of what might have been apprehended in a previous existence. Particular intuitions are not innate, but are 'developed from sense-experience' (100 a 11) by INDUCTION (100 b 4), an operation that gives insight into the real essences of things. Belief in intelligible real essences is necessary for his theory that the natural sciences are like the mathematical sciences in being demonstrative and in yielding conclusions that are necessarily true.

The Soul and the Mind. Aristotle criticises those who, like the Pythagoreans with their doctrine of the transmigration of souls, 'join the soul to a body, or place it in a body, without adding any specification of the reason of their union' (407 b 15). Aristotle himself provides such a specification. It takes the form of a definition of soul in terms of one of two 'grades of actuality'. The possession of a capacity, such as the capacity to be courageous, is more than the mere potentiality of developing the capacity, but it is not the exercise of the capacity. It is what Aristotle calls 'the first grade of actuality' of the capacity. Soul, he says, is the first grade of actuality of any natural body which has, within itself, life, that is, the power of initiating changes in itself and other things. Suppose that an eye were not merely an organ of a body which has life within itself, but that it was itself alive. Then eyesight would be its soul (412 b 20). As eyesight would be to such an eye, so its soul is to any living body, whether plant or animal. Therefore the soul is inseparable from the body (413 a 4), and thus not immortal. May there not be some capacities, such as the capacity to think, that are not the actualities of a body? A soul may not be able to act courageously without involving the body, but is not thinking different? Aristotle thinks so, calls the thinking soul 'the mind', and says 'The mind seems to be an independent substance implanted within the soul and to be incapable of being destroyed' (408 b 18).

The Prime Mover. The term 'moves' is ambiguous: something may itself be moving; or it may be moving another thing, being a cause of motion. Furthermore, a cause of motion may be an 'instrumental' mover (it passes on motion derived from something else), or it may be a 'responsible' mover. A responsible mover may be either motionless or moved by itself. It may be immediately responsible for a given motion, or responsible for it only mediately, that is, through the mediation of one or more instrumental movers. In terms of these and other conceptual distinctions Aristotle develops an argument for the conclusion that there is an eternal, motionless first or prime mover that is immediately responsible for the eternal unchanging rotatory movement of a fifth element (in addition to earth, fire, air and water) at the circumference of the universe, and thereby mediately responsible for the movement of everything else (259 a 1–13). This motionless Prime Mover has a form, but no matter. It produces the rotatory movement of the fifth element as the object of love moves the lover (1072 b 3). In some respects Aristotle's theory is like a monistic version of Plato's theory in the *Laws* (894 a–907 b). One respect in which they differ is that Plato's gods were said to be 'mindful of us', whereas Aristotle's one Prime Mover is aloof. It can think only of the most excellent of things, namely itself (1074 b 34).

The Good Life. In Plato's THEORY OF FORMS there is one supreme Form, the Form of the Good. Similarly, in his *Nicomachean Ethics*, Aristotle says that there is one supreme or final end for all human endeavour. Plato's theory, Aristotle says, is not about something to be attained by man (1096 b 34). Hence it does not tell us in what the one final end consists. Aristotle takes it to be happiness (1097 b 21). What is happiness? Aristotle supposes that just as we say that a flute-player or a carpenter, as such, has a function (a defining activity) so we can talk of man, as such, having a function (1097 b 32). Man's function is what is peculiar to man, namely the activity of reasoning. Happiness for man, then, is the good performance of this activity, and the good life is the life in which this is kept up, 'for one swallow does not make a summer' (1098 a 19).

Arnauld, Antoine (1612–1694), born in Paris and ordained a priest, Arnauld was a disciple of J. Cornelius Jansen, whose book *Augustinus*, published posthumously in 1641, was critical of scholastic theology and censorious of the Jesuits. Arnauld's sister, Angelique, was the abbess of Port-Royal, where Jansen's book was adopted as the standard text. In 1643 Arnauld published a popular exposition of Jansenism, *Frequent Communion*. This led to him being persecuted, along with other Jansenists, by the Jesuits, which did not prevent him making notable contributions to philosophy, often in the form of criticism of, or correspondence with, other philosophers.

Arnauld contributed the fourth set of *Objections* to DESCARTES's *Meditations*, published with the first edition in 1641. Two of his objections are well known. The first was an objection to Descartes's argument for the conclusion, 'I am in reality distinct from my body and can exist apart from it'. Arnauld traced the argument back to the proposition that a person can both doubt the existence of MATTER and be certain of his own existence. Arnauld objected that by the same reasoning someone with a limited knowledge of geometry could satisfy himself that it does not belong to the ESSENCE of a right-angled triangle that the square on the hypotenuse should be equal to those on the other sides, since he could be certain that a triangle was right-angled and yet be uncertain about the consequences. The second well-known objection related to Descartes's argument for our being able to rely on what we clearly and distinctly perceive. Arnauld held it to be circular: the argument for the existence of a GOD who would not allow us to be deceived in what we clearly and distinctly perceive is itself based on our having a CLEAR and distinct IDEA of God.

Together with another associate of the Port-Royal, Pierre NICOLE, Arnauld wrote *Logic, or the Art of Thinking* (1662), better known as the Port-Royal Logic. Cartesian in outlook (see CARTESIANISM), it elaborated the theory of clear and distinct ideas, and contributed, in Bk. 1, Ch. 5, to the ABSTRACTIONISM of LOCKE.

Nicolas MALEBRANCHE, in his *Search after Truth* (1674–1675), had held that we cannot be directly aware of material objects, and that in having clear and distinct ideas of the essence of matter, EXTENSION, we are perceiving what are actually God's ideas. Arnauld's main work in philosophy, *Treatise on True and False Ideas* (1683), is a detailed refutation both of Malebranche's REPRESENTATIVE THEORY OF PERCEPTION and of what has been called his doctrine of 'vision in God'. Arnauld argued against Malebranche that 'objective presence' to a mind does not require 'local presence'; and that for something to be objectively present to a mind is not the same thing as for it to be causally active on it. Intermediary entities called 'ideas' are needed neither as local presences nor as effects. The only 'ideas' are acts of perception, and these in no sense come between the perceiver and the OBJECT perceived. The CONCEPT of MIND is such that we should not wonder how material objects can be present to it.

LEIBNIZ met Arnauld during his stay in Paris from 1672–1676, and in

1686 sent him a summary of his *Discourse on Metaphysics*. Arnauld's contributions to the ensuing correspondence in 1686 and 1687 helped Leibniz to clarify the implications of his doctrine that in every true PROPOSITION about an individual substance the concept of the PREDICATE is included in that of the SUBJECT. Leibniz may have succeeded in showing that FATALISM is not an implication of his doctrine, but did not succeed in showing how it could be used to explain such details of the relation of body and mind as that a mind feels pain when the body is pricked during sleep.

association of ideas, in the philosophy of LOCKE, who was the first to use the expression, is a connection of IDEAS which is 'wholly owing to chance and circumstance'. For example, someone who learnt to dance in a room in which there happened to be an old trunk might so connect being able to dance with the presence of the trunk that he could thereafter dance well only in a room containing the trunk or one like it (*Essay*, 4th ed., II xxxiii 16). Locke contrasted ideas associated in this way with those which have 'a natural correspondence and connexion with one another'. It is the task of our reason to trace natural connections. Unnatural connections, such as that of the trunk and dancing, can be understood only as a chance product of our physiology: 'Custom settles habits of thinking in the understanding, as well as of determining in the will, and of motions in the body: all which seem to be but trains of motion in the animal spirits, which, once set a-going, continue in the same steps they have been used to' (*Essay* II xxxiii 6).

Locke neither thought it worthwhile to list the ways in which ideas come to be associated (though the principle of association in his trunk-dancing example is plainly that of contiguity), nor gave the association of ideas any useful, and identical, role to play in how everyone's mind works. Here HUME is in sharp contrast with Locke. Besides contiguity, Hume gives two other principles of association: resemblance (which Locke regarded as a natural connection, since resemblance of ideas is the result of nature making things alike), and causation (see CAUSE). Whereas Locke disparaged the association of ideas as a chance affair, and concentrated on how *dissimilar* associations in different people make the opinions, reasonings and actions of other people seem odd and extravagant, Hume contrasted ideas being associated in accordance with universal principles with their being joined by chance, and used the universality of the principles of association to explain how it is that different people make *similar* associations. He was particularly concerned with simple ideas being associated to form complex ones. It is because, in general, different people associate the same simple ideas to form the same complex ones that 'languages so nearly correspond to each other'. Thus, whereas the association of ideas is an uncontroversial afterthought in Locke's philosophy, in Hume's it is a central tenet in the controversial theory that simple ideas, otherwise 'entirely loose and unconnected', are combined to form complex ones. Hume likened the association of ideas in his account of the workings of the mind to NEWTON's gravitational attraction in his account of the workings of the physical world: 'Here is a kind of attraction, which in the mental world will be found to have as extraordinary effects as in the natural' (*Treatise* I i 4).

Hume had recourse to physiology only to explain what he regarded as mistakes in the association of ideas. His theory was that when the mind desires to survey a particular idea it dispatches the animal spirits into that region of the brain in which the idea is located, so as to excite it, but the animal spirits naturally wobble about a bit and may fall into a contiguous trace, thus exciting some other idea than the one intended. That we are not aware of having excited the wrong idea is, Hume says, 'the cause of many mistakes and sophisms in philosophy'.

Unlike Hume, David HARTLEY in his *Observations on Man, His Frame, His Duty, and His Expectations* (1749) developed a systematic psycho-physiology in which the association of ideas in the mind was presented as the effect of vibrations in the nervous system. He was no less hopeful than Hume about the usefulness of the doctrine: 'One may hope that by pursuing and perfecting the doctrine of association, we may some time or other be enabled to analyse all that vast variety of complex ideas into their simple compounding parts, i.e. into the simple ideas of sensation, of which they consist'. One philosopher who undertook the task of pursuing and perfecting the doctrine was JAMES MILL in *The Analysis of the Human Mind* (1829). His son, JOHN STUART MILL, however, abandoned any hope of analysis, holding the properties of mental compounds not to be deducible from the properties of the alleged sensory elements.

The severest philosophical criticism of associationism in the 19th century was that of F. H. BRADLEY. He accepted as a psychological fact the association of ideas in the non-technical sense of 'idea' (as in Locke's example of an idea of a trunk being associated with being able to dance well), but dismissed the notion, common to Hume, Hartley and James Mill, that 'simple ideas' can be associated. A simple idea, like the impression from which it is derived, 'exists only for a moment'. The notion that it can recur, as is implied in the doctrine that simple ideas can be associated to form complex ones, should be repudiated as one of the 'touching beliefs of a pious legend'. On somewhat similar lines William JAMES argued that the association is of objects thought-of, not of 'ideas'. See BEHAVIOURISM, CONDITIONING, PSYCHOLOGY.

atheism, *n.* (from Greek *a* not, *theos* god hence godlessness) a position that asserts that there is no GOD. In this, atheism goes further than AGNOSTICISM, which merely says that we cannot know whether there is or not. This in turn differs from the Aristotelian COSMOLOGICAL ARGUMENT which infers a prime mover from the fact of motion, but tells us nothing about his nature. AQUINAS agreed that we can know on metaphysical grounds that God exists, but revelation is needed to tell us what He is like. An atheist cannot base ethical theories on the existence of divine authority, but must find some other way to establish them. The traditional arguments for the existence of God, both *a priori* and *a posteriori*, are all unsound, as has been shown repeatedly. Indeed, the stark reality of evil in the world always sits uneasily with the notion of an all-benevolent God (see EVIL, PROBLEM OF). It has been argued against atheism that it makes the world a sinister place to live in: this has no force, for life is indeed quite often a messy business; besides, this line of reasoning presupposes that the world must be a cosy place, which it is not and which the objectors certainly have not established. The position of Aristotle allows that there is a God of sorts, but not one that takes any interest in human affairs.

atomism, *n.* (from Greek *atomos* uncuttable) regards the universe as composed of many indivisible particles, too small to see. Its originators, Leucippus and DEMOCRITUS (5th century BC) were reacting against the Eleatics, who argued that for there to be many things there would have to be a void to separate them, but a void is nothing, so does not exist, so the universe is indivisible, or 'one' (see ELEATICISM). Leucippus affirmed the existence of the void, postulated many 'ones', or ATOMS, and explained changes in the SENSIBLE world quantitatively as due to the movements of atoms of different sizes and shapes. The atoms are indivisible because they contain no void; they are 'the full' as against 'the empty' (Aristotle, *Metaphysics*, 985 b 4).

The theory explained certain phenomena, such as evaporation, but was not applicable widely enough to succeed against rival approaches. For ARISTOTLE the primary substances are the visible things around us, and change is explained in terms of 'final' rather than 'motor' causes

ATTRIBUTE

(*De Partibus Animalium*, 639 b 15) (see FINAL CAUSE). PLATO rejected the atomists' MATERIALISM for his THEORY OF FORMS (*Sophist*, 246). EPICURUS (341–270 BC), however, favoured atomism and influenced Pierre GASSENDI (1592–1655), who made atomism seem less materialistic by holding that it presupposes THEISM: GOD creates the atoms, and makes them move. Other philosophers saw difficulties in the notions of the void and indivisibility. DESCARTES made EXTENSION the ESSENCE of MATTER, which meant rejecting extension without matter, the void: parts of 'the full' are distinguishable by moving together, which they can do only in closed chains, or 'vortices'. For LEIBNIZ, whatever has extension is divisible, so atoms cannot be extended; they are soul-like, with phenomenal extension only. In spite of these philosophical difficulties, 17th century science found the atomic hypothesis highly useful.

attribute, *n.* in LOGIC, that which may be predicated (see PREDICATE) of anything, as 'green' may be predicated of grass. In METAPHYSICS a distinction is made between essential and accidental attributes (see ESSENCE and ACCIDENT).

Augustine, St (Aurelius Augustinus) (AD 354–430), born in Tagaste in the Roman province of Numidia, now Souk-Ahras in Algeria. Augustine became interested in philosophy on reading Cicero's now lost treatise, *Hortensius*. He was attracted to MANICHEISM, a syncretist religion based on Persian DUALISM together with elements from CHRISTIANITY and BUDDHISM. One of the basic doctrines of Manicheism was that of the opposed principles of Light (goodness) and Darkness (evil). The struggle between them was held to extend into man himself, the soul being good and the body evil. Later, influenced by NEO-PLATONISM, Augustine rejected the idea that evil is a positive principle, and the associated idea that it is a man's body rather than the man himself who is responsible for his sins. In 383, Augustine left Carthage, where he had been teaching rhetoric, spent a year in Rome, and then became a professor of rhetoric at Milan. Following contact with Ambrose, Bishop of Milan, Augustine's early doubts about the reasonableness of orthodox Christianity were resolved in favour of a synthesis of Neo-Platonism and the Christian doctrine of revelation. He defended the PLATONIC notion of the possibility of KNOWLEDGE against the Sceptics (see SCEPTICISM) of the ACADEMY with an argument which has sometimes been likened to the COGITO, *ero sum* of DESCARTES. 'He who is not can certainly not be deceived; therefore, if I am deceived I am.' He was baptised in 387 in Milan, returned to Africa, was ordained presbyter in 390, and from 395 to his death was Bishop of Hippo. He was the author of a great many books, sermons and letters. Most relevant to philosophy are his *Confessions* (AD 400), *On the Trinity* (AD 400–416), *On Christian Doctrine* (397–426), *The City of God* (413–426) and *Retractions* (427).

Much of the philosophical interest of Augustine lies in how he adapted Platonist and Neo-Platonist ideas to provide a theoretical framework for the Christian faith, and in how he dealt with certain attendant problems. (a) In Plato's THEORY OF FORMS, the Form of the Good is somehow superior to all the others. It is said to be related to our apprehension of the other Forms as the sun is related to our apprehension of visible objects. In the mathematicised version of the theory the Form of the Good becomes 'the One'. According to Augustine 'The One' is GOD, and the other Forms are ideas in God's mind, the archetypes for his creation. (b) Plato, in the *Timaeus*, had given to a Demiurge, a craftsman, the power to reproduce likenesses of the Forms in an independently existing 'matter' or 'receiving principle'. Augustine's God is not a mere craftsman working with independently existing materials. He not only gives FORM to MATTER; he creates the formless matter, to which he gives form, out of nothing. This is part of Augustine's controversial interpretation of the first chapter of Genesis, defended in Books XI–XII of the *Confessions*. (c) Plato held that we have had direct knowledge of the Forms in a prior disembodied existence, and that visible things serve to remind us of what we had earlier known directly. This was his theory of *anamnesis*, recollection. Augustine rejected this theory and put in its place the theory that God illuminates a human soul, suitably prepared by holiness and purity, with the Forms, so that they are visible to the inner eye of intelligence. (d) One of the problems consequent upon the doctrine of creation had to do with God and time: What was God doing before he made heaven and earth? Augustine dismissed the frivolous answer, 'He was preparing Hell for people who pry into mysteries'; and gave what amounts to the answer that there was no 'before' in which God could have been doing anything. Time came into existence with the creation of heaven and earth. Augustine recognised the need to explain further, and devoted most of Book XI of the *Confessions* to the task. He approached the question 'What is time?' via the question 'How is time measured?', and in Chapter 27 concluded that if time is measured at all then, since only what exists now can be measured, and neither the past nor the future exist now, time must be something subjective, the impression made in the mind by something as it passes and moves into the past. (e) Another problem consequent upon the doctrine of creation was that of how our actions can be forseen by God if we are truly responsible for them. Augustine's solution was that God is able to forsee free acts of choice no less than man's 'natural' behaviour.

Austin, John Langshaw (1911–1960), Oxford philosopher best known for holding, after the Second World War, that a necessary pre-requisite of philosophical investigation of a concept such as PERCEPTION, KNOWLEDGE or freewill (see FREEWILL AND DETERMIN-ISM) is a thorough examination of relevant ordinary language. For example, before starting to consider how statements about material things are related to ones about sense-data we should methodically examine our everyday use of such terms as 'looks', 'appears', 'seems' and 'real'. Such an examination may reveal that the philosopher's talk of 'sense-data' ('*sensa*', '*sensibilia*') is ill-founded (see SENSE-DATUM).

Austin's concern for what people ordinarily say became the mark of his philosophical method only after the war. In a paper published just before the war ('Are there *a priori* concepts?', *Proceedings of the Aristotelian Society*. Supp. Vol XII, 1939) he had himself used the term '*sensa*', in expounding and criticising an argument to prove the existence of UNIVERSALS, without any preliminary research into what we ordinarily say we sense. In his post-war lectures on perception, from the manuscript notes of which G. J. Warnock reconstructed a book, *Sense and Sensibilia* (Oxford, 1962), Austin cited A. J. AYER and H. H. Price as holders of the allegedly ill-founded doctrine that what we directly perceive are not material things but sense-data. Despite Austin's painstaking attention to what we ordinarily say when talking about what we see, and so on, Ayer held that in the lectures he 'entirely failed' to establish the falsity of the doctrine that we must have evidence, provided by sense-data, for what we say about material things.

Austin's best-remembered paper, published along with nine others in *Philosophical Papers* (ed. J. O. Urmson and G. J. Warnock, Oxford, 1961), was a contribution to a symposium with John Wisdom and A. J. Ayer on 'Other Minds' (*Arist. Soc.* Supp. Vol XX, 1946) It is remembered for Austin's remark about the metaphysician typically asking 'Is it real?' without specifying with what 'real' is being contrasted, for Austin's endorsement of the view that 'any description of a taste or sound or smell (or colour) or of a feeling, involves (is) saying that it is like one or some that we have experienced before' (the view criticised by WITTGENSTEIN in *Brown Book II* (Oxford, 1958, *The Blue and Brown Books*)), but primarily for Austin's drawing attention to what he called 'the descriptive fallacy' in philosophy. The fallacy is exemplified in a philosopher's remark that in saying 'I know' I am describing my mental state. Austin says, instead, that 'when I say "I know" I give others my word: I give others my authority for saying "*S* is *P*"'. Just as saying 'I promise' is *doing* something (promising) so saying 'I know' is *doing* something (avowing). Though not in this paper, Austin used the technical terms 'performative' to refer to utterances, such as 'I promise', which are the performances of an act by the speaker, and 'constative' to refer to ones, like 'he promised', that are naturally called true or false. Later he came to regard this as an oversimplification, and, in *How to Do Things with Words* (Oxford, 1962) replaced it with a more complex 'theory of illocutionary forces'.

authority, *n.* (from Latin *auctoritas*) in POLITICAL PHILOSOPHY, a power held more or less securely on a variety of more or less acceptable grounds. Wherever in a State the final authority rests, it can prevail only if it can either impose itself or command sufficient support. Some would say that only GOD has absolute authority, however this be realised.

automaton, *n.* a mechanism that simulates the behaviour of a living being, for example a clockwork mouse. DESCARTES held that man is not an automaton, since he acts voluntarily (*Principles of Philosophy*, 1644, Pt. I, Sect. 37). T. H. HUXLEY held that man is an automaton, but a conscious one. See BEHAVIOURISM.

autonomy, *n.* (from Greek *autos* self, *nomos* law) in philosophy the fact of being self-determined, instead of being determined from outside. Thus in ETHICS the demand for autonomy is the notion that ethical rules must be freely arrived at as being conformable to reason, rather than imposed. This view was strongly defended by KANT.

avowal, *n.* some utterances beginning with the first person singular pronoun (such as 'I hope he'll come' and 'I'm tired', but not 'I weigh 140 pounds') have been called 'avowals' by some philosophers, who are opposed to the notion that it is sensible to ask someone who says 'I hope he'll come', *how he knows* that he is hoping, and not expecting, and how he knows what he hopes. The traditional answer to the 'How do you know?' question is 'By INTROSPECTION', this being thought of as like sense-perception, only directed inwards (LOCKE, *Essay*, II i 4). In the case of 'I'm tired' the point of calling it an avowal is to assimilate it to yawning; the utterance is not a report of something one has observed, but an expression of one's state. See PRIVACY.

axiom, *n.* (from Greek *axioma* a self-evident statement; literally, something worthy of respect) in LOGIC and other FORMAL systems, a PROPOSITION which is assumed without proof and serves in turn to help in the proof of other propositions in the system. A typical example is the principle of excluded middle (a proposition is either true or false), which is adopted by most systems of logic (though not by INTUITIONISM); this seems so basic that we seem neither able to prove it nor convinced that we need to.

Ayer, Sir Alfred Jules (1910–1989) British philosopher, professor at University College London (1946–1959) and at Oxford (1959–1977), became known early for his *Language, Truth and Logic* (1936), through which the logical positivist doctrines of the VIENNA CIRCLE first came to be widely known amongst English readers. At the same time Ayer shows how this line of thought is linked with the earlier British empiricist tradition, as well as with the philosophy of RUSSELL and in some ways WITTGENSTEIN. Like HUME, he rejects statements that have neither logical nor empirical content, taking them as meaningless. This disposes of METAPHYSICS in general, and of theology in particular. The task of philosophy is then simply to clarify areas not yet occupied by scientific investigation. In *The Foundations of Empirical Knowledge* (1940), he emphasizes the use of sense-data language (see SENSE-DATUM) as the most suitable for discussing problems of PERCEPTION, thus developing his position of PHENOMENALISM. In *The Problem of Knowledge* (1956), he examines the nature of sceptical argument, concluding that we sometimes do have KNOWLEDGE. In his later work, he shows a certain widening of philosophic sympathies. Throughout, his writings are marked by great elegance and clarity.

B

Bacon, Francis (1561–1626), born in London, Bacon studied at Trinity College, Cambridge, and entered Parliament in 1584. His ambitions were such as might befit a present-day Minister for Science and Technology. He was appointed Lord Chancellor in 1618. In 1621 he was accused of accepting gifts from litigants. His plea, that he did not allow them to influence his judgment, was not accepted and he was deprived of his offices. In his remaining five years he continued his pursuit of the advancement of science.

Bacon's life-work, unfinished, was to have been a book of which the full title was *The Great Instauration of the Power of Man over the Universe*. The first part of it was a revised and extended version of his *The Advancement of Learning* (1605). The second part, the *Novum Organon (New Instrument for Scientific Investigation)* appeared in 1620. The 'power of man over the universe', referred to in the full title of *The Great Instauration*, was man's dominion over all the earth, promised in the first chapter of Genesis, but thought of as involving science; specifically, a science capable of practical application to yield inventions and techniques for bettering man's lot on earth. Bacon thought that some of the Pre-Socratic philosophers, DEMOCRITUS in particular, had shown signs of developing such a science. However, any science capable of constructive application had been caught, like a fly in a spider's web, in the word-spinning of ARISTOTLE, where it had remained trapped for nearly 2000 years. The scholastics, by adopting Aristotelianism as the philosophical underpinning for CHRISTIANITY, had made it all the more difficult to break Aristotle's stranglehold over men's minds (see SCHOLASTIC). A revolution in the principles and methods of science was made to seem like a revolution against Christianity itself. What was needed, Bacon saw, was, in religion, a return from Aristotle's *Physics* and *Metaphysics* to the simple piety and faith of the Bible, and, in science, a method which would almost automatically yield genuinely useful knowledge. In a posthumously published address, *The Reputation of Philosophies*, Bacon identified the required method in the works of one of the despised Greek philosophers, PLATO. It was the method of INDUCTION involved in attaining knowledge of FORMS. These two parts of Plato's philosophy, Bacon said, are truly divine, but Plato 'corrupted them and made them fruitless by aiming only at abstract Forms and taking the material for his Inductions only from superficial and vulgar EXPERIENCE'. The 'forms' which Bacon held we should try to discover by induction are not the separately-existing Platonic Forms but something much more like the internal 'real constitutions' of which LOCKE was to write later in the 17th century, 'the real constitution on which the SENSIBLE qualities of bodies depend'. The sort of induction required for the discovery of such forms, moreover, was not merely a preliminary to what really mattered, DIALECTIC; it was itself the key to their discovery, and a key which could be turned by anyone. It involved the drawing up of three 'Tables of Investigation'. In the 'Table of Affirmation' would be listed various instances of the presence of the PHENOMENON under investigation. In the 'Table of Negation' there would be cases which lacked the phenomenon but were otherwise as similar as possible to those in which it occurred. The 'Table of Comparison' would contain examples of variations in degrees of presence and absence. Additionally, note was to be made of instances which, for one reason or another, were outstanding. Bacon distinguished as many as 27 types of such 'prerogative instances'. He described the whole method as the way of *'literate experience'*, the art or place for an honest interpretation of nature, a true path from sense to intellect'. He also described it as the way of the bee. 'The Empiricists, like ants, gather and consume. The Rationalists, like spiders, spin webs out of themselves. The bee adopts the middle course, drawing her material from the flowers of the garden or field, but transforming it by a faculty peculiar to herself.' (See EMPIRICISM, RATIONALISM).

Bacon has been criticised for giving too little recognition, in his account of scientific method, the work of the bee, to the role of HYPO-THESIS, the making of inspired guesses to guide further experimental investigation. Still, at the time, his proposals were both original and seminal. They were to be largely reproduced, over 200 years later, as JOHN STUART MILL's *Methods of Induction*. Bacon saw resistance to their acceptance as evidence of the power of certain false notions he called 'Idols'. These were of four main types. The idols of the tribe, so called because they are 'inherent in human nature and the very tribe or race of men', are such things as the tendency to accept uncritically what our senses tell us, to believe what we want to believe, and to interpret nature anthropomorphically. An example of the last is Aristotle's liking for explaining things as though there were purposes operative in nature. 'Inquiry into final causes', Bacon says, 'is sterile and, like a virgin consecrated to God, produces nothing'. The idols of the den or cave (after Plato's myth, in the *Republic*, of people living in a cave) are each person's tendency to interpret nature from his own peculiar viewpoint. The idols of the market place are those of commonly-accepted language. We tend to assume that if there is a word, such as 'fortune', in common use, there must be such a thing as fortune. Finally, there are the idols of the theatre. These are the dogmas of past philosophical systems. To accept them would be like mistaking a stage-play for real life.

Bacon, Roger (*c.*1215–1292), English Franciscan philosopher who studied and taught at Paris and Oxford, was important above all for his rejection of blind obedience to received AUTHORITY, and his growing interest in experimental science as against following the conventional Aristotelianism of his time. Still, he himself was not always critical towards other people's scientific claims. His independent approach led to a period of imprisonment.

bad faith, *n.* in ETHICS and PSYCHOLOGY, a state of mind that shows itself in insincere action. It is related to the notion of false consciousness found in existentialist writers (see EXISTENTIALISM). The difference is that one who is in bad faith knows that he is, whereas one who has false consciousness does not know that he has.

basic statements, those statements, if any, into which complex statements are said to be ultimately analysable. All KNOWLEDGE is supposed to rest on them, and they are regarded as the expression of indubitable flashes of immediate EXPERIENCE. Whether there are such basic statements remains controversial.

Bayle, Pierre (1647–1706), French philosopher, author of a massive *Historical and Critical Dictionary* (2 vols, 1695, 1697), aptly described by R. H. Popkin, translator of selections from it (Indianapolis, 1965) as 'a *Summa Sceptica* that deftly undermined all the foundations of the 17th century intellectual world'. Of particular interest to early 18th century philosophers like BERKELEY and HUME was Bayle's treatment of the foundations in Greek ATOMISM, with its distinction between what came to be called PRIMARY AND SECONDARY QUALITIES, of the 'new philosophy' of DESCARTES, GASSENDI, HOBBES, LOCKE and others.

beauty, *n.* an important feature (some would say the most important) studied in AESTHETICS. Two questions arise: what is beauty, and how do we recognise it? As to the former, the Ancients held that one could define the beautiful, whereas some modern thinkers regard it as indefinable. Moreover, some regard beauty as belonging to things, while others take it to be a relation between beholder and beheld. As for recognising it, if beauty is an OBJECTIVE quality, then we perceive it as we do other qualities. Just as we can learn to distinguish colours, so we can learn to discern beauty, and just as some people are better than others at the first, so with the second. If, however, beauty is somehow a result of one's way of looking at things, it rests in one's EMOTIONS and becomes a matter of taste, about which there is no disputing, as the Latin tag has it. In either case, there is an element of approval when one declares something to be beautiful: people who deliberately and consistently despise the beautiful are abnormal. The notion of beauty shades off into that of elegance, as when we recognise a certain harmony between means and ends in the solution of a practical problem, such as the building of a bridge. At the same time, we recognise beauty not only in human artefacts or affairs, but also in the world of nature that surrounds us.

behaviourism, *n.* either a methodological doctrine in early 20th century PSYCHOLOGY, or a reductionist (see REDUCTIONISM) solution to the OTHER MINDS PROBLEM in philosophy.

The methodological doctrine was that the proper kind of observation to employ in psychology is not the inward observation of private happenings (i.e. INTROSPECTION of mental events and processes), but the outward observation of public happenings. It was called behaviourism on the assumption that how someone behaves is something that is in principle open to anyone to observe, so that theories about behaviour can be confirmed or disconfirmed in broadly the same way as can theories in such natural sciences as biology.

In the early 20th century the use of introspection in psychology had led to seemingly unresolvable disputes about, for example, whether there is imageless thought. Observations of animal behaviour, begun in the late 19th century to test Darwin's theory of the continuity between animals and man (see DARWINISM), were yielding results on which investigators could agree. Some of the theories could be tested under laboratory conditions. There seemed to be a strong case for using the same observational methods in the study of humans as had proved fruitful in the study of animals.

Behaviourists tend also to be materialists (see MATERIALISM). This can be understood best in the context of CARTESIAN DUALISM. For DESCARTES, there were two quite different ways in which bodily movements might be caused. First, 'animal spirits' reaching the brain through sensory channels may automatically be 'reflected' into motor channels, producing what we call 'involuntary' movements. Second, the SOUL, by willing, can make the part of the brain with which it is united move in the way requisite for producing the bodily movement aimed at in the VOLITION. Such a movement is said to be 'voluntary'.

The 'reflex' explanation of involuntary movements was taken a stage further with Pavlov's discovery that a reflex such as salivation can be made to occur as a response to a different stimulus from its natural one, food. This suggested to behaviourist psychologists an analogue of the ASSOCIATION OF IDEAS in introspectionist psychology. Instead of acquired associations of ideas there are acquired associations of physical stimuli and behavioural responses. The implication was obvious. If Descartes could be shown to be wrong about some movements having a mental cause then the new S–R (stimulus–response) associationism would provide just what was needed to put psychology on an equal footing with even the most deterministic and mechanistic of the natural sciences. A contemporary of Darwin, T. H. HUXLEY (1825–1895) had shown the way, declaring man to be a conscious AUTOMATON, and saying that 'the feeling we call volition is not the cause of a voluntary act, but the symbol of that state of the brain which is the immediate cause of the act'. Mind, the province of the introspectionist, could be explained away as an 'epiphenomenon' (see EPIPHENOMENALISM). In this spirit, J. B. WATSON (1879–1958) the best-known pioneer of behaviourism, held THINKING to be identical with movements in the brain and larynx, EMOTIONS to be implicit visceral reactions, and both to be amenable to CONDITIONING.

Sooner or later behaviourists had to turn from attacking DUALISM and introspectionism to explaining what they meant by 'behaviour'. Can we justifiably assume that how someone behaves is something that is in principle open to anyone to observe? A turning point was the publication of E. C. Tolman's *Purposive Behaviour in Animals and Men* (New York, 1932). Tolman distinguished between what he called 'molecular' and 'molar' behaviour. Molecular behaviour is the bodily motions studied by the physiologist. Molar behaviour is the behaviour studied by the psychologist. Some behaviourists had tried to deduce molar behaviour from molecular. Tolman held such a deduction to be impossible; molar behaviour has descriptive and defining properties that make it irreducible to molecular behaviour. It is essentially purposive.

The crucial question in a philosophical critique of behaviourism is this: who is to say with what purpose something is done? Is not the agent in a unique position to say what he is up to? Does not our ordinary notion of ourselves as responsible agents imply that he is? Yet the behaviourist, by assuming that how someone behaves is something that is in principle open to anyone to observe, seems to imply the contrary. Such an implication seems to be evident in the writings of the foremost behaviourist of the second half of the 20th century, B. F. Skinner (1904–   ).

The reductionist solution to the other minds problem in philosophy is to say that a proposition about someone else's mind, such as that someone else is in pain, is to be analysed in terms of behaviour.

being, *n.* the fact that something is. ARISTOTLE in *Metaphysics* Book 5 Chapter 7 (1017 a 9–b 9) discusses the various meanings of being, or senses of 'is'. Before him, PLATO had examined what happens if we fail to distinguish these (*Sophist*, 243 d–245 e). Some of the seemingly absurd views of PARMENIDES arise from just this neglect. Very much later, KANT put it succinctly in saying that existence is not a PREDICATE. For example, to say that Pegasus does not exist is simply short for no horse has wings. To be is to be of a certain kind. To say that Pegasus does exist is as it were short for an imaginary animal figures in Greek myth. Here, in appropriate senses, the two seemingly contradictory statements are perfectly compatible. The insight that existence and non-existence are not predicates like red and non-red has not always been clearly understood. Thus, many SCHOLASTIC thinkers sought to define GOD as that in which existence coincides with ESSENCE and tried from this to develop a proof that God exists. If we recognise that there is no such state as barely being and no more, but that whatever 'is' must be such and such, that is, have a describable quality or feature, then the apparent puzzles about being and nothingness, much canvassed by existentialists (see EXISTENTIALISM) in our own time, will simply vanish.

belief, *n.* the act of (a) believing that something is so,

(b) believing someone who says it is so, or

(c) believing in someone or something (e.g. belief in a religious creed).

In believing that something is so, belief is opposed to KNOWLEDGE:

one says one only believes that something is so when one feels unjustified in claiming to know that it is.

There is a connection between what one believes and how one acts, but one cannot analyse 'the belief that *p*' as 'the disposition to act as if *p* were true': a person can believe he is unselfish, and yet act as selfishly as anyone else.

Bentham, Jeremy (1748–1832), English philosopher and central figure of the utilitarian movement of his time (see UTILITARIANISM). He was the son of a London lawyer and himself trained for the law. He did not practise it for long but became instead a philosopher and writer on law. Inspired by the notion that the good is to be found in the greatest happiness of the greatest number (a view with ancient roots but expressed in modern times by HUTCHESON (1694–1747) and others), sometimes called the utilitarian principle, he sought to set the theory and practice of law on a new and scientific basis, which ran straight against the natural law tradition of jurisprudence. He was an active advocate of reform in law, the handling of the convicted (he devised a new layout for building prisons), parliamentary institutions, political economy and education (he helped to found University College, London, as a place where non-Anglicans could gain a higher education; hence the nick-name of the College as 'the Godless of Gower Street'). However, his approach was down-to-earth and opposed to some of the more romantic outcrops of the French Revolution. Thus he said of Human Rights that they were 'nonsense on stilts'.

Much of his writing was collected and edited after his death. The most influential of his works to be published in England during his lifetime was *An Introduction to the Principles of Morals and Legislation* (1789), where he explains his general utilitarian theory. What moves us to act is finding pleasure and shunning pain. We should do this with due regard to the pleasures and pains of others, so that in sum the outcome is the most that can be got of the former and the least of the latter. The trouble, as with all forms of utilitarianism, is that we have no agreed measures to perform the calculation. Besides, it seems un-attractive that the convenience of the many should be bought at the price of inflicting pain even on one alone. To this there is no viable reply. Still, many practical decisions are so made.

Berdyaev, Nicolas (1874–1948), Russian religious philosopher whose aim was to realise the Christian commonwealth here on earth. In the wake of the Russian Revolution, he was expelled and went first to Germany and then to France. He distinguished between the material and the spiritual world: man sits astride both, and as having spirit and seeking freedom, belongs to the latter.

Bergson, Henri (1859–1941), a French philosopher, became professor at the Collège de France (1900) and gained the 1927 Nobel prize for literature. He is best known for his view of psychological time and his theory of creative evolution. As regards time, he points out that what we experience is not the spatialised time of physical science, but some kind of intuitive duration that cannot be described in spatial metaphors. It is this time that gives human beings a moral dimension, and it is in this time that we are free agents. The time of physics is a medium where strict determinism prevails: free will resides in duration (see FREEWILL AND DETERMINISM).

Agreeing with the evolutionist notions of his time, he gives them a peculiar twist of his own. He regards evolution in Darwin's mould (see DARWINISM) as too mechanical to account for the processes it describes. Instead, Bergson considers these developments to be due to the operation of an *'élan vital'* or vital impetus which enacts the changes that occur in evolution. This is set out in his *Creative Evolution* (1907, translated 1911).

His theory of MEMORY likewise makes use of the notion of intuitive duration: it, rather than physical time, is the medium in which we remember. He exercised a deep influence on the French novelist Marcel Proust and was himself a lecturer of great clarity and elegance. However, his philosophical views were on the whole received with reservations, not least because the original concepts central to his position were left so vague.

Berkeley, George (1685–1753), born near Kilkenny in Ireland. Berkeley entered Trinity College, Dublin in 1700, and became a Fellow of the College in 1707. In that year and the next he filled two notebooks, now called the *Philosophical Commentaries*, with what were, in germ, the ideas he developed in *An Essay Towards a New Theory of Vision* (1709), *A Treatise Concerning the Principles of Human Knowledge* (1710), and *Three Dialogues Between Hylas and Philonous* (1713), his three best-known works. In 1713–14, and again from 1716 to 1720, he travelled on the Continent and in 1721 published an essay entitled *Of Motion*, containing criticisms of NEWTON's philosophy of nature and LEIBNIZ's theory of force. These criticisms have led to his being described as a precursor of MACH and EINSTEIN. In 1724 Berkeley resigned his Fellowship to become Dean of Derry. He attempted, but failed, to establish a college in Bermuda to educate Negroes, native

Indians, and the sons of American colonists. In 1734 he was made Bishop of Cloyne, Ireland. He settled in Oxford in 1752 and died the following year.

Berkeley's philosophy can best be understood in the context of the philosophies of René DESCARTES (1596–1650), John LOCKE (1632–1704) and Nicolas MALEBRANCHE (1638–1715). Berkeley referred to Descartes and Locke as 'corpuscularian philosophers', and rejected their notion that the objects of knowledge, IDEAS, are caused by CORPUSCLES of matter affecting our senses, on the grounds that this notion was a cause of error and difficulty in the sciences, and was conducive to SCEPTICISM and ATHEISM. Descartes had explained how matter can affect mind in terms of a person's MIND being united with his body (see MIND–BODY PROBLEM). Malebranche held that the only way to understand the union of mind and matter was by supposing that GOD, on the occasion of an event in a person's body, wills an event in the person's mind, and vice versa. This was known as the doctrine of 'OCCASIONALISM'. It involved holding that the real cause of our ideas is God, not external material things. In theory God could put ideas of material things into our minds without creating material things for them to be ideas of. But Malebranche, like Descartes, held that God would not have given us an inclination to believe in the existence of material things if He had not created them, and Malebranche could think of no good reason to deny their existence.

Berkeley agreed with Malebranche, against Descartes and Locke, that the cause of our ideas is God. However, he denied the existence of material things, holding that our inclination to believe in their existence is not God-given, but is the product of illegitimate ABSTRACTION. The being of SENSIBLE things, he said, is to be perceived (*esse est percipi*), and to suppose that they can exist unperceived is illegitimately to abstract their existence from their being perceived. Moreover, unlike Malebranche, he held that there is a good reason to deny that they exist. The corpuscularian philosopher's conception of matter, he held, involves a contradiction: a non-sentient substance, such as the corpuscularian philosophers supposed matter to be, cannot be the substratum of ideas.

Since his conclusion was to be that the corpuscularian philosophy is false, Berkeley was not in a position to define the word 'idea' as an effect of corpuscles of matter affecting our senses. The impression conveyed by the opening section of Part I of the *Principles of Human Knowledge*, that by 'idea' Berkeley meant what Locke meant, is accordingly misleading, and one needs to look elsewhere for a definition.

To make sense of Berkeley's philosophy one needs a definition of 'idea' which will suit the various sorts of arguments he employs. One argument, that can be elicited from Sections 2, 16 and 41 of *An Essay Towards a New Theory of Vision*, is as follows. Since distance is a line directed end-wise to the eye it projects only one point in the back of the eye, which point remains the same whether the distance be longer or shorter. So there is nothing in the stimulation of the eye which varies with the distance of the object, and which could thus be the physical basis for non-inferential awareness of distance. So it must be the case that distance is suggested, by ancillary sensations, such as the SENSATION of the eyes turning inwards to focus on an object close enough to touch, rather than actually seen. The capacity of the sensation to suggest a certain distance depends on the perceiver having had EXPERIENCE of the conjunction of the sensation with the object being close. A man born blind, who was given sight, would not have had the relevant experience. So to him the object would not have any 'outness', near or far. So the object would not have 'outness' in respect of his mind. It would be an object in his mind, what we call an 'idea'.

The argument is invalid on at least two counts. First, even if there were nothing in the stimulation of one eye which varies systematically with the distance of the object, it would not follow that there is nothing in the stimulation of two eyes; and there is, as is evident in the making of stereoscopes. Second, even if an object did not seem, to a man born blind who was given sight, to have outness, in the sense of being at a distance from him, it would not follow that the object seemed to him not to have outness with respect to his mind. For the last part of the argument to seem valid one's concept of 'idea' must be defined in terms that are spatial but equivocal ('outness' meaning either 'external to a perceiver' or 'external to the mind').

Berkeley had got the unusual word 'outness' from Malebranche, in translation, and may have got his CONCEPT of an 'idea' from him, too. Malebranche (in *The Search after Truth*, 1674/5, Bk. III, Pt. 2, Chap. 1) had defined 'idea' in equivocally spatial terms, as what, because it is 'intimately joined' to the SOUL, can mediate perception of objects which cannot be perceived immediately because they are at a distance.

Others of Berkeley's arguments seem to call for other definitions of 'idea'. The argument in Section 44 of the *Essay Towards a New Theory of Vision* seems to require that 'idea' be defined in terms of how things appear, according to the laws of perspective. In *The Theory of Vision Vindicated and Explained* (1733), the immediate objects of visual perception are said to be 'pictures', relative to the images which would be projected on 'a diaphanous plane erected near the eye, perpendicular to the horizon' (Section 55).

An argument about heat and pain, near the beginning of the first of his *Three Dialogues*, suggests that Berkeley may have been thinking of 'ideas' as bodily sensations. What lies behind the argument is the question 'Does the word "hot" used to describe a fire mean the same as the word "hot" used to describe how one feels?' If the answer given is 'Yes' then one is open to the argument that since a fire is an unperceiving thing it cannot be the SUBJECT of heat, that is, cannot really feel hot. If the answer given is 'No' then one is open to the argument that since the word 'hot' used to describe the fire does not mean the same as the word 'hot' used to describe one's sensations, in calling a fire 'hot' one is not saying that a sensation of heat, or anything like it, is in the fire. And if one accepts this conclusion one may be inclined to accept that in calling a fire 'hot' one is really saying no more than that it has a power to produce sensations of being hot in people.

To Berkeley it seemed that his philosophy, which has been described positively as 'IDEALISM' and negatively as 'IMMATERIALISM', had three main merits, relating to SCEPTICISM, ATHEISM, and science. The proneness of the corpuscularian philosophy to sceptical doubts about the existence of material things had been brought to his attention by reading the *Critical and Historical Dictionary* (1697), of Pierre BAYLE (1647–1706). He saw that if the existence of apples, stones, trees, books, and so on, were to be defined in terms of their being perceived (in other words, if they are declared to be collections of ideas) then, given the appropriate ideas, there would be no room for doubts about their existence.

Furthermore, if ideas are said to be imprinted on our senses not as the result of the motions of corpuscles of matter but by God, then the existence of God is thereby rendered even more certain than the existence of other men, 'everything we see, hear, feel or anywise perceive by sense, being a sign or effect of the Power of God; as is our perception of those very motions, which are produced by men' (*Principles of Human Knowledge*, Section 148). A corollary of this is that belief in the existence of other human minds is made dependent on belief that God would not give me ideas of motions of other men without other men existing.

Berkeley's immaterialism and his doctrine that God wills our ideas had consequences for science. He rejects the notions of absolute space and time, which he attributes to the doctrine of abstract ideas, in favour of operationalist notions (see *Principles of Human Knowledge*, Section 116). 'Force', 'gravity' and 'attraction' are said to be useful notions interpreted operationally in mathematical hypotheses, but not real causes of motion. (A mathematical HYPOTHESIS claims only that its consequences agree with the phenomena.) The science of real efficient causes is not physics, but METAPHYSICS, for the real causes are spiritual. The physicist should realise that he is not dealing with real causes, but only with secondary or OCCASIONAL CAUSES, an occasional cause being a sign, that God gives us, of what we may expect. There are no necessary connections in nature. Essentialist explanations, of either the Aristotelian or Cartesian kind, are amongst the 'chief causes of error and difficulty in the sciences', and their elimination is a way of 'rendering the sciences more easy, useful and compendious'. Although, in Descartes's philosophy, God is needed to sustain the world in existence, His creative work is done when He has set it up. It operates thereafter according to mechanical laws. In Berkeley's philosophy God is constantly active, willing the ideas which, for us, constitute nature. These ideas are the language in which He speaks to us. See PRIMARY AND SECONDARY QUALITIES, PROPER OBJECT, SUBSTANCE.

body–mind problem, see MIND–BODY PROBLEM.

Boethius, Anicius Manlius Severinus (*c.*480–524), born in Rome, was educated in the liberal arts and philosophy, entered public life, and, like his father, became a consul. Towards the end of the reign of Theodoric, the Ostrogoth ruler in Rome from 500, Boethius was arrested on a charge of conspiring against Theodoric, and, in spite of his denials, was condemned, sent to the prison at Pavia, and executed in 524.

Apart from his translations into Latin of ARISTOTLE's logical treatise, his main philosophical works were a commentary on Porphyry's *Isagoge* (an introduction to the elementary concepts of LOGIC), and the famous book he wrote in prison, *The Consolation of Philosophy*, translated into Anglo-Saxon by Alfred the Great and into English by Chaucer.

Porphyry had surveyed various accounts of the nature of UNIVERSALS, but had not pronounced on them. Boethius, in his commentary, distinguished between a seen likeness and a thought likeness, and between a thought such as that of a centaur and a thought such as that of a geometrical line. Two men can be seen to be alike in both being human. This sensible likeness exists in the individuals. The likeness as thought, however, is a universal and is not in the individuals. It does not follow that the universal, the species human, has a merely fictional existence, like that of a centaur. Its mode of existence is like that of a line, something which has no real existence apart from sensible bodies, but of which the thought, nevertheless, is not false.

Boethius added that PLATO had gone further than this, in holding that universals, or 'FORMS', do have a real existence apart from SENSIBLE things. Boethius's formulation of these issues considerably influenced later discussions of the problem of universals.

Faced with death, Boethius found consolation in Stoic and neo-Platonist philosophy (see STOICISM, NEO-PLATONISM). The fifth and last book of the *Consolation* is of particular interest. In it Boethius, like AUGUSTINE before him, sought to reconcile man's freedom with God's foreknowledge of his actions (see FREEWILL AND DETERMINISM). The reconciliation is achieved by denying that God's knowledge is un-equivocally foreknowledge. 'Since God lives in an eternal present, his knowledge transcends all temporal change and abides in the simplicity of his "now". Embracing the infinite stretch of past and future, it views all things in its simple comprehension as if they were going on now.' Human knowledge that someone is walking now does not entail that the person is not walking voluntarily (see VOLITION). Similarly, God's knowledge of someone's walking (in what from our time-conditioned point of view is the past, present or future) does not entail that the person's walk is not voluntary.

Boolean algebra, *n.* a logical CALCULUS invented by the English mathematician George Boole (1815–1864). He denotes a class by a letter, say x, and the complementary class, namely what is not x, by $\bar{x}$ or $1-x$. The proposition all x are y then becomes $x\,(1-y)=0$, that is, the x that are not y amount to the empty class. Along such lines, the valid arguments of traditional logic can readily be exhibited. Boolean algebra is the forerunner of modern mathematical LOGIC.

Bradley, Francis Herbert (1846–1924), English idealist philosopher (see IDEALISM), studied at Oxford where he became a fellow in 1870 and stayed for the rest of his life without ever having to teach. Strongly influenced by HEGEL, he nevertheless maintained a position of his own and was a writer of great power and brilliance.

In his *Ethical Studies* (1876), the prime target is UTILITARIANISM, especially J. S. MILL. He attacks the individualist psychological assumptions

of utilitarian ethics, based as it is on Hume's principle of the ASSOCIA-
TION OF IDEAS. Instead, he emphasizes man as formed by the social
setting in which he lives, through the traditions that this involves. In
the *Principles of Logic* (1883), he gives an account of the various forms
of argument, pointing out the incompleteness of traditional LOGIC,
which neglects relational arguments, and the fallacy in the inductive
logic of Mill (see INDUCTION), which purports to go from particular to
universal. At the same time he insists that logic must be severed from
psychology, a position that is at the core of modern logic. His best
known work is *Appearance and Reality* (1893), where he develops a
metaphysical position in the idealist mould. All the separate parts of the
world and our experience of it are necessarily incomplete, for all of it
points to things and events that lie outside it. Hence none of our
ordinary EXPERIENCE has the status of full thinghood or reality: it
remains at the level of appearance (see APPEARANCE, REALITY). Only
the totality of all things, the universe as a whole with all that inhabits
it, can have reality.

Bradley's work had a powerful critical influence in the transition
from 19th century idealism to the new tendencies in Oxford and
Cambridge after 1900.

Brentano, Franz (1838–1917), German-Austrian philosopher who
wrote on many aspects of philosophy but is best-known for his *Psychology from an Empirical Standpoint* (Leipzig, 1874, English edition ed.
L. L. McAlister, London 1973). In it Brentano rejected not-being-
extended as what distinguishes mental phenomena from physical, on
the ground that sounds and smells are not apprehended as extended
and yet are not regarded as mental; he instead proposed to characterise
mental phenomena in terms of 'reference to a content, direction
toward an object, or immanent objectivity'. He called this 'the intentional inexistence of an object', and provided no further explanation of
it, beyond saying, in the second edition, that it is not a relation (the
object need not exist), but is 'relation like'. He influenced Alexius
MEINONG (1853–1920) (and, through Meinong, RUSSELL, MOORE and
other British and American realists), and Edmund HUSSERL (1859–
1938), whose PHENOMENOLOGY is based on, but goes far beyond,
Brentano's descriptive PSYCHOLOGY. See INTENTIONALITY.

Buber, Martin (1878–1965), Jewish philosopher of religion (see JEWISH
PHILOSOPHY) born in Vienna, was an active member of the Zionist
movement and during the Weimar Republic Professor of Jewish
Religious Philosophy at Frankfurt. He remained engaged in Jewish

adult education in Germany till 1938, but then emigrated to Palestine and received the Chair of Sociology of Religion at the Hebrew University in Jerusalem. In philosophy, he is known for his distinction between viewing things from without as OBJECTS on the one hand, and entering into a full two-way relationship on the other: thus, we silently observe things, but normally enter into discourse with fellow-humans. This is the famous distinction between the 'I–It' and the 'I–Thou' relation. In a way, only the second involves our full being and establishes a personal relation. It is in the 'I–Thou' relation that we stand to GOD, for example in prayer, and to other people when we acknowledge the divine spark in them. The 'I–Thou' relation is open-ended and risky, because not rationally predictable. This is reminiscent of KIERKEGAARD's 'leap of faith', and allows one to describe Buber's position as a form of EXISTENTIALISM. He applied his views particularly to interpreting the Old Testament, as documenting the encounter of the Children of Israel with their God, involving trust in His being reliable. In contrast, the theology of CHRISTIANITY, rooted in Greek philosophy, has produced Creeds, sets of propositions that must be taken on trust.

Buddhism, *n.* an Eastern religion, started in India about 500 BC, and called after Buddha ('the enlightened one'), the traditional founder and propounder of its doctrines. Its principles are very simple, perhaps by reaction against the complex formalities of the prevailing Hinduism of that time. Basically, we must recognise that life is a painful business, because of our greed for things. To remedy this, we must renounce our cravings by following the eight-fold path of right views, right intention, right speech, right action, right livelihood, right effort, right mindfulness and right concentration. This is a mixture of a proper recognition of how things are with proper behaviour and proper mental application to that end. Buddhism denies the existence of everlasting souls and takes a commonsense view of how the world and its furniture and inhabitants are made up. Nor is there any supernatural deity. In its search for release from the wheel of birth, which makes a given consciousness reappear in a different guise, higher or lower in the animal scale, according to merit in the previous life, that consciousness may through following the eight-fold path eventually attain enlightenment and so pass into nirvana or nothingness.

On this fundamental outlook three main schools of Buddhism (the Greater, Lesser, and Diamond Vehicles) have developed over the years with various emphases and metaphysical accretions. India has now very few Buddhists, the main centres having shifted to Southeast Asia, Sri Lanka, Tibet, China and Japan.

Butler, Joseph (1692–1752), Anglican bishop and moral philosopher, who sought to show that the basis of morality lay not so much in some divine will, but rather in the nature of things. In this he was following a generally naturalist tendency that had arisen in the 17th century. He is, however, original in recognising that human nature is neither totally self-regarding nor totally un-self-regarding: we are all partly selfish and partly benevolent, and this is acceptable if properly balanced. The basis of morality then lies in a unique feature of the human animal, namely its having a CONSCIENCE that of itself tells its possessor what is right and wrong. This is a typical ENLIGHTENMENT view (perhaps most memorably expressed in GOETHE's *Faust*, Prologue in Heaven: 'a good man in his dark striving is well aware of the right way'). At the same time, Butler was a Christian, and as such believed that his naturalist notions were quite compatible with Christian doctrine, each in some way making one expect the other, a position developed in his *Analogy of Religion* (1736).

As for the origin of human conscience, Butler takes a clear Christian stand, holding that it has been ordained for us by GOD. It is this that gives us our IDENTITY as human beings, for it makes us aware not just of being in the world, but of being so as moral agents.

C

calculus, *n.* (*Latin* pebble) a system of rules for doing certain sums. The term goes back to ancient times when such operations were carried out with pebbles. In LOGIC it is applied to ways of setting out FORMAL arguments, in particular to systems for which one lays down some basic formulae or AXIOMS with the help of which other formulae are to be deduced. In UTILITARIANISM we hear of a *felicific calculus*; that is, the method to be followed to make the assessment of positive (pleasure-bringing) and negative (pain-causing) elements in a given proposed action.

Cambridge Platonists, *n.* a group of divines, mainly Cambridge dons, who looked back to Plato, or Plato as interpreted by PLOTINUS, for their philosophical ideas. In the *Sophist* (246) PLATO referred to an 'interminable battle' between two camps, those who 'define reality as the same thing as body' and those, like himself, who maintain that 'true reality consists in certain intelligible and bodiless FORMS'. The acknowledged leaders of the first camp, in ancient Greece, were the atomists, Leucippus and DEMOCRITUS (see ATOMISM). About 2000 years later, in 17th century England, the camp leader for MATERIALISM was Thomas HOBBES. Like Democritus, but unlike DESCARTES, Hobbes gave a materialistic account even of human thought processes. SENSATIONS are motions in our heads, and IDEAS arise from sensations. In the 'interminable battle', opposition to Hobbes' MATERIALISM and EMPIRICISM was provided by the 'Cambridge Platonists'. Among their number were Henry MORE (1614–1687) and Ralph CUDWORTH (1617–1688).

More corresponded with Descartes, in 1649, about the denial of thought to animals, and about the definition of body exclusively in terms of EXTENSION. On the former, Descartes's position was that 'it has never yet been observed that any brute animal reached the stage of using real speech, that is to say, of indicating by word or sign something pertaining to pure thought and not to natural impulse'. Natural impulse, Descartes held, could be explained mechanically.

More disagreed both about animals being AUTOMATA and about the definition of body. His final position was that 'there is no purely mechanical phenomenon in the whole universe'. The universe is pervaded by 'Spirit'. This 'Spirit' is a 'Spirit of Nature', not God.

On the issue of empiricism More expressed his opposition to Hobbes sometimes in terminology like that of Descartes (sensations are only the 'extrinsical occasion' for having ideas), sometimes like that of Plato (external objects are rather 'the reminders than the first begetters or implanters of our knowledge').

Cudworth, in his immense *The True Intellectual System of the Universe* (1678, ed. J. Harrison, London, 1845) scorned the notion 'that *Life* and *Sense* could . . . spring out of *Dead* and *Senseless* Matter'. GOD creates things whose ESSENCES correspond to intelligible ideas and, at the same time, gives us intuitions of these ideas. He does not immediately and miraculously bring about changes in the material world. Under God 'there is a *Plastik Nature* which as an Inferior and Subordinate Instrument doth drudgingly execute that part of his Providence which consists in the Regular and Orderly Motion of Matter'.

With More's theory of a 'Spirit of Nature' and Cudworth's theory of a 'Plastik Nature' may be contrasted MALEBRANCHE's doctrine of 'OCCASIONALISM'. It turned out to be Malebranche, rather than the Cambridge Platonists, who had more influence in philosophy, even on philosophers writing in English, like BERKELEY and HUME. Still, had it not been for the Cambridge Platonists, LOCKE would not have felt the need to begin his *Essay* (1690) with an attack on the doctrine of INNATE IDEAS.

Camus, Albert (1913–1960), French writer and moralist from Algeria, who has had considerable influence in France after the war. Active in the Resistance, he became linked with the existentialists (see EXISTENTIALISM) through his early nihilist phase, although he disclaimed the connection. In any case he soon moved in a direction of his own, which is better described as a form of stoic humanism, as described in the novel *La Peste* (*The Plague*, 1947) and in his study *L'Homme révolté* (*The Rebel*, 1951). He regards all systems of values as rationally ungrounded, which leaves man to do the best he can to help his fellows and so himself. In particular, the grandiose 'issues' of our time are sham solutions that disregard the individual and lead to terror and bloodshed. The notion of revolt, central to his own position, has nothing to do with barricades but rather with an unwillingness passively to accept evil.

Carnap, Rudolf (1891–1970), German philosopher and leading exponent of LOGICAL POSITIVISM. He taught at Vienna and Prague, and in 1936 emigrated to the United States, teaching first at Chicago and from 1954 in Los Angeles. An early member of the VIENNA CIRCLE, he shared its general concerns and anti-metaphysical bent. As a criterion for meaningful discourse he used the principle of VERIFIABILITY, which accepts as meaningful only what can be directly verified by observation. This rules out all theoretical statements and was therefore found too sweeping: a milder form of verification was therefore adopted, where it was enough that some relevant consequence of a statement should be observable. At first, Carnap held that all significant experience can be reduced to sense-data, although that, too, proved to be too radical a proposal. In *The Logical Syntax of Language* (1934) he argued that LOGIC and MATHEMATICS were mere systems of signs combined by fixed rules but without any other MEANING or content: that is what made them necessary. As for philosophical problems, these arise when instead of making syntactic statements, we talk about various things as if they were genuine OBJECTS. Thus he excludes any talk about how signs are related to what they signify. Here again he later changed his view and did allow some concern with SEMANTICS. In his last years, he became interested in PROBABILITY THEORY, taking the view that probability was a logical relation between a HYPOTHESIS and the evidence on which it is based.

Cartesian dualism, *n.* DESCARTES'S theory that there are just two created SUBSTANCES: MIND, the ESSENCE of which is THINKING, and MATTER, the essence of which is EXTENSION.

Cartesianism, *n.* the philosophy of DESCARTES, and of those of his contemporaries, notably MALEBRANCHE, ARNAULD, SPINOZA, LOCKE and LEIBNIZ, who can be regarded as attempting to make good what they saw as deficiencies in his philosophy. Descartes seemed to some of his contemporaries to provide no adequate explanations (a) of how we are to understand the 'union' of MIND and body in a human being, given that mind and body are distinct SUBSTANCES (we can have a CLEAR and distinct idea of each without having to think of the other), and of how mind and body can act on one another (see MIND–BODY PROBLEM), (b) of what the term 'substance' means as applied to God, on the one hand, and to mind and body, on the other, given that the latter 'need the co-operation of God in order to exist', (c) of how bodies can be impenetrable, and so move one another by impulse, given that the essence of body is EXTENSION, (d) of the nature of ideas, given that they are *particular* things that occur in us on the occasion of our sense-organs being stimulated, on the one hand, and that we have ideas of what *general* words signify, on the other, and, finally, (e) of our being justified in believing in the existence of external material things, given that we are not immediately aware of them.

The Cartesians addressed themselves to these, and other, perceived deficiencies of Descartes's philosophy and, in doing so, modified his doctrines more, or less, profoundly. Spinoza, for example, replaced Descartes's substance-dualism with substance-monism. Someone who departed from Descartes too fundamentally, say by rejecting the notion of substance altogether, would not be counted a Cartesian.

Cassirer, Ernst (1874–1945), German Jewish neo-Kantian thinker, was professor in Hamburg for many years. In 1933 he emigrated and after some time in England and Sweden settled at Yale. He adopted a general Kantian point of view, but regarded KANT's system as too static and too narrow: the CATEGORIES must be allowed to develop, and fields other than the physical sciences must be recognised as having their own categorial features. For Cassirer, what characterises man is his capacity to symbolise his EXPERIENCE, that is, to set it down in symbolic form and so to understand it, in gesture, language and scientific theory. His main work is the *Philosophy of Symbolic Forms* (1923–29, translated 1953–57).

categorical imperative, *n.* a technical notion due to KANT, who regarded it as the central CRITERION for right conduct: always act in such a way that the principle underlying the action could be conceived as turned into a general law. It is a FORMAL principle and might be simply viewed as a bar against special pleading on one's own behalf.

category, *n.* a term introduced by ARISTOTLE for a general aspect under which one can describe a thing. He recognised 10 of these, as set out in his work *Categories:* substance, quantity, quality, relation, place, time, position, state, action and affection. As he put it, 'each uncombined expression means one of these: what, how large, what kind, related to what, where, when, how placed, in what state, acting or suffering' (1 b 25–28). For example, a man may be five foot six and a writer, a student of philosophy at his desk at midnight, sitting down and writing, and suffering from the cold. It is not clear how Aristotle arrived at 10 categories, perhaps the Pythagorean importance of that number had some bearing on it; at any rate the scheme is hardly systematic. The categories are taken as the highest kinds, not being in turn species of still higher ones. This theory more or less prevailed until KANT, who exhibits categories as linked with the structure of PROPOSITIONS. Thus as to quantity, these are universal, particular or singular in quantity; as to quality, affirmative, negative or infinite; as to relation, categorical, hypothetical or disjunctive; and as to modality, problematic, assertoric or apodeictic (i.e. possible, actual or necessary). From this, he arrives at his table of 12 categories (*Critique of Pure Reason*, B106). His list itself was perhaps less important than the systematic linking of categories with propositional structure, which has influenced later philosophers, in particular HEGEL.

That confusion arises if one mislocates an expression has always been recognised, and the term 'category mistake' is well known from the work of RYLE, who uses it freely. However, he does not himself develop a theory of categories.

cartharsis, *n.* (*Greek* a cleansing) a term used by early medical writers for purging, both of body and soul. It is a Pythagorean notion, and figures in PLATO's *Phaedo*, where philosophy is said to purge the soul (67c–d). In the *Poetics* (1449 b 28), ARISTOTLE speaks of the performance of tragedy producing a 'purging of the emotions'. The notion is used also in connection with mystical religious rites.

cause, *n.* a factor in the explanation of something being as it is. Prephilosophical explanations were in terms of the caprices of anthropomorphic gods. The first philosophers sought the explanation of natural things within nature itself, and speculated as to what the basic stuff (water, air, the boundless) of the world might be. ARISTOTLE called this the search for 'MATERIAL CAUSES'. ANAXAGORAS attributed movement or change in the stuff to NOUS (mind). PLATO contrasted the explanation of human actions in terms of MIND with an explanation in terms of the agent's body being composed of bones and sinew, the sinews by relaxing and contracting enabling him to bend his limbs, and so on. He called only the former 'the cause', and scorned those who were 'unable to distinguish between the cause of a thing, and the condition without which it could not be a cause' (*Phaedo* 99b). Since mind acts for an end, to explain things by reference to mind was to provide a teleological ('FINAL CAUSE') explanation. Plato's own approach to causality was part of his THEORY OF FORMS. The cause of something's being beautiful is 'the presence in it, or association with it, of absolute beauty' (100d). Absolute BEAUTY may be said to be the 'FORMAL CAUSE' of the thing being beautiful. Plato's theory is ultimately teleological since he postulates a supreme FORM, which has a role in the apprehension of the other Forms comparable to that of the sun in the apprehension of visible things, and this supreme Form is said to be the Form of the Good.

To the 'material', 'final' and 'formal' causes, Aristotle added the concept of an 'EFFICIENT CAUSE', defined as 'the primary source of the change', and illustrated by the examples of the man who gives advice being a cause, and the father being cause of the child (194 b 30). To a 17th century corpuscular philosopher like DESCARTES the obvious example would be that of one CORPUSCLE of MATTER in MOTION impelling another corpuscle of matter to move. Descartes gave himself a problem by specifying, in this example, *how* the efficient cause works (by impulse). This is possible since cause and EFFECT have a common quality, that of being spatially extended. Mind and body lack a common quality, save that of being created by GOD. So how does mind act on body, and vice versa? Some of Descartes's followers took the drastic step of declaring God to be the only efficient cause. Changes in minds and bodies are merely the occasions for God to will other changes. They are merely occasional causes, not real ones (see OCCASIONALISM).

Empiricist philosophers (see EMPIRICISM) had a different problem. From what EXPERIENCE do we derive our IDEA of an efficient cause, that is, something which has the power to necessitate some change? Is the experience such that we are justified in distinguishing between a causally connected sequence of events and one which merely occurs regularly? This was a question to which LOCKE and HUME addressed themselves. Hume's answer being criticised by KANT, who held the CONCEPT of cause to be A PRIORI.

certainty, *n.* (from Latin *certus* decided) is used both to describe a mental state (as when a person feels certain about something) or a feature of a PROPOSITION. Whether propositions are certain except if people are certain about them is indeed doubtful. The point of introducing certainty is as a guarantee for KNOWLEDGE: however, feeling certain that something is so does not ensure that it is so. The question remains controversial. A variety of philosophers from ancient times onward have taken as certain reflections (e.g. logic) that are purely conducted by the mind, and the immediate EXPERIENCE of the senses. However, the implied distinction is itself not beyond criticism. At the same time, many philosophers have regarded statements about other minds as uncertain, in contrast with statements about one's own mind, which are held to be certain. Some have put forward a universal

SCEPTICISM, according to which nothing is certain and therefore nothing is knowable, although they cannot explain how they know that. Finally, there is a very down-to-earth sense of certainty that goes back to the root meaning of something that has been decided: if, for example, we decide to set up a certain verbal DEFINITION, then nothing further remains to be said: it is certain. Some thinkers regard FORMAL systems as being thus decided and therefore certain.

Chinese philosophy, *n.* the philosophic thought of Chinese civilisation which has on the whole been governed by a practical outlook. Where the philosophy of Greece had been dominated by the notion of *logos* (word, account, explanation), that of China is guided by the concept of *tao* (see TAOISM), the way: it aims to show the path to be followed to achieve a harmonious existence of the individual not as such but as functioning in society in all its facets, from life in the family to the proper organisation of the State.

To start with, Chinese philosophy was grounded in the cumulative folk wisdom of Chinese history. This began to be treated in a somewhat more systematic manner from the 6th century BC onwards. CONFUCIUS (551–479 BC) and Laotse were the main figures of that period. Whereas the former regarded the *tao* as a doctrine of ethical truth, the latter saw in *tao* nature herself, so that following the path becomes living in tune with nature (somewhat in the manner of the Stoics) (see STOICISM). From each of them derives a school, called the Confucian and Taoist. Both are concerned with man and his place in society, but Taoism developed in a somewhat more abstract way, while Confucianism remained more closely in touch with the variety of actual life. The two main followers of Confucius were Mencius (372–298 BC) who taught that man was essentially good, and Hsun Tze (313–238 BC) who held on the contrary that man was originally evil. Opposed to Confucianism was the school of Mo Tzu (468–376 BC) who taught a doctrine of universal benevolence rather than the measured benevolence of Confucius. Moreover, he was opposed to the ritual performances that were important to the Confucian school. Another influential movement began at this time, based on the doctrine of the two principles of *yin* and *yang* (passive and active) which are seen as governing everything. It is under the influence of this doctrine that the *Book of Changes* arose to become a classic of Confucianism. It is an account of how the two principles arose, and from them the world that we know.

From the late 3rd century BC, under the Han dynasty, philosophical thought became syncretic, in particular coming up against elements from BUDDHISM. From the 10th century AD, a number of neo-Confucian orientations began to develop and continued right up to modern times. Since the communist revolution in China, the official philosophy has been a brand of dialectical materialism.

Chomsky, Noam (1928-   ), American linguist known in philosophy for his theory of the nature of language and the attendant views as to the constitution of the mind. According to Chomsky, a human being has an inherent linguistic competence which consists in an inborn structural disposition that comes to manifest itself in the ability to speak the language amongst whose speakers one grows up. Spoken languages differ widely, each having its own 'surface structure'. On the other hand, all languages share a 'deep structure' and it is this which we all have potential command of. What we do in learning an actual language is to apply a set of transformation rules that generate the particular surface structure from the universal deep structure. This, Chomsky holds, can explain why a competent speaker of a natural language can form an unlimited number of new sentences that he might never have heard. The empiricist account of language learning would have to rely on practice through repeated utterance and could thus not explain linguistic competence (see EMPIRICISM). Philosophically, Chomsky's theory comes close to the Cartesian notion of INNATE IDEAS. In any case, his account of language learning does not accord well with what we observe children doing when they learn to speak: they do in fact practice sounds by repetition, often provoking adults to correct them. MEANING is acquired piecemeal over a longer period, through use and further correction. The ability to form sentences not previously heard comes later at an advanced stage of language learning. See LANGUAGE, PHILOSOPHY OF.

Christianity, *n.* as a religious doctrine, consists of a set of beliefs of widely differing age and origins. First there is the figure of GOD, creator of heaven and earth, invisible and all-powerful, creating out of nothing and enjoining mankind to obey his laws. This is the God of the Jews, as seen in the Old Testament, as a Creator in Genesis, and as a Lawgiver in Exodus. Next comes the person of Joshua ben Joseph, the carpenter's son from Nazareth, better known to us as Jesus, the 'anointed one' (in Greek *christos*), whom some Jews regarded as the saviour announced by the prophets, while others did not. Jesus was in line with a new movement that gave the Scriptures a more generous interpretation (the sabbath is made for man, not man for the sabbath). As a Jew, Jesus would not have regarded himself as any more than a teacher, albeit an inspired one. However, his doctrine was addressed to all men, not only to Jews, and his followers came to regard him as the incarnate son of God, immaculately conceived and born of a human mother, Mary. The story of his ministry is told in the four Gospels, Greek documents from the late 1st to mid-2nd centuries AD. Through the mediation of Jesus, fallen mankind can achieve everlasting life after death, by repentance and belief in the Master. During the next four centuries there gradually emerged the basic framework of Christian theology, which tries to give some kind of rational account, insofar as this is possible, of Christian doctrine, using Greek META-PHYSICS as a basis, in particular neo-Platonic, Aristotelian and Stoic speculations (see NEO-PLATONISM, ARISTOTLE, STOICISM). Thus arose an orthodox line of Christian belief, all deviations being branded as heresies. One difficulty was to explain the relation of God the Father to God the Son. For example, some denied that the Son ever was truly human (Docetism), while others denied that he was always divine, because he must have been created by the Father (Arianism). The orthodox dogma finally decreed at the Council of Nicaea (325) that Father and Son were of the same substance *(omoousioi)*, not as Arius had said of similar substance *(omoiousioi)*. A further doctrine that was gradually elaborated was that of the Holy Trinity: God as Father, Son and Holy Spirit, three aspects of the one God.

The set of Christian dogmata as a whole is a somewhat varied lot that do not all go comfortably together. In theory, an adherent is supposed to declare his belief in them. In practice, it is not easy either to check this, or make out what it amounts to. However, neither of these things is necessary for the religion to have inspired many generations of men to implement their beliefs to the best of their limited powers.

class, *n*. in POLITICAL PHILOSOPHY, denotes a group of people who enjoy similarity of status on the grounds of often ill-defined and varied features, that may differ from one society to another. Thus, in some places men are classified according to their income, in others according to their education, or their attainments, or their outlook. A special sense is given to the term class in Marxist doctrine: there, it denotes people who stand in the same relation to the means of production. Much confusion is generated by not keeping clearly in view what criterion is being used in a particular instance.

clear, *adj*. DESCARTES says that 'we never go wrong when we assent only to what we clearly and distinctly perceive' (*Principles of Philosophy*, Pt. 1, Sect. 43). A PERCEPTION is clear 'when it is present and accessible to the attentive mind'. It is distinct 'if, as well as being clear, it is so sharply separated from all other perceptions that it contains within itself only what is clear'. His example is that when someone is in pain his perception of the pain is clear, but it is not distinct: he confuses his perception of the pain with an obscure judgment he makes concerning the nature of something he thinks exists in the painful spot. Really, the pain is in his mind; but he seems to feel it in some part of his body; so his perception of it, while clear, is not distinct in that he fails to distinguish it from something bodily.

cogito (short for Latin *cogito, ergo sum* I think, therefore I am), the famous proposition of which DESCARTES said, in his *Discourse on the Method of Rightly Conducting the Reason* (1637), IV, that it 'was so certain and so assured that all the most extravagant suppositions brought forward by the sceptics (see SCEPTICISM) were incapable of shaking it'. Descartes intended using its certainty in his attempts

(a) to justify treating the clearness and distinctness with which *anything* is perceived as a CRITERION of its being true;

(b) to prove that the MIND is a SUBSTANCE distinct from the body (from which it would follow that the mind can survive the corruption of the body).

The first argument goes as follows. I am certain of the truth of the *cogito*. All that assures me of its truth is that I conceive it clearly and distinctly. Therefore clearness and distinctness must be a sufficient criterion of truth in general.

Descartes himself decided that the *cogito* was not sufficient for this purpose. In the same part of the *Discourse* he wrote: 'But if we did not know that all that is in us of reality and truth proceeds from a perfect and infinite Being, however clear and distinct were our ideas, we should not have any reason to assure ourselves that they had the perfection of being true.' In addition to the *cogito* he needed a proof of the existence of an undeceiving god.

The second argument goes like this. I cannot doubt that I think. I can doubt everything else, e.g. that I have bodily attributes. God, being omnipotent, could have made me without those attributes I can doubt myself having. Therefore, essentially, I am distinct from 'my' body, even though I am, in fact, united with it in this life.

How far Descartes succeeds in his attempts has remained controversial, agreement being made harder by his formulating the premiss of the arguments differently in his *Meditations on First Philosophy* (1640), II. Two of the points that have been made about the phrase 'I think' are (a) that Descartes, while he is thinking, is entitled to say, with certainty, that THINKING is going on, but not that the PREDICATE 'think' has a particular subject, the one referred to by 'I'; and (b) that a peculiarity of 'I think', as thought, is that it is self-verifying (like 'I am speaking', *said* by someone). Alternatively it has been maintained, on the basis of Descartes's exposition in the *Meditations*, that what matters is that a person's thoughts are 'evident' to him in a special sense; he is 'immediately conscious' of them (see IMMEDIATE). What 'evidence' and 'CONSCIOUSNESS' mean in this connection some regard as unclear. See CARTESIANISM.

cognition, see KNOWLEDGE.

Collingwood, Robin George (1889–1943), English philosopher and historian and archaeologist of Roman Britain, who became professor at Oxford. His philosophical position is complex and changed with time, but in general terms it is based on idealist assumptions, even if he is critical about certain aspects of IDEALISM. From an earlier view that the task of philosophy was to provide a rational account of our knowledge (*Essay on Philosophical Method*, 1933) he later proceeded to the position that philosophy had to lay bare the basic presuppositions that underlie our thinking (*Essay on Metaphysics*, 1940), which are different at various periods, so that the task becomes a historical one; a view that has some affinity with the doctrine of CROCE. His notion of history as the story of human thinking has Hegelian undertones (see HEGEL). His aesthetic theory, too, is close to that of Croce.

communism, *n.* is a social system in which the community as a whole is the owner of all assets, and all members of the society work for the group to the best of their abilities. In return, the group will give to each member goods according to his or her needs ('from each according to his ability, to each according to his needs'). Whether such a system has ever in fact existed on a large scale is doubtful. Perhaps the nearest that we come to it is the internal functioning of a Kibbutz. Such an institution in an environment that is organised differently must indeed operate differently in its dealings with the outside. Whether a full-blown arrangement of this type holding throughout the world is possible is likewise extremely unlikely: it presupposes a centralised 'owner' whose benevolent ministrations look to the universal distribution of goods. This requires a bureaucracy that would crush itself under its own weight.

The communist idea has a long history and may be traced back to PLATO's *Republic*, although he does not advance it as a practical political plan but rather as a speculative argument. It is indeed a utopian dream which assumes that the problem of production has already been solved (see UTOPIANISM). It is then a matter of sharing equitably. The source of all evil is seen in the competitive spirit, which is regarded as setting men against each other: it encourages men to acquire unfair shares for themselves. The extreme form of this view was expressed by the French political writer, Proudhon, in 1840: 'property is theft'. Moreover, since a communist system requires loyalty to the group above all else, any other focus of loyalty becomes suspect. In particular, the structure of the family may be regarded as a threat to the system, and some theorists demand that family ties must be loosened if not destroyed. In practice, this seems to be more difficult, because it is arguable that the survival of this form of organisation has considerable value for survival in the sense of evolution. To return to the example of the Kibbutz, the work to be done requires that children are looked after together during the day, and adults take their meals together in canteens, but at night family units are reunited. As for the assumption that in the absence of property there will be no further incitement to overstepping the mark and that therefore there will be no need for laws and their enforcement, this seems romantic in the extreme. So is the Marxist notion that, given a communist system, the State will ultimately wither away. See MARX.

A rather more down-to-earth political arrangement is that of socialism, where what is held in common are the means of production. This is a much more recent notion, since it is based on the existence of large-scale industrial installations. Here a strong centralised organising power is frankly admitted as necessary. It was LENIN who thought that once the socialist system had solved the problem of production, it could give way to communism, viewed as a kind of kingdom of heaven on earth.

Comte, Auguste (1798–1857), French philosopher who founded POSITIVISM. In his *Course of Positive Philosophy* (1830–1842, trans. 1853), he gave an account of the three stages in the history of each science: the theological, metaphysical and positive. The various sciences form a hierarchy in which the later depend on the earlier: mathematics, astronomy, physics (including chemistry), biology (including psychology) and sociology (his term). Each of these sciences eventually reach the positive stage, in the order of their place in the hierarchy. Sociology, or the science of society, in its positive stage, will ensure a return of social harmony: just as people do not fall out over questions of astronomy, which has reached its positive stage, neither will they over social questions when sociology has. In his later years, Comte had reservations about social cohesion in the absence of religion. He therefore advocated a kind of rational positive cult somewhat reminiscent of similar efforts at the time of the French Revolution.

concept, *n.* what enables one to use a word correctly, recognise something as being of the sort referred to by the word, define the word. Someone or something could still have the concept that lacked one of these capacities. Animals who cannot talk can be trained to react to triangles differently from the way they react to other shapes, and so may be said to have the concept triangle. Someone who could not recognise triangles because he had lost the senses of sight and touch has not for that reason lost the concept. Someone who could use the term 'triangle' correctly should be able to provide some sort of DEFINITION, but there are other words, such as 'time', that people can use correctly though they cannot define them. Having a concept does mean having certain capacities, but none of those mentioned is essential.

Two issues remain controversial: What is the explanation of our having capacities? What is it for the use of a word to be correct?

For some, to have the concept of triangularity is to have an 'abstract idea' of triangularity, obtained by ABSTRACTION from the SENSATIONS we have on looking at triangles. Even those who hold this theory acknowledge difficulties in it. LOCKE says that the abstract idea of a triangle is, in effect, something that cannot exist (*Essay*, IV vii 9). Recently philosophers have rejected explanation of concept-acquisition in terms of abstraction. WITTGENSTEIN, for instance, says that one acquires a concept in acquiring the relevant linguistic competence, by being brought up to use the word according to the rules of practice implicitly accepted by the members of one's linguistic community. For correct use of a word, see UNIVERSALS.

Condillac, Étienne Bonnot de (1715–1780), French philosopher, inspired by VOLTAIRE's praise of LOCKE to attempt, in his *Essai sur l'origine des connaissances humaines (Essay on the Origin of Human Knowledge)* (Paris, 1746, re-edited by the author, 1771) and his *Traité des sensations (Treatise of Sensations)* (Paris, 1754, re-edited 1778), to 'reduce to one single principle all that concerns human understanding'. The one principle was that of SENSE-IMPRESSIONS occasioned by stimulation of sense-organs. In brief, perceiving (see PERCEPTION) is simply the occurrence of the sense-impression; attending is its being vivacious; if the vivacious impression persists there is MEMORY; if two impressions are related there is judgment; and so on. This went beyond the scope of Locke's *Essay*, for Locke believed in understanding as something distinct from sense.

In attempting a systematic sensationalist (see SENSATIONALISM) analysis Condillac might seem to be, like BERKELEY, an immaterialist, but he was not. He sought to explain awareness of external material things in terms of the difference between the two feelings of contact which one has on touching one's own body and the single feeling one has on touching an OBJECT other than one's body.

Condillac's manner of presenting his sensationalist analysis is particularly memorable. He imagined a marble statue to which he successively attributed various sensory capacities, beginning with smell, and built up, from that beginning, a being with all the capacities and BELIEFS of a human being.

conditionals, *n.* are sentences of the 'if . . ., then . . .' type. The if-clause may be false, in which case the conditional is said to be counter-factual. How these are to be analysed remains a controversial question. The ordinary conditional, where one assumes the if-clause to be true, is a straightforward implication (see IMPLICATION AND ENTAILMENT) ('if the barometer falls, then it will rain'). In other words, the if-clause is a reason for stating the then–clause: there is some link between the two. This is not to be confused with material implication (written '$p \supset q$' and read 'if p, then q'), where no such link exists.

conditioning, *n.* either a method whereby something an animal does automatically (e.g. salivating), as a reflex response to something (food), is made to occur in response to something else (e.g. a bell ringing); or a method whereby an animal can be got to do again something it does voluntarily (e.g. a cat pulling a piece of string, or a rat pressing a lever) by rewarding it (e.g. releasing it from a cage, or giving it food) for doing it. Conditioning in the first sense is sometimes called 'Pavlovian conditioning' after I. P. Pavlov (1849–1936) who had found that digestive secretions take place in a dog not only in response to food, but also in response to what he called a 'psychic stimulus' such as the sound of the rattling of dishes in the preparation of food.

Conditioning in the second sense was a method used by E. L. Thorndike (1874–1949) in his investigation of learning in animals, and, later, by B. F. Skinner (1904–   ), who called it 'operant conditioning' because it is based on the animal operating on its environment in some way. Thorndike found that in a problem-solving situation such as that of having to escape from a maze, the animal would indulge in what he called 'trial and error' behaviour; if some particular 'try' was successful the animal would tend to repeat it; Thorndike would then say that the tendency to repeat it had been 'stamped-in' as a result of its effectiveness. If learning could be explained by reference to 'the law of effect' then there would be no need to invoke something not open to public observation, 'insight'. It is understandable, therefore, that the notions of trial and error learning, and of conditioning, should appeal to behaviourists. See BEHAVIOURISM.

confirmation, *n.* is the support given to a HYPOTHESIS by the evidence that can be found in its favour. Since there can always be further evidence, this process is never complete. However, a single unfavourable piece of evidence can disconfirm or invalidate a hypothesis.

Confucius, (K'ung Fu Tse, Master Kung) (551–479 BC) is the first and best-known Chinese philosopher (see CHINESE PHILOSOPHY). He came from a noble but impoverished family. Trained in the arts of men of his class, he worked in various capacities as a civil servant in his native state of Lu. After his patron had died, Confucius, with a group of followers, began a period of wandering, in search of employment elsewhere. After nearly a decade, he returned home and set up a school in which he taught his doctrine to a select circle of adherents. The important new feature of his teaching was that the leading of the good life (in the ethical sense) must be severed from the external performance of ritual practices and be changed to an internal respect for justice and propriety. Men had lost the instinctive knowledge of the right way, so that ritual had become empty. Therefore it was necessary to cultivate a deliberate and informed pursuit of human virtue, to enable people to restore social harmony, which was sadly lacking at that time.

connotation, *n.* of a term, is everything the term signifies (the set of PREDICATES of all true statements of which the term is the SUBJECT). Thus, the connotation of the term 'man' includes such items as being rational, two-legged, mortal and so on. See DENOTATION.

conscience, *n.* (from Latin *conscientia* awareness) is now used for the awareness of the moral qualities of one's own behaviour in the first instance and of human actions in general. In the writings of HUME, the term often means what we now call CONSCIOUSNESS, the two being expressed in French by the one word *conscience*. Moral awareness is an essential characteristic of human beings as living in social groups. A total lack of it is abnormal and indeed dangerous both for him who lacks it and for the other members of his society.

consciousness, *n.* a psychologist once described 'conscious' as 'what we are more and more, as the noise of the crowd outside tardily arouses us from our after-dinner nap' (Ladd, G. T., *Psychology, Descriptive and Explanatory*, N.Y., 1894, p. 30). An 'object of consciousness', in this ordinary sense of 'conscious', would be some such thing as 'the noise of the crowd outside'. There is a philosophical use of the term, which is different. LOCKE (*Essay*, II i 19) says that consciousness is 'the perception of what passes in a man's own mind'. Whereas in the ordinary use of 'conscious', consciousness is opposed to unconsciousness, in this philosopher's usage mental events or operations are opposed to physical ones.

Two questions arise. (a) There can be a crowd outside without my being conscious of it. Can things pass in my mind without my being conscious of them? (b) It makes perfectly good sense to talk of my 'perceiving the crowd outside'. Does it make equally good sense to talk of my 'perceiving what passes in my mind'?

It is evident (from *Essay*, II i 19, and II xxvii 9) that Locke's answer to the first question is 'No', and (from *Essay*, II i 4, 8) that his answer to the second is 'Yes'. Both answers may be disputed. DESCARTES, Locke thought, would have had to dispute the first, since he defined the SOUL as a SUBSTANCE that always thinks, and people are not constantly conscious of THINKING. Psychoanalysts would dispute it because it is part of their theory and practice that people have unconscious desires (see PSYCHOANALYSIS).

That it makes good sense to talk of 'perceiving what passes in one's mind' may be disputed on the ground that whereas circumstances are easily imaginable in which the question 'How do you know, or what evidence have you, that there is a crowd outside?' is a perfectly sensible question to ask, it is difficult to imagine circumstances which would make 'How do you know, or what evidence have you, *that you think* there is a crowd outside?' a sensible question to ask. It is to this esoteric question that 'By consciousness' is the philosopher-made answer. For example, about the 'operations of our minds' (thinking, remembering, reasoning) Thomas REID says that 'consciousness is the evidence, the only evidence, which we have or can have of their existence' (*Essays on the Intellectual Powers of Man*, Bk. 1, Ch. 2).

Reid's remark may be countered in two different ways. One is to say, with Sydney Shoemaker (*Self-knowledge and Self-identity*, Ithaca,

New York, 1963, p. 122), 'It is a distinguishing characteristic of first-person-experience statements . . . that it is simply their being true, and not the observation that they are true, or the possession of evidence that they are true, that entitles one to assert them'. The other way is to dispute even what Shoemaker accepts, namely that the question 'Is one entitled to assert them?' arises in the case of utterances like 'I think there's a crowd outside' and 'I hope it will soon go away'. A positive way of putting this is to say that such utterances are AVOWALS. See INTROSPECTION.

consequentialism, *n.* the theory that ACTIONS are to be judged by their outcome. An example is UTILITARIANISM, in which it is held that useful ends justify the means for attaining them. Thus, compulsory purchase of land for the sake of building a road is sometimes declared to be justified because the usefulness of the finished highway is regarded as outweighing the evil of destroying the homes of those who lived on the repurchased land.

contingent and necessary statements, logicians distinguish between those statements that happen to be true as a matter of fact (grass happens to be green, though it might have been red for all we know before we observed it), and those other statements that are true because of their very FORM, no matter what else may be the case. The former statements are called contingent, the latter necessary. As to what statements, if any, are necessary, opinions differ. Some say that mathematical statements are necessary, as here defined, but others deny this.

contradiction, *n.* (from Latin *contra* against, *dictio* a saying) a gainsaying, the act of saying the opposite of or denying what another has said. By extension, the opposite statement itself. If a statement is true, then its denial contradicts it, and the two are in contradiction. The *principle of contradiction* (see ARISTOTLE) states that a statement is either true or false.

conventionalism, *n.* is the view that the truths of MATHEMATICS are mere useful conventions, rather than independent facts about the world. This position was put forward by the French mathematician, Henri Poincaré (1854–1912).

Copernicus, Nicolas (1473–1543), Polish cleric who had studied medicine and astronomy as well, and in due course revived the ancient heliocentric hypothesis of Aristarchus of Samos, the Greek astronomer (3rd century BC). Instead of the then current Ptolemaic system, based on the old Aristotelian geocentric system with the earth at the centre (see ARISTOTLE), Copernicus advanced the theory that the planets move in circular paths about the sun as their common centre. The advantage of this was that it provided a simple and unified explanation of observed stellar positions. It was not yet a complete theory of celestial motion; for this to develop, two further stages were needed: Kepler's findings that planetary orbits were elliptical and traced out according to definite quantitative laws, and NEWTON's law of universal gravitation (the inverse square law). Nevertheless, the fact that Copernicus displaced man from the central position in the universe, against all established authority, clerical and scientific, caused a complete change in outlook: medieval ways of thinking had been undermined, and fairly quickly gave way to the modern approach. The book in which this theory was expounded is entitled *De Revolutionibus Orbium Coelestium* (1543), that is 'on the rotations of the heavenly bodies'. It is interesting that the term 'revolution', in the sense of sudden change in outlook or in social and political organisation, first appears in the mid-16th century. The new outlook in astronomy came to be called the Copernican Revolution.

corpuscle, *n.* a minute particle of MATTER. The term 'corpuscularian philosophers' was used, with opprobrium, by BERKELEY, to describe DESCARTES and LOCKE. Berkeley held that ideas are caused, not by corpuscles of matter affecting our sense-organs, but by GOD.

cosmology, *n.* (from Greek *cosmos* order, *logos* account) in philosophy, an 18th century term, now out of fashion, for the study of space, time, number, matter and motion. In physics, the term is used for the science that studies the physical structure of the universe as a whole.

cosmological argument, *n.* any one of a set of arguments aiming to start from a feature of the world as it is and thence establish that GOD exists. Examples are ARISTOTLE's conception of a first and unmoved mover (an agent which is ultimately the cause of all MOTION), AQUINAS's first and uncaused CAUSE (which is the ground of all causality in the world), and the notion of a NECESSARY being as ground for all the contingent beings in the actual world. None of these arguments is valid. They each depend on an assumption that contradicts the initial observation. Take causality: if every effect has a cause, it follows that there can be no first cause, precisely because such an item would not itself have a cause. The so-called proof of Aquinas, however, states that if every effect must have a cause, there must be a first and uncaused cause, which simply contradicts the principle of causality.

creation, *n.* the doctrine of how the world was made. In Greek thought, the world, if it was made, was constructed from pre-existing matter by some divine architect. In the Judaeo-Christian tradition, GOD made the ingredients as well: the world was created by him *ex nihilo* (out of nothing). Such an act of creation being a definite event, the world that results has at any time had a finite length of existence behind it and is totally dependent on its creator. One is tempted to ask (but discouraged from doing so) who created the creator, to which there is no answer. In the absence of a creator, the world need not have had a beginning: given any point in time, there have been earlier ones.

criterion, *n.* (*Greek*) a means of judging. The Stoics (see STOICISM) sought for a 'means of judging' that could be used to distinguish veridical (trustworthy) SENSE-IMPRESSIONS from others. In modern philosophy DESCARTES was concerned with the question whether the criterion of something's being true is its being clearly and distinctly perceived (see CLEAR). KANT said that truth, formally, is the agreement of KNOWLEDGE with its OBJECT, but that since the objects of knowledge vary, the content of knowledge varies, so 'it is quite impossible, and indeed absurd, to ask for a general test of truth' (*Critique of Pure Reason*, A59).

In recent philosophy the term 'criterion' has been used, not in talk of a general criterion of truth, but in other related ways. G. E. MOORE, for example, wrote of a characteristic 'which cannot be said to be a "MEANING" of the term "mental", but which may be and has been proposed as a criterion of what is mental . . . namely, that any entity which *can be directly known by one mind only* is a mental entity' ('The Subject-matter of Psychology', *Proc. Arist. Soc.*, 1909–10). Moore's point was that being directly knowable by one mind only, while not what we mean by 'mental entity', may be something which happens to be true of all mental entities. Someone who said that in a case of so-called 'multiple personality' there are two minds, and who accepted that one of them sometimes directly knows what goes on in the other, would have to deny that being directly knowable by one mind only is a criterion of something being a mental entity.

WITTGENSTEIN, in *The Blue and Brown Books* (Oxford, 1958) used the term 'criterion' in a way that is almost the opposite of the way Moore used it. He contrasted the 'defining criterion' of a disease, which might be the presence of a specific bacillus, with the symptoms of the disease. Then, in the *Philosophical Investigations* (Oxford, 1953) he went on to use the term in another way, because amongst the conditions of the meaningfulness of an utterance he distinguished between agreement in DEFINITIONS and a different sort of agreement. Human beings (and higher animals) agree in reacting instinctively to cuts, knocks, and the like, by crying out. In human beings the linguistic utterance 'It hurts', or 'I'm in pain', comes to be used in place of the instinctive behaviour, to attract attention, sympathy, and so on. Someone who says 'It hurts' is not describing his behaviour, but without the aforementioned common behavioural response and tie-up between behaviour and utterances, his utterance would not have the meaning (use) it has. Therefore there is an internal relation between being in pain and behaving in certain ways. It is this internal relation between them that is marked by calling the behaviour a criterion of the so-called 'inner process', the pain.

One important respect in which a criterion, as Wittgenstein used the term in the *Philosophical Investigations*, differs from a criterion as envisaged by the Stoics and Descartes, is that it is not a truth-condition. It is a means of judging, but not one which guarantees the truth of the judgment.

critical realism, *n*. a theory of KNOWLEDGE opposed both to IDEALISM and naive REALISM. The critical realist opposes the former for its view that what we perceive is our own mental furniture (sense-data and the like) (see SENSE-DATUM), and the latter for supposing that we grasp the physical world directly. Instead, the critical realist regards our perceiving and cognising as conveying the external world to us. This is not to ignore these processes, but to put them into proper perspective: our SENSATIONS are in a sense symbols (stand for) the world of independent things. Critical realism was put forward by the American philosopher, R. W. Sellars in a book of that title in 1916.

Croce, Benedetto (1866–1952), Italian philosopher, was in his time the most influential if critical follower of Hegelian principles. From HEGEL, he derives the central emphasis on the historical dimension in all aspects of human affairs. History itself he described as 'the story of liberty', and liberty in turn is taken as the supreme value. Croce's aesthetic theory (see AESTHETICS) owes much to VICO as well, whom he brought back into prominence. According to Croce, aesthetic understanding is based on a kind of insight (intuition) *sui generis*, different both from conceptual formulation and from emotive feeling. Genuine historical experience does enable us to make statements of which we can properly say that they are true, or false. In contrast, the statements of scientific theory are ABSTRACTIONS, and although they are often useful, they could lead to genuine KNOWLEDGE only if we could grasp PLATO's 'FORMS'. Croce had independent means and was therefore able to devote his life to his literary, historical and philosophical studies. An early opponent of the Fascist movement, he was a life-long liberal and after the Second World War became briefly drafted into government office. His influence on intellectual life in Italy has been enormous.

Cudworth, Ralph (1617–1688), see CAMBRIDGE PLATONISM.

cynics, *n.* a group of thinkers during Hellenistic times, who were disenchanted with the established way of life and sought happiness through a form of indifference to material comforts. Their name means 'the dog-like ones', probably because the first of the line, Diogenes of Sinope (4th century BC), is said to have lived in a dog's hut. The general outlook of the Cynics was to disregard artificial features of life (like wealth and social position) and to concentrate on self-knowledge and on acting in a virtuous manner. Their aim was to become self-determining and thus free, by living in accordance with nature. These views seem to have had some influence on the ethical doctrines of the Stoics (see STOICISM).

D

Darwinism, *n.* the theory of EVOLUTION of new species by natural selection: some offspring of members of a species are mutants; some of these mutants chance to be better adapted to the environment than non-mutant offspring; because of this the mutant offspring have more offspring, also mutant, than the non-mutant; and the mutants eventually crowd out the non-mutants. The theory was propounded by Charles Robert Darwin (1809–1882) and Alfred Russel Wallace (1823–1913), and was well summed up in the title of Darwin's book, *On the Origin of Species by Means of Natural Selection, or the Preservation of Favoured Races in the Struggle for Life* (1859).

The significance of Darwinism in philosophy lies in its opposition to traditional Aristotelian views about things happening not by chance but for ends (see ARISTOTLE); and any changes, such as the members of a species growing their front teeth sharper, fitted for tearing, and their molars broader, useful for grinding (*Physics*, Bk. 2, Ch. 8) serving the end of the continuation of the existing species rather than the origination of a new species. Species, as such, are immutable. These Aristotelian views had become sacrosanct. They were challenged by Darwin's theory of natural selection as applied not to the characteristics of species, but to species themselves.

There is empirical evidence of the evolution by natural selection of new characteristics of existing species, such as the camouflaging darkness of the small peppered moth in grimy industrial areas in the 19th century. However, the theory of the origin of new species by natural selection is programmatic, and what it predicts is not always to be found. Fossil evidence of transitional species, which one would expect to find on Darwin's theory, is virtually missing. (An exception is *Archaeopteryx*, the link between birds and dinosaurs.) On the contrary, the fossil evidence suggests that evolution occurs by jumps, rather than gradually. Alternative mechanisms of evolution are being sought. Nevertheless, Darwin's imaginative theory remains of immense value.

Davidson, Donald (1917-   ), American philosopher, professor at Chicago University, is best known for his work on human ACTION, and how the explanation of an action is related to the reasons for which it is taken. While distinguishing between reasons and CAUSES, we may say that the primary reason for an action is indeed its cause, but not that there is a causal law linking reasons with actions. He has extensively examined the truth conditions of indirect discourse, rejecting AUSTIN'S view that performatives are neither true nor false. For the attendant SEMANTICS, he adopts TARSKI'S theory of truth.

deduction, *n.* the logical process by which one derives one PROPOSITION (the conclusion) from one or more others (the premisses), following certain general rules. A conclusion so obtained must be true if the premisses are. The premisses are then said to entail the conclusion. (See IMPLICATION AND ENTAILMENT). The field in which the process of deduction stands out perhaps most clearly (outside LOGIC itself) is MATHEMATICS. That is one reason why mathematical education since the time of PLATO has rightly been regarded as important.

definition, *n.* defining justice is either saying what the ESSENCE of justice really is ('real' definition), or it is saying what the MEANING of the word 'justice' is ('nominal' definition). If the latter, it may be either describing the meaning with which the word is currently used ('descriptive' or 'dictionary' definition) or prescribing a meaning for it ('prescriptive' or 'stipulative' definition). In a dictionary one commonly finds two sorts of definition, examples of which are: 'nephew: a brother's or sister's son' and 'red: the colour of blood and fire'. In the first sort an expression is supplied which is equivalent to, and so can be substituted for, the word being defined. In place of the second sort of dictionary definition the meaning of 'red' may be suggested by pointing at blood and saying 'That is called "red"' ('ostensive' definition). A paradoxical utterance like 'The service of God is perfect freedom', although not in the form either of a dictionary or of a prescriptive definition, may be regarded as a sort of definition. Being intended to persuade people to think of things differently, it may be called a 'persuasive' definition.

PLATO and ARISTOTLE believed in real definitions, the former because of his THEORY OF FORMS, the latter because of his doctrine of real intelligible essences. The distinction between 'real' and 'nominal' definitions was a commonplace in philosophy at least up to the time of LOCKE but, being associated with outdated views, such as

Aristotelianism in science, it is now of mainly historic interest. The term 'ostensive definition' was introduced into philosophy as recently as 1921, by a Cambridge logician W. E. Johnson in his *Logic* (Cambridge, 1921, Pt. 1, Ch. VI, 7). WITTGENSTEIN used it to attack the view that sense can be given to a term like 'pain' by a sort of private ostensive definition, and in his general attack on the empiricist (see EMPIRICISM) notion that language is founded on EXPERIENCE. The term 'persuasive definition' was introduced, even more recently, by an American moral philosopher, C. L. Stevenson, and used in his exposition of an emotivist theory of ETHICS in *Ethics and Language* (New Haven, 1944) (see EMOTIVISM).

deism, *n.* (from Latin *deus* god) a line of rationalistic religious thought that affirms that there is a GOD but denies that he should be understood in any mystical way. The antecedents of deism go back to ARISTOTLE's First Mover, who moved 'the first heaven' at the circumference of the universe but is otherwise unconcerned with human affairs. Deism proper arose with the RENAISSANCE and particularly the ENLIGHTENMENT. It is not a school in any sense, but rather typifies a general approach to religion: individualistic, non-mystical, non-institutional and often anti-clerical. To mention only two great philosophical figures, both LOCKE and KANT took a deist position. As an anti-authoritarian way of thinking, deism in modern times is one of the results of the Protestant REFORMATION. Insofar as it implies a general spirit of tolerance (witness Frederick the Great's dictum that in his realm everyone could save his soul in his own fashion), deism remains in effect a living force today. Besides, toleration in religious matters tends to spread to other human concerns, particularly social and political.

demiurge, *n.* (from Greek *demiourgos* craftsman) the term used by PLATO, in the *Timaeus*, for the being who copies the FORMS onto the receptacle for them, space, thereby producing the many SENSIBLE things which share in the Forms.

democracy, *n.* (from Greek *demos* people, *kratos* strength) a form of government in which power rests with the people, either directly, where numbers are small enough (now almost extinct), or through representatives, chosen for a given term either by lot (as in ancient Athens) or by ballot (as universally the case today). See POLITICAL PHILOSOPHY.

Democritus (*c.*460–*c.*370 BC), of Abdera, a former Greek city on the coast of Thrace not far from the mouth of the Nestos River, was a pupil or associate of Leucippus. Leucippus (*fl. c.*440–435 BC), who was probably born in Miletus and may have visited Elea and Abdera, was credited by ARISTOTLE (*On Generation and Corruption* 325 a 23) with originating the theory of ATOMISM. But whereas Leucippus wrote only two books (*On Mind* and the *Great World-system*), hardly any fragments of which have survived, Democritus wrote well over 50, and it is with his name that 5th-century atomism is usually associated.

By definition, an atom is something that is indivisible. If 'atomism' meant merely that, the Eleatics, PARMENIDES, Zeno and MELISSUS, who held that only one thing exists, and that it is indivisible, would be atomists (see ELEATICISM). The term 'atomism' is used only of those who hold that there are many atoms. Nevertheless the atomism of LEUCIPPUS and Democritus has a lot in common with Eleaticism. Indeed it is more than likely that Melissus gave Leucippus the idea of atomism by remarking that *if* there were many things, each would have to be like the Eleatic One: ungenerated and imperishable, without any qualities, and indivisible.

According to Eleaticism, if there were many things there would have to be a void between one thing and the next. Otherwise why call them two things rather than one? However, a void is nothing, and cannot have being: to talk of a void is to talk of not-being. Leucippus boldly broke the logical rules of Eleaticism, and said that the void, not-being, exists. This freed him to postulate a plurality of Eleatic Ones, differing only in shape and size, in eternal motion in the void. This makes it possible to explain change in the world of the senses, which the Eleatics had had to dismiss as illusory.

The atoms Leucippus postulated are sub-microscopic, but their shapes are such that some of them, when they collide because of their motion, attach themselves to one another and so give rise to sizable aggregates. Although they have no sensible qualities, the interaction of aggregates of atoms of certain shapes and sizes with those of sentient bodies is such that it appears to people that there is a world of things that are sweet or bitter, hot or cold, and so on. All this is mere appearance; it is on the side of belief, not of truth. In truth, all that exists is (a) the atoms, of which all that can be said is that they have certain shapes and sizes and that there is no void in them to permit divisibility (they are 'full'); and (b) the void, empty space. As Aristotle put it (*Metaphysics* 985 b 4) 'Leucippus and his associate Democritus say that the full and the empty are the elements'.

Atomism is not the only pluralistic (see PLURALISM) alternative to

Eleatic MONISM. There are also the theories of EMPEDOCLES and ANAX-AGORAS. The atomists differed from Empedocles and Anaxagoras in recognising the need to allow the void, not-being, some sort of existence for there to be many things, but above all in trying to explain absolutely everything in terms of the coming together and separating of atoms. They did not invoke some extraneous moving cause, like the Love and Strife of Empedocles, or the NOUS of Anaxagoras. Even man's soul was to be explained atomically. Democritus held that some atoms are specially fine and round, so that they can easily penetrate the whole body and control its functions. PERCEPTION arises from the interaction of these soul-atoms with external aggregates of atoms. In visual perception, for example, the air between the eye and the object of sight is contracted and stamped by the object seen and the seer with an image which then enters the eye. (Democritus seems to have taken over the theory of 'effluences' of Empedocles.) Thought, similarly, depends on the impact of an image. At death the soul-atoms disperse and are scattered.

denotation, *n*. in LOGIC, the set of things a given term refers to; that is, the denotation of the given term is the set of SUBJECT terms which with the given term as PREDICATE form true PROPOSITIONS. Thus, the denotation of *animal* is the set of terms *X* such that *X* is an animal is true. See CONNOTATION.

Deontology, *n*, (from Greek *deon* that which should be, DUTY), the science of DUTY, but now more specifically a form of ethical theory where duties are ABSOLUTE, no matter what the consequences. This view is opposed to the empirical insight that circumstances alter cases.

Derrida, Jacques (1930–   ), French philosopher and professor at the École Normale Supérieure in Paris, belongs to the post-STRUCTURALIST movement and practises a kind of investigation that he calls 'deconstruction', by which he means interpretation in terms of the implicit cultural assumptions of the author of the text. This is perhaps a philosophical form of literary criticism rather than a concern with traditional problems of philosophy. It is a style of philosophising relying heavily on literary material and allusions, and steeped in a mode of playing with words familiar from HEGEL and the later HEIDEGGER. On this view we must approach the work of writers without preconceived theoretical views and are therefore compelled to accept a text as a given, unalterable fact, with a kind of scriptural reverence. To deconstruct is to dismantle; next, we take a look at the pieces, and then put them together again, after which the whole cycle may recur, for we cannot take things to bits without some prior notions. This procedure often throws interesting light in unexpected directions, but neither can nor seeks to be systematic.

Descartes, René (1596–1650), born at La Haye, now called La Haye-Descartes in his honour, near Tours in France. Descartes entered the Jesuit School at La Flèche in 1604, where he studied Latin and Greek and the classical authors, and acquired respect for the certainty of MATHEMATICS and distaste for the theories of ARISTOTLE as developed by medieval commentators. In 1619 he took a degree in law at the University of Poitiers. There followed a period during which he studied 'the book of the world' by travelling, for some of the time as a gentleman-officer in the armies of Maurice of Nassau, Prince of Orange, and Maximilian, Duke of Bavaria. In 1625 he returned to Paris and renewed his acquaintance with Father Marin Mersenne, through whom Descartes's views later became known to many of the famous intellectuals in Europe. From 1628 to 1649 he lived in Holland and worked out in detail the scientific, philosophical and mathematical ideas that had engaged him during his travels. His main philosophical works are *Rules for the Direction of the Mind* (written in 1629–30 but not published until 1701), *Discourse on Method* (1637), *Meditations* (1640), *Principles of Philosophy* (1644), and *Treatise on the Passions* (1649). In 1649 Descartes accepted an invitation to visit the Queen of Sweden and instruct her in philosophy. He succumbed to the rigorous climate, and died in February 1650.

Like FRANCIS BACON and HOBBES, Descartes rejected the Aristotelian view of the world as comprising things of many different natural kinds, each kind having its own intelligible ESSENCE prescribing the ends towards which things of that kind develop. Like Bacon and Hobbes, he sought to meet the challenge of SCEPTICISM, recently posed afresh by MONTAIGNE. Bacon's way of meeting the challenge was that of the empiricist: a new, more systematic, method of INDUCTION from what is evident to the senses. For Descartes the senses were far from being the source of anything evident. Sense perceptions may be CLEAR, as when one clearly sees what is present to one's gaze, but they are not distinct, since they involve the dubious attribution to a material thing of something resembling the SENSATION in one's MIND.

It was in MATHEMATICS that Descartes saw hope of deliverance from scepticism. He had founded analytical geometry, which shows how every geometrical object or relation can be given numerical expression. He saw that if EXTENSION in space is the single ESSENCE of all that is to be known, and if the PROPOSITIONS of mathematics can be accepted as immune from the sceptic's doubt, then the ancient Greek idea that the universe is through and through penetrable by human reason, and knowable with CERTAINTY, will be vindicated. Scepticism will give way, not to EMPIRICISM, but to a more thoroughgoing RATIONALISM than ever before. PLATO is said to have regarded MATTER as an impediment to the exact mirroring of the mathematical FORMS in the SENSIBLE world. For Descartes there was no such impediment: matter's essence is no more and no less than quantifiable extension. Everything can be explained mechanically, in terms of matter in motion. However, there were problems:

(1) The notion that the essence of everything is quantifiable EXTENSION does not seem to fit the very things of which we are most directly aware, our own thoughts.

(2) The propositions of MATHEMATICS are, in fact, not immune from the sceptic's doubt: 'the certainty of mathematical propositions' does not mean 'our immunity from being wrong about what is true in mathematics'; we can be wrong in mathematics as in anything else.

(3) The notion that the essence of everything is quantifiable extension does not seem to fit even the things we feel, see, hear, around us; they seem to be hard or soft, hot or cold, coloured, and so on: they seem to have qualities other than just those of shape and size.

(4) If we abandon the commonsense view, that we know the SENSIBLE world exists because we see it and feel it, what reason have we to think that anything objective corresponds to our IDEAS?

(5) If the essence of matter is simply extension then wherever there is extension there should be matter; all of space should be full of matter, but it is not. If it were, MOTION would not be possible; there must be some empty spaces for things to move into.

(6) There must be a difference between extension and whatever has extension. The thing which has a certain extension must have some other property as well, to account for the resistance it offers to the entry of anything else into the space it occupies.

(7) There is no room for contingency in mathematics, so there should be no room in Descartes's philosophy for HYPOTHESES, and their confirmation or disconfirmation by observation and experiment.

(1) Descartes's solution of the first problem was to accept the

implication: there are things, souls or minds, of which the essence is not extension, but thought or CONSCIOUSNESS. This helps him to meet the challenge of scepticism. That minds are distinct from bodies, in the sense of being theoretically able to exist apart from them, seemed to him to follow from an intuition, 'I think, therefore I am' *(cogito, ergo sum)*, which he took to be true without any possible doubt (see 'COGITO'). If he could only perceive what it was about the *cogito* intuition which assured him of its truth then, he thought, he would have a CRITERION of truth which he could apply generally. What assured him of the truth of the *cogito* was his CLEAR and distinct perception of it. This, then, must be the general mark of truth. (Another reason for excluding minds from the realm of extension was that, God willing, the soul might then survive the death of the body.)

(2) Descartes's solution of the second problem was to recognise that there is, after all, more to a proposition's being true than that we seem to have a clear and distinct perception of it. Perhaps there is some all-powerful malicious demon who makes things appear true to us which are not. There could not be both an all-powerful malicious demon and an all-powerful perfect God. We have a clear and distinct idea of the latter. It is evident by the light of nature that this idea must be caused by something with at least as much reality as that attributed in the idea. So there must be an all-powerful perfect God. Moreover, the necessary existence of a perfect God follows from this perfection, since existence is a perfection (Descartes's version of the ONTOLOGICAL ARGUMENT). This guarantees the truthfulness of what is genuinely clear and distinct to us, such as the propositions of mathematics, since a perfect God would not allow us to be deceived about what we clearly and distinctly perceive.

(3) All that is clearly and distinctly perceived in any material thing, such as a piece of wax, is that it is extended. Our ideas of hardness or softness, hotness or coldness, colour, and so on, are innate, occurring when something transmitted through the sense-organs is the occasion for the mind to have them.

(4) We know by the light of nature that our ideas of material things must be caused by something with at least as much reality as is attributed in the ideas. We have a natural impulse to believe the causes to resemble the ideas, that is, to be material things. One alternative would be that God should have given us the ideas directly, without there

actually being any material things. However, God is not deceitful, so we can rely on the natural impulse he has given us to believe the causes to be material things (though not on the impulse to believe that they possess such qualities as hardness or softness, hotness or coldness, and so on).

(5) It is inconceivable that nothing should possess extension, so there cannot be a space in which there is no matter. Motion takes place by all the CORPUSCLES of matter in a circle displacing one another.

(6) There is a conceptual, though not a real distinction between a substance and its essence. We say that a corpuscle of matter *has* a certain shape, size and motion, but that is all it has. The so-called 'resistance' of one material thing to another's occupying the same place is a confused understanding of the contradiction involved in the idea of there being two things simultaneously occupying the same place.

(7) There *is* more to science than mathematics. We cannot determine A PRIORI the size and shape of the corpuscles of matter, how quickly they move, or what circles they describe. We have to make assumptions about what God has done—for example, that He has made the corpuscles of water eel-shaped and those of oil branch-shaped—and see whether or not our assumptions agree with EXPERIENCE.

Some of Descartes's solutions, and their elements, are not original. The solution of the fifth problem is reminiscent of PARMENIDES. The solution of the third, the distinction between what came to be called PRIMARY AND SECONDARY QUALITIES, is to be found in DEMOCRITUS. The doctrine of the 'natural light', which occurs in the solutions of the second and fourth problems, seems to be a version of St AUGUSTINE'S theory of divine illumination. Descartes's *cogito, ergo sum* is Augustine's 'He who is not can certainly not be deceived; therefore, if I am deceived I am', put to a new use—to prove the existence of a soul distinct from the body, and to authenticate the 'clear and distinct' criterion of truth. His ontological argument is a version of St ANSELM'S. The philosophical tools he uses, the terms 'substance', 'essence', 'idea', 'innate', had been in use for centuries, and Descartes was inevitably heir to the theories and problems with which some of them had become laden.

Descartes's conception of philosophy as the quest for certainty, his mechanistic view of the physical world, and his separation, via the *cogito* argument, of the soul from the world so viewed, all had a profound influence. Many of the developments in modern philosophy, up to the present day, cannot be characterised adequately without reference, in particular, to CARTESIAN DUALISM, the doctrine that there are two God-created substances: matter, the essence of which is quantifiable extension, and mind, the essence of which is introspectible thinking. (a) Some of the developments arose out of the difficulty of understanding how two substances with no affinity can interact, or form a unity, an embodied mind. Some philosophers, called 'occasionalists', seized on Descartes's talk of a motion in the brain giving the mind the occasion to have its innate sensory ideas. The real cause, they supposed, must be God, who constantly adjusts the mental realm to the physical realm in perception, and vice versa in voluntary action (see VOLITION). Others looked for a more radical version of the doctrine about substance. SPINOZA held that there was only one substance, of which thought and extension are two attributes. This led to various 'double-aspect' or 'identity' theories of the mind–body relation. LEIBNIZ held that there were many soul-like substances developing in harmony according to a divinely pre-established plan. (b) Other developments grew out of dissatisfaction with Descartes's solution of the fifth and sixth problems. His solution of the fifth problem was felt to be sophistical, and to be at odds with empirical facts about the possibility of a vacuum. Dissatisfaction with his solution of the sixth problem led LOCKE, for example, to ascribe solidity to material things. Implicit in these developments was the notion that while mathematics may have a central place in *science*, it does not have the place Descartes gave it in *nature*. (c) Still other developments, particularly those of the British Empiricists, Locke, BERKELEY and HUME, can be understood in terms of (i) the epistemological concern promoted by Descartes's conception of philosophy as providing an answer to the sceptic, (ii) the distinction between the indubitable mind and its ideas as against the dubitable 'external world', the supposed cause of those ideas, and (iii) the rejection of rationalist epistemology in favour of an empiricist one. 'Men must think and know for themselves', as Locke put it. These developments inevitably favoured the analysis of such concepts as causation, the external world, and even the self, in terms of ideas and their relations. (d) The reaction came with KANT, whose TRANSCENDENTAL idealism relates to Descartes via both the rationalist and empiricist lines of development. The recognition of certain concepts as *a priori* can be regarded as a mark of the rationalist, but the restriction of the knowledge obtainable by their employment to things that can be experienced justifies Kant's entitling his major work *The Critique of Pure Reason*.

HEGEL called Descartes 'the father of modern philosophy'. That his sons, over the years, should have rejected nearly all his most cherished philosophical views, sometimes even with such expressions as 'the myth of the ghost in the machine' (RYLE), does not invalidate this description.

descriptions, theory of, *n.* a device introduced by Bertrand RUSSELL (in an article entitled 'On Denoting', *Mind*, 1905) in order to deal with a range of logical problems concerning the way in which expressions refer. To take one of his examples: how are we to analyse 'the present King of France is bald'? Is it true or false? To avoid having to say it is meaningless (which it clearly is not), Russell analyses this statement thus: 'There is one and only one King of France, and he is bald.' If any part of this is false, so is the whole. Since there is now no King of France, the statement is false. (Of course, a French royalist might disagree and urge that the Comte de Paris is the present King of France, and he is actually a bit thin on top. However, Russell is concerned not with this *material* question, but with the FORMAL question of analysing the statement.)

A similar procedure is used to get rid of proper names by substituting definite descriptions, and to deal with questions of non-existence where we appear first to name something and then go on to say that 'it' does not exist.

determinism, *n.* the view that events, including people's ACTIONS, do not occur by chance, but are caused to occur (see CAUSE), usually with the implication that they could not be otherwise than they are. There is this implication in the case of physical determinism, that is, determinism by preceding events in the course of nature, and in the case of divine determinism, that is, GOD creating everything and preordaining what will happen to it. The implication is absent in the case of self-determinism (meaning that an agent is the cause of his own actions) since he could have decided to act otherwise than he did. Determinism is opposed to indeterminism. Physical indeterminism is sometimes held to follow from the so-called 'principle of indeterminacy', the principle that the position and momentum of an electron cannot be determined simultaneously.

Dewey, John (1859–1952), American philosopher, professor at Chicago (1894–1904) and Columbia University (1904–1930), belonging to the pragmatist tradition (see PRAGMATISM), but with a twist of his own: he preferred to call his position 'instrumentalism', and he regarded enquiry as something based on the model of scientific experimentation. He therefore rejected the notion of a fixed human nature from which an ethical position could be derived by analysis. On the contrary, we must base our morality on our ever expanding EXPERIENCE. The sort of social arrangement best suited for this happens to be democracy, and the generally favourable orientation a liberal one. On this philosophical background he bases his views on education, which have been the most influential aspect of his work. The learning process is an activity that seeks to remove uncertainties and thus issues in a state of intellectual relief. Education thus has to start from what is actually experienced (and not from what authority imposes). In this way we expand our scope and gradually become better adapted in our world, which is currently undergoing deep changes owing to the growth of science and technology. See EDUCATION, PHILOSOPHY OF.

dialectic, *n.* (from Greek *dialektikē technē* art of discussion) a form of philosophic debating attributed in the first instance to the Eleatic ZENO, and practised by him for example in PLATO's *Parmenides*. The procedure was to accept an opponent's view provisionally and to elicit from it contradictory consequences. This was a device much used by the SOPHISTS, whence the pejorative sense of the word as idle logic chopping. The Socrates of Plato's dialogues used dialectic as a method of question and answer in the framing of sound definitions of terms, a philosophic process that ultimately leads to the apprehension of the FORM of the Good. For ARISTOTLE, dialectic is used for argument from unsubstantiated opinion, which cannot establish conclusions (as against demonstrative reasoning which starts from the premises and leads to KNOWLEDGE). For the Stoics (see STOICISM), and thereafter throughout the Middle Ages, dialectic was simply the art of reasoning. A special sense is given to the word by KANT, for whom it is the illicit attempt at using the understanding beyond its proper bounds, namely the domain of EXPERIENCE. For HEGEL, dialectic is a driving force that informs the historical character of particular things, generating change in them, so that new features arise 'contradicting' previous ones. This aspect of Hegel was adopted by MARX and forms the guideline of his historical materialism, standing Hegel on his head (since for him the dialectic was a process of the spirit). From this developed the so-called dialectical materialism of our own time (the term was coined by Plekhanov in 1891), long the official doctrine of the USSR.

Diderot, Denis (1713–1784), French thinker, editor of the famous *Encyclopédie*, a typical ENLIGHTENMENT figure, and a firm supporter of the new scientific spirit, opposed to abstract speculation and greatly influenced by LOCKE's theory of KNOWLEDGE in terms of SENSATIONS. Like others amongst the Encyclopaedists, he favoured an empiricist approach based on observation and experiment. The function of IMAGINATION was to detect general connections put forward as HYPO-THESES to further scientific enquiry. In this he was ahead of the empiricist tradition of his time, which rather discounted the constructive imaginative contributions. Holding that everything was MATTER in MOTION, he attributed a form of sensitivity to all matter and thus sought to give a unified account of both arts and sciences. In particular, he put forward a theory of biological development and heredity that in some ways hints at notions that were not devised till over a century later.

Diogenes Laertius (3rd century AD), author of *The Lives and Opinions of Eminent Philosophers*, an extensive compilation of material on ancient Greek philosophers from THALES to EPICURUS.

direct realism, see PERCEPTION.

distinct, see CLEAR.

double aspect theory, DESCARTES, being a dualist (see DUALISM), held that MIND and body are two distinct things that interact causally, but SPINOZA, a monist (see MONISM), said that a mental event, such as a decision, and a bodily event, such as whatever happens in his brain when someone makes a decision, are 'one and the same thing, which when considered under the attribute of thought . . . we call a decision, and when considered under the attribute of extension . . . we call a determination of the body' (*Ethics*, 1677, Bk. 3, Prop. 2, Note). The phrase 'considered under an attribute' is part of the terminology of the metaphysical theory of monism. Someone who preferred Spinoza's view of the relation of mind and body to Descartes's, but wanted to avoid metaphysical terminology, might say he held a 'double aspect' theory of the relation of mind and body. Thus R. J. Hirst (*Human Senses and Perception*, Edinburgh and London, 1964, p. 321) says that mental and brain activities are, respectively, inner and outer aspects of the same activity. He goes on to deny that the activity of which they are aspects is a third thing distinct from the aspects.

In the absence of a neutral thing to present the mental and physical aspects there is a tendency for one of the aspects to be regarded as the REALITY and the other as its APPEARANCE. If the mental aspect is regarded as the reality, the theory is that of PSYCHICAL MONISM or spiritualism, a theory KANT held we can never know to be true or false (*Critique of Pure Reason*, 1781, A359), but nevertheless endorsed by the German philosopher-psychologist G. T. Fechner (1801–1887). If the physical aspect is regarded as the reality, the theory is that of physical monism, PHYSICALISM or MATERIALISM. Instead of calling it an 'aspect' of the brain-event, the mental event may be said to *be*, or be *identical* with, the brain-event. A step in this direction was taken by the American philosopher R. W. Sellars when he wrote (*The Philosophy of Physical Realism*, New York, 1932, p. 414): 'Consciousness is the qualitative dimension of a brain-event. It is the patterned brain-event as sentient. It is because of its status that we, as conscious, participate in the being of brain-events. Here, and here alone, are we, as conscious beings, on the inside of reality.' Sellars clearly thought of the reality we are inside as physical. See IDENTITY HYPOTHESIS.

dualism, *n.* a theory in which a fundamental two-fold distinction is drawn. In the history of religion the term 'dualist' is used of men who regard GOD and the devil as two coeternal principles. In philosophy the term is used most frequently of DESCARTES'S distinction between two SUBSTANCES, MIND and MATTER, but any fundamental two-fold distinction, such as PLATO'S distinction between the INTELLIGIBLE and the SENSIBLE, or FICHTE'S, between the ego and the non-ego, may be described as dualistic.

Duns Scotus, John (*c.*1266–1308), Scottish philosopher and Franciscan cleric, taught at Oxford and Paris, and sought to reconcile the current Aristotelianism with the requirements of Christian theology. For his ingenious way of doing this he came to be known as the 'Subtle Doctor'. Central to his position is the view that existence is univocal (means the same) in all contexts, but our finite minds can acquire KNOWLEDGE only through our senses. Thus METAPHYSICAL knowledge is abstract and involves making mental distinctions of things that actually are inseparable (somewhat as FORM and MATTER in ARISTOTLE). What makes individual things what they are is their form of *haecceity* or 'thisness'. As to the human soul, he regards it as created by GOD, and as immortal though not demonstrably so, differing in this from AQUINAS.

Durkheim, Émile (1858–1917), French sociologist, professor at Bordeaux and later at the Sorbonne, supported the POSITIVISM of COMTE and founded the modern science of sociology. He regarded society as an irreducible object for enquiry, and examined its various collective features, such as language, institutions and professional traditions. Individuals who are not marked by these features are anomic (lawless) and therefore abnormal. This is one cause that may lead to suicide. In general, all social facts are caused by other social facts.

duty, *n.* in moral philosophy, that which it behoves us to do, either because it is laid down in some moral code, or because it imposes itself, as it were, through our moral consciousness. Conflict occurs where a number of duties make irreconcilable demands on us. This has been a topic for tragedians throughout the ages.

E

education, philosophy of, *n*. the first philosopher in this field was
PLATO, in the *Republic*. He there provides an account of education,
how it should be pursued and to what end. All later philosophy of
education in some measure covers aspects of Plato's account. For him
the object of education is to create social and individual balance,
which is achieved by sorting people into three classes: those who work
for gain (trade, commerce), those who offer protection (the soldiers)
and those who govern (the rulers). The first two need certain special
skills to fulfil their functions, while education proper is reserved to the
last, who undergo a long course of preparatory studies and finally are
ready to tackle philosophy, after which they have the wisdom needed
to govern the state. Amongst the preliminary studies, MATHEMATICS is
central as a training of the mind. This is a Pythagorean notion, which
remains in conscious practice in French education to this day.

The general Platonic outlook is reflected in the study of the seven
liberal arts in the medieval universities of Europe (grammar, rhetoric,
logic (the 'trivium'); and arithmetic, music, geometry, astronomy (the
'quadrivium')). This was followed by tackling philosophy and
theology. The aim here was no longer that of Plato, but rather to
redeem man's fallen nature (according to Christian doctrine) and to
restore a proper balance between the earthly powers of State and
Church. This, roughly, was the doctrine put forward by St AUGUSTINE
(354–430), the Bishop of Hippo. Education, as with the Ancients,
remains the preserve of the few.

When a revival of learning sprang up in the RENAISSANCE, education
became more widespread, and after the Protestant REFORMATION, the
idea of the State providing compulsory elementary education for all
was put forward. It was first implemented in 18th century Prussia.
Meanwhile, a more optimistic outlook on human nature developed in
the wake of the humanist movement (see HUMANISM). Man, though
sinful, was nevertheless perfectible, and could improve himself by
learning: this he was encouraged to do to the limits of his abilities. The

Bohemian thinker Comenius (1592–1670) advocated that educational institutions at all levels should be promoted by the State.

With John LOCKE (1632–1704) educational theory was taken a step further in that he sought to sever the link with theology. The object was simply to enhance the kind of parliamentary government established after the revolution of 1688. Learning must be respected, and acquired as far as lies within each person's scope, preferably not in an institution, but by private tuition at home.

The 18th century brought to the fore some romantic notions of education through ROUSSEAU (1712–1778), who based his views on the notion that man in the initial state of nature had been free and it was civilisation that had shackled him (this is directly opposed to the more realistic notion of HOBBES). In an instructional novel *(Émile)*, Rousseau outlines the proper education of children through direct and active experience under suitable tutorial guidance. The object is to let each person develop in such a way that his aspirations are matched by his abilities.

In KANT (1724–1804), the aim of education was likewise to give full scope to the individual's abilities, with a view to securing a condition of peace throughout the world. As against this international outlook, a narrow nationalistic aim was pursued in the educational thought of FICHTE (1762–1814), who was less sanguine about human nature.

The utilitarian thinkers (see UTILITARIANISM) of the 19th century pursued an educational notion not very different from Kant's, but for quite different reasons. To them, the end of all human activity was the greatest good for the greatest number, and this, they felt, could be achieved by letting everyone develop as far as possible. The same tendency informs the 20th century pragmatic views of education.

If one were to add a word about the state of things today, one might say that what we need is more learning and less education: that is, greater stress on acquiring knowledge from a desire to learn, and less emphasis on institutions and the attendant bureaucracy.

effect, *n.* that which is produced by a CAUSE.

efficient cause, *n.* that which has what LOCKE called 'a power to make a change', as, for example, a moving billiard ball has a power to move a billiard ball it strikes.

Philosophical controversy has centred round the question whether there is any such power in nature. Locke, an empiricist (see EMPIRICISM), asked from what EXPERIENCE we derive the IDEA of it. His answer was that I am aware of power in myself when, by an act of will, I move part of my body (*Essay*, II xxi 4). HUME objected that if I was aware of power in myself I would see a necessary connection between the act of will and the bodily motion, whereas such a connection is inexplicable, given the natures of MIND and MATTER (*Treatise*, appendix). He concluded that any IDEA we may have of necessary connection must have arisen in some other way than by our being immediately aware of power, and speculated as to what this other way might be. Having seen two events constantly occurring together (e.g. a match being struck, and a flame), we are strongly inclined on seeing the first to think of the second. We experience this 'custom-produced propensity' as a 'determination of the mind', rather as, on hearing the first words of the familiar nursery rhyme 'Mary had a little . . .', we feel committed to think 'lamb'. This subjective feeling of being determined, Hume concludes, is the real source of our so-called idea of necessary connection, a conclusion which has the unfortunate consequence that 'necessity is something that exists in the mind, not in objects' (*Treatise*, I iii 4). If Hume is right about the source of our idea of necessary connection, then our having it does not entitle us to suppose regular sequences of events (motion in one billiard ball followed by motion in another, matches being struck followed by flames, etc.) to be anything more than regular sequences; anything more is the product of an illegitimate projection of a feeling in ourselves onto the world.

This makes it hard to explain our addiction to the practice of distinguishing between cases of causation and coincidence (in the *Oxford English Dictionary* sense of 'a notable concurrence of events or circumstances having no apparent causal connexion'), and our relying on the former, but not on the latter, when we want to produce some change in the world. Two possibilities are, first, that there is a justification for this practice, but not of the sort Locke supposed; and, second, that the practice in general does not have or need any justification.

The first possibility was taken up by Kant, who distinguished between empirical CONCEPTS, which are employed without question from anyone, since EXPERIENCE is always available for the proof of their objective reality, and concepts such as CAUSE, which are not acquired through experience and for which there is consequently a problem as to how they relate to objects (*Critique of Pure Reason* A84–5). His solution of the problem involved the claim, argued for at length but not entirely convincingly, that it is only by accepting that all events are caused that we can experience the world as we do, namely as a world in which we can discriminate real from merely apparent succession. Even if the argument were valid, causality would be proved to hold only within the world as we experience it, not amongst things in themselves.

None of this is to say that particular claims, e.g. that such-and-such a concurrence of events is not a coincidence, do not have or need any justification. We are accustomed to providing such justification, but there is much philosophical dispute when it comes to showing clearly *how* we do it. This involves analysing the statement '*X*-type events are not only regularly followed by *Y*-type events, they cause them', and this is easier said than done. One seemingly plausible analysis, in terms of necessary and sufficient conditions, has the curious consequence that a later event can cause an earlier one. Uncertainty as to how to articulate our practice contrasts strikingly with the unquestioning instinctive behaviour in which the cause-and-effect language is rooted, for example our immediate discriminating reaction to what has hit us when we feel a pain. See CAUSE, FINAL CAUSE, VOLITION.

egoism and altruism, in moral philosophy, are two opposed ways for an individual to behave: either purely in a self-regarding way, or with a view of the well-being of others (that is, mankind). The term 'altruism' was invented by the French thinker, Auguste COMTE (1798–1857).

Einstein, Albert (1879–1955), German Jewish by origin, world famous physicist, after 1933 at Princeton Institute of Advanced Studies, is of philosophical import for his theories of RELATIVITY, which rejected the notions of absolute time and space till then prevailing (and still operating implicitly in the conduct of our daily lives). It had been assumed that SPACE AND TIME were simply there to be measured, whereas for Einstein the process of measurement must be analysed in terms of the signals involved. In this way, attempts at unifying mechanics and electro-dynamics led him to the special theory of relativity (1905), and the study of universal gravitation to the general theory of relativity (1916). This last is a way of turning physics into a form of geometry, much in the spirit of PYTHAGORAS. Attempts at a unified field theory, involving both electricity and gravitation, remain unrealised to this day. Meanwhile, the theory of relativity has stressed the notion of LAWS OF NATURE being expressed as 'invariants' (the same in whatever reference frame they are stated).

Eleaticism, *n.* so called from its seat in the Greek colony of Elea, seventy miles south-east of Naples, was one of the principal schools of

PRE-SOCRATIC PHILOSOPHY. Philosophers of the MILESIAN SCHOOL had based their theorising about the world mainly on shaky analogies drawn from their everyday experience. The Eleatics, on the other hand, deduced the features of reality from the conditions for speaking and THINKING of anything. Reason, unaided by EXPERIENCE, was their sole guide. Their understanding of how language works was such that it seemed evident to them, by the light of reason, that only one thing exists, that it is characterless, and that it is eternal. Accordingly they had to dismiss the everyday world of many different things, with changes in quality, position, and so forth, as illusory.

Chief among the Eleatics were PARMENIDES and ZENO OF ELEA. Parmenides argued directly for there being one eternal thing. Zeno argued indirectly for the same conclusion, by trying to show that the common-sense view, that there are many things, that they move from one place to another, and so on, involves paradoxes from which there is no escape. Melissus of Samos (*fl. c.*440 BC) argued – badly, according to ARISTOTLE (*Physics* 186 a 8) – for rather similar conclusions.

Two of the reactions to Eleaticism were, first, that of the pluralists (see PLURALISM), EMPEDOCLES and ANAXAGORAS, and the atomists (see ATOMISM), Leucippus and DEMOCRITUS, all of whom accepted in some version or other the ban on ultimate coming-into-being and perishing; and, second, that of PLATO. In the *Sophist* Plato put into the mouth of the Stranger (identified as a native of Elea and a member of the school of Parmenides and Zeno) the admission that 'when we speak of "that which is not", it seems that we do not mean something contrary to what is but only something that is different' (257 b), thus showing Parmenides 'results in a field which he forbade us even to explore' (258 c).

elements, *n.* the components of which something is made. EM-PEDOCLES held that everything is made of just four elements: earth, air, fire and water.

emotion, *n.* a person may say that on some occasion he was, or felt, frightened, angry, embarrassed, indignant, joyful or sad. These are emotions. They have OBJECTS: a person is frightened of someone, angry about something, and so on. They are reasonable or unreasonable: a person can be right or wrong in appraising some situation as dangerous. Internal bodily changes, such as the secretion of adrenalin, may occur. There are also characteristic external bodily changes, which people recognise as expressions of particular emotions. An embarrassed person blushes, an angry person may clench his fists. Emotions are connected with motivation and behaviour. A person is motivated to avoid being harmed, so flees from what frightens him. However, emotions do not always help one to deal satisfactorily with an emotional situation. Someone may be so emotionally disturbed that he does things that in fact increase rather than diminish the danger he is in.

The concept of emotion is thus multi-faceted, and includes feeling, appraisal, justification, internal and external bodily changes, motivation, and behaviour (both useful in dealing with the situation, and the opposite). Which facet should be stressed in an account of the concept? A person's opinion about this is likely to reflect his general philosophical approach and his interests.

ARISTOTLE stressed the elements of motivation, appraisal, and useful behaviour. Feelings occur as accompaniments, and are of pain or pleasure. He defined anger, for example, as 'an impulse, accompanied by pain, to a conspicuous revenge for a conspicuous slight' (*Rhetoric*, 1378a 31). DESCARTES thought of emotions as being essentially feelings, though feelings with important mental and bodily effects. 'The principal effect of all the passions in men is that they incite and dispose their soul to desire those things for which they prepare their body, so that the feeling of fear incites it to desire to fly, that of courage to desire to fight, and so on' (*Passions of the Soul*, 1649, Art. 40). HUME, like Descartes, categorised emotions as feelings ('reflective impressions'); he distinguished them from SENSATIONS of pain and pleasure; and said that we cannot define them, but can describe them 'by an enumeration of such circumstances as attend them'. A DEFINITION is not necessary since all of us experience the impressions for which emotion words stand. The impressions of pride and humility, for example, are so common that 'every one, of himself, will be able to form a just idea of them, without any danger of mistake' (*Treatise of Human Nature*, 1739, II i 2).

If emotion is identified with feeling, and the connection between feeling and behaviour is thought of as accidental (i.e. causal or circumstantial), then the way is opened for unresolvable doubt as to whether the emotion one person calls 'fear' may not be what another would call 'anger' if only he could see into the first person's mind. Can the connection between feeling and behaviour be strengthened somehow? One theory that does so is the James–Lange theory, advanced by the American philosopher-psychologist William JAMES and the Danish physiologist C. Lange. They hold that the feeling we call the emotional feeling is not something that exists in its own right, so to speak, but is a feeling of the bodily changes that follow our perception of the situation. In his *Principles of Psychology* (New York, 1890, Ch. 25) James expounds the theory as follows:

> The hypothesis here to be defended says that . . . we feel sorry because we cry, angry because we strike, afraid because we tremble, and not that we cry, strike, or tremble, because we are sorry, angry or fearful, as the case may be. Without the bodily states following on the perception, the latter would be purely cognitive in form, pale, colorless, destitute of emotional warmth.

The James–Lange theory strengthens the feeling–behaviour connection by subordinating feeling to behaviour: the feeling is of the behaviour. Thereby the concept of emotion is made to cover both feeling and behaviour, and the sceptical problem attendant on Hume's account cannot arise. The need for a CONCEPT which covers both has been recognised by many philosophers (e.g. P. F. STRAWSON, *Individuals*, London, 1959, Ch. 3), but without general agreement on how it comes about that the concept does cover both.

Hume, like Aristotle, was interested in emotion primarily as a moral philosopher, not an epistemologist (see EPISTEMOLOGY). In moral philosophy the concept of emotion is important because what account one gives of the connection between the various facets determines how one conceives of disagreement about the rightness or wrongness of some action. The important connection here is between feelings (of 'approval' or 'disapproval') and moral appraisals. Holding the connection to be causal or circumstantial means regarding disagreement in morals as like disagreement in taste, not something about which there can be argument. In much the same way as William James strengthened the connection between feeling and behaviour by denying that emotional feelings exist in their own right, so to speak, and identifying them with feelings of bodily changes, so the Oxford moral philosopher, R. M. HARE, has strengthened the connection between feelings of approval and disapproval and moral appraisals by saying

> 'I approve of *A*' is merely a more complicated and circumlocutory way of saying '*A* is right'. It is not a statement, verifiable by observation, that I have a recognizable feeling or recurrent frame of mind; it is a value-judgment; if I ask 'Do I approve of *A*?' my answer is a moral decision, not an observation of introspective fact. (*The Language of Morals*, Oxford, 1952, Ch. 1).

Hare is on the side of Aristotle rather than Hume.

emotivism, *n.* a theory of ETHICS that regards PROPOSITIONS of ethics as stating only preferences, feelings or attitudes, rather than independently verifiable facts (see VERIFIABILITY). This view is widely held and was put forward by C. L. Stevenson and A. J. AYER. The function of ethical statements is then to express or recommend certain attitudes, and to encourage certain ways of acting, or even to command them. A similar emotive approach is followed by many writers on AESTHETICS, where this way of seeing things is well adapted to the notion that matters of taste are not subject to debate.

Empedocles, (*c*.492–*c*.432 BC), poet–philosopher with active interests in politics, medicine and religion. He was a leading citizen of Acragas, now Agrigento, in the centre of the south-west coast of Sicily. He wrote two poems, entitled *On Nature* and *Purifications*, of which about 450 lines have survived. He found much to admire in the teachings of such diverse philosophers as PARMENIDES, PYTHAGORAS, and HERACLITUS; and attempted a synthesis of them. That it was not entirely successful is reflected in the remark of one commentator: 'The important thing in understanding him is to stop thinking at the right moment.' The right moment may be before one tries to reconcile the Pythagorean doctrine of the transmigration of souls, to be found in *Purifications*, with the physical philosophy of *On Nature*, according to which thought is 'the blood around the heart'.

As regards religion, Empedocles thought of himself as one whose wheel of incarnations had turned full circle. There is a legend that his final immortality-winning act of purification was a leap into the crater of Etna. More probably he died in exile in the Peloponnese, having made political enemies in his native city and province.

Empedocles's major contribution to philosophy lay in the repeal of the Eleatic embargo on movement and change (see ELEATICISM). By sacrificing only one of Parmenides's principles, the MONISM which Parmenides shared with XENOPHANES, in favour of a set of four 'roots of all things' or ELEMENTS (earth, air, fire and water) and by invoking two forces, Love and Strife, which motivate the 'roots' to combine (Love) or separate (Strife), Empedocles sought to explain the generation and destruction of everyday things, which is so obvious to our senses. The apparent coming-to-be of something is really the combination of portions of the elements; and the destruction, their separation. Empedocles applied to his four elements the Parmenidean principle that something cannot arise out of nothing, or perish into nothing. In effect they were, for him, the eternal One of Parmenides quadruplicated.

It is not clear precisely how the combination and separation of the elements was thought to take place. ARISTOTLE (*On Generation and Corruption*, 324 b 35) remarked that some philosophers, including Empedocles, said that combination takes place 'only between bodies whose pores are in reciprocal sympathy'; and Plutarch preserved a line of Empedocles about 'effluences from all things that come into being'. The general idea seems to have been that portions of the elements, inspired by Love and Strife, flow into, or out of, one another, their flowing being easy or difficult depending on their sub-microscopic pore-structure. An appropriate flowing-in constitutes the coming-to-be of something; a flowing-out, its destruction.

empiricism, *n.* (from Greek *empeiria* EXPERIENCE) a term variously used in philosophy to denote certain ways in which experience is engaged in such KNOWLEDGE as we do or can have. The opposite view, which denies that experience is involved at all, is called RATIONALISM, suggesting that we can learn things merely by THINKING. In some measure we are indeed all empiricists in practice, whatever we call ourselves, but a number of rather different and specific things have been asserted by thinkers who would call themselves empiricists. Moreover, although as a whole they are opposed to various forms of traditional METAPHYSICS, they often unwittingly set up metaphysical doctrines of their own which are no more plausible than those they wish to supplant; witness the modern view that what we experience are 'sense-data' (see SENSE-DATUM), a kind of basic unit of experience not further describable. Probably no one disputes that in order to find out anything, you must start by looking at the world round you. However, PLATO held that sense PERCEPTION leads only to opinion, while knowledge, being of FORMS, comes only through the operation of reason. Aristotle rejected Plato's THEORY OF FORMS, and held that sense-experience is necessary for scientific knowledge.

A special problem arises about the propositions of pure MATHEMATICS and the principles of LOGIC: these are generally held to be necessary, and therefore not answerable to experience. Empiricists have held various views on this. LOCKE maintained that only logical principles are necessary, because they are really about the meanings of words. For HUME, the necessary concerns relations between IDEAS (in his sense of that term). A 'critical' approach was put forward by KANT, who maintained that all knowledge starts with experience but is not grounded in it: the form that knowledge takes depends on our cognitive equipment. He thus holds that mathematical propositions, amongst others, are *a priori synthetic*. J. S. MILL's view that mathematics are purely empirical has found no followers. Modern empiricists of the logical positivist school (see LOGICAL POSITIVISM) regard logic as necessary but tautological, saying nothing, somewhat in the Lockean tradition. As to mathematics, they favour the view that it is reducible to logic and therefore equally tautological. One thing that all empiricists agree on is that we do not have in our minds some knowledge that was with us from birth, what DESCARTES called INNATE IDEAS. As to the learning process, the Humean view that it is based on constant repetition is not borne out by the facts: some things we learn at one single stroke. Experience can be decisive at once. It is thus not a part of genuine empiricism that what is based on experience can only ever be probable.

Engels, Friedrich (1820–1895), German social philosopher and textile manufacturer, was a close friend and supporter (both material and doctrinal) of Karl MARX. His own philosophical writings are mainly in defence and explanation of Marx's works. In contrast (no doubt unconsciously) to Marx's historical materialism, he put forward a form of materialism more strictly modelled on Hegelian logic (see HEGEL) and later called 'dialectical materialism', or diamat for short. In this he sought to show that the dialectical principle governs not only the way scientific activity proceeds, but the very structure of scientific theory. This last part has not been successful as regards natural science and is now largely discredited, certainly amongst working scientists.

Enlightenment, *n.* the name of a general intellectual movement in 18th century France, Germany and Great Britain. As the term suggests, the period saw greater light shed on the conduct of human affairs: the dark mysteries of traditional attitudes in religion and political life were pushed back, and in their place a new outlook grew up, informed by reason and the power of scientific research and discovery. Old superstitions were discarded, and a new, more reasonable approach grew up. This showed itself in all departments of social life (for example, the abolition of judicial torture, a renewed interest in education as a means towards reform). The philosophic father figure was John LOCKE. In France the so-called *philosophes* and the Encyclopaedia are typical Enlightenment phenomena. HUME and KANT were perhaps the greatest philosophers of that era. In politics, the great enlightened despots of the time were Frederick the Great, King of Prussia and the Habsburg

Emperor, Joseph II of Austria, both of whom supported the principle of religious toleration.

Epicurus (341–270 BC), born on Samos, he came to Athens in 323 BC, travelled in Ionia, taught at Mytilene and Lampsacus, and in 306 BC returned to Athens where he founded a school in a garden. He was a prolific writer, but our knowledge of him is chiefly based on three letters preserved by DIOGENES LAERTIUS and on a poem in praise of him, *De Rerum Natura*, by LUCRETIUS. From what we know through these sources it seems likely that his philosophy was a reaction against the 'other-worldliness' of Plato's THEORY OF FORMS. Whereas for Plato KNOWLEDGE was of intelligible Forms, and the CRITERION of the truth of a HYPOTHESIS about the DEFINITION of a FORM was that it should survive a Socratic testing by question and answer, for Epicurus the criterion of truth was SENSATION, and employment of this criterion favoured the theory with which Plato explicitly contrasted the Theory of Forms (*Sophist* 246 a – d), namely the MATERIALISM of the atomists, Leucippus and DEMOCRITUS. This meant a reaction, also, against the Platonic theory of the IMMORTALITY of the soul. For a sensationist, someone for whom sensation is all-important, talk of life after death is meaningless: 'Death is nothing to us; for that which is dissolved is devoid of sensation, and that which is devoid of sensation is nothing to us'. This, in Epicurus's eyes, was a gain, not a loss. He saw the thought of possible torment at the hands of the gods in a life after death as being one of the main sources of anxiety in this life. Like other philosophers of his time, his aim was to teach wisdom. He saw the goal of wisdom as being *ataraxia*, peace of mind. Someone could not have a quiet mind whose thoughts were forever turning to an unknown future.

In ETHICS Epicurus, like ARISTOTLE, was a naturalist. That is, he sought to derive a view about how we ought to live from a view about our nature. Whereas for Aristotle, who took the function peculiar to man to be the activity of THINKING, the good life was one spent mainly in contemplation of eternal truths, for Epicurus the product of SENSATIONISM was a concern with pleasure and pain, and he took the natural end of man's activity to be 'freedom from pain in the body and from trouble in the mind'. He was sometimes treated as advocating a life devoted to the pleasures of the senses, but this was a misrepresentation which drew attention away from social aspects of his version of HEDONISM, such as the high value he placed on friendship.

In his atomistic theory Epicurus explained the formation of

compounds by reference to an arbitrary 'swerve' in the movement of the atoms. Judging from Lucretius he intended this to explain, also, the freedom of motion of man and animals.

Epicurus's ideas did not die with him. His sensationism finds a modern counterpart in that of the 18th century French philosopher CONDILLAC, his atomism, in that of the 17th century philosopher GASSENDI, two of whose principal works were on Epicureanism. Discussion of his hedonism is a starting point for evaluating the moral philosophy of HUME, ADAM SMITH, BENTHAM and J. S. MILL. The explanation of freedom Lucretius attributes to him is rather like that of some recent physicists in terms of indeterminacy.

epiphenomenalism, *n.* the doctrine that states of CONSCIOUSNESS, including VOLITIONS, are merely by-products of the working of the brain, and, in the words of T. H. HUXLEY (*On the Hypothesis that Animals are Automata*, 1874), are 'as completely without any power of modifying that working as the steam-whistle which accompanies the working of a locomotive engine is without influence upon its machinery'.

epistemology, *n.* (from Greek *episteme* knowledge) the branch of philosophy concerned with the justification of KNOWLEDGE-claims in the face of two kinds of SCEPTICISM, and hence with the nature of knowledge and the things that can be known.

The first kind of scepticism is about there being 'any principle of correctness in names other than convention and agreement' (PLATO, *Cratylus* 384d). Is the meaning of 'beauty', 'largeness', 'holiness', and so on, something we can be said to *know*, or is it something we *decide*, by agreeing to use a word in a certain way? This question, raised by the Sophists' antithesis of nature and convention, is answered by Plato's THEORY OF FORMS: there is a reality, that of the FORMS, to which language must conform if it is to be correct.

Crucial to Plato's theory is a distinction between what is INTELLIGIBLE and what is SENSIBLE. The reality to which language should conform, Plato held, is intelligible. His reasoning for this involved the Heraclitean notion that someone who is, say, beautiful by comparison with an ape, is ugly by comparison with a GOD (*Greater Hippias* 289a) (see HERACLITUS). In anything visible, beauty is confounded with its opposite, ugliness, largeness with its opposite, smallness, and so on. Largeness itself is an OBJECT of intellect: we can think, but not see, what largeness itself is (*Republic* VII 523–524d).

One might hold that the Heraclitean notion applies only to terms with an opposite, that a term like 'blue' has no opposite, and that there is therefore no need to postulate an intelligible reality for it to conform to. The reality it conforms to is visible. A version of this alternative language-justifying doctrine is to be found in LOCKE: the word 'white' stands for our IDEA of SENSATION of whiteness, but this is the effect in us of a power in something outside us, and so it 'agrees to the reality of things' (*Essay*, II xxx 2). This is the sensationalist, or empiricist, form of the doctrine that correct language conforms to an objective reality. Plato held the doctrine in what may be called its rationalist form. A fundamental difference between the two is that whereas a Platonic Form is propositional (i.e. in knowing the Form one knows *that* something is such-and-such, e.g. in knowing the Form of shape one knows that shape is 'that in which a solid terminates'—*Meno* 76a), neither a Lockean power nor its effect in us, a sensation, is propositional. If we can be said to know something, in having a sensation, it is by what RUSSELL later called 'knowledge by acquaintance'.

Besides the kind of scepticism that is answered with the doctrine (rationalist or empiricist) that there is a reality to which language conforms, there is a second, quite different, kind of scepticism. Even if the terms we use have objective reality, can we be sure that what we say, using those terms, is factually correct? Our senses sometimes deceive us. This being so, are we ever justified in claiming to know things about the sensible world? In general, has anything the sort of certainty that would justify knowledge-claims?

To the last question we may reply that whereas we can be mistaken about the truth of such a proposition as 'It is raining' (since now it is raining, now it is not), such propositions as that triangles on equal bases and between parallels are equal in area must always be true. Their truth is not contingent on the changeable world perceived by the senses; it follows logically from that of the DEFINITIONS and AXIOMS of the system. Moreover, our ideas of the objects of MATHEMATICS are CLEAR and distinct, unlike those of SENSIBLE things. Yet the propositions of geometry and arithmetic are not irrelevant to the sensible world. There is a numerical basis for some sensible phenomena, namely MUSICAL CONCORDANCES, and this raises hopes that a mathematical basis may be found for others, such as the orbits of the heavenly bodies. It may thus seem not only that mathematical propositions are necessarily true but also that they are not true merely by convention, that is by virtue of definitions and axioms on which we have arbitrarily decided. Being necessarily true they may seem to be prime candidates for being propositions we can be certain about, and so know. However, there is a problem arising from their being neither merely conventional, nor empirical. *How* do we know the definitions and axioms, given that our awareness of things from birth onwards is conditioned by our senses? The view of the status of mathematical propositions is that of the Pythagoreans (see PYTHAGO-REANISM). Another Pythagorean belief, that in the transmigration of souls, suggests a solution to the problem: we had knowledge of the definitions and axioms when we enjoyed an existence as pure unembodied intelligences before birth, and can now be reminded of them by sensible things. Seeing equal stones and sticks, for example, reminds us of the definition of 'equal' we knew, non-sensibly, before birth.

Plato amalgamated the Pythagorean view of MATHEMATICS with his theory that there is an intelligible principle of correctness for words like 'large' and 'beautiful'. Like the Forms, the objects of mathematics belong to the intelligible world, and mathematics is to be recommended as one of the 'studies that force the soul to turn its vision round to the region where dwells the most blessed part of reality' (*Republic* VII 526e). Further, like the definitions and axioms of mathematical theory, the Forms were known before birth. (Whether Plato held there to be an even closer connection between Forms and the objects of mathematics is controversial.)

The association, in Plato's theory, of anti-conventionalism in the philosophy of language with veneration for geometry as 'knowledge of the eternally existent' had profound implications for subsequent epistemology. It became a 'quest for certainty', but one in which the rationalists and empiricists start from different positions and work down and up respectively. The rationalist, thinking of mathematics as a deductive system, looks for a relatively small number of propositions possessing a necessity comparable to that of mathematical axioms, and tries to work down to the things he wants to prove. The empiricist starts from sensations and tries to work up: sensations, for him, are the *foundations* of empirical knowledge. For a pure rationalist none of our concepts or principles would be derived from EXPERIENCE, they would all be innate (see INNATE IDEAS). For a pure empiricist they would all be derived from experience. Whether any actual philosopher is a pure rationalist or a pure empiricist is doubtful, but the above-mentioned rationalist features are more evident in the epistemology of those philosophers traditionally classified as rationalists, such as DESCARTES,

SPINOZA and LEIBNIZ, than they are in the epistemology of those classified as empiricists, such as LOCKE, BERKELEY and HUME; and vice versa for the empiricist features.

Not all philosophers accept the notion that language either is a matter of convention or conforms either to an intelligible or to a sensible reality. Nor do they all accept the notion that the justification of knowledge-claims involves a quest for certainty. KANT and WITTGENSTEIN fall outside the trichotomy of conventionalism, rationalism and empiricism. Kant held the principle that everything which happens has a CAUSE, for example, to be true but neither as a matter of definition nor as something discovered through sense-experience. It is synthetic but A PRIORI. Neither reason nor experience justifies the employment we make of the concept of cause. The explanation of the manner in which the concept relates to objects is one that breaks entirely new epistemological ground, which Kant called the TRANSCENDENTAL deduction of the concept.

In his later philosophy, Wittgenstein rejected the notion that language conforms to reality, but also rejected the notion that we simply agree to use words in certain ways. Rather, he held, we agree *in* using them as we do, and this is a matter of our sharing in 'forms of life'.

The notion that the justification of knowledge-claims involves a quest for certainty is said by some present-day philosophers to rest on a confusion. Consider the remark that 'what is not true cannot properly be said to be known' (A. J. AYER). If 'properly' means 'truthfully' then the remark is unobjectionable, for it is certainly a feature of our everyday use of 'know' that if someone says he knows something, and what he says he knows turns out to be false, then we say he did not know it after all. However, 'properly' may be taken as in 'something of which one is not conscious cannot properly be said to be a desire', uttered by someone on first hearing about psychoanalytic theory. This means that a person has no right to say he knows something, no matter how good his grounds, if, unbeknown to him, it is in fact false. That is certainly not how we ordinarily use 'know', but it is a big step on the way to saying that one can know only what cannot be false and about which one cannot be wrong. We had best not take this step, since for rationalist and empiricist alike it leads to the conclusion that no knowledge at all is possible. Propositions, like those of mathematics and LOGIC, which are necessarily true, cannot be false, but it does not follow that we cannot be wrong about them. One cannot be wrong in having a sensation, but it does not follow that one is right about something, for sensations are non-propositional.

equality, *n.* in social theory, refers to sameness in some named respect, for instance, equality of opportunity, or of income, or of entitlement. Absolute equality, that is in all conceivable respects, is an illegitimate abstract extension of the notion, and as such is often used by political demagogues and propagandists.

eschatology, *n.* (from Greek *eschatos* the last) the study of last things, particularly the end of the world, in a religious sense. The Day of Judgement, in Christian doctrine, is an eschatological notion. The term is not applied to physical theories of the world's long-term fate.

essence, *n.* in PLATO'S philosophy, to know the essence of, say, BEAUTY is to know, by intelligence, what is necessarily true about beauty in itself, as opposed to being of the opinion, by SENSATION, that some particular thing is beautiful by comparison with certain other things. In ARISTOTLE'S philosophy, one knows the essence of something, e.g. Socrates, in knowing the DEFINITION of the species, man, to which Socrates belongs. 'Essence' is here contrasted with 'ACCIDENT'. Socrates could change in respect of that which is an 'accident', such as his height, and still be Socrates, but this is not true of what is essential to his being Socrates, namely that he is a man.

Both Plato and Aristotle held that what is essential to a thing is not just a matter of convention; it is not determined by how we happen to define the word we use to describe the thing. If it were, the essence would change with changes in our linguistic conventions. Essence, according to Plato and Aristotle, is immutable.

This is sometimes expressed by saying that Plato and Aristotle believed in 'real', not just 'nominal', essences. This way of putting it can be misleading, for the term 'real essence' was used by LOCKE not only to describe the Aristotelian view he regarded as 'wholly useless and unserviceable to any part of our knowledge' (*Essay*, III iii 17); it was also used by him to describe what he called 'the other and more rational opinion', namely that things are constituted, in some way we do not know, out of parts too small for us to sense, the manner of constitution determining 'those sensible qualities which serve us to distinguish them one from another' *(ibid.)*. The manner of constitution is the 'real essence' in the sense of that expression approved of by Locke. A significant difference between an Aristotelian 'real essence' and a Lockean one is that an Aristotelian real essence is immutable, whereas Lockean real essences 'may be changed as easily by that hand that made them, as the internal frame of a watch' (Locke, *First Letter* to Stillingfleet).

Whether the notion of a real essence in the Aristotelian sense is as useless as Locke supposed is a subject of current debate.

ethics, *n.* or **moral philosophy** (from Greek *ethikos*, Latin *moralis* concerning custom), the branch of philosophy treating of good and evil. It is, in the literal sense, a practical study, having to do with the ACTIONS of human beings as members of social groups. Thus we meet questions such as what is goodness and how is one to lead an ethically good life? From this in turn we are led to enquire into what kind of conduct is conducive to such a life, and this raises problems as to duties and obligations. We are thus not merely concerned with questions of obeying commands issuing from an authority that can enforce compliance more or less successfully: this kind of authoritarian ethic (you must act thus because the leader says so) is always open to the logical objection that the ethical question (namely, is the action commanded good?) is simply side-stepped. There are, indeed, some who deny that there is any such objective question, and that, on the contrary, it is all a matter of emotional attitudes. To this extent the whole problem remains controversial. However this may be, in any given case one must first ascertain what kind of question is being asked. Moreover, there is much disagreement as to what constitutes the good life, and it is not clear whether there can be a definitive resolution of such divergencies.

For the Socrates of PLATO'S dialogues, the one overriding good is in the end simply KNOWLEDGE, namely a vision of the FORMS under the Form of the Good. It is in this sense that one must take his view that nobody willingly does evil: if an agent were sufficiently informed he would see that the doing of evil ultimately harms the doer above all, so that if he knew enough he would not do it: surely nobody will knowingly harm himself? This rationalistic doctrine has a grain of truth in it, for it reminds us that by taking precipitate if well-meaning action, we may do more harm than good: being well-disposed is not enough, we must try to be well-informed too. On the other hand, evil is unfortunately a very real thing and is often perpetrated deliberately. ARISTOTLE takes a more down-to-earth view and seeks goodness in moderate conduct (nothing too much, nor too little), which is learned through practice: the good man becomes good through acting in a good manner. The proper setting for this is the city: it is by being members of the city-state that human beings have the scope to fulfil themselves as doers of good actions. This is what he meant by saying that man is a political animal (from Greek *polis* city).

The Stoic ethic (see STOICISM) sees the proper aim of man as being a life lived as closely as possible to the nature of things, a good attained by adapting oneself to the LAWS OF NATURE as much as possible. (In one sense, of course, nobody can help but do just that: we cannot break the laws of nature, they break us.) As against this, the Epicureans (see EPICURUS) saw the goal of life in seeking as much pleasure, and avoiding as much pain, as possible: whereas Plato and Aristotle considered that the good life requires involvement in the life of the city, Epicurus aimed at a state of complete detachment, in which a person remains unruffled by the turbulence of human affairs. All these approaches to ethics are centred on man: the gods play a minor and marginal role in Greek thinking.

By contrast, the ethical views that are linked with the Jewish and Christian religions are God-centred: leading the good life is there a matter of obeying the commandments of GOD, made known to men in various miraculous ways. Disregard of the commandments leads to dire punishment, and it is not for us to reason why: clearly quite the opposite attitude to the inquisitiveness of the Greeks. At the same time, of the famous Ten Commandments, three express necessary conditions of any social existence: indiscriminate killing, stealing and lying make life in a group impossible.

Most ethical doctrines since stress one or several of the features found in ancient ethics. The variability of human nature, customs and institutions is not as great as some contemporary students of society would have us believe. In the rationalist tradition, DESCARTES held that we have an INNATE IDEA of GOD, and from this a God-centred ethic follows at once. SPINOZA's ethics has much in common with Stoic doctrine. He held that God permeates the universe and is indeed identical with it. We ourselves become attuned to the divine by living in accordance with nature. By his Christian contemporaries, he was reviled as a dangerous atheist. KANT's ethics is based on a formal device that is meant to bridge the gap between 'ought' and 'is'; his famous CATEGORICAL IMPERATIVE, which tells us to act always in such a manner that we could wish the principle of our action to be a universal law. Whether this helps one to decide how to act in any given case is doubtful, but as a formula it does ensure some measure of impartiality and discourages special pleading. The ethical notions of justice in John RAWLS's theory partly go back to a similar notion.

On the other side, we have the utilitarian doctrine (see UTILITARIANISM), which decides problems of good and evil in terms of the greatest good of the greatest number. As a theory, it fails to cope with injustice inflicted on the individual for the sake of supposed benefit to the community (for example, compulsory purchase of somebody's home at a contrivedly low price in order that a road may be built), but as a practical procedure it is much used for weighing private against public interest (that notion itself needs examining).

Perhaps the most widespread view about good and evil, as held by the ordinary unreflective, is that we call good what we want to have, and evil what we want to reject or avoid. This works as far as it goes, but a Socratic reminder is called for here: we may not be fully informed of the circumstances (for example, you may call smoking good because you like it, but you might feel differently if you knew that it injures your lungs, which you may not like).

An associated question is that of merit as against EQUALITY. For example, is it right or wrong that, given like access to education, some do better than others? This is an ethical question on which different people hold widely different and often incompatible views. Problems of this kind are common in everyday life. To solve them adequately requires ethical reflection, not just from experts, but from all of us.

evil, *n.* raises a particular problem for those who regard GOD as both all-powerful and all-benevolent: if God is the former, why does he not prevent it, and if the latter, why does he seem not to wish to prevent it? The difficulty seems to have no obvious solution. In Christian theology, the view often occurs that God, having endowed man with free will, must allow him to exercise it, even if he stumbles into disaster through his own fault. What are we to say in the case of a person who, although well-intentioned and well-behaved, lands in trouble because he could not reasonably foresee all the circumstances? After all, we are finite and fallible, it is only God who in his infinity knows everything and can act accordingly. An even more intractable problem arises in the case of natural disasters, where normal precautions are of no avail. The Lisbon earthquake in 1755 claimed some 40 000 victims: was this the act of an all-benevolent deity? In sum, there is no entirely convincing answer to this puzzle. To say that God's way is not our way, and what we see as evil is really good in the end, if only we could see all the facts, is an evasion of the problem, just as in those ethical theories that deny the reality of evil. See ETHICS.

evolution, *n.* (from Latin *evolvere* to roll out) the process of development of characteristics, such as sharp front teeth to tear food with, in existing kinds of living organisms, or of new kinds of organism from existing species. One theory of how new species originate from existing species (as opposed to being due to 'special creation' by GOD) is usually called the doctrine, or theory, of evolution, or DARWINISM.

existentialism, *n.* a philosophic tendency that stresses man in his total setting in the world as the fundamental starting point of philosophic reflection. It is concerned with human experience as a concrete event that has been lived through. As such, it is opposed to lines of abstract philosophising, for example, RATIONALISM, IDEALISM, MATERIALISM and even abstract EMPIRICISM, insofar as that involves generalities divorced from actual life as lived by actual people. Aspects of this approach can be found a long way back, but modern existentialism is rightly taken to start with the 19th century Danish thinker, S. KIERKE-GAARD, who reacted against the all-embracing systematic philosophy of HEGEL. While existentialist thinkers take very different views of many problems, so much so that some decline the label of existentialism, what unites them is a concern with man as a sentient being living and struggling in the world. It is thus a practical rather than a theoretical philosophy, and is closely linked with ethical rather than logical and epistemological problems. For Kierkegaard, the central issue is man's relation to GOD, and the leap of faith into the unknown which is involved in committing oneself to any course of action. What is essential here is not so much the notion of God, but the breaking away from an outlook centred on the self, in favour of an acceptance that to live is to be related to others who are both like us and yet different. The I–thou relation at the heart of Martin BUBER's theological thought is an example of this. SARTRE, for his part, sees in the other not a fellow creature but an enemy, against whom one must maintain oneself. In either case, man is the architect of his own character (there are traces of ARISTOTLE here) and fate. Whereas Sartre was the main representative of atheistic existentialism, MARCEL was a deeply religious Christian: his existentialist approach sees the other as a necessary element for proper understanding of oneself. HEIDEGGER emphasises the fact that others live along with us and interact with us, but is otherwise atheistic in outlook. He is much concerned with the meaning of human existence, as was Sartre after him. Both speculated about being and nothingness, in a somewhat unclear and abstract fashion which rather runs against the central existentialist concern.

(This is perhaps a timely reminder that in the history of human thought, most of the outstanding figures are after all human enough to entangle themselves in their own peculiar contradictions, a fact that poets have often been more aware of than the rest of us.) Finally, we must mention JASPERS, who was a psychiatrist before he became a philosopher. He insisted that we come to know ourselves most vividly in what he called limiting situations, such as the presence of great danger, mortal threats issuing from others or from nature, and the reality of death itself.

Insofar as existentialist thinking relies heavily on raw experience, it has made use of the work of PHENOMENOLOGY, which attempts to capture experience without imposing on it any prior theoretical views held by the observer. In a purely formal sense, existentialism seeks to emphasise that something is, rather than how it is: the fact of its being, rather than describing the features it has. This has been simply put in the tag that existence comes before ESSENCE. Existence (from Latin *exsisto* to stand out there) is what we have as standing in the world, essence (from Latin *essentia* the being of this or that kind) belongs to a description of us in terms of CONCEPTS.

experience, *n.* the term has a common use, as in talk of 'a man of experience', and a philosophical use. The latter is found in the empiricist philosophy of LOCKE and his successors.

To be a man of experience, according to ARISTOTLE (*Metaphysics*, Bk. 1, Ch. 1) is to have perceived things, to have made judgments, to have remembered the judgments, and to have connected them, with a view to ACTION. For example, someone sees some potion administered to Callias, whose fever subsides, and judges that the potion did him good. He sees the same potion administered to Socrates and to many other feverish individuals, with the same results, remembers making these judgments, and acts accordingly when someone else has a fever. Experience, Aristotle says, is KNOWLEDGE of individuals, and the resultant action relates to an individual. Someone who understands *why* the action would be right in *any* similar circumstances is a man of 'science and art'. For practical purposes, he says, the man of science is not necessarily to be preferred to the man of experience, for 'if a man has the theory without the experience, and recognizes the universal but does not know the individual included in this, he will often fail to cure; for it is the individual that is to be cured' (981 a 20).

Having experience of something (e.g. alleviating fever in individuals), for Aristotle, is not simply a matter of perceiving things; judgment and

109

memory are needed, and experience is 'with a view to action'. For Locke, on the other hand, having experience of something may simply be a matter of having SENSATIONS, for sensation is the 'great source of most of the IDEAS we have' (*Essay*, II i 3), and Locke's concern is with experience as the source of ideas (as opposed to ideas being innate), not with experience (as opposed to knowledge of theory) as a guide to action.

Both Aristotle and Locke followed PLATO (*Theaetetus*, 191c) in imagining that our minds contain a block of wax which, when we perceive something, has an impression imprinted on it as a seal ring imprints an impression on wax, but they used this image differently. Aristotle, like Plato, used it in his account of memory. Memory is the persistence of the 'sense-impression' (*Posterior Analytics*, 99 b 36). To explain sense-perception itself he used his notions of FORM and MATTER: a sense is 'what has the power of receiving into itself the sensible forms of things without the matter' (*De Anima*, 424 a 18). Locke used the image not only in his account of memory, but also in what he said about sense-perception. This led him to postulate, within sense-perception, an ELEMENT, sensation, in respect of which the perceiver is, like the wax, passive, and an element, judgment, in which he is active; and to distinguish between them in terms of whether or not the perceiver can properly be said to be right or wrong: he cannot be if he only senses, he must be if he judges.

Locke's use, to explain perception itself, of the image of a seal imprinting an impression on wax, raises a question. How does the perceiver, given the sense-impression or sensation, arrive at a judgment? The answer is a development of the imprinting image. A seal may imprint words on wax in a foreign language. They have to be interpreted. Likewise, in perception, the perceiver 'interprets' the sensation. He interprets it in the light of past experience, and judges accordingly. The act of interpretation takes place so quickly that he does not notice it, and mistakes what is actually judgment for sensation (*Essay*, II ix 8–10).

The SENSE-IMPRESSION notion of experience, under various descriptions ('the given', 'sense-data') has played a major role in EPISTEMOLOGY since Locke's day, though without general agreement about it, even among philosophers who agree in regarding epistemology as a search for foundations of knowledge. Not all philosophers do so agree: foremost among those who do not are KANT and WITTGENSTEIN. See APPEARANCE, PERCEPTION, SENSE-DATUM.

extension, *n.* **1.** the property of being spatially extended. DESCARTES held that the ESSENCE of MATTER is quantifiable extension.

2. in LOGIC, the range of a term as measured by the number of objects to which it applies; the term denotes these objects (see DENOTATION). Extension in sense 2 is opposed to INTENSION (or comprehension), the sum of the attributes comprehended in a term; the term connotes these attributes (see CONNOTATION).

F

facts and values, two kinds of entity that are often distinguished as to status: a fact concerns what is, a value what ought to be. According to HUME, 'is' cannot imply 'ought'. Thus ethical values (and by extension aesthetic ones) come to be viewed as not independent, but linked to human demands and desires. Whether the distinction is quite so clear-cut is, however, not beyond controversy.

fallacy, *n.* (from Latin *fallo* I deceive) A FORMAL mistake in argument, occurs when people reason invalidly. By extension, the term is sometimes used for the making of false assumptions (it is a fallacy that all rich are wicked, and all poor virtuous). This example is closely related to a fallacy often committed, namely to argue that if all *X* are *Y*, then all *non-X* are *non-Y*. AMBIGUITY of terms is a common cause of fallacy: if the meaning of a term shifts in the course of an argument, the conclusion will not follow from the premises (see DEDUCTION). Likewise, an argument often fails because one makes an assumption that begs the question at issue. If in arguing one ignores the point at issue, another fallacy occurs. A fallacy often found in ethical argument is the passage from categorical premises to a modal conclusion (the argument that given the world is such and such, we must do this or that). Fallacies can be avoided by clearly stating the essentials of an argument.

falsifiability, *n.* that feature of PROPOSITIONS which allows them to be tested by experiment and rejected if they fail the test. A proposition that is necessary cannot be falsified. Indeed, a proposition that is true cannot be falsified either. To say that a proposition is falsifiable is thus a somewhat misleading way of insisting that it be tested, where we allow that it might be false.

fatalism, *n.* (from Latin *fatum* what is decreed) the doctrine that what will happen is bound to happen; there is nothing we can do to prevent it. The doctrine is theological, rather than philosophical. It would seem to be implied in the seventeenth of the 39 articles of religion ('Of Predestination and Election') of the Church of England (1562).

Consideration of predestination, according to this article, is 'full of sweet, pleasant, and unspeakable comfort to godly persons', but a cause of desperation for 'curious and carnal persons, lacking the spirit of Christ'.

Feuerbach, Ludwig Andreas (1804–1872), German philosopher, decided to abandon his academic career when the authorship of an anonymous essay of his on the subject of belief in immortality became known (1832). At first a Hegelian (see HEGEL), he came to place more importance on sense experience. His main importance lies in the field of religious thought, where he pronounced the radical view that theology was basically an anthropological pursuit: in religion, we seek to make up for our own inadequacies as finite beings. This view greatly influenced the young MARX, although he accused Feuerbach of not giving sufficient weight to the social aspects.

Fichte, Johann Gottlieb (1762–1814), German philosopher, came from a very humble background and became professor of philosophy and first rector of the new university of Berlin (1810–11). As a young tutor he was greatly impressed by KANT and wrote a 'critique of all revelation' (1792) which was accidentally published without his name and at first attributed to Kant. In 1794 he became professor at Jena. During his editorship of a philosophic journal, a colleague published an article in it in which he defined god as the moral order in the world. As a result of this, the so-called controversy on ATHEISM *(Atheismusstreit)* broke out, which in 1799 led to his leaving for Berlin. It was there that he published his book on the closed trading state, in which he advocated an early form of socialist economy (1800). By this time he had already published (1797) his theory of KNOWLEDGE *(Wissenschaftslehre)* which is perhaps his philosophically most important contribution. Here, he developed what came to be known as the DIALECTIC method: the I (by which he means something like self-awareness) posits itself and distinguishes itself from the not-I (the world), and then recognises how each limits and bears on the other. By this tripartite step-like process we advance our knowledge (for example, I recognise gold, distinguish it from silver and understand it as a metal with specific properties; in general, I recognise x as real, set it over against *not-x* and then subsume both under a higher concept). This method had some influence on the philosophy of HEGEL, although he did not strictly follow the tripartite step.

fideism, *n.* is the view that certain beliefs, particularly religious ones, require the operation of faith and remain inaccessible to reason alone.

FINAL CAUSE

It is thus an anti-rationalist view (see RATIONALISM), to the extent that it places limits on the powers of reason, but it is also irrationalist, in setting aside a group of beliefs as beyond the scope of any reason.

final cause, *n.* that for the sake of which a thing exists, or for the sake of which something happens. For example, a thermostat exists for the sake of keeping the temperature constant; a plant's leaves turn towards the light to enable photosynthesis (the conversion of water and carbon dioxide from the air into carbohydrates) to take place in the plant-cells. That there are final causes or teleological (from Greek *telos* an end) explanations of things does not rule out other sorts of explanation of the same things. The turning of the leaves can be explained as a reaction to certain stimuli, the latter being EFFICIENT CAUSES.

Philosophers have disagreed about the range of things that can be explained in terms of final causes or purposes, and about the relative importance of final-cause and efficient-cause explanation.

ARISTOTLE proposed final-cause explanations even of such things as the motions of the stars, saying that 'We are inclined to think of the stars as mere bodies or units occurring in a certain order but completely lifeless; whereas we ought to think of them as partaking of life and initiative' (292 a 20). GALILEO rejected this whole idea, and in its place advocated a new scientific methodology in which only locomotion (changes in the place of things over time) counts for explanatory purposes, and the manner of such motion is described in exclusively mathematical terms. DESCARTES provided a metaphysical basis for the new methodology by declaring EXTENSION to be the sole ESSENCE of MATTER, and by founding analytical geometry, which shows how every geometrical object or relation can be given numerical expression. (He assumed the properties of physical and geometrical space to be the same.)

Aristotle gave priority to final-cause explanations not only for human actions, and for things made for a purpose ('works of art' as he called them), but also for works of nature, saying that the final cause 'is the Reason, and the Reason forms the starting-point, alike in the works of art and in works of nature' (639 b 15). The starting point he meant was that for understanding why things of various kinds develop as they do. However, whereas the ancients mainly sought to *understand* nature, the moderns seek to *control* it and for that efficient causes alone matter. One can understand why some strange-looking piece of apparatus exists if told that it is to keep the temperature constant, but this information, by itself, is of no use if one's task is to make, or repair, one of them. For that, one needs to be an engineer or mechanic, that is, someone who can apply his knowledge of efficient causes. See CAUSE.

First Mover or **Prime Mover**, *n*. in ARISTOTLE'S philosophy the external motionless CAUSE of the eternal rotatory movement of a fifth ELEMENT (the other four being earth, fire, air and water) at the circumference of the universe, and thereby the cause of the movement of everything else in the universe (*Physics*, Bk. VIII, Ch. 6, 259 a 1–13). The First Mover is a cause of MOTION in things through infinite time (*Metaphysics*, Bk. XII, Ch. 7, 1073 a 6); that is, it does not simply initiate motion which then continues of its own accord. It causes motion as an object of love moves a lover (*ibid.*, 1072 b 3). It is GOD, 'a living being, eternal, most good' (*ibid.*, 1072 b 28).

AQUINAS incorporated Aristotle's notion of a First Mover into his idea of God, the argument for a First Mover being, he said, the most obvious of five ways of proving God's existence. Aquinas's God, however, differs from Aristotle's in being a cause not only of movement but of the existence of the things that move. That is, He is a Creator. See DEISM.

form, *n*. the more common and more easily understood of the two uses of the term is as the correlative of 'MATTER' in talk of the 'form and matter' of things, as when we say of two beds, one made of iron and one made of wood, that their form is the same but their matter is different. The use of the term is extended to cover qualities like colour, which is referred to as a 'sensible form', apprehended by one of the senses. In general, the 'form' of something is anything about it we care to mention for purposes of classification.

The less common use of the term is in a theory, the so-called THEORY OF FORMS (or theory of Ideas) originated by PLATO but also to be found in a revised version in Aristotelian philosophy. Here we write it with a capital: 'Form'. The theory is many-sided, reflecting Plato's debts to SOCRATES, HERACLITUS, PYTHAGORAS, PARMENIDES and others.

It would seem, from the sort of questions Socrates asked, that he thought that someone cannot be said to know what, say, justice is simply on the ground that he applies the term 'just' as the rest of us do; he must be able to provide a 'real' DEFINITION of justice, i.e. say what justice really and essentially is, apart from whatever our conventional linguistic practice may be with the term 'just'.

From Heraclitus Plato derived the notion that nothing in the

SENSIBLE world is beautiful, or large, or wise, without at the same time being ugly, or small or stupid. Man is both wise, by comparison with an ape, and stupid, by comparison with a GOD. The 'opposites', wise and stupid, are confounded in sensible things. Plato concluded that they must also exist separately, in themselves.

Next, Plato combined this with what he derived from Socrates: the opposites in themselves are intelligible, i.e. have definitions we can, in principle, know.

Thus far the theory might seem to be restricted to terms that are obviously comparative, like 'just' and 'unjust', 'large' and 'small'. It might seem not to be about terms like 'finger', since a finger is a finger regardless of what one compares it with. However, something which is a finger at one time will not be so at another, when the body has decomposed. So although something cannot be both a finger and not-a-finger at the same time, something can be both a finger and not-a-finger from the viewpoint of eternity. Plato's next development of the theory involves adopting this viewpoint. He adopts it because, like other philosophers of the time, he holds that only what is eternally true can properly be said to be known. Everything in the sensible world is in a state of 'flux', i.e. is not eternally what it is at any one time. So nothing in the sensible world qualifies as an object of KNOWLEDGE. Hence there must be intelligible Forms, existing separately, not only for opposites like large and small, which are confounded at the same time in sensible things; but also for opposites like finger and not-a-finger, or man and not-a-man, which are confounded in sensible things only over a period of time.

The next development of the theory is to meet an epistemological problem (see EPISTEMOLOGY). Our awareness of things, from birth onwards, is by the senses. Sense-perception is not awareness of what is eternal. It would seem to follow that we can have knowledge of things only through having existed before we acquired senses, i.e. before birth. Plato welcomes this conclusion as confirmation of the Pythagorean belief that we exist both before birth and after death. He holds that we knew the Forms before birth, when our mode of existence was purely intellectual, and that we can now be brought to recollect them in favourable circumstances.

Whereas the more common use of the term 'form' is classificatory, Plato's theory of Forms is advanced as being explanatory, in some sense. In his dialogue *Phaedo*, he introduces the theory in the context of an account Socrates gives of his thoughts about the comparative merits of different kinds of explanation. He concludes that there is 'only one thing for a man to consider, with regard both to himself and to anything else, namely the best and highest good' (*Phaedo* 96 d). He then represents explanation by reference to a Form (e.g. explanation of something being beautiful by reference to its 'partaking' of beauty in itself) as a makeshift approach, i.e. as a falling off from the ideal of explanation by reference to 'the best and highest good'. Elsewhere Plato posits a supreme Form, which he calls 'the Form of the Good'. He gives it a role in the apprehension of the other Forms comparable to that of the sun in the apprehension of visible things. The ultimate aim of the philosopher is to attain the apprehension of this Form. It is, he says, 'the limit of the intelligible' (*Republic* VII, 532b). This is Plato's way of representing his theory as consistent with the Socratic ideal of explanation by reference to 'the best and highest good'.

The difference between the classificatory use of the term 'form' in talk of many articles of furniture all having the same form, bed, or many flowers all having the same sensible form, red, and the use of the term 'Form' in Plato's theory is very great. The classificatory use does not involve questionable assumptions about things having real definitions, about knowledge being of what is eternally true, about existence before birth, and so forth. Not surprisingly Plato occasionally represents his theory of Forms as if it were a theory of forms. For example, he remarks that 'we are in the habit of postulating one single form for each class of particulars to which we give the same name' (*Republic* X 596a), though he recognizes the need to give an account of how Forms are related to forms. He thinks of Forms, *qua* eternal, as being more substantial than sensible things, and, in keeping with this, employs the metaphor of an original, or 'archetype', and a copy. The question of the relation of Forms to forms accordingly becomes that of how it is that a single Form can have one or many copies. Plato's answer is: through there being a 'receptacle' for copies, which is space. A divine artificer, with his eye on the Forms, copies them in various parts of space, whence there are many things with the same form.

Plato's pupil, ARISTOTLE, gives an account of Plato's theory of Forms (*Metaphysics*, Bk. 1, Ch. 6, 987 b 6; cf. Bk. 13, Ch. 3, 1078 b 15) in which he mentions three of the main ingredients of the theory, namely the part about there being definitions which express the essential nature of things, the part about knowledge being limited to what is eternal and unchanging, and the part about the sensible world being in a state of 'flux', but, inexplicably, makes no mention at all of what Plato calls 'the origin of the designation *intelligible*' (*Republic* VII, 524 c), namely the reflection that opposites are confounded in sensible things and so must exist separately, in themselves. With the omission of any mention of opposites, Aristotle is able to represent Plato as holding the theory that the forms (not Forms) of things are substantial, and exist apart from the things of which they are forms; and to present himself in a much more favourable light as the holder of the theory that forms exist *in* the things of which they are forms. In the primary sense of 'SUBSTANCE', Aristotle says, it is the individual things we see around us that comprise the substance of the world.

One might suppose that Aristotle, having ignored what Plato called 'the origin of the designation *intelligible*' would reject the notion of things having definable essences. In fact he embraced it wholeheartedly, saying that the definitions are of 'natural kinds' to which the individual things we see around us belong. In the case of the individual thing, Socrates, the natural kind is the species, man. The difference between a kind in general, and a natural kind, is given by the facts of generation. We may describe an individual as a good runner, or as a man. The latter is the natural kind, since men beget men but not necessarily good runners. One of Aristotle's most delightful examples to illustrate the difference is that of a wooden bed being buried. If it sprouted, Aristotle says, what would come up would be little trees, not little beds. Bed is a kind of thing, but not a natural kind. The concept of a natural kind is a teleological concept: things develop to be things of a certain natural kind. Aristotle extended the notion of TELEOLOGY beyond the organic world, and even said that 'we ought to think of stars as partaking of life and initiative' (*De Caelo*, Bk. 2, Ch. 12, 292 a 18). If there is anything in Aristotle's teleological theory which corresponds to Plato's Form of the Good, it is his 'Prime Mover'. The Prime Mover is immediately, or mediately, responsible for the movement of everything, and moves as a 'being for whose good an action is done' (*Metaphysics*, Bk. 12, Ch. 6, 1072 b 2).

Aristotle said that species and genera are substance in a secondary sense. In keeping with this, medieval philosophers called a form such as man, but not a form such as runner, a 'substantial form'. The scientist's foremost task, for a believer in substantial forms, is to discover their intelligible essences. This conception of the scientist's task came under fierce attack in the 17th century, by GALILEO, GASSENDI and DESCARTES amongst others. The use of the term 'form' in talk of the 'form and matter' of things has survived and passed into common usage.

formal, *adj*. **1**. referring to the FORM of something, rather than to its content or matter; 'grass is green' and 'water is wet' are two sentences of the same form but with different content or matter.

2. denotes strictness in exposition as against informal talk.

formal cause, *n*. the FORM of a thing considered as a factor in the explanation of the thing being as it is. See ARISTOTLE, CAUSE, MATTER.

freewill and determinism, the problem whether we ever act freely if everything is determined. Three possible solutions are:

(a) not everything is physically determined, and physical indeterminism allows for human actions to be determined mentally, by the will.

(b) everything is determined, and freedom is an illusion.

(c) freewill and determinism are compatible.

A version of the first solution seems to have been propounded by EPICURUS. In his atomistic theory (see ATOMISM) he explained the formation of compounds in terms of an arbitrary 'swerve' in the movement of the atoms. Judging from LUCRETIUS he meant this to explain, also, the freedom of movement of man and animals. A present-day version of this first solution has been advanced by the physiologist, J. C. Eccles, who holds that since quantum mechanics admits the existence of unpredictable events there are no scientific grounds for denying that actions can be controlled voluntarily. Presumably the thought behind this solution, at least in Eccles's version, is the thought that voluntary control of actions can be explained in terms of the mind stepping in where there is physical indeterminism, and influencing the atoms in the brain in a way such as to determine what bodily movement takes place. A possible objection is that nobody is conscious of exercising such an influence on the atoms in his brain, and hence nobody could tell whether or not he had acted freely.

A version of the second solution is proposed by SPINOZA. In *Ethics* Book II, Prop. 48, Spinoza says: 'In the mind there is no absolute or free will; but the mind is determined to will this or that by a cause, which has been determined by another cause, and this last by another cause, and so on to infinity.' A man thinks he is free only because he is ignorant of the causes of his willing to do this or that. Spinoza's denial of freewill is qualified: he holds that a man is free, in a sense, in so far as he manifests the power of God. This sense of 'free' is far removed from the ordinary sense, which seems to have no more to do with God than it has to do with atoms in the brain.

The third solution may take various forms. 'Determined' may be analysed so as to be compatible with 'free', or conversely. Some philosophers have held determinism to be necessarily true. LEIBNIZ (*Discourse on Metaphysics*, VI) said that if a number of points are jotted down on a sheet of paper then no matter how many points there are, and how randomly they may seem to be distributed, there is bound to be a formula which will yield a line which goes through all of them, even though the formula may be too complex for us to work out. Equally, there is bound to be regularity or orderliness in the world, no matter what happens. On this analysis orderliness in general (i.e. provided the kinds of order, or 'laws of nature', are not specified, and the orderliness can be indefinitely complex) puts no constraint on what can happen. What happens determines what the LAWS OF NATURE can be just as much as the laws of nature determine what can happen. Determinism in this necessary, general, reciprocal sense is compatible with anything we do, and hence has not the implications that we are bound to act as we do.

The problem remains, however, if things are determined in a different sense, namely, if God 'preordains' what we are and do. Even this kind of determinism has been regarded as compatible with our being free, at least in a negative sense of 'free'. Someone is not free if his actions are brought about in what might be called an 'external' way. Suppose I kick someone, but only as a result of a neurologist passing an electric current through part of my brain so as to produce the motion of my foot. There is a sense in which it would not be something *I* did. For a bodily movement to be one for which I can be held accountable the action must not be determined in this external way. The question is: Is God's creating us, with a given nature, external determination? Perhaps not, on the ground that prior to being created we do not exist, and so have no nature of our own by contrast with which anything God might decree for us would be an external determination. The question of externality would not arise, and so God's preordination of our having the nature we have would not be incompatible with our being free, in the negative sense of there being things we do which are not externally determined, or against our nature.

Such an analysis of 'free' will satisfy only those who accept the system according to which they are created with a given nature, for which they are not themselves responsible. Not all philosophers are prepared to accept this. Thus in *The Vocation of Man*, Book 1, F. G. FICHTE writes

> What I had desired was this: that I myself, that of which I am conscious as my own being and person, but which in this system appears as only the manifestation of a higher existence, that this 'I' would be independent, would be something which exists not by another or through another, but of myself, and, as such, would be the final root of all my determinations. The rank which in this system is assumed by an original power of Nature I would myself assume; with this difference, that my nature would not be determined by any foreign power.

See VOLITION.

Frege, Gottlob (1848–1925), German philosopher and mathematician, professor at Jena, was a precursor of RUSSELL and WHITEHEAD in developing a FORMAL system of modern LOGIC with a view to showing that MATHEMATICS is, in a certain sense, reducible to logical notions alone. This was done in his *Begriffsschrift* (1879), in which a 'conceptual script' was developed, following a project first mooted by LEIBNIZ nearly two centuries earlier. This he applied to arithmetic in *Grundgesetze der Arithmetik* (1893) where he defines a cardinal number as the class of all classes similar to a given class, a procedure adopted independently by Russell afterwards. Russell seems to have been one of the rare readers of Frege to understand his work. At the same time, he shook Frege's confidence by the well-known PARADOX of the class of all classes not members of themselves, which Russell later solved in terms of the theory of types (see TYPES, THEORY OF). In logic, Frege's most important philosophic contribution is his systematic treatment of QUANTIFIERS.

His logical notation was not adopted, but superseded by that of Russell and Whitehead. A distinction of some importance in later developments was that between sense and reference (1892, in an article so named). The sense of a word is roughly its MEANING, while its reference is the OBJECT we are talking about. (Some confusion has been caused by this, because Frege wilfully used for 'reference' the German word for 'meaning', when another quite usual word was available.)

function, *n.* (from Latin *fungor* I perform) has a number of senses in philosophy. There is first the mathematical notion of one quantity depending systematically on another. By extension, this is used in LOGIC where a sentence frame or propositional function (Bertrand RUSSELL'S term) takes various values when an open place in it is occupied by particular 'values'. Likewise with the notion that the truth-value of an argument is a function of the truth-values of its constituents. Another sense that is closer to the term's etymology occurs when we say that the function of a part is to contribute in certain ways to the action of the whole. This sense, common in biology, is widespread in ARISTOTLE'S works.

G

Galilei, Galileo, (1564–1642), born at Pisa, where he entered the university in 1581 to study medicine. His interest turned to MATHEMATICS and from 1592 to 1610 he held the Chair of Mathematics at the University of Padua. He applied mathematics to the study of MOTION, both astronomical and terrestrial. He became convinced of the Copernican theory that the planets revolve about the sun (see COPERNICUS), and, with the aid of a telescope he had built, made other observations which conflicted with the teachings, derived mainly from ARISTOTLE and the Bible, of SCHOLASTIC philosophers and the Catholic Church. In 1610 he left Padua to become 'first philosopher and mathematician' to the grand duke of Tuscany. His publications of greatest philosophical interest are *The Assayer* (1623), in which he ridicules the Aristotelian philosophy and expounds the new scientific method, including the distinction between PRIMARY AND SECONDARY QUALITIES, and the *Dialogue Concerning the Two Chief World Systems–Ptolemaic and Copernican* (1632). When it was realised that the *Dialogue* was in fact a defence of the Copernican system Galileo was prosecuted for heresy and spent the last eight years of his life under house arrest.

Although Galileo was not primarily a philosopher it was as a result of the revolution in scientific method, to which he made a major contribution, that modern philosophy acquired one of its most characteristic interests. He rejected the received Aristotelian scientific methodology based on there being things of fixed natural kinds, whose changes were to be explained teleologically (see TELEOLOGY) in terms of inbuilt ends. In its place he advocated a new methodology in which only what Aristotle called 'local motion' (changes in the place of things over time) counts for explanatory purposes, and the manner of such motion is described in exclusively mathematical terms. This revolution in scientific methodology meant a fundamental reassessment of man's position *vis-à-vis* the world as an object of knowledge. Instead of man being privileged to have an intellectual insight into the ESSENCES of things of various natural kinds, in a world that is much as it appears to ordinary sense-perception, man has now to rely on his ability to detect regularities in the movements of atoms of matter in a world that is distinct from what we perceive and possesses only those features that are amenable to mathematical treatment. Tastes and smells, colours and sounds are no more a part of the objective world than is the tickling caused by a feather. With the doctrine of primary and secondary qualities the real world is distanced from man, and modern philosophy acquires its most characteristic interest, that in the theory of knowledge, EPISTEMOLOGY, to bring them together again.

Galileo's interest was methodological rather than philosophical. He would have rejected, as not answerable by the scientist as such, the question why the book of nature is, as he put it, 'written in the mathematical language'. It was enough that GOD had chosen so to write it. He left it to DESCARTES, HOBBES and others to debate the place of man in the mechanistic world of his science.

Gassendi, Pierre (1592–1655), French priest, scientist and philosopher. He was as devoted as DESCARTES to reconciling science and religion, but severely critical of Descartes's brand of mathematical RATIONALISM. He contributed the fifth set of objections to Descartes's *Meditations* (1641), challenging the beliefs that we can know when we clearly (see CLEAR) and distinctly perceive something (Descartes's criterion of its being true), and that we can clearly and distinctly perceive the nature of a material thing, such as a piece of wax, not by 'acts of vision, touch and imagination' but by 'an intuition of the mind' *(Second Meditation)*.

Although Gassendi followed SEXTUS EMPIRICUS in being sceptical about there being a CRITERION of truth that can in fact be applied, he departed from Sextus in allowing that what we sense can be a sign to us of what we cannot sense. For example, the sweat we see is a sign to us of the existence, in the skin, of the pores we cannot see. Paradoxically, such empirical reasoning from sign to signified, 'can so emend the perception of sense as to receive therefrom no sign until it be emended' *(Syntagma Philosophicum*, published posthumously 1658, *Institutio logica*, cap. 1). This 'emendation' typically occurs in the perception of things as being near or far, or large or small. It has the result that, as LOCKE put it *(Essay*, II ix 9) 'we take that for the perception of our sensation which is an idea formed by our judgment'.

Reasoning from, and emending, the signs given by sense, Gassendi held, yields what can be accepted as knowledge for practical purposes, without there being any guarantee of its truth, such as its satisfying the criterion of clearness and distinctness. Gassendi rejected Descartes's rationalist theory that the ESSENCE OF MATTER is EXTENSION (the same extension as in Euclidean geometry), and its corollary, that there is no extension without matter (i.e. no 'void'). In its place he put the empiricist theory that the best model for explaining nature is an ATOMISM of solid, weighty, bodies, in MOTION or rest in absolute SPACE AND TIME. This theory, expounded at length in the form of historical studies of EPICURUS, and in the *Syntagma philosophicum*, was his *via media* between the Pyrrhonian scepticism (see PYRRHONISM) exhibited in his first work (*Exercitationes paradoxicae adversus Aristoteleos*, 1624) and the dogmatism of the mathematical rationalists.

Gestalt psychology, *n.* a school of PSYCHOLOGY founded by Max Wertheimer, Wolfgang Köhler and Kurt Koffka in Germany in the second decade of the 20th century. A Gestalt is a pattern, configuration or grouping which characterises a whole and is not present in the parts. A melody, for example, is not present in the individual tones of which it is composed. Moreover, there can be the same melody with different tones, if the key is changed.

Gestalt psychologists stressed those aspects of perceptual experience that cannot be inferred from the stimulation of the sense-organ. A favourite example is that of apparent movement. If someone looks at two stationary lights, close together, which successively go on and off at intervals of about 0.06 second, he will seem to see one light, moving. Wertheimer postulated cortical processes to explain this effect.

Gestalt psychologists rejected the sensationalist/associationist approach to PERCEPTION, but they merely substitute one given (the cortically-determined percept) for another (the stimulus-determined sensation). Their explanations still fall within the traditional stimulus-response framework, unlike those of present-day researchers who assimilate a percept to an HYPOTHESIS.

Geulincx, Arnold (1624–1669), Belgian follower of DESCARTES, best known for his philosophy of ACTION. In works on ETHICS and META-PHYSICS, published in 1665 and 1691, and reprinted in his *Opera Philosophica*, (3 volumes, ed. J. P. N. Land, The Hague, 1891–93), he drew the consequences of the principle that 'it is impossible that he should do a thing who is ignorant of how it is done' (*ibid.*, III 33).

The significance of this principle can be seen by contrasting the Cartesian conception of responsibility with that of PLATO and ARISTOTLE. Plato acknowledged that a man's being able to cause his limbs to move is conditional on his bones being rigid, his muscles able to contract and relax, and so on. However, he insisted on a distinction between the *cause* of the limb-movements (the man), and the *conditions* without which the man could not be a cause (*Phaedo*, 99 b). In his *Physics*, Bk. VIII, Ch. 5, Aristotle, likewise, conceived of a man as responsible, directly, for the movement of his hand: responsible, in that he is not an instrument in someone else's movement of his hand; directly, in that he does not have to do something else to make it move. The conditions of his being able to move his hand are not things he does. For a Cartesian, however, this way of conceiving the matter is ruled out. A man is really a non-extended thinking substance united with a body via a brain. What is to take the place of the earlier way of conceiving responsibility? At first it might seem that only a small change is needed: what Plato thought of as *conditions* of a *man's* causality become, for Descartes, *instruments* of a *mind's* causality. However, this will not do, for the mind is not conscious of employing any instruments to effect the hand-movement and is ignorant of how it can cause movement in the supposed instruments, the bones and muscles. The conclusion seems inevitable: either the mind does not really do anything at all; or if it does do things they are restricted to things of a purely mental kind, 'acts of VOLITION', and we are left with the question how these mental acts can possibly bring about movements in, and of, the body.

Geulincx's answer to this last question involved an extension of something Descartes said in the Synopsis of his *Meditations on First Philosophy* (1641), about the relation of a human body to body (matter) in general. Just as Descartes related a human body to body in general so Geulincx related a human mind to mind in general, which he identified with GOD. God, being omniscient and omnipotent, can do what we cannot do. So it is God who really moves the hand, on the occasion of the human act of volition. Furthermore He is the real cause behind all the sequences we ordinarily think of as causal. Just as coins have no purchasing power in virtue of the metal they are made of, but only because of human institution, so what we think of as causes have no real efficacy in themselves, but only because of divine institution. See MALEBRANCHE, OCCASIONALISM.

gnosticism, *n.* (from Greek *gnosis* insight) is a religious and philosophic tendency of the 2nd century AD which arose from a mixture of Hellenistic and Eastern influences. The Greek element is Neo-Platonic (see NEO-PLATONISM), the Eastern aspects come from Egypt and Persia. Some gnostic sects were close to CHRISTIANITY and attacked by the

Church as heretical. According to gnostic doctrine, we attain salvation through gaining esoteric KNOWLEDGE concerning GOD and the world. There is a strong DUALISM of matter and spirit, the former being essentially EVIL. Gnostic doctrines have greatly influenced both Jewish and Christian mysticism in the Middle Ages and traces of them can be found in idealist philosophies (see IDEALISM).

god, the ultimate power on which the world and all that is in it depend, is found in one form or another in all religious thinking and in many philosophic positions. The empirical prerequisite that leads to this notion lies in our coming up against powers that vastly exceed our own: this is part of every human being's ordinary experience beginning with the child's position *vis-à-vis* its parents, and issuing in the untamable forces of nature, including the awareness that our lives are finite and end in physical death. In the thinking of philosophers, the idea of god has taken many different forms. For PLATO, god is a DEMIURGE who fashions the world out of chaos, the original matter being simply there. ARISTOTLE saw god as the FIRST MOVER, who set the whole world going. For the Greeks in general, god was a remote and unconcerned figure that had organised the world system and then let it run without further regard to the fate of man. Opposed to this is the view of god in Jewish and Christian religion: here god is the creator of heaven and earth and all that dwell therein; man is made in the image of god, who retains a close interest in how our lives proceed and who gives us guidelines on how we should conduct our human affairs. By contrast, for the Greeks, god is made in the image of man. In either case, the idea of a divinity answers to the feeling that something or other must be behind, or responsible for, or giving meaning to, everything that is and that happens, the world and what goes on in it. There are those who do not have this feeling, who simply hold that we are intricate parts of a highly intricate world that is there to be looked at and lived in: such people are called atheists (see ATHEISM), who see no positive need for divinities. For the rest it is a very natural habit of ours to assume that if we cannot grasp something there must be something else behind it. That seems to be the point of VOLTAIRE's remark, that if God did not exist, we should have to invent him.

The God of the Bible is transcendent, he lies beyond our grasp, and can be known and recognised only through some act on his part, namely, the granting of divine grace. According to AQUINAS and following Aristotle, his existence can be grasped by unaided reason, but knowing his nature requires the grace of revelation. In Protestant theology, God in all his aspects is unknowable and must be revealed. The 'people of the Book' (Jews, Christians, Muslims) recognise one single God (the triune God of the Christians is to be understood as one God with three main aspects). The Ancients recognised many gods (polytheism), roughly one for each main department of human activities. There is yet a further possibility, namely the view that God is identical with the world and therefore present in every single part of it: this theory of all-presence is called PANTHEISM, most explicitly found in the ethics of SPINOZA. In this case we speak of God as immanent, or in the world. Quite unjustly, Spinoza's contemporaries called him an atheist. In these various notions of God, very different views have been held as to his attributes. The Greek gods were certainly regarded as powerful, but not as benevolent. Indeed, the attribute of power seems to be the fundamental aspect common to all concepts of a deity. Every tribe considered its god or gods more powerful than those of their enemies. If defeated, a people might well go over to the stronger gods of the victors. What makes the God of the Jews, and later the Christians, different from these, is that even in defeat the Children of Israel remained faithful to their God, who was one and supreme, and therefore beyond defeat.

Gödel, Kurt (1906–1984), Austrian logician and mathematician who became American and worked at the Princeton Institute for Advanced Studies. In 1930, he proved the completeness of first-order predicate calculus (the set of sentences that have 'one-place' predicates such as 'black', 'solid', 'round'). Shortly afterwards he established that in the logical system of *Principia Mathematica* (RUSSELL and WHITEHEAD), one can formulate PROPOSITIONS that can neither be proved nor disproved. Thus, if MATHEMATICS is reducible to LOGIC, as *Principia Mathematica* maintains, then mathematics is undecidable (that is, it contains propositions neither provable nor disprovable from the AXIOMS). The undecidability proof itself proceeds through a special mathematical encoding of any formula in mathematics. From it he concluded that a proof that a system of elementary mathematics is consistent (if it is) cannot be given within that system.

Goethe, Johann Wolfgang von (1749–1832), the great German poet and writer, who was interested also in biology and in scientific method. In connection with botanical enquiries he coined the term 'morphology', the study of form or shape, which goes back largely to him. As regards method, he was opposed to the mathematical approach of NEWTON and his followers, and rejected Newton's findings that white light was composed of all the colours. His own approach was in terms of immediate EXPERIENCE of the observer, and in his work on colour he brought out important aspects of complementarity. In fact, his disagreement with Newton rests on a misunderstanding: he did not really grasp the Newtonian method, which was aimed at problems different from those in which he was interested.

Goodman's paradox, *n.* a difficulty (not the only one) in the theory of CONFIRMATION, first noticed by the American philosopher Nelson Goodman (1906–). Suppose we define 'grue' as applicable to all things examined before time *t* just in case they are green but to other things just in case they are blue. Then at *t*, for every evidence statement that a given emerald is green, there is a parallel statement that it is grue. It thus seems that the prediction that all emeralds examined later will be green, and that they will be grue, are equally confirmed by past evidence statements describing the same observation. However, if we do later examine an emerald and it is grue, it is blue and therefore not green. Moreover, if confirmation is defined in terms of past success, by suitably contriving a strange PREDICATE, anything can be made to confirm anything else. The objection to confirmation theory is well taken, but the device of a predicate with a built-in time switch is itself objectionable.

Greek Academy, *n.* the name given to the school of philosophy founded by PLATO. It was named after a public park, called Academia, just outside Athens, where Plato started teaching in about 385 BC. It is customary to distinguish different periods in the school's long history. In the Old Academy discussion tended to revolve round Plato's own philosophy, and in particular his THEORY OF FORMS. Some way of combining Plato's theory with Pythagorean number theory was sought. The Middle Academy was dominated by the dogmatic SCEPTICISM of Arcesilaus of Pitane (*c.*315–240 BC); and the New Academy by the Pyrrhonian scepticism of Carneades of Cyrene (*c.*213–129 BC). See PYRRHONISM, PYTHAGOREANISM.

Green, Thomas Hill (1836–1882), English philosopher, studied and later taught at Oxford, introducing to his public the philosophies of KANT and HEGEL at a time when the utilitarian and empiricist doctrines of J. S. MILL were dominant. His own views were on the contrary based on the idealist notion that all KNOWLEDGE is essentially dependent on self-awareness (see IDEALISM). Thus the real world consisted of a system of relations one term of which was always in the end the self as aware of itself, somewhat in the manner of Hegel. This approach is extended to moral philosophy, in that a human being's wishes and aspirations cannot be considered in isolation but must somehow be viewed as a whole. However, while allowing that self-fulfilment had a social setting, he does not see the individual as subordinated to society and to the state, as Hegel does. In the end, Green's native liberalism and his idealist metaphysic pull in opposite directions, and leave his position with unresolved contradictions.

H

Hare, Richard Mervin (1919–), Oxford philosopher, mainly known for his view that moral facts are not descriptive, but prescriptive (see ETHICS). Moral discourse is not so much an account of human affairs, but rather a guide to ACTION. There may indeed be some descriptive material, but only incidentally: the peculiarly moral aspect is prescriptive. This guidance to action somewhat resembles the function of ordering, as in imperative statements. However, they differ in that moral statements must be universalisable, which is not the case with all imperatives. Thus moral prescriptions contain an evaluative element, which distinguishes them from mere orders. The attendant question whether we can combine freedom with a rational observance of universal moral principles is answered affirmatively.

Hartley, David (1705–1757), English philosopher, physician and psychologist. In his *Observations on Man, His Frame, His Duty and His Expectations* (1749) he followed HUME in giving an account of human nature based on the ASSOCIATION OF IDEAS. Hume thought of the association as being an effect, in the mind, of something that happens in the brain. Hartley was more specific: SENSATIONS in the mind are caused by vibrations on the surface of the nerves and in the brain. IDEAS of sensations correspond to the diminutive vibrations that are the vestiges of these vibrations. These diminutive vibrations become associated by joint occurrence, so that the occurrence of one predisposes another to occur. The association of ideas is the representation in the mind of this association of diminutive vibrations in the brain (*Observations*, etc., Pt. I, Sect. ii, Prop. 8). Hartley followed Hume in what he said about the same MOTIVES always producing the same ACTIONS, and stated categorically that motives are mechanical causes of actions. This meant denying what is generally termed 'freewill' (see FREEWILL AND DETERMINISM). Later philosophers think that motives are better thought of as FINAL CAUSES than as EFFICIENT CAUSES.

hedonism, *n.* (from Greek *hedone* pleasure) is the doctrine that sees the attainment of maximum pleasure as the mainspring of human action in pursuit of the good life. This view was first put forward by Aristippus of Cyrene (435–356 BC). Two problems arose at once: first, we must devise some method of weighing pleasures against pains, a *'felicific calculus'*, as it were; and second, we must decide how to assess intense transient pleasures as against moderate but lasting ones. EPICURUS seems to have been in favour of the latter, finding pleasure in *ataraxia* or unruffledness, achieved through detachment.

The hedonistic principle lies at the base of utilitarian ethics (see UTILITARIANISM). However, J. S. MILL raised the question of quality of pleasure and recognised that there are higher and lower pleasures. Amongst the former he counted the pursuit of disinterested enquiry, and now we are not far removed from a Socratic position. As soon as one raises the question as to quality, it becomes clear that there is no agreed common scale on which pleasures can be assessed. As a simple rule of practice, there is of course no difficulty in accepting that we should seek to avoid all avoidable pain in pursuing a particular good.

Hegel, Georg Wilhelm Friedrich (1770–1831), German philosopher who studied philosophy and theology at Tübingen, became a tutor and lecturer at Jena, editor of a journal in Bamberg, director of Nürnberg Gymnasium, Professor at Heidelberg (1816) and Berlin (from 1818). His philosophy is a vast system which presents the reflective examination of things as such, the most comprehensive absolute idealist account of human endeavour (see IDEALISM). In his lifetime he published *Phenomenology of Spirit* (1807), *Science of Logic* (1812–16), *Encyclopaedia of philosophic sciences* (1817) and *Philosophy of Right* (1821). The rest of his voluminous writings was published posthumously from lecture notes taken by students and disciples.

The system starts from the most general, comprehensive and unquestionable concept, namely that of BEING. From it, by means of the DIALECTIC method described by FICHTE, all other CONCEPTS are gradually evolved. The procedure is to pass from a given position or thesis to its opposite or antithesis and from these two together to a higher position or synthesis. This is indeed an astute piece of observation of how intellectual progress is made, both by the individual in the process of learning and by science in the gradual advance and refinement of insights. Hegel regarded the development of Pre-Socratic philosophy from the notion that everything moves (HERACLITUS) to the view that nothing moves (PARMENIDES) to the proper compromise in PLATO as a prime example of the dialectic at work. While the dialectic gives a fair account of the psychology of how we advance in KNOWLEDGE, it is not of much use in describing natural science, and the attempt to treat that in dialectic terms is as useless here as later in Marxist thought. On the other hand, it is suggestive in the study of history. To Hegel the historical process had found its ultimate goal in the Prussian State of his time. As regards the realm of concepts and of MATHEMATICS, what links things together is the relation of ground and consequence, that is timeless logical relations. In the world of nature, the link becomes causal (see CAUSE) and therefore temporal. In the spiritual or mental sphere, these two come together, for human action is to be understood both in its causal and in its purely rational aspects. Nature itself, being accessible to our rational grasp, is ultimately spiritual. The system as a whole is a kind of pantheistic whole, not unlike that of SPINOZA. In it, the historical process is a gradual striving for freedom, and that consists in recognising necessity as it actually occurs. At each stage, history both preserves and repeals all previous stages (Hegel here uses an ambiguity of the German verb *aufheben* which renders the senses of both the English ones above). The purpose of history, through its various cultural stages, is to overcome all differences and to issue in a final condition of rational order, when the absolute spirit alone prevails. One need not accept Hegel's view of the final stage of this process, or even that it has such a stage, but as a guideline to historical studies his account has been most influential and is in any case a great deal more serviceable than any historical tools that come from the empiricist tradition (see EMPIRICISM). Hegelians in the sequel split into a right (Old Hegelians) who followed a conservative theistic line, and a left (Young Hegelians) who eventually merged with the materialist tendency, especially as later represented by MARX.

Heidegger, Martin (1889–1976), German philosopher, student of HUSSERL whom he succeeded as professor at Freiburg, is reckoned as the main German existentialist (see EXISTENTIALISM). When the National Socialists came to power in 1933, he applauded the new regime and disavowed Husserl who was Jewish (albeit baptised, since otherwise he would have been barred from a university chair in pre-1914 Germany). Ironically, his best known work, an essay on *Being and Time* (1927) was dedicated to Husserl (who published it in his yearbook for philosophy and phenomenological research (1913–1930)). Heidegger himself disowned the title of existentialist, though admitting that he was vitally concerned with the nature of 'being'. However, his account of it, while purporting to be a logical enquiry, is more an anthropological study, concerned with various essentially human situations. Much of this material is very obscure and his later speculations on PRE-SOCRATIC PHILOSOPHY are even more so. He is fond of vertiginous plays on words which make Hegel seem child's play. In this way, he reifies nothingness (makes nothingness into a thing), inventing a verb (by analogy with other cases) that is supposed to describe what nothingness 'does'. His scattered insights into important psychological aspects of human existence are of interest, but his philosophical import is slight.

Heraclitus (*c.*540–*c.*475 BC), an aristocrat from Ephesus, on the Ionian coast 30 miles north of Miletus. His epigrammatic style later earned him the sobriquet 'the Dark'. He saw himself as the mouthpiece of an insight available to all if only they would 'search themselves', instead of going round collecting ideas from others. Above all, he attacked PYTHAGORAS who chose bits from the writings of others and 'claimed for his own wisdom what was but a knowledge of many things and an imposture'.

Heraclitus held that things are not as we ordinarily see and describe them. The wise man realises that what is called by one name, and so is commonly thought of as a unity, contains opposites (the sea is drinkable for fish, undrinkable for man; fr. 61), and, conversely, that opposites coexist in what is one and the same (upwards and downwards, in a road; fr. 60). Moreover, this unity-in-opposites marks the whole cosmos, expressing the plan of a single all-powerful deity who, as fire, is the cause of all change in the world. This deity is 'the *Logos*'. A man can become wise, that is, can recognise this principle, by 'searching himself', since his soul consists of a share in the *Logos* deity. The metaphysical notion of opposed predicates in a single thing marks Heraclitus's philosophy off from the proto-science of the Milesians. See MILESIAN SCHOOL.

Fragment 12 says: 'Upon those who step into the same river, there flow different waters in different cases'. A river is such that if we step into it at different times at the same place, the water must be different, or else there is no river (flowing water). Cratylus, a late 5th century self-styled follower of Heraclitus, says: 'You could not step twice into the same river', which both PLATO (*Cratylus* 402A) and ARISTOTLE (*Metaphysics* 1010 a 10–15) call a Heraclitean saying. Elsewhere Heraclitus says: 'All is in flux'.

Aristotle (*Metaphysics* 987 a 32) states that Plato's familiarity with Cratylus and 'the Heraclitean theories that all sensible things are for ever flowing' partly led him to deny that we can know the SENSIBLE world, and hence to his THEORY OF FORMS as unchanging non-SENSIBLE OBJECTS of KNOWLEDGE. Co-existence of opposites may have influenced Plato's early theory of Forms as universal flux influenced his later version.

history, *n.* gives rise to two kinds of questions that are dealt with under the title of 'philosophy of history'. There is first the question of the development of human affairs through time. The Greeks tended to see history as a cyclical process, which after a given length of time leads to a great cataclysm followed by a repetition of what had gone before, and so on indefinitely. As against this, Christian thinkers saw history as a gradual process towards salvation. This same attitude is found in philosophers like HEGEL, who view history as the gradual liberation of humanity from ignorance, the KNOWLEDGE gained in this process being an awareness of NECESSITY, that is an acknowledgement of a set of limitations. Again the phases of civilisation (mystical, metaphysical and scientific) in the POSITIVISM of COMTE are of this type, as is MARX's notion of the historical development from slave-ownership through feudalism, capitalism and COMMUNISM to the withering away of the State in a kind of paradise on Earth. The second kind of question concerns the nature of history itself, and of the study of historical events and processes. Is there such a thing as objective history, and how does it differ from individual experience of the passage of time? Problems of this kind greatly exercised 19th century historians, particularly in Germany. It is of course a commonplace that there are enormous differences in how various people experience historical events (for example, in war, the front-line soldier as against the official at the War Office). In this same area arise problems as to historical necessity and as to what, if anything, one can learn from history. Moreover, there is the problem of how to go about conducting historical enquiries, how to sift and assess material and documentary evidence (it is a salutary reminder that Caesar's *Gallic Wars* were written with political ends in view. Generals, in their memoirs, have been doing this ever since).

On the whole, the first kind of question looks ahead, while the second looks back. The first is linked with our destiny, if we have one, the second with our actual past, such as it is.

Hobbes, Thomas (1588–1679), born at Malmesbury (Wiltshire), was educated at Oxford, and lived in England and France. He met GALILEO in Italy and was inspired with the idea of explaining not only physical events, but man and society, in terms of MOTION. His best-known work is *Leviathan* (1651).

Like William of OCKHAM, Hobbes was a NOMINALIST, denying the existence of REAL ESSENCES. He held genuine explanation to be in terms of material bodies in motion. This applies even to the MIND. Pleasure, for example, is 'nothing really but motion about the heart, as conception is nothing but motion in the head'. Actions (see ACTION), similarly, he reduced to motions; for he reduced the CONCEPT of a FINAL CAUSE, in terms of which actions might be distinguished from motions, to that of an EFFICIENT CAUSE. Actions are motions either towards something or away from something. A motion towards something is the fulfilment of the endeavour, or small beginning of motion, called 'appetite' or 'desire'; motion away is the fulfilment of 'hate' or 'aversion'. When there is deliberation, also explained mechanically, the last appetite is called 'will'. The will, like everything else, is 'necessitated'. What is commonly called 'freewill' (see FREEWILL AND DETERMINISM) is really absence of external compulsion. Man's freedom 'consisteth in this, that he finds no stop, in doing what he has the will, desire, or inclination to do'. What he desires, or hates, determines what is, for him, good, or evil. 'Whatsoever is the object of any man's appetite or desire, that is it which he for his part calleth *good*: and the object of his hate or aversion, *evil*.' The point of praising and blaming, rewarding and punishing, is to influence deliberations. Hobbes is the 17th century equivalent of B. F. Skinner.

It is for the extension of his model of explanation into the study of man in society that Hobbes is best known. The datum for political theory is psychological: man's concern for his own preservation. How is this end to be achieved when there are a multitude of men, with conflicting interests? In a hypothetical state of nature man's existence would be nasty, brutish and short. It is as if they had contracted with one another to form a commonwealth in which all power is vested in a sovereign capable of preserving peace and order among them. The sovereign rules, not by divine right but in virtue of the SOCIAL CONTRACT. 'Covenants, without the Sword, are but Words and of no strength to secure a man at all'; hence the sovereign is not a party to the contract, since that would require enforcing by a higher power, and so he would not be the sovereign. The sovereign's command is law. The only law a subject is not obliged to obey is one which 'frustrates the End for which the Sovereignty was ordained', that is, self-preservation. Nevertheless, the sovereign has duties to further the end for which the commonwealth was established. If he neglects these duties, or loses the power to rule, the subjects' concern for their self-preservation will lead them to rebel.

humanism, *n.* an intellectual movement that brings out one central feature of the RENAISSANCE: a revaluation of man and human affairs, as against the god-centred speculations of the Middle Ages. The movement began in 14th century Italy and spread with the Renaissance. The thinkers in this tradition stressed the value of liberty and tolerance, and helped to promote the attitudes that enabled men to disown existing authorities and to initiate the scientific revolution of the 16th century. This general outlook has followers who call themselves humanists to this day.

Hume, David (1711–1776), born in Scotland and attended Edinburgh University. In 1734, after a brief spell in a merchant's office in Bristol, he went to France to write the book about which he had been thinking for some time, *A Treatise of Human Nature*, published anonymously in 1739 (Books I and II) and 1740 (Book III). An *Abstract*, also anonymous and written as if by someone other than the author of the *Treatise*, appeared about the same time, and provides an invaluable account, in a brief compass, of what Hume thought most important about the *Treatise*. The *Treatise* was not well received, and Hume was unsuccessful in his candidature for the chair of moral philosophy at Edinburgh. He rewrote Book I of the *Treatise*, adding a controversial discussion of miracles and providence; and a revision of this was published as *An Enquiry Concerning Human Understanding* in 1758. His *Enquiry Concerning the Principles of Morals*, which was a rewriting of Book III of the *Treatise*, was published in 1751, and his *Dissertation on the Passions*, corresponding to Book II of the *Treatise*, but with significant omissions, such as the account of the psychological mechanism of sympathy, in 1757. In 1752 he had been made keeper of the Advocates' Library at Edinburgh, and he wrote a six-volume *History of England* which, at the time, brought him more approbation than his philosophy. During this time he wrote the *Dialogues concerning Natural Religion*, published posthumously in 1779. In 1763 he became secretary to the British Embassy in Paris. He returned to London in 1766, and a year later was Undersecretary of State. In 1769 he retired to Edinburgh and worked on final editions of his writings, and on an autobiography, dated April 18, 1776, a few months before his death.

In the Introduction to the *Treatise* Hume says that 'as the science of man is the only solid foundation for the other sciences, so the only solid foundation we can give this science itself must be laid on experience and observation.' In the Cartesian tradition, laying the foundation of the science of man on experience and observation meant, for Hume, adopting a reformulated version of LOCKE's Way of Ideas, and explaining the relations of ideas in terms of 'association'. Hume distinguishes between what is present to the mind when we employ our senses or are actuated with passion and what is present to the mind when we exercise our thought and reflection, a distinction 'as evident as that betwixt feeling and thinking'. He accordingly used two words, 'impressions' and 'ideas', where Locke had used one, 'ideas'. He brought the two together again by saying that ideas, unless they are fictitious, are derived from impressions, and differ from them only in force and vivacity: 'impressions are our lively and strong perceptions; ideas are the fainter and weaker'.

The second main ingredient in Hume's 'empirical' science of man, his theory of the ASSOCIATION OF IDEAS, goes beyond Locke's remarks (*Essay*, IVth ed. II xxxiii 5) on the subject. According to Hume the connections arise from the resemblance, contiguity in time or place, or causal relationship, of the corresponding impressions, and are highly important. They are the equivalent in the mental world of NEWTON's gravitation in the physical. Hume, who followed Locke's Way of Ideas to the bitter end, was able to say that the principles of association 'are really *to us* the cement of the universe'. To complete his equipment of explanatory principles for a mechanics of the mind Hume added to the doctrines of strong impressions and weak ideas derived from them, and of a three-fold association of ideas, one further principle: if an IDEA (weak) is closely associated with an impression (strong) some of the strength of the impression will transfer to the idea. So equipped, Hume embarked on his LOGIC, his attempt 'to explain the principles and operations of our reasoning faculty'.

Rather as Locke had distinguished between connections between ideas which our reason can trace, and ones which are due to chance and custom, so Hume distinguished between relations of ideas which 'depend entirely on the ideas, which we compare together, and such as may be changed without any change in the ideas'. That the three angles of a triangle are equal to two right angles depends entirely on our idea of a triangle. It is a relation on which demonstrative reasoning can be based. With a matter of fact, such as that this billiard ball is adjacent to the cushion, there is no basis in our ideas for demonstrative reasoning. The idea of the billiard ball would be no different were it not adjacent to the cushion. All reasonings concerning matters of fact, Hume says, are founded on the relation of CAUSE AND EFFECT; we explain the position of the billiard ball causally: it moved to its present position as a result of having been struck by another billiard ball. All causal relations are such that they could not be foreseen from a knowledge of the respective ideas. It is not demonstrable even that everything has a cause. Any beliefs we have about causation are based on EXPERIENCE, not demonstrative reasoning. If reasoning about matter of fact is based on causal beliefs and is genuine reasoning then we must be able to *infer* the effect from the cause, to do which there must be a necessary connection between cause and effect. However, there is not the sort of necessary connection we find in mathematics. Besides, when we look at one billiard ball causing motion in another we do not *see* any necessary connection. Repetition of the experience does not help. Hume reverses roles: instead of the inference depending on a necessary connection, the idea of a necessary connection somehow arises out of the inference, considered psychologically. Seeing the billiard ball moving is an impression, associated by resemblance with the ideas of moving billiard balls seen in the past, each of which is associated by contiguity with the idea of another billiard ball striking it. So, on seeing the billiard ball moving, we cannot help but think of the associated idea. We have a custom-produced propensity to pass from the present impression to the idea of another billiard ball. The passage is the inference, experienced as a felt 'determination of the thought'; and the idea of a necessary connection is derived from this internal impression, and mistaken for an idea of something objective. We do not merely think of the other billiard ball; we believe it to exist. He deals with this by supposing belief to differ from mere thought in the strength of the idea entertained, and by supposing that the present impression infects the associated idea with its strength.

All this may make it appear that Hume's main concern was with causal reasoning about matters of fact. Yet he described the *Treatise*, on the title-page, as 'an attempt to introduce the experimental method of reasoning into moral subjects'. In what respect are moral judgments like causal ones? Hume held that just as the necessary connection between cause and effect 'is something that exists in the mind, not in objects', so the reality of vice and virtue is something internal: '. . . when you pronounce any action or character to be vicious, you mean nothing, but that from the constitution of your nature you have a feeling or sentiment of blame from the contemplation of it' (*Treatise* 3.1.1).

By 'the constitution of your nature', here, Hume does not mean the original constitution. We are not born to feel a sentiment of disapprobation about an act of injustice towards someone else, for example. What happens is that we notice that if the rules of conduct are not obeyed so far as we ourselves are concerned, that is, if others are unjust to us, we suffer; and then, if the injustice involves somebody else 'we partake of their uneasiness by sympathy'. Sympathy makes it possible for us to feel about injustice in general what, without it, we would only feel about injustice to ourselves, and it is 'only when a character is considered in general, without reference to our particular interest, that it causes such a feeling or sentiment as denominates it morally good or evil' (*Treatise* 3.1.2. Cf. 3.2.2). In other words, without the working of sympathy there would be no moral judgments as such.

The operation of sympathy he explains as follows. We observe certain external signs in the countenance and conversation of another person from which, by virtue of the association in ourselves of this sort of behaviour with having a certain passion, we infer the existence of a passion resembling one of our own, in the other person. This inference gives rise only to an *idea* of the passion in question. We do not yet really *feel* for the other person. Somehow the idea must be strengthened so as 'to become the very passion itself, and produce an equal emotion, as any original affection'. This happens by transference of strength. The idea we have of the other person is related by resemblance to the idea we have of ourselves, thus facilitating a transfer of strength from the idea of ourselves, if it is strong enough (and he says it is), to the idea we have of the other person's passion.

It is evident that the idea, or rather impression of ourselves is always intimately present with us, and that our consciousness gives us so lively a conception of our own person, that it is not possible to imagine, that any thing can in this particular go beyond it. Whatever object, therefore, is related to ourselves must be conceived with a like vivacity of conception, according to the foregoing principles.

All this, Hume concludes, 'is an object of the plainest experience' (*Treatise* 2.1.11). He has succeeded in his attempt to introduce EMPIRICISM into the moral sciences. However, in Book I Hume had denied that a person has any impression or idea of his self or person. A person is 'nothing but a bundle or collection of different perceptions, which succeed each other with an inconceivable rapidity, and are in a perpetual flux and movement' (*Treatise* 1.4.6). If he means something different by 'person' in Book I and Book II he does not explain the difference, so as to remove the apparent contradiction. Moreover, a self over and above the different perceptions seems to be assumed in his account of causal inference and in an account he gives of our beliefs about things continuing to exist when unperceived.

Hume was aware of this difficulty (in the Appendix to the *Treatise*). In his rewriting of the *Treatise* the sections on personal identity and sympathy are left out. See BENTHAM, HUTCHESON, KANT, MALEBRANCHE, PERSONAL IDENTITY, REID, UTILITARIANISM.

Husserl, Edmund (1859–1938), Austrian Jewish philosopher, student under BRENTANO at Vienna, professor at Göttingen and Freiburg, who began teaching at Halle in 1887 (for an academic career he had to become a Protestant). He is the founder of an orientation called PHENOMENOLOGY, a method that he first outlined in his *Logical Investigations* (1900). The point of this approach is to study everything as it appears to the conscious mind, as an intentional content (that is, one directed to some item or goal). This is to be undertaken as a logical enquiry, keeping in abeyance for the time being the actual furniture of the world (he calls this process 'bracketing'). Only when this has been accomplished can we proceed to the empirical study of the various sciences, including psychology. Thus we have first to go through a phenomenological analysis before we can consider anything else. This approach is somewhat reminiscent of KANT's *Critique of Pure Reason*, where a preliminary study is made of the scope and nature of the human mind. However, in practice Husserl finds great difficulty in carrying out his programme. Indeed, he often seems to make use of concepts, such as 'intuition', which really ought to figure only in a later study, namely psychology, rather than in this propaedeutic phase of phenomenology. In the end, this analysis requires the suspension at a TRANSCENDENTAL level, of all belief, and yet the appearances to be analysed are themselves items that invite belief. As a result, Husserl's accounts become increasingly metaphysical and severed from the real world. Nevertheless, his early insights on the intentional nature of thought have had much influence on later continental thought.

Hutcheson, Francis (1694–1746), Scottish philosopher, became Professor of Moral Philosophy at Glasgow in 1729. Following Shaftesbury, he developed a theory of the MORAL SENSE, against HOBBES's view that man is essentially selfish. His view is echoed in HUME's basic notion of sympathy as the driving force in human affairs.

hylozoism, *n.* (from Greek *hyle* matter, *zoe* life) the doctrine that the MATTER of all things is alive. See ANAXIMENES.

hypothesis, *n.* **1.** in science, a provisional explanation, that observation and experiment may or may not confirm. If confirmed, it is accepted as a theory, or LAW OF NATURE.

2. in LOGIC, an assumption on the basis of which other PROPOSITIONS are obtained. If the latter turn out to be false, then the hypothesis is disproved.

I

idea, *n.* the term occurs most conspicuously in the philosophy of PLATO and, many centuries later, in that of DESCARTES, MALEBRANCHE, LOCKE, BERKELEY and HUME. The use of the term by the modern philosophers, however, contrasts so sharply with its use by Plato that no single definition can cover them. To avoid confusion Plato's 'ideas' will be called 'Forms' (see FORM). According to Plato, Forms are things grasped by the MIND, and SENSIBLE things are, in some sense, derived from them. In the dialogue *Parmenides* (132 b) Plato rejects the notion that a Form 'is a thought, which cannot properly exist anywhere but in a mind'. According to Locke, ideas are 'materials of thinking'; and they come from SENSATION or REFLECTION (INTROSPECTION), the latter being so very like sensation that it 'might properly enough be called internal sense' (*Essay*, II i 2, 4). Thus for Plato Forms are outside the mind and prior to what is sensed, but for Locke ideas are inside the mind and subsequent to what is sensed.

Such a reversal of meaning calls for an explanation. Plato gave an account of how the many sensible things which share the same character, say that of being beautiful, are related to the one Form of BEAUTY. He thought of Forms as eternal and therefore more substantial than sensible things, and employed the metaphor of an original, or 'archetype', and a copy. Sensible things are copies of Forms. In one of his later dialogues, *Timaeus*, Plato explained how it is that there can be many copies of the same Form. The 'receptacle' for the copies is space. A divine artificer, with his mind's eye on a Form, copies it in various parts of space. This introduction, into the THEORY OF FORMS, of the notion that the sensible world has a Maker paved the way for ideas being constituents of human minds. In the Christian NEO-PLATONISM of St AUGUSTINE (*De Diversis Quaestionibus* LXXXIII Question 46) Forms became archetypal ideas in the mind of GOD, and in the part of Malebranche's philosophy inspired by Augustine human minds were 'placed' in God's mind and so shared, in a limited way, in God's ideas.

Philosophers did not have to accept Malebranche's doctrine of 'seeing all things in God' to use the term 'idea'. Malebranche himself supplied another, quite different, definition of the term in the context of a REPRESENTATIVE THEORY OF PERCEPTION of material OBJECTS. He argued that the mind cannot perceive objects external to it, i.e. at a distance from it, by themselves, since they are not present to it, and concluded that there must be an intermediary object that *is* present to it: 'our mind's immediate object when it sees the sun, for example, is not the sun, but something that is intimately joined to our soul, and this is what I call an *idea*' (*Search after Truth*, III ii 1). Berkeley rejected Malebranche's 'seeing all things in God' doctrine (*Principles*, I 148), and the associated Neo-Platonic use of 'idea', but he accepted what Malebranche said about the significance of material objects being distant from us. Where Malebranche talked about external objects not being 'present to' the mind Berkeley talked about their being 'without' the mind (*New Theory of Vision*, 41), but for both the significance was the same: there must be something other than a distant material object, something which *is* 'present to', or *not* 'without', the mind, for there to be perception.

Malebranche thought that everyone would agree that 'we do not perceive objects external to us by themselves' but not everyone did agree with him. Antoine ARNAULD, for example, accused him of trading on the equivocality of the word 'presence'. It does not follow, Arnauld said, from something's not having 'local presence' that it does not have 'objective presence' (i.e. presence as an object of CONSCIOUSNESS) (*Concerning true and false ideas*, Ch. 8). And Locke, in his *Examination of Malebranche's Doctrine of Seeing All Things in the Mind of God* (17, 18) attacked Malebranche's remark that ideas are 'real things'. Just how Locke conceived of ideas is not clear. According to the traditional interpretation of his earlier major work, the *Essay Concerning Human Understanding*, Locke, like Malebranche, held a representative theory of perception. This interpretation has been disputed recently, notably by two editors of Locke's works.

There is at least one passage in Locke's *Essay* (II viii 18) which suggests that he thought of ideas as being like SENSATIONS of pain or sickness. This is not compatible with calling ideas 'materials of thinking', for thoughts, whatever else they may be, are *of* or *about* things external to themselves, and bodily sensations do not have this representative or 'intentional' character. That ideas do have it was recognised by Descartes, who, in the *Third Meditation*, contrasted ideas thought of as images (i.e. as representing things) with ideas thought of only as occurrences in the mind.

It is more plausible to view THINKING as consisting in bringing different ideas into relationship, if they are thought of as images, in Descartes's sense, than if they are thought of only as mental occurrences, like sensations of pain or sickness. Still, there remain difficulties in Locke's apparent assumption that the term 'idea' means the same in 'ideas are materials of thinking' as it means in 'ideas come from sensation or reflection'. How can we identify the experiences of sensation or REFLECTION, which, according to the theory, should be the source of the most widely used materials of thinking, such as the ideas of SUBSTANCE and CAUSE? In the case of an idea such as that of whiteness, how can it be caused in us by looking at white things? Locke saw the problem: effects are particular whereas the ideas we use to think with must be general. He thought he could solve this problem with a doctrine of ABSTRACTION. A related view of the problem is that an idea of whiteness, unlike a sensation of eye-strain, does not seem to be the sort of thing that could be caused by looking at something. Locke wrongly seemed to want 'Looking at white things causes an idea of whiteness' to be understood on the model of 'Eating indigestible food causes a sensation of sickness'. The idea of whiteness is not so much a mental occurrence as a mental capacity (to recognise things as white, to use 'white' as other people do, and so on). People have capacities, but not in the same way as they have sensations.

The difficulty about ideas such as those of substance and cause, led KANT to reject EMPIRICISM and to postulate a class of 'A PRIORI concepts of the understanding'. He remarked that anyone familiar with Plato's works, as he was, 'must find it intolerable to hear the representation of the colour, red, called an idea' (*Critique of Pure Reason*, A320/ B377). The only concepts for which Kant used the term 'idea' were regulative ones like those of God, freedom and immortality, which have to do with our conduct in, not our understanding of, the empirical world.

The Lockean use of the term 'idea' survived in the doctrine of 'ASSOCIATION OF IDEAS' of Hume, HARTLEY and JAMES MILL. Ideas, simple and complex, were the stock-in-trade of early introspective psychology, just as reflexes, unconditioned and conditioned, were of early behaviouristic psychology (see BEHAVIOURISM). However, since ideas are not particular psychological occurrences, the technical term in philosophy was eventually abandoned, particularly through the work of F. H. BRADLEY (*Principles of Logic*, Bk. 2, Pt. 2, Ch. 1). The everyday use of the term survives.

IDEALISM

idealism, *n.* (from Greek *idea* a thing seen) strictly 'idea-ism' in philosophy, is a doctrine that holds the world to be essentially a mental vision, as against the common-sense realist view that it is something 'out there' and independent of us (see REALISM). Although PLATO uses the word 'ideas' for FORMS (the other-worldly patterns that genuinely are, rather than the perceptual semblances accessible to the senses), it is a mistake to describe his theory as idealism (even if some writers rashly speak of ontological idealism here). Indeed, what is remarkable about Greek philosophy of the classical period is precisely that it is free from idealism. Not until the rise of NEO-PLATONISM (3rd century AD) do we find the world described as mental emanations, and then they come from the divine mind. The notion that IDEAS are something inside the human mind is due to DESCARTES, who on this account is rightly regarded as the founder of modern philosophy. The term 'idealism' did not come into use until the 18th century.

Idealist philosophy takes different forms depending on what opposing theories different thinkers are attacking. Thus, LEIBNIZ (1646–1716) argued against the independent reality of MATTER because it was inert and composite, whereas actuality belongs only to active simples, what he called 'MONADS'. The position of BERKELEY (1685–1710), which he called immaterialism, arises from his criticisms of LOCKE's theory of abstract ideas (e.g. the idea of a triangle in general, of no specific kind). This leads Berkeley to the view that to be is to be perceived; that is, there can be no unperceived things, all we know are our own perceptions. For the rest, the Cartesian 'way of ideas' (Locke's phrase) is kept in play, KNOWLEDGE being construed in terms of ideas in the mind (although these are always acquired by EXPERIENCE, while for DESCARTES some are innate). KANT (1724–1804) puts forward what may be called a theory of critical idealism, where the mind has equipment of its own (the concepts of SPACE AND TIME as forms of sensibility, and the CATEGORIES as concepts of understanding) with which to digest experience, while nothing can be said about 'things in themselves'. The vital point as against the Cartesians is that knowing involves an active mind, not just a clean mirror that reflects CLEAR and distinct ideas. The high point of idealist philosophy is the absolute, metaphysical idealism of the late 18th century and early 19th century German school. FICHTE (1762–1814) took a step further than Kant and saw the focus of reality in the self-conscious 'I' or *ego* confronted with the not-I. A systematic elaboration of this approach was produced by Schelling (1775–1854) and above all by HEGEL (1770–1831), who describes his idealism as objective, in contrast with subjective forms based on perception as with Berkeley. In contrast, Hegel's theory is metaphysical, and asserts that anything short of totality is not fully real, a view that echoes the Pre-Socratic notions of PARMENIDES. This aspect recurs in the neo-Hegelian philosophy of BRADLEY (1846–1924) and Royce (1855–1916).

In the natural sciences, idealism has never been a convincing point of view. However, in the social field, the conceptual framework of idealism is in some ways more suggestive than the attempts at dealing with human affairs in positivist terms (see POSITIVISM). This is because of the emphasis on active mental effort, which obviously will not upset the stars in their courses but does have much to do with how people act and interact. At the same time, absolute idealism, in its Hegelian form, does exhibit the feature of systematic treatment that is also aspired to by theoretical development in natural science (witness Newtonian physics).

identity, *n.* (from Latin *idem* the same) used in several senses in philosophy. There is first the notion of one thing being the same as another: if and only if the two coincide in every feature, they are identical. If there is the slightest difference, they are not identical. Less plausibly, one says that a thing is identical with itself. The so-called principle of identity (*A* is *A*) was traditionally counted as a law of thought. However, judgments of identity need not be tautologous (saying the same): if one and the same OBJECT is known under two descriptions, we may well learn something new when the two are said to refer to the same thing: a child will recognise the morning star and the evening star without knowing that they are the same star. In FREGE's terms, there is here one reference, and two senses (an earlier terminology speaks of DENOTATION and CONNOTATION). In another sense, one speaks of the identity of a single object maintaining itself through the passage of various outside influences: a strip of countryside remains the same strip, although it undergoes the impact of seasonal changes. Closely related to this is the notion of PERSONAL IDENTITY, which remains the same throughout one's lifetime: it is our sense of identity that makes us into individuals. This notion of identity is an important psychological characteristic: a failure of the feeling of identity can lead to serious mental disturbance. Finally there is a FORMAL sense of identity used in MATHEMATICS and LOGIC: a formula is called an identity if it holds good for any values given to the variables in it.

identity hypothesis, *n.* the HYPOTHESIS that mental events are in fact identical with neural events. See MATERIALISM and MIND–BODY PROBLEM.

illusion, argument from, *n.* normally we see, feel, hear, things as they are; but exceptionally our senses deceive us: the moon looks bigger when it is near the horizon but, of course, it is not any bigger; a pencil held between crossed fingers feels like two pencils, and so on. The argument from illusion is, in fact, one or other of two arguments, the first of which is invalid, the second valid.

The invalid argument is that if some of our experiences are illusory then we ought not to trust any of them. This ignores the way in which we settle whether an EXPERIENCE is illusory. It is only by trusting some experiences that we can identify others as illusory: it is by trusting our eyes that we identify as illusory the feeling of there being two pencils when there is one, between our crossed fingers. No one can have a reason to think that everything is illusory; the fact that some experiences are illusory cannot be a reason for thinking that all are.

The valid argument is that if some of our experiences are illusory then the direct realist theory of perception is false, where 'direct' means that questions of truth or falsity do not arise (as in the case of 'SENSATIONS' in the REPRESENTATIVE THEORY OF PERCEPTION).

That the direct realist theory is false does not entail that the representative theory is true. See APPEARANCE, PERCEPTION.

imagination, *n.* in PHILOSOPHY, is the power we have to put things to ourselves in images. The Greek term for this is *phantasia*, which in ARISTOTLE means the faculty of imagination. The notion involves mental appearances that are somehow evoked in the process of THINKING or REFLECTION. It has a central role in KANT's *Critique of Pure Reason*, where it provides the mechanism of binding different perceptions into a whole that can be called EXPERIENCE. In the moral sphere, imagination is necessary if we are to activate that feeling of human sympathy which, for HUME, is the mainspring of our actions as civilised beings. This brings us close to the meaning of imagination in the arts. An imaginative writer will catch, in his accounts, the lives of people as they are actually lived. At the same time, there is a current usage of the term imagination that is pejorative, being contrasted with a sense for reality: somebody who is full of fanciful notions, does not know how things really are.

immaterialism, *n.* the theory that MATTER (as opposed to mind) does not exist. BERKELEY used the term to describe his own theory, that IDEAS are caused, not by CORPUSCLES of matter affecting our sense-organs, but by GOD. See IDEALISM.

immediate, *adj.* not separated from, by something coming between. What is immediate in time is what happens without any delay. What is immediate in movement is what is moved without any instrument being employed: a man can move his hand, but not a stone, immediately (ARISTOTLE, *Physics*, Bk. VIII, Ch. 5). What is immediate in awareness is what we are aware of without making any inference: we are immediately aware of our thoughts, but not of the consequences of our thoughts. For example, we are immediately aware of the operations of the will, but not of the voluntary movements they originate (DESCARTES, *Arguments proving the existence of God*, Def. 1). What is immediate in inference is what is inferred from a premiss without requiring a further premiss. For example, from the premiss that all men are mortal it can be immediately inferred that all immortals are non-men.

immortality, *n.* the survival, for ever, after death. DESCARTES claimed it as one of the advantages of his mind–body DUALISM, that it is a prerequisite of immortality (*Meditations*, Synopsis): a mind can survive death because it is distinct from a body even though it is somehow united with one. However, CARTESIAN DUALISM is not required for immortality in the traditional Christian sense, which relies simply on GOD's promise of resurrection. See SOUL.

implication and entailment, *n.* (from Latin *implico* to enfold) in LOGIC, the relation between two connected PROPOSITIONS such that if the first holds, so does the second. The term was used in this sense until the 20th century, when it was usurped by RUSSELL for what is now more properly called 'material implication', where the two propositions need no longer be connected. In that case we obtain several paradoxical results. For example, if a proposition is false, it implies every proposition, and if it is true, it is implied by every proposition. To recover the old sense of 'implication', G. E. MOORE invented (1920) a new term, 'entailment', which is the converse of 'deducible from': if *q* is deducible from *p*, then *p* entails *q* (see DEDUCTION). The relation of entailment holds only when there is some appropriate connection between the two propositions. What this connection is cannot be readily displayed beyond repeating that it amounts to deducibility. Some modern logicians here speak of relevance, which is no more explicit. At any rate, the entailment relation is not truth-functional, nor indeed can it be explicated in terms of C. I. Lewis's 'strict implication', that is in terms of NECESSITY and possibility. Strict implication generates its own PARADOXES that are even more pointed than those of the material variety. In any case, the relation that figures in DEDUCTION is entailment.

Indian philosophy, *n.* unlike that of the West, is grounded not in early scientific speculations, but in theological ones. Where the central guiding notion of Greek philosophy was that of the *logos*, as a rational account, in Indian philosophy we find the concept of *brahman*, which amounts to a ritual verbal gesture or formula, a kind of prayer, which governs man's relation to the GODS by the intermediary of a priestly caste. Along with this goes a view of the transmigration of souls, each soul becoming re-embodied in a higher or lower creature depending on the worth of its deeds in the previous life. Moreover, the direction of thought is not towards the outside, but inwards to the very core of the self *(atman)*: it is there that union with the divine, or *brahman*, is ultimately achieved. All this is to be found in the *Upanishads*, a body of early mystical writings. In the later, Buddhist philosophy (see BUDDHISM), release from the cycle of being is obtained through escape into nothingness, the highest achievement of the soul. A more philosophical approach in the Western sense is found in the Samkhyte tradition of the early centuries of our era. Here we are given a contrast between spirit and nature, of which the former is in a state of being while the latter is constantly becoming. The human soul survives the disintegration of the body at death and thus has to go over into a new body. The constant change of the material world is due to ever changing mixtures of the basic constituents which are roughly identifiable as light, air and earth. We are somewhat reminded here of Pre-Socratic and Stoic notions. This system of philosophy in the course of time became atheistic, and salvation then consists in recognising that the soul is not tied to the body. This alone will free the soul from suffering. The necessary inward concentration and detachment is furthered particularly by the practice of yoga, a set of procedures designed to master and control our bodies.

induction, *n.* (from Latin *inductio* a leading into) in LOGIC, the process of moving from the particular to the general, and as such is not demonstrative (that is, an inductive argument does not prove its conclusions, as a deductive one does (see DEDUCTION); we exclude complete enumerations which do not properly belong here). It is first mentioned by ARISTOTLE. Perhaps the best known example is HUME's theory of causality in terms of constant conjunction in the past. Ever since induction has been noticed, many philosophers have either been apologetic about it for not being demonstrative, or have tried to show that somehow it really is demonstrative in a roundabout way, or at least respectable in spite of not doing what deduction does. This is the so-called problem of induction. Of course, if one allows that induction is not demonstrative, no amount of chicanery will make it so. Attempts in this direction, numerous and ingenious though they be, are bound to fail. One way out of this dead-end is to recognise the general features in the particular case. Thus, if I observe the sun rising today and no more, it might seem rash to infer that it will do likewise tomorrow. However, if in seeing it rise today, I recognise this fact as linked with the laws of planetary motion, themselves an application of the theory of universal gravitation, then my forecast of sunrise tomorrow is quite conclusive. Provided, of course, that no astronomic catastrophe supervenes in the meantime, but that is a different story.

inference rules, *n*. that part of formal systems that stipulates how we may move from one set of PROPOSITIONS to another. Thus, from the proposition *p* and the fact that *p* entails *q*, we can move to the proposition *q*. There are various such patterns, and these collectively are called the rules of inference. Any general procedure that enables us to transform one expression into another different one, is an instance of this. Depending on what rules we stipulate, we obtain diverse FORMAL systems. The choice is not entirely arbitrary, since we must observe certain requirements of consistency and absence of ambiguity if the resultant systems are to make sense. If the system is to serve to summarise the findings in a certain concrete field of enquiry, it must of course be such that this aim is approached, which keeps such choices within narrow limits. See DEDUCTION.

innate ideas, *n*. according to DESCARTES, those IDEAS which we have from birth before any EXPERIENCE. That there could be such ideas was vigorously denied by empiricist philosophers from LOCKE onwards. Descartes held that the idea of GOD was innate. So are the notions of OBJECT, truth and reason. LEIBNIZ adopted a similar view, in that he regarded the disposition for having certain beliefs as innate: for him, this includes the whole of arithmetic and geometry, which are discoverable by orderly ratiocination alone. Along with HUME, KANT agreed that all KNOWLEDGE has to come through experience. However, he held that the categorial framework under which we know is innate or born with us, we do not acquire that as well through experience. The theory of innate ideas, widely criticised though it has been, has lately found a new champion in N. CHOMSKY, who holds that human beings have a built-in grasp of the deep structure of language, issuing in the surface structure of our mother tongue. In general, the theory of innate ideas forestalls the question of how experience begins. As such it is a hindrance to psychological enquiry concerning the earliest stages of learning. There may, of course, be a sense in which the order of procedure (seeing that we cannot do everything at once) depends on our own structure as sentient beings. Thus, there seems to be some physiological evidence that in the eye, the receptors that locate come before those that discern qualities such as colour and shape. Perhaps that is why in a PROPOSITION we put SUBJECT before PREDICATE, but this would not prove that we had innate ideas.

intelligible, *n.* that which can be understood, and hence defined. In PLATO, the intelligible is opposed to the SENSIBLE, that which can be perceived by the senses. See DEFINITION, FORM, ESSENCE.

intension, *n.* in LOGIC, the sum of the attributes comprehended in a term; opposed to EXTENSION, the range of a term as measured by the number of OBJECTS to which it applies. See DENOTATION, CONNOTATION.

intentionality, *n.* (from Latin *intendere* to stretch) the metaphorical stretching of CONSCIOUSNESS to be *of* something, i.e. to have an OBJECT, which may or may not actually exist.

ARISTOTLE may have held that to perceive a quality of something is for the FORM, but not the MATTER, of it to be received, or taken on, by the sense-organ. For example, when I put my hand in hot water my hand gets hot but does not take in the matter, water. Its getting hot is my perceiving the heat of the water. Whether Aristotle actually held this is questionable since he also wrote of the *sense*, not the sense-organ, receiving the form. AQUINAS explicitly distinguished between a 'natural' reception of a form, as when my hand becomes hot, and a 'spiritual' or 'intentional' reception, in which the faculty of soul or mind apprehends the object. DESCARTES, holding mind and body to be distinct substances, construed this apprehension as the occurrence of an IDEA in the MIND on the occasion of the sense-organ being stimulated. Intentionality features in his account in the form of ideas having what he calls 'objective reality'. The degree of objective reality corresponds to the actual reality of whatever the object is. Thus the infinite Being, GOD, having more actual reality than any finite being, the idea of God has more objective reality than that of a finite being. Descartes held that ideas were objectively real and must be caused by something at least equally real, and used this in a proof of the existence of God.

The notion of intentionality was put to a different use by Franz BRENTANO, who developed Aquinas's distinction between two modes of being (*esse naturale* and *esse intentionale*), corresponding to the two ways in which the form of something can be received. He rejected Descartes's describing the mental as not extended in space (see EXTENSION). Brentano noted that sounds and smells, unlike colours, are not apprehended as spatially extended, but nevertheless are not regarded as mental. Something more must be said about judgment, recollection, expectation, joy, sorrow, fear, and so on, than that they are not extended, if they are adequately to be distinguished from these other non-extended phenomena. Brentano proposed that mental phenomena should be defined as 'those that contain an object intentionally within themselves'. He acknowledged, however, that to a superficial observer it may seem that in the case of being cut or burnt there is only the non-intentional PHENOMENON of pain. See HUSSERL.

interactionism, *n.* DESCARTES's theory of the relation of mind and body. See MIND-BODY PROBLEM.

introspection, *n.* defined by William JAMES as 'the looking into our own minds and reporting what we there discover'. Everyone agrees, James said, that we there discover states of CONSCIOUSNESS, such as THINKING; this belief he regards as basic to PSYCHOLOGY (*Principles of Psychology*, I, vii).

Behaviourist psychologists (see BEHAVIOURISM) disputed not so much the CERTAINTY of the belief James attributed to all people, as his contention that in psychology 'Introspective observation is what we have to rely on first and foremost and always'. A scientific theory, they thought, is essentially open to public confirmation or disconfirmation, and whereas someone's thoughts are private (see PRIVACY) his behaviour is something that is in principle publicly observable. If psychology is to be a science its subject-matter and methodology must be appropriate to a science.

What James called 'curious inquiries' about the certainty of the belief that people feel themselves thinking have originated with philosophers rather than with psychologists, and in reaction to what earlier philosophers had said. LOCKE had called INTROSPECTION 'reflection', meaning by it 'that notice which the mind takes of its own operations, and the manner of them, by reason whereof there come to be ideas of these operations in the understanding' (*Essay* II i 4). This has two implications, one for the answer to the question 'What is the difference between, say, hoping and expecting, or knowing and believing?', and one for the answer to the question 'What must a person notice to be entitled to say "I hope . . .", etc.?' To the first question the introspectionist answer is: the difference is one in what can be introspected. To the second, it is: he must have noticed which mental operation (hoping or expecting, knowing or believing) was going on in himself. Anti-introspectionist philosophers say that the difference between hoping, expecting, knowing, believing, and so on, can only be got at by examining how the expressions 'hope', 'expect', and so on, are used in human intercourse; and that for someone to be entitled to say 'I hope such-and-such' he does not have to have observed anything going on in himself (or anything about his behaviour, either). Some of our utterances are reports of what we have observed (e.g. 'The temperature is falling'), but 'I hope such-and-such' is usually not such a report. Rather, it is itself a piece of hopeful behaviour. See AVOWAL.

intuitionism, *n.* in MATHEMATICS, first put forward by the Dutch mathematician, L. E. J. Brouwer (1881–1966). According to him, mathematics is essentially linked with the mental activity of the mathematician and consists in constructing the OBJECTS with which it works. As such it is opposed both to the logicism of FREGE and RUSSELL, who try to reduce mathematics to LOGIC, and to the formalism of Hilbert, for whom mathematics consists in manipulating abstract symbols. Indeed, intuitionist mathematics does not need any special links with logic to get off the ground. Rather, the constructive activity of mathematics itself indicates certain rules of what is called intuitionist logic (first stated systematically by Brouwer's compatriot, A. Heyting, in 1930). This logic differs from the conventional variety in several points. In particular, its notion of NEGATION is different, standing roughly for 'not proved', so that the traditional formula 'x or not-x' no longer holds (we may not be able to prove nor disprove 'x'). The notion of constructivity is especially obvious in dealing with infinity: the Aristotelian idea of infinity as unlimited EXTENSION of the finite (you can always add '1') is constructive, the Cantorian idea of infinite totalities is not.

In ETHICS, intuitionism is the view that moral truths are apprehended by intuition. J. S. MILL (1806–1873) was opposed to intuitionism; G. E. MOORE (1873–1958) defended it.

Islamic philosophy, *n.* the philosophic work of thinkers who were, more or less, followers of the Islamic religion, based on the *Koran*, which is found in many places where that religion established itself, from the Atlantic to the Indian ocean. The Arab conquests of the 7th and 8th centuries spread Islam in the Near East, North Africa and Spain, while the Ottoman Turks extended its hold to Turkey and the Balkans from the 14th to the 16th centuries. Much Islamic philosophy was written in Arabic, though many of the authors were not Arabs (just as much of the later 'Greek' philosophy is due to writers who were not Greeks).

In substance, Islamic philosophy is based on Greek philosophy, mainly ARISTOTLE and NEO-PLATONISM, somewhat distorted through mutual influence and two processes of translation. The originals came to the notice of Islamic scholars in Syriac translation, and were later turned into Arabic, mostly in an intense period of literary activity in the 9th and 10th centuries. Indeed, it was through Latin translations of these Arabic texts in Spain, that much ancient philosophy came to the notice of medieval Europe. Direct recovery of Greek texts came mainly after the fall of Constantinople to the Ottoman Turks in 1453.

Islamic philosophy was faced with a problem that the Greeks did not experience, namely interference from a totalitarian religious faith based on a book (the *Koran*) and backed by powerful groups of populist leaders. Thus developed the somewhat evasive notion that philosophy taught the same doctrine as the *Koran*, but in a form accessible only to the learned few. A not dissimilar attitude was displayed by medieval Christian authorities (see SCHOLASTIC and MEDIEVAL PHILOSOPHY).

Amongst important figures (in chronological order) the first was the 9th century Al-Kindi, who was attached to the caliphate at Baghdad and followed a mainly Neo-Platonist line of thought. More influential was Al-Farabi (875–950), a Persian of Turkish ancestry, whose teachers included Nestorian Christian scholars. In his writings he tried to avoid clashing either with his Shi-ite patrons or with the Sunni population as a whole. He regarded philosophy as the highest doctrine but allowed that religion was a more or less valid symbolic expression of the same truths, Islam being of course the best. Avicenna (980–1037), a Persian, was a thinker of great range and power, who sought to reconcile Greek philosophy with the demands of Koranic religion. He developed his own version of the distinction between ESSENCE and EXISTENCE, in which the latter is entirely dependent on GOD, who is pure existence. This view was rejected by Averroës (1126–1198), who came from Cordova in Spain. He took a somewhat unusual line about the universal nature of the passive intellect reminiscent of the Stoics rather than of Aristotle (see STOICISM). This was rejected by Muslims and Christians alike. His commentaries on Aristotle were widely read in the West and his philosophy was influential at the Sorbonne, only to attract condemnation by the Church towards the end of the 13th century. It was amongst Western followers of Averroës that the problem of reconciling reason and faith took the explicit form of the 'double truth': if rational argument leads to a conclusion at odds with revealed religion, what is one to do? This question has never been satisfactorily resolved.

J

James, William (1842–1910), American philosopher and psychologist. His best-known publications are his *Principles of Psychology* (2 vols, London, 1890) and *The Varieties of Religious Experience* (New York, 1902).

In an address given in 1898, and reprinted as 'The Pragmatic Method' in *The Journal of Philosophy, Psychology and Scientific Method*, Vol. 1 (1904), James referred to a view advanced by C. S. PEIRCE in the *Popular Science Monthly* for January 1878, the view that 'to develop a thought's meaning we need only determine what conduct it is fitted to produce'. Peirce had called this principle 'PRAGMATISM'. James amended the principle, saying that the thought 'inspires that conduct because it first foretells some particular turn to our experience which shall call for just that conduct from us', but called the amended principle by the same name as Peirce had used. He explained the amended principle in terms of answers to the question 'Is matter the producer of all things, or is a God there too?', saying that 'the very meaning of the conception of God lies in those differences which must be made in our experience if the conception be true', and not in hair-splitting abstractions about the metaphysical attributes of GOD.

James's choice of the MATERIALISM/THEISM issue as one in terms of which to explain his experience-orientated version of pragmatism led to his *The Varieties of Religious Experience* (New York, 1902), in the Postscript of which he expressed his own 'piecemeal supernaturalist' belief that 'beyond each man and in a fashion continuous with him there exists a larger power which is friendly to him and to his ideals', a power which need be neither infinite, not unitary (p. 525).

In 'Does "Consciousness" Exist?' (*The Journal of Philosophy, Psychology and Scientific Method*, Vol. 1, 1904) James said that the 'entering wedge' for his view about the relation of a knowing SUBJECT to OBJECTS of KNOWLEDGE 'was fashioned by LOCKE when he made the word "idea" stand indifferently for thing and thought, and by BERKELEY when he said that what common sense means by realities is exactly what the philosopher means by ideas'. His own view is that IDEAS, or experiences, are the 'stuff' not only of physical objects but also of the knowing subject. This is opposed to the neo-kantian view that the duality of knower and known is ultimate (see KANT). James's thesis is that 'there is one primal stuff or material', pure EXPERIENCE, and that 'a given undivided portion of experience, taken in one context of associates, plays the part of a knower, or a state of mind, of "consciousness"; while in a different context the same undivided bit of experience plays the part of a thing known, of an objective "content"'.

James's choice of the term 'experience' for what is supposedly neutral as between knower and known was criticised on the ground that experience 'must be a product, not part of the primary stuff of the universe' (Bertrand RUSSELL, *Analysis of Mind*, London, 1921, p. 24). In its place the term 'neutral-stuff' was used, and the theory became known as 'NEUTRAL MONISM'.

Jaspers, Karl (1883–1969), German philosopher, a psychiatrist before he became a philosopher, was professor at Heidelberg, and from 1948, at Basle. In his philosophy he makes much use of HUSSERL's phenomenological method and takes human EXPERIENCE as his starting point. In this way he is rightly regarded as part of the existentialist movement, although that label is not very informative. Existence, for Jaspers, is threefold: objective, subjective and absolute. We observe OBJECTS, but can never turn ourselves completely into objects for observation. Nor can the ego ultimately grasp existence as something absolute and independent. Therein lies the fact that we are led to a leap of faith (to use KIERKEGAARD's phrase). For Jaspers, the nearest we come to meeting the absolute is in 'boundary situations', such as extreme danger, suffering and death. Jaspers was very active in the intellectual reconstruction of university life after the Second World War, although the half-hearted attitudes of his colleagues eventually drove him to accept the call to Switzerland. For him, the university was a place where the young could learn disinterested enquiry, examining all sides of a question. He therefore deprecated party-political activity amongst students.

Jewish philosophy, *n.* in general terms, the body of thought that over the ages has sought to give a philosophic account of the theological doctrines of the Jewish religion as gleaned from the Old Testament. While the thinkers who have occupied themselves with this task are all of them Jews, it is by no means the case that all Jews who happen to have been philosophers belong to the field of Jewish philosophy.

Samuel ALEXANDER was a Jew, but his philosophy is not Jewish. In some cases, it may be difficult to decide: SPINOZA'S PANTHEISM is hardly Jewish, but his *Tractatus Theologico-Politicus*, which lays the foundations of modern biblical criticism for the Old Testament, may well be counted as such. The lines of division remain unclear. An early philosophical approach to these problems is due to Philo of Alexandria, who at the beginning of our era sought to interpret Judaic tradition in terms of Neo-Platonic conceptions (see NEO-PLATONISM). The greatest of the medieval Jewish philosophers was Maimonides, born in Cordova in 1135, whose *Guide for the Perplexed* sought to reconcile Jews who were conversant with the Greek philosophic tradition with the principles of their own religion. The work of Gersonides of Narbonne (1288–1344) was much influenced by Maimonides. These thinkers, especially in the south of France and in Spain, lived in a cultural atmosphere where Jewish, Muslim and Christian strains freely intermixed, not to mention the overriding importance of ancient sources, such as were available. This came to a sudden end after the expulsion of the Jews from Spain and Portugal in 1492. Many sought refuge in the Netherlands, and it is perhaps no accident that Uriel da Costa (1585–1640) came from Portugal to Amsterdam, and Spinoza (1632–1677) was born there of parents who had fled from Spain via Portugal. An ENLIGHTENMENT figure is the German Jewish thinker, Moses Mendelssohn (1729–1786, grandfather of the composer), a friend of Lessing, who aimed to show the boundaries between philosophy and the Jewish religion, which helped Jews to become less isolated from the rest of society. Whether Martin BUBER (1878–1965) and his analysis of the I–Thou relation of man's meeting with GOD is to be counted as Jewish philosophy is again doubtful, since it has had much bearing on contemporary Christian thought as well.

justice, *n.* (from Latin *justitia* righteousness) in ETHICS is roughly synonymous with fairness. It applies in an economic sense where people compete for scarce resources, but also in human actions in general where these affect others. In a special sense it applies to the law and to its impartial treatment of those who come before it (like cases merit like judgment).

K

Kant, Immanuel (1724–1804), German philosopher, who was born, studied, lived, taught and died at Königsberg in East Prussia (since World War II, Kaliningrad). Brought up on Leibnizian thought (see LEIBNIZ) as presented by Christian Wolff (1679–1754), he retained in his main philosophic writing the latter's tortuous style, but presented a line of development that was new. In his early years as a teacher, he lectured on a great range of scientific and philosophic subjects. To this period belongs his view on the origin of the stellar systems by rotation set up in a primeval cloud of cosmic dust, the so-called Kant–Laplace theory, after the French mathematician of that time who held similar views. Gradually, he moved away from the traditional philosophy of Leibniz towards his own critical approach, first fully propounded in the *Critique of Pure Reason* (1781 (=A), second revised edition 1787 (=B)). Here he turns to an examination of the enquiring mind and its essential limitations. This involves what he calls a Copernican reversal of approach: instead of assuming that all our KNOWLEDGE must conform to OBJECTS, he says, we must 'make trial whether we may not have more success in the tasks of METAPHYSICS, if we suppose that objects must conform to our knowledge' (B xvi), and appear to us accordingly. What we can grasp are those appearances (in Greek *phaenomena*), whereas the 'things in themselves' are not knowable and remain mere thoughts *(noumena)*. As for knowledge, it arises through EXPERIENCE only, except for A PRIORI insights concerning our own rational equipment itself, and this is the subject of the *Critique of Pure Reason*. Such insights include certain general principles at the base of all theoretical enquiry. These principles are not analytic like the logical principles of IDENTITY or excluded middle (a statement is either true or false, there is no further possibility) but synthetic, in that they contribute something positive to the enquiries in question (see ANALYTIC AND SYNTHETIC). Such principles are therefore '*a priori* synthetic', a central notion in Kant's critical philosophy. Whether there be any such principles remains controversial, but according to Kant the whole of pure MATHEMATICS is *a priori* synthetic, as is the principle of causality in science. Space, the form of outer intuition, and time, the form of inner intuition, are, similarly, *a priori*. So, too, is the principle of the unity of APPERCEPTION, which makes it possible for the experiencing mind to regard its experiences as belonging to itself. This is Kant's solution to HUME's puzzle about there being no 'I' or *ego*. The general principles of the understanding (of which causality is one) are exhibited as linked with the structure of PROPOSITIONS. Kant introduces the principles (or 'categories', to use ARISTOTLE's term), by means of a FORMAL device which he calls their 'transcendental deduction': 'TRANSCENDENTAL' as being 'occupied not so much with objects as with the mode of our knowledge of objects in so far as this mode of knowledge is to be possible *a priori*' (A 11–12); 'deduction' from jurists' use of this term to refer to a proof of our right to do something (A 84). A 'transcendental deduction' is accordingly a proof of our right to employ *a priori* concepts, involving an explanation of the manner in which such concepts relate *a priori* to objects so as to yield experience (A 85). Any employment of reason divorced from experience remains purely speculative and therefore beyond being established. Still, for experience to be possible, it must be guided by some conceptual framework ('thoughts without content are empty, intuitions without concepts are blind', B 75).

As far as the *First Critique* goes, human beings living in a world governed by causality are no more free than the stars in their courses. To account for the fact that we feel ourselves to be free, Kant observes that while our natural selves, belonging to the world of phenomena, are indeed determined, our moral selves belong to the world of *noumena* and are therefore free. More precisely, the will is noumenal. The only perfectly good thing is a good will, namely, one that leads us to act in such a way that we could at the same time will the principle of our action to become a universal law. The injunction so to act is what Kant calls the 'categorical imperative', which is central to his ETHICS. This is outlined in *Groundwork of Morals* (1785) and the *Critique of Practical Reason* (1787). The formula as such is rather bare, but it implies that we should not enter special pleas for ourselves. It is perhaps a long-winded way of asking us to treat others as we would have them treat us. In the *Critique of Judgment* (1790), some of the previous ground is covered again, but there is also a discussion of aesthetic theory (in the modern sense of theory of the beautiful; the term 'AESTHETICS' is first so used by Baumgarten (1714–1762)).

KIERKEGAARD

Although Kant was himself a moderate Protestant, it is clear that the *First Critique* completely undermines the possibility of knowing GOD. With some justice it has been said that here lies the origin of the 'God is dead' theology of our own time. Kant states that in setting the boundaries to knowledge he makes room for faith, but this is no more than a pious after-thought. In particular, the *First Critique* shows that none of the traditional proofs for the existence of God are sound. Kant is on less secure ground when he seeks to show that reason on its own tends to entrap itself in contradictions ('antinomies'), giving, for example, proofs both for the world having to have a beginning and for this to be impossible. Such puzzles are resolvable by more careful analysis. The fact remains that untrammelled speculation is apt to be unconvincing and inconclusive.

Although Kant hardly ever moved beyond the city of his birth, he took an active interest in the historical events of his time. In 1795, he published a pamphlet *On Perpetual Peace*, in which he outlines a philosophical approach to the abolition of war. To him, as to other ENLIGHTENMENT thinkers, warfare obstructed the progress of science and trade and hindered human development. The problem remains unresolved to this day.

Although Kant himself becomes involved in metaphysical difficulties (the status of things in themselves is the central one), the critical approach in general is nevertheless a powerful brake on mere speculative metaphysics and on unexamined dogmatism. It was the reading of HUME that had aroused Kant from his 'dogmatic slumbers', and his critical work continues, albeit on a grander scale, what Hume had begun. In his restriction of religion to moral content alone, he follows the general trend of the 18th century Enlightenment.

Kierkegaard, Søren Aabye (1813–1855), Danish philosopher and writer on theology. Opposed to the drift of the Hegelian doctrine of system then dominant (see HEGEL), he held truth to be something highly individual. He distanced himself from the Lutheranism of his youth, though eventually taking orders. His thesis, *The Concept of Irony* (1841), analyses the use of irony, especially as practised by SOCRATES. About that time he broke his inconclusive engagement with the young Regine Olsen, and with the Danish church.

Although he did not use the label, he is rightly regarded as the founder of modern EXISTENTIALISM. According to him, man makes unconditioned choices that involve a 'leap of faith', which marks a transition from ethical to religious action, the life of the senses (the

162

aesthetic sphere) having been left behind when the ethical approach is adopted. This criterionless choice in the end is paradoxical, and reminds one of Tertullian's dictum *'credo quia absurdum'*, 'I believe it because it is absurd'. These notions are examined in detail in a series of books, notably *Either/Or* (1843), *Fear and Trembling* (1843), *The Concept of Dread* (1844), *Concluding Unscientific Postscript* (1846). The fact that his position is not consistent would not have disturbed him greatly—that individuals are erratic in their behaviour is, after all, well-known.

In sum, his *oeuvre* is really an individualistic PSYCHOLOGY in the great romantic style of his time. Thus he treats his opponents not so much as wrong, but as morally misguided. Though opposed to Hegel, he shares the latter's tendency to reify negative states, as HEIDEGGER did later (for example, Nothingness). As the forerunner of 20th century existentialism he remains important, perhaps in theology more than in philosophy.

knowledge, *n.* the word 'know' is used in talk of:

  1. knowing that something is the case
  2. knowing some person or place
  3. knowing how to do something

1. Philosophers agree in distinguishing between knowledge in the first of these senses, and belief. But they differ in their accounts of how they are to be distinguished: (a) are they to be distinguished in terms of their objects, knowledge being exclusively of things that are necessarily true, such as that $2+2=4$? (b) are knowledge and belief mental processes (operations, acts), the difference between them being one that can only be known by introspection? (c) does knowing some proposition, p, imply believing it and, if so, is the difference between knowledge and belief a matter of whether one's belief is caused in a certain way?

(a) Saying that we can know only what is necessarily true is at odds with our ordinary sense of 'know', as in talk of knowing the time, and so is unacceptable to those who hold that philosophy must explicate ordinary usage. However, they accept that for someone to know p, p must be true since, in ordinary usage, someone who, with good reason, claims to know p, is held to have said something false if it turns out that p is false. He has not misused 'know' as he would if he said 'I know p, which is false'.

(b) Locke described knowing and believing as 'operations' or 'actings' of our minds which we observe in ourselves by reflection (*Essay*, I i 4), and the Cambridge philosopher, G. E. Moore, said that the question 'How do you know that?' may be meant to ask 'What sort of a process goes on in your mind, when you know it?' (*Some Main Problems of Philosophy*, London, 1953, p. 25). The assumption in each case is that knowledge and belief are mental processes (operations, acts, and so on), the difference between them being ascertainable by introspection. If so, what is the difference? Various accounts have been given by rationalist philosophers, such as that knowledge that *p* differs from belief that *p* in that one's perception of *p* is 'clear and distinct' (Descartes) or that one's idea of *p* is a 'true idea' (Spinoza), but it is hard to see how anything genuinely introspectible can guarantee the truth of a proposition which is not about the mind. One alternative account dates back at least to Plato (*Theaetetus* 201b *sq.*, 208b *sq.*): knowledge differs from belief in that knowledge is true belief plus good reasons for believing, but this account, rejected by Plato himself, has been found, by E. Gettier ('Is justified true belief knowledge?', *Analysis* 23, 1963) and others, to be open to counter-examples. An alternative account is that of the Oxford linguistic philosopher J. L. Austin: 'When I say "I know" I give others my word: I give others my authority for saying "*S* is *P*"' ('Other Minds', *Arist. Soc.* Supp. Vol. XX, 1946). Saying 'I know' is like saying 'I promise'.

(c) As a rule, knowing implies believing. But if people were being tested to find out if they were any good at telling the sex of chickens, and one of them got it right every time, but was not told this, and so thought that what he said was as likely to be false as true, we might say that he knew, but did not believe, that a certain chicken would be male. Would we say this if we thought there was no causal explanation of his getting it right, if we thought it was a sheer coincidence? If not then we hold a causal theory of knowledge: there must be a satisfactory causal explanation of someone getting something right for him properly to be said to have knowledge, whether or not he believes what he says. Opinions will differ as to what is a satisfactory causal explanation. Will extra-sensory perception do? Does it become satisfactory if some passage of electrical energy from the card in the next room to the brain of the alleged perceiver is discovered, and respected scientists are satisfied? We are used to accepting authority, even if we change our minds as to who or what is an authority.

2. We also say we know people, including ourselves ('Know then thyself', Alexander Pope), places, and feelings, such as grief. Philosophers, notably William James (*Principles of Psychology*, 2 vols, London, 1890. Vol. 1, Ch. 8) and Bertrand Russell (*Problems of Philosophy*, Oxford, 1912, Ch. 5), have distinguished between 'knowledge by acquaintance' and 'knowledge by description', but not so much to shed light on our everyday use of 'know' as to serve the purposes of epistemological theorising (see epistemology). Russell defines 'acquaintance' in terms of the technical concept of 'direct awareness', so that we can be acquainted with 'sense-data' (see SENSE-DATUM) and with 'universals', but not with our bank-manager or grief.

3. Finally, there is knowing how to do something. The Oxford philosopher, Gilbert Ryle, (*The Concept of Mind*, London, 1949, Ch. 2) holds that some philosophers, whom he calls 'champions of the intellectualist legend', try to assimilate knowing *how* to knowing *that*. It is easy to see that knowing how to do something like winking cannot be reduced to knowing that in winking such and such muscles contract or expand: one could be told which muscles are involved and still not be able to wink.

knowledge by acquaintance, see KNOWLEDGE.

knowledge by description, see KNOWLEDGE.

Kripke, Saul (1941–   ), American philosopher, professor at Princeton, is principally known for his work on semantical aspects of modal LOGIC (see SEMANTICS). He introduced the term 'rigid designator' for what in any possible world refers to the same OBJECT. Examples of rigid designators are the natural numbers. This approach leads him to a revision of traditional modal concepts and of our common notion of PERSONAL IDENTITY.

L

language-games, *n.* a term used by WITTGENSTEIN in his reflections on 'the multiplicity of the tools in a language and of the ways they are used'. Some examples of language-games are 'giving orders and obeying them' and 'asking, thanking, cursing, greeting, praying' (*Philosophical Investigations*, Oxford, 1953, I 23). 'The term "language-*game*" is meant to bring into prominence that the *speaking* of language is part of an activity' (*ibid.*). Like games, language-games do not have one thing in common, but exhibit various 'family resemblances'. Wittgenstein is opposed to the idea that language 'always serves the same purpose: to convey thoughts—which may be about houses, pains, good and evil, or anything else you please' (*ibid.*, I 304). Just as there are rules which play various roles in games, so there are 'rules of language', and much variety in what we call 'going by a rule'. For example, 'there is a way of grasping a rule which is *not* an *interpretation*, but which is exhibited in what we call "obeying the rule", and "going against it" in actual cases' (*ibid.*, I 201).

language, philosophy of, *n.* the study of the various areas where language impinges on philosophic enquiry. Since the main method of communication in human affairs is the use of language, either spoken or written, any study whatsoever will at some point involve language. What does remain to this day controversial is whether THINKING occurs essentially in terms of language (expressing one's thoughts obviously does). The ancient problem of UNIVERSALS and particulars was often treated as mainly linguistic, while some mid-20th century philosophers have held that the very business of philosophy consists in philosophical ANALYSIS and clarification. Amongst those who see philosophy as essentially concerned with language, some hold that the idiom we commonly use needs to be illuminated but not corrected (for example, the ordinary language philosophers of Oxford in the 1950s), while others insist that current usage must be revised and improved (RUSSELL). Moreover, philosophers are sometimes concerned with the question how the language we use to speak about the world out there is related to that world. Does language somehow picture the world? In LOGIC, we come up against the actual structure of language. There is evidence suggesting that logical structure at some level is shared by all languages. Many of these problems border on other areas, notably PSYCHOLOGY and social behaviour. See CHOMSKY.

laws of nature, the general PROPOSITIONS that state how and in what order the events in the world around us take place. Of this world, we are ourselves a part, so that our own ways of functioning fall under the same heading as, say, the law of gravitation which governs the motion of heavenly bodies. Our KNOWLEDGE of these laws is never complete, since there are always further problems: enquiry does push back the boundaries of the unknown, but the more we know, the greater our contact with what we do not know. The logical status of laws of nature has been questioned since the turn of the century, because some findings appear to be statistical in kind. However, there is no unanimous view in this area, and the famous EINSTEIN for one did not accept that laws of nature had anything to do with probability ('God does not play dice').

Leibniz, Gottfried Wilhelm (1646–1716), son of the professor of moral philosophy at the University of Leipzig. Leibniz entered the University at the age of 15 and graduated in 1663 with a dissertation on the principle of individuation. In Paris from 1672 to 1676 he made the acquaintance of MALEBRANCHE, ARNAULD, and the Dutch physicist, Christian Huygens. During this time he discovered the differential CALCULUS, independently of, but later than, NEWTON. In 1673 he visited London, and met the chemist, Robert Boyle. In 1676, *en route* to Hanover to become librarian to the Duke of Brunswick, he spent a month in Amsterdam and met SPINOZA. He served three successive dukes at Hanover and died in 1716. Much of his philosophical writing took the form of papers and correspondence. The semi-popular *Theodicy* (1710) was the only longish book to be published in his lifetime. For an understanding of his philosophy the most important works are his *Discourse on Metaphysics* (written 1686), the resulting *Correspondence with Arnauld* (1686–87), *A Specimen of Discoveries* (*c.*1686), *New System, and Explanation of the New System* (1695–96), *Monadology* (1714), and the *Correspondence with Clarke* (1715–16).

Forgetting, for the moment, the world that actually exists, consider the realm of possible worlds, and their constituents. There is no limit either to the number of possible worlds, or to the number of possible constituents of them, although there may be a world with a finite number of constituents. Suppose we are to identify, by means of a DESCRIPTION, a constituent of one of these possible worlds. Since two such worlds might differ in only one constituent, the description must involve a reference to all the other constituents. Since the constituents might be related in other ways in other possible worlds, it must involve a reference to how they are related. So to identify the thing in question we must mention all the other constituents of that possible world and say how they are all related to one another: this description will serve to identify it.

We can talk of a 'notion' or 'complete concept' of the thing such that an omniscient being possessing this notion or concept could assess the TRUTH-VALUE not only of propositions about that thing but also, because of the way it has been identified, about everything else in the possible world of which it is a constituent. The possible world it inhabits is, in a sense, mirrored in the concept of the thing; the concept 'expresses' that world and its inhabitants.

Any property of the thing in question will be contained in its complete CONCEPT, rather as the property of having angles equal to two right angles is contained in the concept of a triangle. The difference is that the propositions of geometry are true in all possible worlds, whereas propositions about the thing in question are true only in one possible world. They are certain, but not NECESSARY; or necessary only on the HYPOTHESIS that that possible world actually exists, not absolutely necessary. Whereas the concept of a triangle admits of a complete ANALYSIS, if the thing in question is a constituent of a world with an infinite number of constituents then although the omniscient being could be said to have an intuitive knowledge of its complete concept, even he would not be able to provide a complete analysis of it.

The complete CONCEPT of a thing covers its entire history. Given the complete concept, one has no need to take account of possible causal interactions with other things in order to predict the thing's future. The manner in which the thing has been identified ensures that everything that has happened or will happen to it is embraced in its complete concept. If the thing possessed intuitive knowledge of its own complete concept it would know, with CERTAINTY, not only what it had done, but also what it was going to do.

The above are purely logical considerations. However, Leibniz was also a metaphysician and a scientist, and, like other philosophers of the time, he wanted to provide a sound metaphysical basis for the new science. DESCARTES's way of doing this had been to treat EXTENSION as the ESSENCE of MATTER, separating the MIND as something both quite distinct from matter and yet somehow conjoined by GOD with those portions of matter we call a human body. Leibniz could not accept this account, either of the reality of material things or of the mind–body relation. Moreover he felt that Descartes had ignored the question of why God had created the world he did create, and had treated as humanly unanswerable the question of how man can be free in a divinely preordained world.

Leibniz advanced a METAPHYSICS in which the SCHOLASTIC notion of a thing having a certain substantial FORM or essence was reinterpreted in the light of the above logical points about possible worlds and their constituents. The constituents have a certain need for existence, or claim to exist, the more so the closer they come to being constituents of a world in which there would be the greatest possible number, an infinity, of constituents, related in ways such that the laws governing their relationship are the fewest and simplest possible. God, like a mathematician who uses the calculus of variations to find an extremal value, chooses to create this world, the most perfect of possible worlds. We know A PRIORI that God exists since 'he must exist if he is possible, and nothing can prevent the possibility of that which has no limits, no negation, and consequently no contradiction'. We know A POSTERIORI that he exists since there must be a sufficient reason for the existence and behaviour of contingent things (PRINCIPLE OF SUFFICIENT REASON), and, being contingent, they do not contain that reason in themselves. Also, we know, he exists as the ground of eternal truths, though these exist by his understanding, not, as Descartes held, by his will.

There cannot be aggregates of things unless there are things which have a true unity, 'MONADS' (from Greek *monas* a unit). Hence, since what is extended is infinitely divisible, the constituents are not extended. The alternative that presents itself is that they are SOULS, or, at any rate, soul-like. Leibniz's concept of a soul is more like ARISTOTLE's than like Descartes's. A monad is a principle of activity or force, rather than a principle of self-awareness. It has an 'appetite' to progress to the next stage in its history but rarely more than a glimmer of what that history will be. Monads are created substances. Having, in a sense, the world in themselves, they are causally independent of other monads. They are dependent only on God. We may talk of changes in one thing causing changes in another but the reality is that in God's planning of the best possible world the plans for one monad have taken precedence over, and so determined, those for another. The causality is that of FINAL CAUSES. This is what underlies our talk of a change in one thing being the EFFICIENT CAUSE of a change in another. Such talk is in keeping with the notion of a monad being a principle of activity or force. We say that a change in one thing is the EFFICIENT CAUSE of a change in another when the changes are expressed more perfectly or distinctly in the former; that is, when we can explain the changes more economically by reference to the former. Without the notion of force it would not be possible to say that one body is in MOTION and another at rest, since motion is change of place, and place is relative. The corpuscular philosophy of efficient causes is not self-sufficient, as Descartes supposed. The principles of mechanics need to be supplemented by the principles of dynamics or force. SPACE AND TIME are not absolute. To suppose, with NEWTON, that they are is to suppose that God does some things without a reason, since he would have no reason for creating the world at a given time and not a year sooner in absolute time, or in one or other of two ways round in absolute space.

The dependence of this system of efficient causes of motions in matter on the system of final causes of changes in monads is such that there is a harmony between the two systems. A special case of this harmony is the harmony between what happens in a person's body and in his soul. Thus the problem of the 'union' of body and soul, bequeathed by Descartes, is solved without recourse to the OCCASION-ALISM of MALEBRANCHE.

There is nothing in the logical considerations mentioned above to prejudice man's freedom, nor is there anything to elucidate the concept of freedom, or to warrant our saying that a man sometimes acts freely. Leibniz saw the logical point and supposed that the in-dependence, or 'spontaneity', of a monad served to explain what it is for man to be free. In the sense of 'free' in which a man sometimes acts freely, sometimes not, Leibniz's explanation is as irrelevant to a man's being free as was KANT's explanation in terms of the soul's being a thing-in-itself, not subject to causality. See BERKELEY, FREEWILL AND DETERMINISM, MIND–BODY PROBLEM, SUBSTANCE.

Lenin, Vladimir Ilyich Ulyanov (1870–1924), leader of the Bolshev-ist (i.e. majority) movement and main architect of the Russian Revolution of 1917, was in his day the elaborator of the theories of MARX and ENGELS into the dialectical materialism ('diamat') that became the official philosophy of the Soviet Union. In particular, he emphasised the role of the Party as a vehicle of continued revolutionary activity and as the expression of the 'dictatorship of the proletariat'. He was opposed to merely theoretical under-pinning and insisted on the need for action, to help the historical process along, towards the ultimate goal of communist society when the state would wither away. His writings are thus on the whole aimed at partisan activity rather than at ANALYSIS. His position was a simple-minded realist materialism (see REALISM), and he was strongly critical of scientific philosophers like E. MACH and his SENSE-DATUM view of the basis of reality. His own view of diamat was squarely based on Hegelian DIALECTIC (see HEGEL).

Leucippus of Miletus, see DEMOCRITUS.

Levi-Strauss, Claude (1908–), French ethnologist, known above all for his structural analysis of the customs of various societies. In this way he shows how their beliefs and practices are linked with their material conditions, and how the underlying structure works itself out in terms of a set of basic oppositions. The notion of structure is ultimately derived from MATHEMATICS.

local sign theory, see SENSATION.

Locke, John (1632–1704), English empiricist philosopher (see EMPIRICISM). Born in Somerset, he went to Westminster School and to Christ Church, Oxford. In 1659 he was elected to a Senior Studentship there, but for political reasons lost it in 1684. He was a friend and adviser of Lord Ashley, afterwards Earl of Shaftesbury. When Shaftesbury died in political disfavour in 1683, Locke went to Holland for five years. He returned shortly after the revolution of 1688 and in 1691 retired to Essex where he died in 1704. His main philosophical work was *An Essay concerning Human Understanding* on which he worked for nearly 20 years before it came out in 1690, when his *Two Treatises of Civil Government* also appeared.

Locke's philosophy has been described as 'The Way of Ideas'. Like DESCARTES, he used 'IDEA' to cover everything of which one is immediately aware: THINKING and perceiving alike involve IDEAS, the former being the MEANINGS of the words we use to express our thoughts, and the latter the effects in us of qualities in external bodies. The ideas of sense are caused by impulse, 'the only way we can conceive bodies operate in' (*Essay*, II vii 11). Sense-ideas such as that of sound can be explained in terms of MOTION (vibration); the external body contains nothing resembling the idea. Qualities like motion are primary, essential to our CONCEPT of body; qualities like sound are secondary. There are simple ideas, such as the coldness and hardness which one feels in a piece of ice, and complex ideas, such as the idea of ice, the latter being formed out of the former. Ideas are real, as against fictitious, if they conform to something objective. All simple ideas are real, being the effects in us of qualities in external bodies (II xxx 1–2). The ideas involved in thinking are general; that is, are used in thinking about many different things, as the word 'white' is used to describe snow, milk, chalk, and so on. Their generality lies in their use; in themselves, ideas, like all other things, are particular. General ideas are acquired by ABSTRACTION. Besides the ideas involved in PERCEPTION, and in thinking, there are ideas of REFLECTION, the operations of our own minds. Reflection is like sense, but internal. Unlike Descartes, Locke held none of our ideas to be innate; they are all founded on experience (II i 1–2).

All these aspects of Locke's 'Way of Ideas' are controversial. He has been generally taken to hold a REPRESENTATIVE THEORY OF PERCEPTION, but this view has recently been challenged: when talking about perception, might he not mean by 'idea' the act of awareness? Indeed, he sometimes equates 'idea' with 'sensation or perception', he is not as concerned about the SCEPTICISM attendant on a representative theory as he should be if he held it, and later he criticised MALEBRANCHE for talking of ideas as entities. However, he also says that the ideas of primary qualities resemble the qualities, and how can an act of awareness resemble a quality? He also assimilates ideas to bodily sensations, like pain (II viii 18).

Locke held that to think is to connect ideas into mental *propositions*. Ideas and mental PROPOSITIONS, however, are private to the person who has them. To convey our thoughts to another and to record them for ourselves, we need signs of our ideas and mental propositions. These are words and verbal propositions. We often overlook that there are mental propositions as well as verbal ones because 'it is unavoidable, in treating of mental propositions, to make use of words, and then the instances given of mental propositions cease immediately to be barely mental and become verbal' (IV v 3). The main problem here is to explain how words have a common meaning. If they have meaning by standing for ideas, and ideas are private (see PRIVACY), how can a man know that his 'words excite the same ideas in the hearer which he makes them stand for in speaking' (III ii 8)? Locke answers that as regards words for simple ideas, it would not matter if they did not excite the same ideas (II xxxii 15). Speaker and hearer might apply the same words to the same qualities but have different ideas. Perhaps ideas are not necessary for communication, so long as people use words in the same way.

He defined knowledge as 'nothing but the perception of the connexion and agreement, or disagreement and repugnancy, of any of our ideas' (IV i 2), but did not have an idealist or phenomenalist conception of reality (see IDEALISM, PHENOMENALISM). For him, external OBJECTS exist and have 'real ESSENCES', understood not in terms of Aristotelian 'substantial forms' (II xxiii 3), but in terms of corpuscular theory and MATHEMATICS. If our senses were more acute we could know the minute corpuscular constitutions of things, and from this deduce, as we deduce the properties of a triangle from the idea of three lines enclosing a space, both why certain qualities necessarily co-exist in particular substances (II xxxi 6), and why bodies interact causally as they do (IV iii 25). As things are, we cannot (IV iii 10–14). At best we have probability, not KNOWLEDGE. Yet we have 'an assurance that deserves the name of knowledge' that there are external objects (IV xi 3), even if our knowledge of them is so limited.

Locke wrote *Two Treatises of Government* 'to establish the Throne of Our Great Restorer, our present King William; and to make good his Title, in the Consent of the People' (Preface). Like HOBBES, he explained political society by reference to a state of nature and a SOCIAL CONTRACT. However, by 'a state of nature' and 'a political society', he did not mean the same as Hobbes. First, his 'state of nature' was subject to a natural moral law which teaches 'that, being all equal and independent, no one ought to harm another in his life, health, liberty or possessions'. His view about possessions is a fore-runner of the labour theory of value: 'God has given the earth to mankind in common', but each man makes part of it his own by using his labour to make it productive. The moral law of nature demands that nobody's property shall be so big as to deprive another of his means of self-preservation. Such property laws must be made legally enforceable, or else the state of nature degenerates into a state of war such as, for Hobbes, indeed it was. Hence the social contract, whereby each man surrenders his 'executive power of the law of nature', in return for a public enforcement of it, with penalties for infringement. Secondly, for Hobbes, the King was sovereign, an absolute monarch whose command was law. For Locke, the people retain sovereignty and exercise it through the legislative, executive and judiciary powers they establish. The social contract is for majority rule. Hence 'absolute monarchy, which by some men is counted the only government in the world, is indeed inconsistent with civil society and so can be no form of civil government at all'. See INTROSPECTION, PERSONAL IDENTITY, PRIMARY AND SECONDARY QUALITIES.

logic, *n.* (from Greek *logos* collection, word, speech, reason, account) the study of how we reason correctly. In order to stress that this has nothing to do with how we feel, one might define it as concerned with the structure of correct reasoning. The first philosopher to present a systematic account of logic was ARISTOTLE, although people did of course reason correctly from time immemorial. Aristotelian logic is treated above all in his *Organon*, particularly in the *Prior* and *Posterior Analytics*, where he explains the notions of term, PROPOSITION, INFERENCE and the like, together with a full account of syllogistic argument. His is essentially a logic of terms. As against this, the Stoics (see STOICISM) developed a logic of propositions. Both survive as parts of modern logic in predicate logic and propositional logic. The logic of Aristotle, as interpreted and arranged by later thinkers, especially during the Middle Ages, has played a dominant role until the 19th century. It is above all a FORMAL doctrine, concerned with the structure of statements and arguments rather than with their contents, or, what comes to the same, applicable to any contents whatever. In this it is similar to that other formal field of studies, MATHEMATICS. Working out a problem in logic much resembles the solving of a mathematical problem. From the outset this has manifested itself in the use of symbols. Thus Aristotle uses letters of the Greek alphabet to stand for terms (in the logical sense of the word). In modern times it was LEIBNIZ who suggested that logic could be elaborated into a universal problem-solving device on the mathematical model: instead of arguing or debating, men would enter their critical views into the device and then calculate: differences of opinion would be settled not by posturing but by calculation. A systematic development of this notion had to wait till the 19th century, when Boole developed his calculus of classes (see BOOLEAN ALGEBRA) and FREGE invented a general conceptual script which operates in an all-embracing logical framework. His formulation was superseded in the 20th century by the work of RUSSELL, and various rival systems of notation have been devised since.

Along with the development of logic there arise certain general questions that do not belong to the operation of the logical calculus itself, but rather to the way in which various components are to be taken. Some of these questions are of recent origin, but others are as old as the subject. Of this latter kind is the question whether terms that figure in statements are to be taken as denoting things that exist ('real terms') or whether this need not be so. Aristotle held that the terms A and B in the statement 'all A are B' must be real. In modern predicate logic, this is not so. Here the statement is presented differently: for any x, if x is A then x is B. There is no call for A to be a real term, since it figures in a hypothetical antecedent of an inference. This being so, certain consequences that can be drawn from the Aristotelian formula no longer follow from the modern formulation. Whether this last is a genuine translation of the Aristotelian statement remains a controversial question that cannot be resolved in terms of the logical formalisms involved.

Another even more basic question of this kind concerns the relation of formal logic to the world in and to which we apply it. Aristotle held that the general principles of logic are directly applicable to the external world. This is in direct contrast with the view that the principles of logic are mere empirical generalisations (not just that we learn them, like anything else, through experience). Then there are those who regard them as rules of language, which are more or less arbitrary conventions. This is related to the conventionalist view of mathematics as based on principles fixed by convention (H. Poincaré). In KANT's epistemology, the principles of logic are part of the cognitive framework of human understanding. Many modern logicians take the principles of logic as abstract, empty formulae or tautologies. The whole question of how logic bears on the world is similar to the problem (if it is a problem) of how mathematics is applicable to practical affairs (the answer, if there is one, is similar too).

Along with a logic of categorical statements (those that contain '. . . is . . .' or '. . . is not . . .') there has been from Aristotle onward a so-called modal logic, where the statements contain modal copulas like '. . . must be . . .', '. . . may be . . .' and others. Modal logic in Aristotle considers questions of possibility and necessity, and their opposites. The detailed study of modal systems has greatly increased in our own time. Depending on various assumptions made concerning basic modal concepts and inferences, a whole range of different modal logics has been developed. Moreover, it has been noticed that the way in which formal systems are set up does not always give an accurate account of how argument in natural language actually proceeds. This has led to further systems being developed to avoid such difficulties. One may well ask whether in the end there are many logics, all independent from each other, or whether they all somehow depend on the logic of ordinary discourse. Here we have yet another controversial issue that cannot be resolved in terms of logical operations within the systems concerned.

Finally, we must mention that in various logical doctrines there arise difficulties of principle that are commonly known as PARADOXES and that are often very awkward to deal with. There is no single method for tackling them, nor is it always agreed whether they should or even can be removed. Paradoxes in logical systems are generated by somewhat freakish examples. If ordinary statements led to such trouble, a system would soon be abandoned. One main use of formal systems is indeed the testing of a set of statements for consistency. Once more, this notion is familiar from mathematics. It is perhaps not surprising that Russell and logicians in his tradition have sought to show that mathematics can be reduced to purely logical notions. The attempt has led to interesting insights concerning logical systems but was not in the end successful: it hinges on whether one regards class membership as a logical or a mathematical CONCEPT. It is perhaps worth recalling in conclusion that formal reasoning alone can never lead us to new discoveries. However, as a method of putting our findings in a systematic order, it has always been recognised as a vital adjunct to enquiry. See REFERENCE, RULE OF; DEDUCTION.

logical constructions, *n.* a term used in PHILOSOPHICAL ANALYSIS. Saying that the average Englishman is a logical construction out of individual Englishmen goes with saying that the statement 'The average Englishman has one and a half children' can be analysed as 'The number of children of Englishmen is one and a half times the number of Englishmen'. The term was introduced by Bertrand RUSSELL in 1905 ('On Denoting', *Mind*, 14, 479–493).

logical positivism, the doctrine of the VIENNA CIRCLE, so called because it recognises only the positive sciences (as against systems of metaphysical speculation) as valid sources of human KNOWLEDGE, and in this process attends to the logical structure of scientific (that is, acceptable) statements. Thus, the doctrine insists on the empirical approach (see EMPIRICISM), in some ways continuing the tradition that goes back to LOCKE and HUME. However, the thorough-going rejection of abstract theorising went too far: theoretical science seemed itself to be inadmissible. This consequence, due to the verification principle in its strong form ('the meaning of a statement is the method of its verification'), excludes as meaningless anything not directly verifiable (see VERIFIABILITY). A weaker form of verification was therefore substituted, so that meaning was saved provided there was at least some link with verification. Logical positivism adopted a theory of logical atomism, which reduces the complex states of affairs we experience to simple 'protocols' that are not further analysable. This is of course itself a metaphysical doctrine and has been widely criticised. So is the correspondence theory of truth involved in the notion of 'protocol statements' as simply mirroring facts (see TRUTH, THEORIES OF). With acceptable statements all belonging to science, and their FORMAL adequacy secured by LOGIC, there is nothing left for philosophy to do except to analyse language. This stark conclusion thus leaves no room for artistic interests that people actually have. However, even as regards the analysis of language, it looks as if the choice of formal linguistic systems we are to use in dealing with the world is somewhat arbitrary: the notion that we can move between such 'languages' by rules that are in principle specifiable remains controversial. Thus it is dubious whether we may express ourselves equally well in 'sense-data language' and in 'physical-object language'. Moreover, the logical positivist approach does not seem to be very helpful in coping with the complications of natural languages. As regards ETHICS, it is likewise not entirely adequate, in that it treats ethical statements as concerned only with our attitudes and not with our activities.

Lucretius, (Titus Lucretius Carus) (*c.*99–55 BC), the author of an instructional poem, *De Rerum Natura* (On the Nature of Things) expounding the MATERIALISM and ATOMISM of EPICURUS. Lucretius held that the SOUL consists of tenuous particles that disperse when leaving the body. The soul does not fulfil any of the conditions of IMMORTALITY. For Lucretius the advantage of this is that man, at death, has nothing to fear for all time to come.

M

Mach, Ernst (1838–1916), Austrian physicist and philosopher, who taught mathematics at Graz (1864–67), physics at Prague (1867–1895) and history of science *(inductive philosophy)* at Vienna (1895–1901). His philosophy was an extreme form of phenomenalistic POSITIVISM: everything we know is based on what we EXPERIENCE by our senses, that is, SENSATIONS. In this he follows the general line of HUME's empiricist account. This means that theories, which are ultimately based on sensations, are only provisional, and are adopted so long as they prove themselves in use. As regards scientific explanation, all we can genuinely do is to describe things in terms of our sensations. Natural laws are our way of coming to terms with the world we inhabit. His best known work, *The Science of Mechanics* (1883), gives a critical historical account of how mechanics developed and makes use of his general approach to our way of acquiring KNOWLEDGE. He was a precursor of the VIENNA CIRCLE who called their first association after him.

Malebranche, Nicolas (1638–1715). Born in Paris, Malebranche attended the Sorbonne, entered the congregation of the Oratory, and was ordained priest in 1664. By 1668 he had begun his life's work of developing and defending a Christian philosophy in the tradition of St AUGUSTINE. His first major work was *Search after Truth* (1674–75), but the best introduction to his philosophy is his *Dialogues on Metaphysics and Religion* (1688). This brought him into conflict with some of his contemporaries, in particular Antoine ARNAULD. His influence extended to the British empiricists, George BERKELEY and David HUME. As with DESCARTES, his starting point is the thought that if mathematically quantifiable spatial EXTENSION constitutes the ESSENCE of MATTER, and colours, sounds, smells, are no more than SENSATIONS in us, then matter is intrinsically intelligible; and the dream of the Platonists, that the universe is wholly penetrable by human reason, is thus far realised. Malebranche, like Descartes, described our ideas of extension as 'CLEAR and distinct'. They diverged, however, in their explanations of why we can rely on what we clearly and distinctly perceive. Malebranche explained this in terms of PLOTINUS and Augustine. The ideas we clearly and distinctly perceive are not subjective, like our sensations of colour, sound and smell; they exist in GOD, being the archetypes he uses in creating the world. We see them, in the intellectual sense of 'see', because we are united with God.

This 'vision in God' does not extend to actual material OBJECTS, but only to the intelligible essence of any possible world God might chose to actualize. Our beliefs about particular material objects rest on the SENSATIONS they produce in us, but since God could have produced the latter without there being any material objects at all, our belief that there is a material world must be justified further, namely by revelation.

Unlike Descartes, Malebranche held that MIND is not as well known as MATTER. If we knew the mind clearly and distinctly, we should know clearly that the mind must be subject to precisely the sort of 'modifications' to which it is subject, such as sensations of pain or colour, and various acts, such as reasoning. However, we do not know this. There is no possibility of DEDUCTION. From the FORMAL defining property of mind, THINKING, we cannot deduce the variety of introspectible mental events and acts. To know what they are, we have to rely on EXPERIENCE.

For Malebranche everything has its *being* in God. There is no causal efficacy save that of God. When, as we say, one material object's motion causes another's, God causes the motion of the second on the occasion of the motion of the first. Malebranche followed De La Forge (*Treatise on the Spirit of Man*, 1665) in using the term 'OCCASIONALISM' for his theory of causation. LEIBNIZ criticised it on the grounds that it required God to be constantly at work adjusting the motions of all the things in the universe to one another. In its place he put his theory of 'pre-established harmony'. As applied to the problem of the relation of body and mind (see MIND–BODY PROBLEM) both theories were held to be open to fewer objections than Descartes's INTERACTIONISM.

Amongst Malebranche's arguments in defence of these views we mention two. The first asserted that an object of perception cannot be at a distance from the perceiver: the mind can perceive only what is present to it; it is not likely that the mind leaves the body and walks about in the heavens to look at the sun and stars. ARNAULD, in his *True and False Ideas* (1683), objected that Malebranche had failed to distinguish between 'local presence' and 'objective presence'. I cannot be hit on the eye by a ball that is not locally present, in contact with my eye, but seeing a ball, or a star, is different: these are at a distance from me but can be objectively present to my mind. This point was made again, by Thomas REID (*Essays on the Intellectual Powers of Man*, 1785, Essay 2, Ch. 4).

The second argument asserts that we are not conscious of causal efficacy. In the motion of bodies we observe only constant conjunctions of events, not a necessary connection (*liaison nécessaire*). Likewise, there is no intrinsic relation between an act of VOLITION and the motion it produces. We do not know how the volition produces the motion, any more than we know how the motion of one body causes that of another. This point of Malebranche was made again in criticism of LOCKE (*Essay*, 1690, Bk. 2, Ch. 21) by Hume (*Enquiry concerning Human Understanding*, 1758, Sect. 7, Part 1).

Manicheism, *n.* a religion named after its Persian founder, Mani (*c*.215–276). There are two opposed principles, Light (goodness) and Darkness (evil). Man's soul is good, his body EVIL. Salvation consists in freeing oneself from the evil material element in one's nature. St AUGUSTINE was initially attracted to Manicheism, but came to reject the idea that evil is an independent positive principle.

Marcel, Gabriel (1889–1973), French philosopher of the Christian wing of the existentialist movement (see EXISTENTIALISM), after conversion to Catholicism at the age of 40. For him, the mystery of existence strikes us most vividly in the presence of others and ultimately of GOD. Like SARTRE, he wrote plays, in which his views are shown in action. As to the existentialist tag, he made no use of it himself.

Marx, Karl (1818–1883), German social theorist and revolutionary, had studied philosophy at Berlin, then still strongly under the influence of HEGEL who had died some years earlier. Marx turned to journalism, first in Cologne, then in Paris whence he was expelled (1845). He went to Brussels, which he had to leave in turn during the 1848 revolution, for his part in writing the *Communist Manifesto* (with ENGELS). Back in Cologne he returned to editing a newspaper. When reaction set in, he was exiled in 1849 and came to live in London, where he led a penurious life, depending on help from Engels, who owned a textile mill in Manchester. Marx henceforth spent his time on his literary researches, mainly at the British Museum, with occasional episodes of political activity, in connection with the First International. The result of his studies was his principal work, *Capital*, the first volume of which was published, in German, in Hamburg in 1867. The remaining two volumes were compiled by Engels from Marx's literary remains. *Capital* contains a detailed analysis of economic theory and an historical account of how economic conditions and activities had governed the various stages of human history. In his early writings he had given a materialist account of history, predicting where the historical process was inevitably moving: through socialism to COMMUNISM, when the State would 'wither away', as LENIN later put it. This utopian streak is in some ways related to Hegel's forecast of the final good of the State as represented by the Kingdom of Prussia. Marx, however, turned Hegel 'upside down', and saw the basic principle as material, being influenced partly by ancient materialists such as EPICURUS and by the 18th century French materialist thinkers. His theory of value, which was supposed to supplant the mercantilist views of ADAM SMITH, rests partly on the economic thought of Ricardo but in any case fails to see that Smith's analysis was basically logical, even if incomplete. Marx recognises only labour as a really important factor of production and argues that the 'surplus value' thereby created is largely taken away from the workers when it should be rightfully theirs. Of course, this sort of exploitation would be overcome when communism had taken over and all goods were communally owned (the French socialist Proudhon hints at similar views (*c.*1840) when he declared that 'property is theft'). Marx is the originator of 'dialectical materialism' (the term was coined later by Plekhanov (the Russian Marxist)), a doctrine which became highly influential, particularly as official philosophies in the USSR and China. His doctrine on the one hand presents history as unrolling according to definite principles towards an inevitable goal, but in his political activities he displayed a form of practical voluntarism. On the whole, the diamat approach, which takes the cultural manifestations of a period, including its philosophy, as an ideological feature of underlying material conditions, underestimates the independence of theoretical findings in science and philosophy. What it does do is to stress the sometimes unrecognised importance of economic conditions in human affairs. See DIALECTIC.

material cause, *n.* the MATTER of a thing (in the Aristotelian sense of 'matter', as opposed to 'FORM') considered as a factor in the explanation of the thing being as it is. See ARISTOTLE.

materialism, *n.* one of two theories that relates to the 'MATTER' of Descartes's mind–matter DUALISM. The less common use of the term

MATERIALISM

'materialist' refers to a philosopher who believes in the existence of material things over and above the sensory IDEAS we have of them. In this sense materialism is opposed to IMMATERIALISM or PHENOMENAL-ISM. BERKELEY called himself an immaterialist, and DESCARTES and LOCKE materialists.

The more common use of the word denotes those who hold that everything in the universe, including MINDS, can be explained in terms of matter in MOTION. In this sense the Pre-Socratic atomists (see ATOMISM), Leucippus and DEMOCRITUS, were materialists; HOBBES, who said that 'all that exists is body, all that occurs motion', was a materialist; Locke, who said that 'since we know not wherein thinking consists' it is 'not much more remote from our comprehension to conceive that GOD can, if he pleases, superadd to matter a faculty of thinking, than that he should superadd to it another substance with a faculty for thinking' (*Essay* IV iii 6), did not rule out a form of materialism; and T. H. HUXLEY, who said that the mind is related to the brain as the whistle made by a locomotive engine when it is working is related to the engine, held a form of materialism. (Materialism is usually restricted to what is in the universe; it is not extended to a Creator of the universe.)

Materialism in the second half of the 20th century took the form of the HYPOTHESIS that mental processes are in fact identical with brain-processes. It is sometimes called 'central state materialism', sometimes 'the contingent mind–brain IDENTITY hypothesis'. The notion of 'mental processes' is Locke's notion that 'perception, thinking, doubting, believing, reasoning, knowing, willing and all the different actings of our own minds' are operations which we perceive within ourselves by something so very like sense-perception that it 'might properly enough be called internal sense' (*Essay* II i 4). The objection to the identification of these inwardly observed operations with brain–processes, that when someone says 'I can see so-and-so' or 'I think such-and-such' he does not mean something about his brain, is met by saying that the objection confuses MEANING and reference. 'I can see so-and-so' does not *mean* 'There is a certain process occurring in my visual cortex', but nevertheless it may in fact *refer* to this process. 'The morning star' does not *mean* 'the evening star' and yet the two expressions do in fact *refer* to the same star. Critics of materialism object that the cases are not parallel. They ask what cor-responds to 'the same star' in the case of the alleged mind – brain identity, or, alternatively, what criteria of IDENTITY are involved in the statement that the mental operation is identical with a brain-process.

An alternative way of combatting CARTESIAN DUALISM, to asserting the identity of mental operations with brain-processes, is to say that utterances like 'I can see so-and-so' and 'I think such-and-such' do not function as reports of operations at all, either inwardly or outwardly observed. This is WITTGENSTEIN'S way, and is associated with calling such utterances 'AVOWALS'.

mathematics, *n.* the science of number and quantity, is of special interest in the history of philosophy, since the rise of Greek philosophic thought went hand in hand with mathematical discovery. The word itself is connected with Greek *mathein* learn, since in the view of PYTHAGORAS all learning was ultimately linked with number. By the 4th century BC, this link, though not forgotten, had faded and the term had come to mean what it still does. Mathematical examples figure in many Greek philosophers, from the earliest to PLATO and ARISTOTLE and beyond, while many modern philosophers have been mathematicians as well, to mention only DESCARTES, LEIBNIZ and RUSSELL. In mathematics, the process of proving a conclusion from premises stands out especially clearly, which makes it useful for the logician. It is mathematics that first gave a full blown example of a logical system, Euclid's Elements of Geometry, which starts from DEFINITIONS and AXIOMS (basic initial assumptions) and deduces a wealth of consequences by FORMAL argument. This procedure became the pattern to which science has aspired ever since, and until the 17th century to adopt the 'geometric mode' was a way of claiming that one's arguments were respectable.

What is of further interest to philosophers is that the findings of mathematics have a kind of solidity that other branches of science seem to lack. Thus, many have held that mathematical KNOWLEDGE was necessary: its PROPOSITIONS are what they are and could not be otherwise (two twos make four and no mistake). It is sometimes said that this is because mathematics does not depend on EXPERIENCE, which can deceive us, but is somehow abstract and independent of the external world. As to that, views differ: mathematics may equally be held to be as worldly as anything else, but that numerical features of that world are discernable with peculiar clarity and can therefore be displayed in a form free from the inaccuracies we meet in other fields.

Ultimately, mathematics goes back to the simple business of

counting. As to its foundations there are, however, competing positions, of which three in particular deserve special notice. Some regard mathematics as just a branch of logic, if we probe deep enough. This view (logicism) was held by FREGE and RUSSELL. Another approach regards mathematics as a juggling with undefined symbols according to certain basic rules; a view (formalism) put forward by the German mathematician David Hilbert. Then there is the outlook that sees mathematics as something directly apprehended and therefore capable of being constructed, which excludes infinite processes that cannot. This theory (INTUITIONISM) was proposed by the Dutch mathematician L. E. J. Brouwer; it demands some radical changes in ordinary logic and has not been as widely adopted as the other two approaches.

Some problems in the foundations of mathematics concern the general properties of whole systems of propositions and might as well be taken to belong to logic. These are questions as to whether in a given system with its definitions and axioms, any formulable proposition is decidable, that is whether we can say that it is true, or false. If this cannot be done, then the system is not complete, or undecidable. About the way in which such enquiries are conducted there is some controversy, and it is not always easy to see what assumptions are being made.

Questions that strictly belong to what we may call the philosophy of mathematics are not of a kind that will be decided by further discoveries in the field of mathematics. Rather, they touch on our general view on what mathematics is and what it does. For example, how is mathematics as such related to its applications in practice ('pure' as against 'applied' mathematics)? Whatever answer we may give, further research will not resolve this. One answer is that all mathematics is in principle applied, but some disagree.

matter, *n.* the stuff of which things are made. Some pre-Socratic speculations as to the nature of this stuff extended to the cause of changes in it. According to ANAXAGORAS, the predominant characteristics of things change under the influence of NOUS, mind. For PARMENIDES, there was only one thing, ungenerated and imperishable, timeless, indivisible and motionless. This brought natural philosophy to a stop, because one cannot deduce the world as we experience it from a motionless unitary being. In quite different ways Parmenides influenced LEUCIPPUS and DEMOCRITUS, on the one hand, and PLATO, on the other.

According to Leucippus and Democritus, in addition to 'what is' (Parmenides's 'one being') there is 'what is not' (a void with a separate existence of its own). Given a void, there can be a plurality of things, since there is something to keep them apart, and there can be movement of the things in the void. Hence, as ARISTOTLE put it (325 a 25), 'Leucippus thought he had a theory which harmonized with sense-perception and would not abolish either coming-to-be and passing-away or motion'. Leucippus patterned his plurality of things on Parmenides's one indivisible being, and hence was regarded as the first atomist (see ATOMISM). The atoms have no SENSIBLE qualities, but when aggregates of them interact with those of sentient bodies such apparent qualities arise. No extraneous moving CAUSE, like the *nous* of Anaxagoras, is invoked, and even man's soul is explained atomistically. Thus this early atomism is a MATERIALISM both as a theory about the stuff of which things are made and as a theory that denies the independent existence of MIND.

Parmenides's 'one being' was the pattern, also, for Plato's eternal intelligible FORMS, but these are certainly not stuff of which things are made. By the time he wrote the *Timaeus* Plato had come to accept that there are Forms of fire, water and earth. These Forms are, in Plato's terminology, 'copied' in the sensible world, but the 'copies' of them are not sensible fire, water and earth conceived of as *things*. They are, rather, the fieriness, the wateriness, and the earthiness of some other 'thing'. Plato calls this other thing, onto which the Form is copied, a 'receptacle' for the copy (*Timaeus* 49a). It must be devoid of character, lest the characters it is to receive get distorted. We shall not be far wrong, Plato says, 'in thinking of it as an invisible and formless being which receives all things and in some mysterious way partakes of the intelligible, and is most incomprehensible' (51a–b). He concludes that it is *space*.

Aristotle's use of the term 'matter', in talk of the 'matter and form' of something, can be explained more readily by reference to Plato than to the Pre-Socratics. To Aristotle it seemed that Plato's self-confessed state of unclarity about how to talk of sensible things and their characteristics called for a new conceptual scheme in which individual sensible things come first, and Forms and space second. 'Matter' was now correlated with a new sense of 'form' (with a small 'f', to indicate that the new 'forms' are not, like Plato's Forms, 'separate' from sensible things). Whereas for Plato the primary things are intelligible Forms, and sensible things are merely copies of them in a receptacle, space, for Aristotle substances 'in the truest and primary and most definite sense of that word' are individual sensible things in various, related, places. These individual things are of a certain matter and have a certain form. 'Matter' is a relative term: the matter which, given a certain form, is a certain thing, a dress, has itself a form, cloth; hence one can ask of what more basic matter any matter consists. The notions of matter and form closely match those of potentiality and actuality: as regards the matter, the cloth, of a dress, there is the potentiality of a table-cloth, curtains and so on; the actuality is the dress, the form the cloth has in fact taken. Matter cannot exist without a form, so actuality is prior to potentiality. Aristotle associates this with the view that everything exists for the sake of an end.

Whereas Aristotle, reacting against Plato, gave us the 'matter' of 'matter and form', DESCARTES, reacting against Aristotle, Plato and, in some respects, the Pre-Socratic atomists, gave us the 'matter' of 'matter and mind'. He rejected Aristotle's view that the world has in it things of many different natural kinds, each having its own intelligible ESSENCE prescribing the ends towards which things of that kind develop. He rejected Plato's view that space is 'most incomprehensible'. While he accepted much of the atomism of Leucippus and Democritus he rejected their opposition of matter and space (the void), maintained that matter is infinitely divisible, and exempted the mind from explanation in atomistic terms.

PYTHAGORAS tried to use his discovery that there is a numerical basis for musical concordances as a key to understanding all nature. The equivalent for Descartes of Pythagoras's discovery of acoustic theory was his discovery of analytical geometry, which shows how every geometrical object or relation can be given numerical expression. Assuming that physical space has the same properties as geometrical space, Descartes realised that if EXTENSION in space is the essence of matter, and if belief in the PROPOSITIONS of MATHEMATICS is justified, then Pythagoras is right and the universe is wholly penetrable by human reason. Everything will be explicable mechanically, in terms of CORPUSCLES of matter in MOTION, except mind.

In sharp contrast with Aristotle's 'primary substances' (individuals of innumerable natural kinds, each developing towards its own end), Descartes's corpuscles of matter, with their one essence, extension, are inert, without energy. In Descartes's philosophy, GOD, as the originator of the motions of the corpuscles of matter and the author of the LAWS OF NATURE according to which they move supplants the FINAL

CAUSES which Aristotle had paradoxically said 'come first' (639 b 15, cf. *Physics* II 8). One reaction against Descartes's view on the ELEMENTS of the material world was that of LEIBNIZ, for whom substances are soul-like extensionless centres of energy, and the material space–time world mere APPEARANCE, albeit *phenomenon bene fundatum*.

One other philosophical use of the term 'matter' deserves mention. KANT, like Aristotle, distinguished between 'matter' and 'form', but in the context of his TRANSCENDENTAL IDEALISM, in which there is a distinction between how things appear to us and how they are in themselves. In an appearance, he said, there is matter and form. Matter is that in the appearance which corresponds to SENSATION, and is given to us A POSTERIORI; form, on the other hand, 'must lie ready for the sensations A PRIORI in the mind' (*Critique of Pure Reason* A20). As for things in themselves, Kant held that I cannot think of them as having any properties 'save only those which my inner sense presents to me' (A266), namely ones analogous to thinking. This, Kant thought, was what had led Leibniz to postulate a plurality of 'simple subjects with powers of representation'. Kant admits the possibility, with this in mind, that what appears to us as matter 'is in itself the possessor of thoughts' (A359), but this, for him, was something that could never be known.

Natural scientists developed the concept of matter in other ways. The Cartesian notion of inert, impenetrable corpuscles, moving one another by impulsion, has gone. NEWTON recognized forces of attraction and repulsion. EINSTEIN held that in some circumstances matter and energy are mutually transformable.

meaning, *n.* **1.** causal meaning, as in 'the meaning of red skies at night' (see CAUSE).

2. linguistic meaning, as in talk of the different meanings of 'She was drawing on the bank'. This is a property of words and sentences, but not a property they have by themselves: they do not mean as such, but mean something to somebody. This holds even for those areas of LOGIC that are primarily concerned not with meaning (SEMANTICS) but with structure (syntax); symbols assembled by mathematicians and logicians are not in themselves meaningful, but are given meaning by certain stipulations about how we are to take them and their combinations. Indeed, a 'symbol' is not complete until this has been done. Of course, we cannot always say who decided, and when, that a certain symbol has this or that meaning. We are born into speech

MEANING

communities in which the linguistic symbols in action have developed over time, and we grow up taking the whole set for granted.

However, meaning is not SUBJECTIVE, something in the MIND of the individual. We can tell when communication is successful, so the meaning of a word is not a Lockean idea (see LOCKE).

Is meaning, then, something OBJECTIVE, the OBJECT to which the expression refers? No, since two different expressions, for example 'the morning star' and 'the evening star', may in fact refer to the same object, the planet Venus, though the user of them may not know this. If we call the reference 'the meaning', people could be ignorant of what they mean by what they say. FREGE allowed this consequence, and distinguished between the reference of an expression, which he called its meaning, and the 'sense'. To someone who does not know that the morning star and the evening star are the same body, the two expressions have different senses, although they have the same meaning (objective reference).

We talk, also, of the meaning of whole sentences, such as 'The morning star is shining'. Frege applied his sense/reference distinction to sentences. For him, the thought contained in the sentence 'The morning star is shining' stands to the sentence as the sense of the expression 'the morning star' stands to the expression. Moreover, the 'truth value' of the sentence stands to the sentence as the reference of the expression 'the morning star' stands to the expression. Hence a declarative sentence (stating that something is so) is 'to be regarded as a proper name, and its meaning . . . is either the True or the False' (Peter Geach and Max Black (eds) *Translations from the Philosophical Writings of Gottlob Frege*, Oxford, 1952, 63). Hence 'on the one hand all true sentences have the same meaning and so, on the other hand, do all false sentences' (*ibid.*, 65).

Intuitively more acceptable is WITTGENSTEIN's 'To understand a proposition means to know what is the case, if it is true' (*Tractatus Logico-Philosophicus*, London, 1922, 4.024). How do we establish that something is the case? In 1929 Wittgenstein said that the meaning of a statement is the method of its verification (*Wittgenstein and the Vienna Circle*, Conversations recorded by Friedrich Waismann, edited by Brian McGuinness, Oxford, 1979, 47). Waismann applied this to propositions about other people's EMOTIONS: 'A proposition cannot say more than is established by means of its verification. If I say "My friend is angry" and establish this in virtue of his displaying a certain perceptible behaviour, I only *mean* that he displays that behaviour' (*ibid.*, 244). This is philosophical BEHAVIOURISM, the product of applying the verification principle (see LOGICAL POSITIVISM) to propositions about people's feelings.

Wittgenstein saw that verificationism leads to behaviourism. He saw, also, that verificationism fits a particular view of language, the view that 'language always serves the same purpose: to convey thoughts—which may be about houses, pains, good and evil, or anything else you please' (*Philosophical Investigations*, Oxford, 1953, Pt. I, 304). He saw that we must reject this view. Someone who cries 'Help' is not doing so to convey his thoughts; he is not describing his mental state (*ibid.*, 24). The speaking of language is 'part of an activity, or of a form of life' (23). There are countless different kinds of use of what we call 'symbols', 'words', 'sentences': asking questions, thanking, cursing, greeting, praying. This multiplicity contrasts with what logicians, including his earlier self, have said about language. In short, 'don't ask for the meaning, ask for the use'.

This is advice which some later philosophers have not found easy to take. The attempt to find a philosophical explanation of linguistic meaning has continued.

medieval philosophy, *n*. The last sentence of a short tract on the Holy Trinity, by BOETHIUS (*c.*480–524) reads: 'As far as you are able, join faith to reason'. Since the 'faith' was the faith of Christian revelation, and 'reason', at the time, stood mainly for pagan Greek philosophy, it is understandable that Boethius should qualify his injunction with 'As far as you are able'. The history of medieval philosophy is largely the history of this ability. At first, the main representative of Greek philosophy was PLATO, as seen through the eyes of PLOTINUS (205–270). When Latin translations of Aristotle's more theoretical works became available in the late 12th and early 13th centuries, and Aristotle became 'the philosopher', the challenge to join faith to reason was taken up anew. It was only when 'reason', in the writings of Francis BACON, Thomas HOBBES, René DESCARTES, and others, came to mean something quite other than, and even opposed to, Greek philosophy, that medieval philosophy was at an end and modern philosophy (divorced from theology) began.

Meinong, Alexis (1853–1920), Austrian philosopher, who studied at Vienna under F. BRENTANO and became professor at Graz. His psychology was influenced by his teacher, and he held that when we think, our minds are directed to (or intend) certain OBJECTS that do not all of them exist but nevertheless are OBJECTS of thought. An example is a

square circle, which is an impossible object, to which the law of CON-
TRADICTION (that a PROPOSITION is either true or false) does not apply.
Quite in general, we can think of things that do not exist, namely
those whose naming involves a false proposition, for example, of
centaurs (no beings exist that have a human torso and a bovine under-
carriage). Moreover, in his *On Assumptions* (1902), he states that the
object of a judgement is an 'objective', something that the thinker
entertains in thought, which is one way of side-stepping what was later
called the problem of counterfactual hypotheticals (assumed statements
known to be false). An objective as such does not depend on someone
entertaining it. The theory of objectives also enters his discussion of
values, since what he regards as basic here are value-feelings the object
of which is an objective (in his technical sense).

Melissus, see ELEATICISM.

memory and imagination. Remembering differs from imagining in
both of two senses of 'imagine'. First, 'Can you remember clothes
being rationed (in Britain in the Second World War)?' differs from
'Can you imagine clothes being rationed?' Second, 'He remembers
clothes being rationed' differs from 'He thinks he remembers, but
really he only imagines it from having heard us talk about it; he was
too young at the time to realize what was happening'.

Consideration of the second difference has led some philosophers to
say that 'to remember an event, a person must not only represent and
have experienced it, but also his experience of it must have been
operative in producing a state or successive states in him finally
operative in producing his representation' (C. B. Martin and M.
Deutscher, 'Remembering', *Phil. Review*, 75, 1966). Other philosophers (e.g. N. Malcolm, *Memory and Mind*, New York, 1977) have
questioned the need for a causal CRITERION.

Empiricist philosophers (see EMPIRICISM) have assumed not only the
NECESSITY of a representation (i.e. that someone could not answer
'Yes', from memory, to 'Was there clothes-rationing?' without
something having come to mind which represents it) but also that the
question 'How do I know whether I am remembering or imagining?'
is a sensible one, and, furthermore, that the answer must be in terms of
the alleged representation, which they call an 'IDEA' or 'image'. HUME,
for example, wrote: 'A man may indulge his fancy in feigning any past
scene of adventure; nor would there be any possibility of distinguishing this from a remembrance of a like kind were not the ideas of
the imagination fainter and more obscure' (*Treatise*, I iii 5). And

Bertrand RUSSELL wrote that whereas memory images 'feel very familiar', imagination images 'feel strange' (*Analysis of Mind*, London, 1921, p. 161). These are different versions of the empiricist theory of memory (criticised by R. F. Holland in 'The Empiricist Theory of Memory', *Mind*, 63, 1954).

If what is at issue in the question 'How do I know whether I am remembering or imagining?' is the second difference (that between remembering and only thinking one remembers) then the question is a sensible one, to be answered by, for example, asking one's parents whether one had had occasion to notice the event at the time. Such things as the strength or faintness of an image cannot be directly relevant; someone who had recently been reading about an event might be able to imagine it much more vividly than someone who remembered it.

If what is at issue concerns the first of the two senses of 'imagine' then the question hardly seems sensible. If someone who says 'I remember clothes-rationing' is asked 'What is it about the representation which justifies your saying you remember, as opposed to imagine, suppose, expect or merely believe?' then the reasonable response is 'Why do you suppose I have no right to say I remember unless there is what you call a representation, and something qualitative about it that is peculiar to memory? Isn't it enough that I have learnt English, and so know the use of "remember", "imagine", "suppose", and so on?' See KNOWLEDGE.

Merleau-Ponty, Maurice (1908–1961), French philosopher, professor at the Collège de France from 1953, who developed an existential (see EXISTENTIALISM) PHENOMENOLOGY, opposed both to the DUALISM of DESCARTES and to HUSSERL'S attempt at leaving questions of existence to one side. Moreover, he rejects SARTRE'S existential dualism of being-in-itself as contrasted with being-for-itself (roughly MATTER and MIND respectively). Hence for him we must base our enquiries on a descriptive account of perceptual EXPERIENCE, allowing that this involves a world of which we have it. Thus he does away with the strict contrast between 'inner' and 'outer', since this inevitably leads us back into dualism. In his *Phenomenology of Perception* (1945) he develops a psychology of PERCEPTION that emphasises the role of the body in perceptual experience, while criticizing traditional accounts, especially SENSE-DATUM theories. In his ethical theories (see ETHICS) he lays stress on the political aspect of moral action, somewhat in a Marxist vein, but insists (as MARX does not) on the vital role of the moral individual.

He rejects the Marxist notion of historical study as scientifically predictive, taking the existentialist view that men make choices that we often cannot foresee.

metalanguage, *n.* a language beyond the original one, in which to talk about the latter. For example, grammar gives an account of how language is built up. In doing this, it involves a metalanguage, the words of which may also figure in the particular object-language at issue. Thus the grammatical word 'verbal' is also a word of ordinary English.

metaphysics, *n.* (from Greek *meta* after, *physica* natural things) so called because early editors of ARISTOTLE put his book on 'first philosophy' after that on 'nature' (physics). It is a branch of enquiry that deals with fundamental questions about BEING (what is involved in saying that something is) and about what kinds of things there are in the world. Different thinkers have taken the term more or less widely, some including under it questions that are now treated under EPISTEMOLOGY (theory of KNOWLEDGE). In any case, since the enquiry is very general and in a sense has to underpin everything else in the world, it proceeds in a general and somewhat abstract manner, seeking to lay bare the logical structure of things. Much of this has been speculative throughout the history of philosophy. The object of this, as indeed of any speculative effort, is somehow to account for what happens in nature and in human affairs. In one sense, if we are to interact with the world we inhabit, we must make some assumptions, although we may be more or less astute in doing so. To that extent, we are all our own metaphysicians, even if we are not usually aware of it. The early Greek philosophers asked some metaphysical questions that have occupied thinkers ever since. In their enquiries they were concerned about the constitution of nature and tried to see it in terms of some underlying stuff or principle, which through a few general processes formed all that can be found in the world. Some thought that reality was an ever transient becoming (HERACLITUS), while others held that it was static and one (PARMENIDES). PLATO sought to reconcile these views in terms of the THEORY OF FORMS, according to which these are each of them one and unchanging, while EXPERIENCE is of a changing world in which opposed FORMS, such as large and small, are confounded. Aristotle, on the other hand, regarded the forms as being in the particular things that exhibit them (what the Medievals expressed by saying that universals are in things). Neo-Platonist metaphysics elaborates the Platonic system into a complicated hierarchy of connected realms that is to account for the world. Medieval thinkers developed these strains in a mainly speculative manner. With DESCARTES, a new approach begins, in that he insists on a rigorous foundation of the subject, rather than allowing the speculative excesses of the later Medievals: everything must be reduced to CLEAR and distinct mental pictures, which then precludes further doubt. This quasi-scientific procedure is followed in principle by the rationalist philosophers of the 17th and 18th centuries too (see RATIONALISM). At the same time, those who reject this approach tend to be pushed into a position of SCEPTICISM, notably with HUME. A new stage is reached with KANT, who rejects both what he calls the dogmatic and the sceptical orientations. Rather, he favours a critical treatment, starting with an examination of our own rational equipment and powers. Speculative metaphysics is for him no more than idle vapourings, indeed impossible. His account, however, leads him to treat all our possible experience as consisting of appearances (phenomena) behind which loom 'things in themselves' (noumena) of which we can know nothing. HEGEL rejects this distinction and develops an OBJECTIVE form of IDEALISM according to which reality is what in the end is fully grasped by the human MIND. One of the excrescences of this approach is a rather fanciful philosophy of nature which was vigorously opposed by 19th century scientists and led to the logical positivist doctrine (MACH, the VIENNA CIRCLE) which spurns such metaphysical speculation and bases its own approach on the apprehension of protocol or simple observation statements as the only foundation of our grasp of the world. This leaves LOGIC and MATHEMATICS somewhat out on a limb, as indeed scientific theory as well: these have to be accommodated more or less artificially. One development from this leads to an attempt at coping with the world by examining how we usually talk about it. This linguistic analysis has the drawback that it tacitly assumes language to be a static feature of our lives. Moreover, much of it is rather narrowly tied to the native language of the enquirer. This makes a genuine study of language impossible. In a sense, the question has not advanced much beyond Aristotle. We all need a first philosophy, even if it often remains implicit. The philosopher tries to lay bare these assumptions. What they must ultimately do is to enable us to give a tenable account of the world, consistent in itself and with what goes on in and around us. At this point philosophic enquiry is the same in kind as that involved in the construction of scientific theories.

Milesian school (c.600–c.525 BC), comprising THALES, ANAXIMANDER, and ANAXIMENES, of Miletus (hence 'Milesian'). All three men sought to explain the natural world otherwise than by reference to the mythical activities of anthropomorphic gods. Moreover, the material for most of their explanations (but not for Anaximander's explanation in terms of a 'boundless' *arche*) came from their experience of natural things, such as water (Thales) or air (Anaximenes). On the other hand, they thought of the material as living. That is, they were 'hylozoists' (from Greek *hyle* matter, *zoe* life).

Mill, James (1773–1836), father of the philosophically more famous JOHN STUART MILL whose severe upbringing by his father is described in J. S. Mill, *Autobiography* (1873). In his *Analysis of the Phenomena of the Human Mind* (1829) James Mill sought to perfect the doctrine of the ASSOCIATION OF IDEAS, that had been propounded by HUME and HARTLEY. In ETHICS he was a disciple of JEREMY BENTHAM.

Mill, John Stuart (1806–1873), born in London, son of the Scottish historian of India, and philosopher, JAMES MILL (1773–1836), by whom he was educated in, among other things, the principles of British EMPIRICISM and Benthamite UTILITARIANISM. Like his father he worked for the East India Company, being in charge of the company's relations with the native states (1836–1856), and head of the examiner's office from 1856 until the powers of the company were transferred in 1858. In 1830 he met Mrs Harriet Taylor to whom, he says in his *Autobiography* (London, 1873) he owed none of his technical doctrines but many of his liberal ideas for the individual and society. He married her, after her husband died, in 1851. She died in 1858. In *On Liberty* (London, 1859) he defended liberal views they had shared, such as that 'the sole end for which mankind are warranted, individually or collectively, in interfering with the liberty of action of any of their number, is self-protection'. He served as an independent Member of Parliament for Westminster (1865–68) and proposed votes for women as an amendment to Disraeli's Franchise Bill. He died where he and Harriet had spent much of their time together, in Avignon, France, in 1873.

The book which established Mill as a philosopher was his *System of Logic* (2 vols, 6 books, London, 1843), described in its full title as 'a connected view of the principles of evidence and the methods of scientific investigation'. Mill attacked INTUITIONISM, rather as LOCKE had attacked the doctrine of INNATE IDEAS. Only in INDUCTION, the main pillar of which is the law of causation, is there real progress of thought, and the law of causation is 'but the familiar truth that invariability of succession is found by observation to obtain between every fact in nature and some other fact which has preceded it' (*Logic*, III v 5). This way of putting it makes the 'finding by observation' that facts in nature have other facts as invariable antecedents seem easy, but, Mill says, 'the order of nature, as perceived at a first glance, presents at every instant a chaos followed by another chaos' and 'we must learn to see in the chaotic antecedent a multitude of distinct antecedents, in the chaotic consequent a multitude of distinct consequents' (III vii 1). To learn to see this is 'a rare talent', and only when it has been exercised can one apply four 'methods of experimental inquiry' he propounds, to eliminate the antecedents of a fact which are not invariable, and to discover its cause.

At the end of Book 6 ('On the logic of the moral sciences') he declares (VI xii 7), without trying to justify it, that there is a general principle to which all rules of practice ought to conform; namely that of 'conduciveness to the happiness of mankind, or rather, of all sentient beings'. For example, we should keep our promises not because we can see intuitively the truth of the precept, but because it passes the utilitarian test. Mill sought to justify this view in his *Utilitarianism* (London, 1863), which critics say involves various fallacies, including what G. E. MOORE calls 'the NATURALISTIC FALLACY' of inferring a moral or 'non-natural' conclusion from 'naturalistic' premises about what people desire. Mill's version of utilitarianism differed from BENTHAM's in that he recognised both quantitative and qualitative differences between pleasures.

Mill commented at length on the views of many of his predecessors and contemporaries. In his *Examination of Sir William Hamilton's Philosophy* (London, 1865) there is a classic formulation of PHENOMENALISM. Mill explains our belief in an external world in terms of two things: that we can expect to have certain SENSATIONS if certain conditions are fulfilled, and that there are laws of ASSOCIATION OF IDEAS. MATTER, he said, 'may be defined, a Permanent Possibility of Sensation'. No such phenomenalist ANALYSIS of MIND is possible: expectations and memories cannot be reduced to present sensations. In the mind itself we have finally arrived at something that cannot be explained in terms of EXPERIENCE.

mind, *n.* in PLATO the term means either what has KNOWLEDGE, which is of what is eternal and hence rare ('mind is the attribute of the gods and of very few men' (*Timaeus*, 51d)); or what 'sets everything in order and arranges each individual thing in the way that is best for it'

(*Phaedo*, 97c)). ARISTOTLE'S use is linked with his theory of sense-PERCEPTION. The sense, or sense-organ, receives the SENSIBLE FORM without the MATTER. For example, when someone puts his hand in hot water his hand becomes hot but it does not become water. Only the form, the quality of heat, is taken in. The matter of a sense-organ is such that it can take in only certain forms. The eye can take in colours but not sounds. Mind, on the other hand, is not limited in what it can take in, so is not itself a combination of matter and form. Before it thinks, it is not actually any real thing; but potentially it is 'whatever is thinkable' (*De Anima*, 429 b 30). 'Mind as passive' 'is what it is by virtue of becoming all things'. But there is also 'mind as active', which 'is what it is by virtue of making all things' (*ibid.*, 430 a 15). Mind as passive is destructible, but mind as active is immortal and eternal.

'For DESCARTES, mind is the SUBSTANCE in which thought resides, thought being 'everything that is within us in such a way that we are IMMEDIATELY aware of it'. Since a person can be immediately aware only of what is in his own mind, mind is inescapably subjective or private (see PRIVACY) (*Arguments proving the existence of God*, etc., Definitions I and VI). Thoughts have 'objective reality'; that is, they are not just private mental events; like aches and pains they relate beyond themselves to something objective (*Third Meditation*). Since mind and body are two distinct substances, the mind can survive the death of the body (*Meditations*, Synopsis).

There is a problem about how mind and body, being distinct substances, join together to form a person (*Sixth Meditation*). A man, having a mind, differs from a machine: 'It is a supreme perfection in man that he acts voluntarily, that is freely; this makes him in a special way the author of his actions and deserving of praise for what he does' (*Principles of Philosophy*, Pt. I, Sect. 37).

Post-Cartesian philosophers have agreed or disagreed with each of these features of Descartes's conception of mind.

LOCKE held that a person's thoughts 'are all within his own breast, invisible and hidden from others' (*Essay*, III ii 1), and that it makes sense to ask 'How is it that a person can say what he himself believes, expects, hopes, etc.?'. He described believing, expecting, etc., as 'internal operations', said that a person observes them by 'reflection' (introspection), and said that reflection 'though it be not sense, as having nothing to do with external objects, yet it is very like it, and might properly enough be called internal sense' (*ibid.*, II i 4).

Wittgenstein rejected the question to which 'by internal sense' was Locke's answer. Utterances like 'I hope he'll come' are not reports about what I have observed internally; they are AVOWALS (see MEANING, RYLE).

BRENTANO agreed with Descartes that thoughts relate beyond themselves to objects: 'Every mental phenomenon is characterised by . . . the intentional (or mental) inexistence of an object' (*Psychology from an Empirical Standpoint*, ed. McAlister, London, 1973, 88) (see INTENTIONALITY).

Some think that a belief in CARTESIAN DUALISM is needed for a belief in IMMORTALITY; others do not.

P. F. Strawson rejects Descartes's DUALISM in favour of a form of MONISM: 'What I mean by the concept of a person is the concept of a type of entity such that *both* predicates ascribing states of consciousness *and* predicates ascribing corporeal characteristics, a physical situation, etc., are equally applicable to a single individual of that single type' (*Individuals*, London, 1959, Ch. 3). Compare Descartes on the union of mind and body as the ordinary man sees it: 'There is one single person who has at once body and consciousness, so that this consciousness can move the body and be aware of the events that happen to it' (Letter to Princess Elizabeth of Bohemia, 28 June 1643).

Unlike Descartes, HARTLEY held that our actions have mechanical causes, namely MOTIVES, so that we do not have 'what is generally termed free-will' (*Observations on Man*, Pt. 1, Conclusion 'Containing some remarks on the mechanism of the human mind'). T. H. HUXLEY held that the brain operates on mechanical principles, and that the mind is no more than an 'epiphenomenon' (see EPIPHENOMENALISM).

In one respect some machines are like minds: the workings of computers, for example, are described in terms of 'information' and 'memory'. It has been said that the relation of mind to brain is that of software to hardware in a computer. Such REDUCTIONISM ignores what Descartes said about people being aware of their thoughts, and about man being 'the author of his . . . actions and deserving of praise for what he does'. Computers are only automata; as Descartes remarked, we praise not automata, but their designers. See MIND–BODY PROBLEM, OTHER MINDS PROBLEM, PSYCHOLOGY, PSYCHOANALYSIS, SOUL.

mind–body problem, *n. phr.* the question how MIND and body are related. Are they two different things (DUALISM), or two 'aspects' of one thing (MONISM), or what? For ancient Greek philosophers the question arose when they distinguished between eternal INTELLIGIBLE things (PLATO's 'FORMS') and transient SENSIBLE things. Plato is a dualist for saying that before birth and after death the soul can have an apprehension of the Forms that is pure because then the soul is 'separate and independent of the body' (*Phaedo* 67a), the bodily senses being an impediment to such apprehension. The question of how mind and body can interact became pressing only when, with DESCARTES, the body had become a 'SUBSTANCE', and the mind a different kind of substance, the two having nothing in common save their dependence for existence on GOD. The mind–body problem, as it occurs in modern philosophy, starts with Descartes.

If the mind is a substance, then ordinary utterances like 'I think it will rain' become reports of mental events. Awareness of these is said to be 'IMMEDIATE', as opposed to the awareness of material things, which is inferential, based on having sensations of them. However, this immediate awareness is also said to be like sense, except that it is internal (LOCKE, *Essay*, II i 4). 'Internal' is a metaphor, the literal meaning being that only one person, the speaker, can be aware of his mental event of thinking it will rain. His access to his own mental events is 'privileged'. Saying that the awareness is like sense leads to talk of 'mental phenomena'. To those who accept these consequences there is no question that there are mental events; the only question is how mental events, or phenomena, cause, and are caused by, certain physical or physiological events, namely, what happens in the brain.

Descartes suggested that mind and brain interact causally through a gland in the brain called the 'pineal gland'. However, this does not tell us how interaction takes place. The model of causation with which scientists had come to operate was that of one body propelling another. The mind, being immaterial, cannot be in spatial contact with, and so cannot propel, anything. When this point was put to him (by a correspondent, Princess Elizabeth of Bohemia, in a letter dated 6–16 May 1643) Descartes replied that we can have some understanding of how mind and body interact in virtue of having a notion of their 'union', a notion we acquire 'just by means of ordinary life and conversation, by abstaining from meditating and from studying things that exercise the imagination' (Descartes to Elizabeth, 28 June 1643). i.e. 'shut up!'

Others have taken this further in various ways. Roughly, treatments of the problem can be divided into those that develop Descartes's CONCEPT of substance (one independently existing substance, GOD, and two dependent substances, mind and MATTER), and those that avoid substance terminology but accept a consequence of mind being a substance, namely that there are 'mental events' or 'mental processes'. Finally, there are those who say that the mind should not be taken as a substance, so that the above consequences disappear.

The theory which departs least from that of Descartes is OCCASIONALISM. Propounded by GEULINCX (1624–1669), MALEBRANCHE (1639–1715), and others, it is the theory that mind and body do not act at all; only God acts. On the occasion (hence 'occasionalism') of a certain sort of brain-event God decrees that there should be an appropriate mental event (say, a 'SENSATION'), and on the occasion of a mental event (say, a 'VOLITION') God decrees that there should be an appropriate brain-event. Malebranche explained Descartes's 'union' in terms of God's action (*Dialogues on Metaphysics and Religion*, 1688, trans. M. Ginsberg, London, 1923). Two theories involving the concept of substance, but not Descartes's concept, are those of LEIBNIZ (1646–1716) and SPINOZA (1632–1697). Leibniz held that there are many soul-like substances of different orders. Lower-order substances comprise the reality of a body. There is a pre-established harmony between substances, hence the appearance of causal interaction between minds and bodies. This harmony seemed to Leibniz to provide the true 'explanation of that great mystery "the union of the soul and the body"', and to be preferable to occasionalism (*Discourse on Metaphysics*, written 1686, Section 33). For Spinoza, there was only one substance, God, with an infinity of attributes. A human mind and body are modifications of two of the attributes of this one substance, related through the mind being the 'idea' whose 'object' is the body. This was Spinoza's account of 'what must be understood by the union of the mind and the body' (*Ethics*, published posthumously 1677, Part 2, Prop. 13).

The spirit, but not the technical terms, of Spinoza's theory is retained in the 'DOUBLE-ASPECT THEORY', which is Spinozism without God, and with attributes replaced by aspects. Mental activities 'present two aspects: an outer one which consists of a complex of brain activity and is on principle, at least, externally observable; and an inner one, the various experiences which the person has, and can introspect, in the actual performance of these activities' (G. M. Wyburn, R. W. Pickford, R. J. Hirst, *Human Senses and Perception*, Edinburgh, 1964, p. 321). What is the thing of which the outer and inner aspects are aspects? The theory provides no answer. We tend to say either that the mind is the thing, and the brain an aspect of it (spiritualism), or that the brain is the thing, and the mind an aspect of it (materialism). The latter leads to the theory that mental events are in fact identical with neural events (the so-called 'IDENTITY' HYPOTHESIS); but in what sense of 'identical'? Opponents object that someone who says 'I think it will rain' is talking about the possibility of rain, not about what is going on in his brain. Adherents (e.g. J. J. C. Smart, 'Sensations and Brain Processes' *Phil. Review*, LXVIII, 1959, 141–156) meet this objection with a theory about the 'reference' of what a person says. If thoughts are in fact brain processes, then, in saying 'I think it will rain', I am talking about a brain process, even if I might not know that I am.

Are the Cartesians right in thinking that 'I think it will rain' is a report of a mental event, i.e. an event which the speaker has observed by what 'might properly enough be called internal sense' (Locke)? (Only if they are, does the further question, 'Is the mental event in fact identical with a brain process?', arise.) Two recent philosophers who think that the Cartesians are not right are RYLE (1900–1976) and WITT-GENSTEIN (1889–1951). Ryle is particularly critical of the notion of PRIVILEGED ACCESS (*The Concept of Mind*, London, 1949); Wittgenstein, of the notion that an utterance like 'I think it will rain' has meaning as a report of a private mental event or process (*Philosophical Investigations*, Oxford, 1953, I 304–342). For someone who finds Ryle and Wittgenstein convincing on these issues the mind–body problem, in its Cartesian form, does not arise.

miracle, *n.* (from Latin *miraculum* something to be wondered at) an event which seems to run counter to strong expectation and to transgress established LAWS OF NATURE, and is therefore regarded as a manifestation of special divine intervention in the course of events. In a strictly OBJECTIVE sense, there can be no miracles, because the laws of nature cannot be broken. In a psychological sense, it is indeed the case that we are often amazed by a turn of events that we find inexplicable. Thus, one who seemed to be at death's door may make a 'miraculous' recovery.

monad (from Greek *monas* unit) in Greek philosophy generally, an individual; in PYTHAGOREANISM, the unity from which the number system, and hence everything that exists, is derived. In modern philosophy the term is mainly associated with LEIBNIZ. His *Monadology* (1714) contrasts with the substance-philosophy of DESCARTES, and of SPINOZA. Descartes defined (material) substance in terms of EXTENSION. What is extended being infinitely divisible, there are no true units. For Leibniz there are true units, monads. They are soul-like, and extension is merely phenomenal. Spinoza defined substance as that which exists in itself, and is conceived through itself. It followed that there is only one substance, GOD. Leibniz defined substance in terms, not of self-existence, but of activity. There is an infinity of monads. A monad does not interact causally with other monads but is, so to speak, 'programmed' by God to develop in a way which makes its development harmonise with that of other monads.

monism, *n*. either the theory that there is really only one thing, or the theory that there are many things but that they are all of one fundamental kind. SPINOZA's philosophy is a monism in the first of these senses. The one thing is GOD, a SUBSTANCE with infinite ATTRIBUTES, two of which, the mental and the bodily, are known to us. A monism in the second sense is, for example, the MATERIALISM of those who hold that sensations are identical with brain processes. The opposite form of monism to materialism is the theory that the things that appear to us as material are, in themselves, spiritual. A monism which is neutral between the two ('neutral monism') is the theory that MINDS, on the one hand, and bodies, on the other, are differently collected assemblages of things of one kind, SENSATIONS. This theory was advanced by William JAMES and by Bertrand RUSSELL.

Montaigne, Michel Eyquem de (1533–1592), French humanist, whose principal philosophical work, *Apology for Raimond Sebond*, was published in a collection of essays in 1588. Sebond was a 15th century theologian who maintained that the articles of the Christian religion can be established by reason. Despite his work being entitled *Apology* (defence), Montaigne's main contentions were those of SCEPTICISM about the possibility of KNOWLEDGE in general, and of the priority of faith over reason in religion ('FIDEISM'). The scepticism was the Pyrrhonist scepticism of SEXTUS EMPIRICUS, whose writings had recently been translated from the original Greek into Latin, in which language Montaigne was brought up.

Among the questions discussed by Sextus had been those of the CRITERION by which any experience is judged to be veridical, and of what, if anything, differentiates man's rationality from that of the beasts, exhibited in their behaviour. Coming at a time when ARISTOTLE's scientific outlook was under attack, Montaigne's 'new Pyrrhonism' had to be met by those, like GASSENDI and DESCARTES, who sought to replace Aristotelianism with a new outlook.

Moore, George Edward (1873–1958), Cambridge philosopher best known for his rejection of NATURALISM in ETHICS, his defence of common-sense beliefs against IDEALISM, his practice of PHILOSOPHICAL ANALYSIS in his treatment of, in particular, PERCEPTION, and, among aspiring philosophers, his editorship of the philosophical journal, *Mind*, 1921–1947.

His rejection of naturalism in ethics, in his influential first book, *Principia Ethica* (Cambridge, 1903), took the form of accusing philosophers such as the utilitarians (see UTILITARIANISM) of committing 'the NATURALISTIC FALLACY'. This, in effect, is a matter of identifying the 'is' in 'pleasure is good' (the 'is' of attribution) with the 'is' in 'a brother is a male sibling' (the 'is' of IDENTITY). It means, in Moore's terms, identifying a 'non-natural' quality, goodness, with some 'natural' one, such as that of being pleasurable. Years later, in response to criticism by a Cambridge colleague, C. D. Broad, Moore admitted to having not given 'any tenable explanation of what I meant by saying that "good" was not a natural property' (*The Philosophy of G. E. Moore*, ed. P. A. Schilpp, Evanston and Chicago, 1942, p. 582).

In 'The Refutation of Idealism' (*Mind*, 1903, reprinted in *Philosophical Studies*, London, 1922) Moore accused BERKELEY and J. S. MILL of failing to distinguish consciousness and the OBJECT of consciousness. The idealists hold that *esse* is *percipi* (to be is to be perceived) 'solely because *what is experienced* is held to be identical with *the experience* of it'. Experiencing something is an 'act of consciousness'. Whereas the act of consciousness is 'somewhere within my body', what is experienced may be on the surface of a material thing (lecture given in 1910, in *Some Main Problems of Philosophy*, London, 1953, p. 31). In later papers (some of which are collected in *Philosophical Papers*, London, 1959) Moore often returns to his contention that there is an 'act of consciousness' distinct from the object of the act, but does not defend it against objections, such as that no such act is empirically discoverable (Bertrand RUSSELL, *Analysis of Mind*, London, 1921, p. 17).

Moore called the object of the act of consciousness in sense-perception a 'SENSE-DATUM'. His treatment of perception consisted in a series of attempts to discover what precisely is the relation between sense-data and material things.

moral philosophy, see ETHICS.

moral sense, *n.* the ability to grasp and make moral judgments, also called CONSCIENCE. This is a prerequisite for social existence. One who lacks it completely is a psychopath, who will never develop the sense of human sympathy that holds communities together, and is likely to do himself and others pointless harm.

More, Henry (1614–1687), see CAMBRIDGE PLATONISM.

motion, *n.* **1.** generally, any change (ARISTOTLE).

2. more specifically, a change in the spatial location of bodies relative to one another.

motive, *n.* that which moves a person to act in one way rather than another; for example, Socrates to sit, submitting to punishment, rather than to take to his heels and run away (Plato, *Phaedo*, 99a). The phrase 'that which moves a person . . . to sit' might be taken to refer to the contraction and relaxation of muscles. PLATO says it would be absurd to call things like that CAUSES: 'Fancy being unable to distinguish between the cause of a thing and the condition without which it could not be a cause!' Socrates sits because he thinks it best to submit to whatever penalty Athens orders. That is the cause, the 'real reason'. People, not sinews and bones, are 'impelled by a conviction of what is best'.

The same distinction, but expressed in different terminology, is made by recent writers on motivation, such as R. S. Peters (*The Concept of Motivation*, London, 1958). The change in terminology reflects the contraction in the concept of cause so as to exclude what ARISTOTLE called 'FINAL CAUSES'. Things like muscle-movements are now called 'causes', and are contrasted with reasons for actions, such as the wish to submit to punishment, which are called 'motives'. To say that what is done has a point, or is motivated, 'is *ipso facto* to deny that it can be *sufficiently explained* in terms of causes . . . in the sense of *necessary* conditions' (*ibid.*, p. 12).

However, are not motives causes in *some* sense? Are not questions about people's intentions in doing certain things questions about introspectible mental events or states (occurrences of wanting to do something, for some reason) which precede, lead up to, and somehow produce, appropriate bodily MOTIONS? It has been suggested that, rather, they are questions about how people would describe their actions (G. E. M. Anscombe, *Intention*, Oxford, 1959). Whether a motivational explanation is not somehow causal remains controversial (D. Davidson, *Essays on Actions and Events*, Oxford, 1980).

Having reasons is not the same thing as being able to reason. HUME raised the question whether being able to reason, alone, move us to act in one way rather than another, and denied that it does.

musical concordances and the harmony of the spheres, PYTHA-

GORAS (*c*.570–*c*.504 BC) used his discovery that there is a numerical basis for musical concordances as a key to the understanding of all nature.

Vibrations are heard as notes, the pitch of the note being proportional to the frequency of the vibration—the greater the frequency of the vibration, the higher the note. The frequency of the vibration of two similar strings (of the same thickness, under the same tension) is inversely proportional to their length. Two notes of different pitch, heard in succession, may or may not be heard as being the same, in spite of being different in pitch; they are, or are not, 'concordant'. (There was no such thing as harmony in classical Greek music, but to say of two notes, heard in succession, that they are concordant, is equivalent to saying that, heard together, they harmonise.) Two notes are concordant if, and only if, the length of two similar vibrating strings producing them is in the ratio 2:1, 3:2 or 4:3. Notes produced by similar vibrating strings of length in the ratio 2:1 are further apart on the scale of notes (of greater difference in pitch) than ones produced by similar vibrating strings of length in the ratio 3:2. In other words, the concordant interval is greater. The greatest concordant interval (corresponding to strings of lengths in the ratio 2:1) was called, by the Greeks, *diapásón* (and, by us, the octave); the next greatest (3:2), the *dia pente* (the fifth) and the next (4:3), the *diatessaron* (the fourth).

Pythagoras discovered concordant notes—perhaps by using a single string which could be stopped at different intervals by a movable bridge. He probably did not know about frequency; even a century or more later it was common to confuse the frequency of vibration producing a sound and the speed of sound itself (cf. PLATO, *Timaeus* 80a).

Such a confusion may have contributed to the Pythagorean theory of 'the harmony of the spheres': the stars, moving at different speeds in their spherical orbits, produce sounds of different pitch, and the sound is concordant because the speed of the stars, judged by their distances, is in the ratio of the musical consonances (Aristotle, *De Caelo* 291 a 8). It is this view that one finds, with imaginative elaboration, in Plato (*Republic* 616b), in Cicero (*Dream of Scipio*) and in Shakespeare (*Merchant of Venice* V. i. 160–65).

mysticism, *n.* (from Greek *mystikos* secret) is a speculative streak in religion and philosophy, seeking to attain a state of union with GOD and the world, by means that are essentially hidden and arcane. The notion goes back to the mystery cults of Greece, of which those of

Eleusis were the most famous. In philosophy, there is a strong mystical streak in many Neo-Platonic writers, and more recently in the work of existentialists (see NEO-PLATONISM, EXISTENTIALISM). There have been mystical trends in Judaism, Islam and CHRISTIANITY. Christian mysticism has always been one facet of the religion, although more striking at some times than at others. The Church authorities, tending towards orthodox conservatism, have always opposed this tendency, and mystics from within the Church have often been denounced as heretics.

N

naturalistic fallacy, *n.* a term introduced by the Cambridge philosopher, G. E. MOORE (1873–1958), in *Principia Ethica* (1903), to denote what he saw as the mistake of regarding moral properties, such as the goodness of courage, as being natural in the way yellowness is a natural property of buttercups. Supposing happiness to be natural, we would, on Moore's view, commit the naturalistic fallacy if we analysed 'courage is good' as meaning simply that courage is, on the whole, conducive to happiness. Moore was criticised by his Cambridge colleague, C. D. Broad, for not making the MEANING of 'natural' and 'non-natural' clear. He accepted the criticism, saying: 'I agree that in *Principia* I did not give any tenable explanation of what I meant by saying that "good" was not a natural property'.

necessary, *n.* needful, as in 'I prepared all things necessary for my journey', or inevitably determined or fixed, either by the operation of causal laws (physical necessity) or by an inherent necessity (absolute or metaphysical necessity). For LEIBNIZ, the Being 'to whose essence existence belongs' (GOD) is metaphysically necessary; the truths of MATHEMATICS are absolutely necessary. On a recent view, inherent necessity is merely conventional: a statement is necessary because of the way we have defined our terms.

necessary and sufficient conditions, for a PROPOSITION to hold, are those other propositions that guarantee its holding. A condition is necessary for *p* if without it *p* cannot hold. A condition is sufficient for *p* if with it *p* must hold. In the process of seeking to establish a proposition *p* we often find that we have various necessary conditions, but lack some items that would make the set sufficient as well, which is usually more difficult to achieve. In geometry we often find that one condition is both necessary and sufficient to guarantee another. Thus, for three points to lie on the same line, it is necessary and sufficient that the area of the triangle having them as vertices be zero. In general, if *p* is necessary for *q*, then *q* is sufficient for *p*; while if *p* is sufficient for *q*, then *q* is necessary for *p*.

negation, *n.* the act of contradicting a PROPOSITION, and by extension, that contradictory itself. The negation of a proposition *p* is *not-p*. If *p* is true, its negation is false, and vice versa. For example, 'all timber will float in water' is in fact false, whereas its negation 'it is not the case that all timber will float', or 'some hardwoods will sink in water', is true. See CONTRADICTION.

neutral monism, see WILLIAM JAMES, MONISM.

Neo-Platonism, *n.* a term we now use for a group of Platonist thinkers of late antiquity, who in fact combined aspects of various ancient philosophies: PLATO, ARISTOTLE, STOICISM and EPICUREANISM. A central figure is PLOTINUS. An influence of Neo-Platonism on later Christian thinking has been to make Christians less willing to make extremely precise dogmatic statements about GOD. We can say what God is not, but not what God is. This is sometimes referred to as 'the Negative Way' of the Neo-Platonists. We can know God in the sense of *becoming one with God*, but not in the sense of *knowing about God*. See AUGUSTINE; RELIGION, PHILOSOPHY OF.

Newton, Isaac (1642–1727), English 'natural philosopher' (physicist), for many years professor of MATHEMATICS at Cambridge and later Master of the Mint in London, was co-inventor (with LEIBNIZ) of the CALCULUS and in his *Principia* (1687) presented a general account of mechanical science, universal gravitation (the famous inverse square law of attraction) and planetary motion. Philosophically, what interests us here is his scientific method. He started from ordinary observation and experimental findings, and then tried to exhibit these in mathematical form as consequences of general laws in particular circumstances. He is often misquoted as despising hypotheses ('*hypotheses non fingo*'—I do not frame hypotheses), but this is merely taking things out of context. What he says is that he has no HYPOTHESIS to give as to what causes gravitation: he is content to proceed from observation and experiment. In his *Optics* (1704) he does indeed advance hypotheses, albeit in a provisional vein. It would indeed be strange if he did not, since that is what we must do to advance science: the principle of universal gravitation was an hypothesis of genius and has become so well confirmed that it is now taken for granted. It was accepted for some 150 years after the publication of Newton's work that all natural phenomena were ultimately explicable in terms of mechanics.

Nicole, Pierre (1625–1695), a French philosopher who collaborated with Antoine ARNAULD on the Logic of the School of Port Royal.

Nietzche, Friedrich (1844–1900), German philosopher and critic of culture, studied at Bonn and was professor of classics at Basle (1870–1878). There he met J. Burckhardt, the historian of art and of the Italian Renaissance. His own works began with a study on *The Birth of Tragedy* (1872), in which he developed his distinction between Apollonian and Dionysian (roughly the rational and the emotional) aspects of Greek life, especially as regards drama. Perhaps his best known book is *Thus Spoke Zarathustra* (1883–1891), a tale written in poetic prose and containing his basic philosophic position. He holds that the one MOTIVE force in human affairs is the will to power. This is best exemplified in a type of human being that has overcome the claims of weakness and attained the status of 'overman' (Übermensch). He was explicitly opposed to CHRISTIANITY as involving a slave morality, and he despised the newly arising mass societies with their egalitarian tendencies. Some have seen him as a precursor of 20th century totalitarian movements: this is quite wrong. He would have been the first to reject them. One of his constant targets for attack was German nationalism as it developed after 1870. As to morality, he came to the conclusion that this is an individual matter and cannot be formulated in general theoretical terms. This is outlined in *Beyond Good and Evil* (1886), where the distinction between the moralities of slave and master is stated. He is under strong Aristotelian influence here and describes his type of master much in the way the Nicomachean Ethics speaks of the magnanimous man (see ARISTOTLE). His literary style is simple and colourful, the very opposite of academic jargon, and his influence on later literature was considerable, as also on modern depth psychology and on existentialist philosophy. See EXISTENTIALISM.

nominal, *adj.* (from Latin *nomen* name) in name only. A nominal definition says what the MEANING of a word, e.g. 'justice', is; a real DEFINITION says what the real ESSENCE of justice is. PLATO believed in real definitions, since he believed in real essences, apprehended by intelligence. LOCKE gave the name 'real essence' to something else, 'the real internal constitution of things on which their discoverable qualities depend' (*Essay*, III iii 15). Locke's 'real essences' are molecular; they would be apprehended by sense, if only we had 'microscopical eyes' (*ibid.*, II xxiii 12), not by intelligence. NOMINALISM is the view that UNIVERSALS are mere names; they are not real entities either in the world or in the MIND.

nominal essence, see NOMINAL, ESSENCE.

nominalism, see ABELARD, HOBBES, WILLIAM OF OCKHAM, UNIVERSALS.

nous, *n.* (*Greek* mind, reason) sometimes thought of as the cause of movement or change. See ANAXAGORAS.

O

object, *n.* that of which we are, or can be, conscious, as opposed to SUBJECT.

objective, 1. *adj.* having a real existence as opposed to a merely SUBJECTIVE one.

2. *n.* that at which someone aims, as in 'His objective was to win the race'.

occasionalism, *n.* the theory that when one event appears to cause another what really happens is that GOD, on the occasion of the first, causes the second: the first event is not the real or primary CAUSE of the second, but only its occasional or secondary cause. The term was introduced by the Cartesian philosopher Louis de la Forge in his *Treatise on the Spirit of Man* (1665), and used by other so-called 'occasionalists', of whom the best known is Nicolas MALEBRANCHE. See, also, Arnold GEULINCX. Some followers of DESCARTES thought it impossible that a MIND (a substance of which the ESSENCE is THINKING) should interact causally with a brain (made of MATTER, the essence of which is EXTENSION). Occasionalism states that they do not really interact; they merely seem to, as a result of GOD willing brain-events on the occasion of mind-events, and vice versa. See MIND–BODY PROBLEM.

Ockham, William of (*c.*1285–1349), born at Ockham, near Guildford in Surrey, was a student at Oxford, entered the Franciscan order, and taught at Oxford from about 1315 to 1323. He gave a course of lectures on Peter Lombard's *Sentences* which was unorthodox in its EMPIRICISM and rejection of the largely Aristotelian philosophy which St Thomas AQUINAS and other philosopher-theologians had adopted in the 13th century. He was therefore summoned to the papal court at Avignon in 1324 to answer charges of heresy. He remained there for four years and in 1328 left Avignon with the General of the Franciscan order, Michael of Cesena, who had opposed the Pope on the doctrine of absolute poverty practised by the Mendicants of the Franciscan order. He was excommunicated and took up residence in Munich under the protection of the Emperor, Louis of Bavaria. It is believed that he died of the Black Death. His most important nonpolitical writings, apart from his lectures on the *Sentences*, known as the *Ordinatio*, were commentaries on some of Aristotle's logical works, and on Porphyry's *Isagoge*, and a systematic treatise entitled *Summa Logicae*.

Ockham is best known for a principle of economy in the choice of explanatory hypotheses, and for rejecting the traditional realist theory of UNIVERSALS in favour of a nominalist theory. The principle of economy, one formulation of which was 'What can be done with fewer assumptions is done in vain with more', became known as 'OCKHAM'S RAZOR'. His rejection of realism in favour of nominalism is one application of the razor, for realism is the theory that the explanation of our being able to use words like 'just' and 'human' of any number of individual things requires the assumption of real, single, definable 'FORMS' or 'ESSENCES', and nominalism seeks to explain our ability without any such assumption. A nominalist (from Latin *nominalis* belonging to a name) holds that universality is a property of names or signs. Ockham's version of nominalism involved a two-fold classification of signs and a theory about two kinds of cognition, one derived from the other.

In addition to the distinction between natural signs (smoke signifies fire) and conventional signs ('smoke' signifies smoke), Ockham distinguished between linguistic and mental signs. A linguistic sign may be a natural sign, as for example when a spoken word signifies that the speaker has a cold. Linguistic signs are conventional in so far as they are intended to mean what they signify. A mental sign, sometimes described as a spiritual directing *(intentio animae)*, is in no language, and hence is not the sort of thing of which it makes sense to talk of understanding or misunderstanding. It can be said to mean primarily what a linguistic sign can mean only secondarily. Moreover, it is a natural sign of what it signifies.

This involves understanding the theory of two kinds of cognition. Intuitive cognition, the immediate awareness either of the objects of the senses or, reflexively, of the mind's activities about them, is basic. From intuitive cognition is derived abstractive cognition, the derivation being such that the CONCEPT involved is not peculiar to a single thing apprehended intuitively. Although the individual things apprehended intuitively (e.g. Socrates and Plato) do not, as the realists assumed, share a common nature, they are similar, and the abstractive concept, of which the linguistic sign is 'man', reflects this similarity. That is, the abstractive concept derived from the intuitive cognition of

Socrates can be used as a sign of Plato, Aristotle, and so on. This mental sign can be used in such a mental PROPOSITION as would correspond to the linguistic proposition 'Man is rational'. (Mental signs are formed to be part of mental propositions.) When so used the mental sign is a universal. The term 'universal' refers secondarily to the corresponding linguistic sign. Unlike the linguistic sign, which is chosen and differs from one linguistic community to another, the mental sign is natural. Just as fire gives rise to smoke, so that smoke is a natural sign of fire, so a certain intuitive cognition gives rise to a certain abstractive cognition, so that the concept involved can serve as a natural sign of all the things that are similar to the one intuitively cognised.

The main problem with this theory is that Socrates and Plato are similar in any number of ways, though some may seem more obvious, or 'natural', than others. They are both philosophers, for example, as well as both being men. A thing has as many characters for anyone as he has words to describe it. Recognition of this may lead one to a different kind of nominalism from Ockham's, one in which his own razor is used on mental signs, and concept-formation is seen as language-acquisition.

The best known and most influential realist theory of universals was Plato's THEORY OF FORMS. The theory was adapted by philosopher-theologians to harmonise with religious faith in a GOD who created the world by making the Forms into ideas in his mind, patterns for his creative enterprise. So adapted, the Platonic theory figures in St AUGUSTINE and in St AQUINAS, though the latter makes it clear that the ideas are not independent of God's essence. Ockham saw this doctrine of ideas in God's mind as a constraint on God's absolute freedom and power to create things just as and how he willed; and he rejected it. The corollary of this rejection, for our KNOWLEDGE of created things, is that we are utterly dependent on EXPERIENCE. There are no necessary connections in nature into which we may hope to have an intellectual insight. ARISTOTLE is sometimes opposed, as an empiricist, to Plato, as a rationalist. Ockham is considerably further on the road to empiricism than Aristotle.

Ockham's version of nominalism led to the philosophy of language of HOBBES and LOCKE, and to the ABSTRACTIONISM of Locke and empiricism of HUME. His rejection of necessary connections in nature formed an element in Hume's treatment of causation. There were other departures from Aristotelianism which found a place in later philosophy. He rejected the Aristotelian conception of matter as potentiality in favour of a view that cleared the way for the Cartesian definition of material substance in terms of spatial EXTENSION, and for the distinction between PRIMARY AND SECONDARY QUALITIES. He rejected the Aristotelian conception of FINAL CAUSES operative in nature. This, together with his rejection of ARISTOTLE'S view of matter and doctrine of essences, left the field clear for attending to EFFICIENT CAUSES, a move which contributed to the scientific revolution of the 17th century. Finally, his rejection of Aristotle's secondary substance, the intelligible essence, cleared the way for acceptance of Aristotle's primary substance, the individual thing, which Ockham conceived in a way that anticipated Locke's conception of substance as a substratum, a 'support of such qualities which are capable of producing simple ideas in us' (*Essay*, II xxiii 1).

Ockham's razor, *n*. the principle of parsimony or economy evident in the NOMINALISM of WILLIAM OF OCKHAM (*c*.1285–1349): entities not known to exist should not be postulated as existing unless absolutely necessary to an explanation of the phenomena. Unnecessary entities should be erased (hence 'razor'). The usual wording, in Latin, of the principle is *Entia non sunt multiplicanda praeter necessitatem* ('Entities are not to be multiplied beyond necessity'), but this wording does not actually occur in Ockham's writings.

ontological argument, *n*. a form of proof for the existence of GOD, first given by ANSELM (1033–1109), Archbishop of Canterbury. If God is defined as that than which nothing greater can be conceived, which he regards clearly as something conceivable, then that thing must have amongst its properties existence, otherwise something greater could be conceived, which is absurd, given the DEFINITION. Hence God so defined must exist. This argument was conclusively refuted by KANT, who denied that existence was a PREDICATE. Rather, it is used to mark synthetic connections between terms. Thus, in the case of the ontological argument, the statement that some being is perfect in every respect is synthetic, not analytic (see ANALYTIC AND SYNTHETIC), and therefore devoid of necessary truth. A very similar approach is evident in RUSSELL'S theory of descriptions (see DESCRIPTIONS, THEORY OF). Various attempts have been made to rescue the ontological argument, none of them sound. In theology, it did not long survive because it was rejected by AQUINAS, who preferred to argue for God's existence from what he took to be the need for a first CAUSE (cosmological argument). In Protestant theology, the existence of God is regarded as not establishable by argument at all; it must be grasped through revelation.

ostensive definition, *n.* the explanation of the MEANING of a term to someone by showing him the things to which the term applies. See DEFINITION.

other minds problem, *n.* the philosophical puzzle of how one can know that there are other minds, given that one can have IMMEDIATE awareness only of the contents of one's own MIND. This has usually been tackled by an argument from analogy: I know, in my own case, that there is a feeling of pain behind the pain-expressing behaviour I exhibit; likewise, it seems reasonable for me to suppose, there is a feeling of pain behind the pain-expressing behaviour I see exhibited by someone else. The reasoning is necessarily based on the observation of a single instance (there being mental phenomena behind the behaviour *I* exhibit), and we cannot discover the conclusion of the argument to be true (any thoughts or feelings of which I had immediate awareness would necessarily be *my* thoughts or feelings, not someone else's).

The problem is presented as one of KNOWLEDGE, like 'How can I know there are invisible currents of electricity behind the electrical behaviour (e.g. if I touch it it gives me a shock) exhibited by this bare wire?', except that nobody can see the currents but I can see the contents of my mind.

What more there is to the problem has been considered by WITTGEN-STEIN and philosophers influenced by him. Behind the knowledge problem there is one of MEANING. How does talk of 'pain' have meaning for me? If 'pain' is a name I give to my own feeling, by a private act of OSTENSIVE DEFINITION, then I should not even be able to *understand* talk of pain I do not feel, never mind *believe* the conclusion of the argument from analogy for other minds, that there exist pains I do not feel.

On what does the meaningfulness of 'I am in pain' depend? In place of the private ostensive definition account Wittgenstein proposes one which explains how 'pain' has a common, public meaning. The meaningfulness depends on there being a natural expression of pain, and a natural reaction to this expression in others: 'Words are connected with the primitive, the natural, expressions of the sensation and used in their place. A child has hurt himself and he cries; and then adults talk to him and teach him exclamations and, later, sentences. They teach the child new pain-behaviour' (*Philosophical Investigations*, I, 244). See AVOWAL, PRIVACY.

P

panpsychism, see ANIMISM.

pantheism, *n.* (from Greek *pan* everything, *theos* God) is a theory that regards GOD as residing in everything, rather than being set above or alongside the world. A modern example of this is SPINOZA's equating God with the world as a whole. On such a view there can be no creation of the world, since that would mean God creating himself.

paradox, *n.* (from Greek *para* alongside, *doxa* belief) is what we call a statement that is 'beyond belief', or against what we should normally expect. Thus, we may obtain strange conclusions from premisses that seem acceptable. This happens, for example, in the paradox of ZENO OF ELEA that MOTION is impossible. What we need to do here is to have another look at our premisses. More puzzling are the PARADOXES that occur in LOGIC. Of these, one is ancient, the so-called 'Liar': a Cretan says that all Cretans are liars. If true, it is false; if false, true. A whole series of paradoxes have surfaced in connection with modern logic. The most famous of these is RUSSELL's paradox of the set of all sets that are not members of themselves: if it is a member of itself, it is not, and if it is not, it is. Can these puzzles be resolved? Many attempts have been made and the question remains controversial. At any rate, each such connundrum has to be tackled in its own detail. One would like to think that with careful attention to the proper formulation of such statements, a way out will show itself. One general point to be remembered is that merely being able to give a verbal DEFINITION of something does not ensure that we finish up with a genuine item. We can give a definition of a round square, but there are none.

Parmenides (*c.*515–*c.*440 BC) of Elea, 70 miles south-east of Naples, the most original and influential metaphysician and epistemologist before PLATO, who named a dialogue after him. The school he founded, of which ZENO OF ELEA and MELISSUS OF SAMOS were members, became known as ELEATICISM.

In a poem, *On Nature*, Parmenides distinguished three ways of enquiry. The first, the way of Truth, is defined by the proposition 'that it *is*, and cannot not be' (Fr. 2). The second, the way of Ignorance is 'that it *is not*, and must necessarily not be' (*ibid*.). What is this 'it'? Judging from an objection to the second way, it is 'whatever is for thinking and saying' (Fr. 6), that is, the object of thought or knowledge. The way of Ignorance is dismissed on the ground that since the OBJECT of thought or KNOWLEDGE can exist, but what is not cannot exist, the object of thought or knowledge must exist (the way of Truth).

Some understanding of the way of Truth can be gleaned by contrasting it with a third way, the way of Seeming. On one plausible interpretation, the way of Seeming is a cosmogony, in opposition to those of ANAXIMANDER, ANAXIMENES, HERACLITUS and the Pythagoreans. However, Parmenides may have meant, by 'the way of Seeming', 'the beliefs of mortals', chief amongst them being that sense-perception is reliable. Now, of what we perceive we may say that it is (at one time, or at one place) *and* is not (at another time, or at another place). That something should be *and* not be, can be seen by reason, as opposed to the senses, to be impossible. Hence change (existence and non-existence at different times) and difference (existence and non-existence in different places) are impossible. Hence the object of thought and knowledge must be unchanging and undifferentiated, a single, eternal, indivisible, homogeneous whole. Parmenides ends his account of the way of Truth by saying that what exists is 'perfect from every angle, equally matched from the middle in every way, like the mass of a well-rounded ball' (Fr. 8.42–44). Taken literally this favours interpreting the way of Truth as a cosmogony, rather than as a plea for the use of reason or intelligence as against the senses.

Parmenides influenced EMPEDOCLES, the atomists (see ATOMISM) (LEUCIPPUS and DEMOCRITUS), and Plato, whose distinction between the FORMS and the SENSIBLE world corresponds to Parmenides' distinction between the objects of the ways of Truth and of Seeming. However, Plato takes account of Heraclitus, and produces a distinction between *being*, 'apprehended by intelligence and reason', and *becoming*, 'conceived by opinion with the help of sensation' (*Timaeus* 27d–28a). In Platonic terms, Parmenides severed all links between the worlds of being and becoming, by construing the former as what can exist and the latter as what cannot. In his THEORY OF FORMS Plato sought to bring the worlds of being and becoming together again. Whether, and how, this can be done, is the subject of his dialogue, *Parmenides*.

Peirce, Charles Sanders (1839–1914), American scientist and philosopher, was the founder of PRAGMATISM. He insisted that the significance of assertions lay in whatever practical consequences they might have. Things have MEANING for us insofar as they affect our actual lives. In line with his scientific background he assimilates the structure of all KNOWLEDGE to that of scientific knowledge. As for the CRITERION for what can be accepted as such, he insisted on the consensus of the scientific community as a whole, although no state of information is ever complete. Here he overlooks the fact that prevailing views may be wrong and the isolated heretic right. Nonetheless he does stress the need for conscientious appraisal in the pursuit of enquiry, a kind of morality of research. In LOGIC he made a special study of relations and discovered the device of quantification (see QUANTIFIER) independently of FREGE. All this was later absorbed in RUSSELL and WHITEHEAD's *Principia Mathematica*.

Like KANT, through whose work he came to philosophy, he sought to establish a system of CATEGORIES, in his case to account for the form of our sense-experience: Firstness, which concerns independent existence; Secondness, concerning the reactions between things; and Thirdness, the operation of laws or continuity. Perhaps his most original views relate to scientific method: the formation of hypotheses consequent on observation he calls 'abduction', while the testing of hypotheses is a matter of 'INDUCTION'. On the whole, his work has not received the attention it deserves.

perception, *n.* the cognitive apprehension of something. For example, one can perceive the validity of a valid argument. Hallucination, being merely the apparent perception of something, is not perception. In a narrow sense ('sense-perception'), cognitive apprehension depends on the stimulation of the sense-organs.

Behind the 'REPRESENTATIVE THEORY' of perception lie three philosophical assumptions: (a) only judgments (thoughts, PROPOSITIONS, which are non-sensory) can be true or false. (b) a person, to be justified, must have some basis for judging as he does. (c) the basis must ultimately be something other than another judgment.

Thus there must be an ELEMENT that is *not* a judgment (and so *not* true or false). This might correspond to the stimulation of the sense-organs, but be mental (such that the perceiver is conscious of it) and the basis for the judgment the perceiver makes. This element is called a SENSATION or IDEA, is said to 'represent' the external OBJECT, and to be, by 'interpretation', the basis for the judgment that there is an external object, with such-and-such qualities. Perception is accordingly defined as 'the interpretation of sensations to yield knowledge of the external world'. That the external world exists is postulated in the act of interpreting, and so KNOWLEDGE of it is 'mediated' or 'indirect', while the perceiver is 'immediately' or 'directly' acquainted with the sensation. Another theory states that we are directly aware of external objects ('direct realism'). Holders of the first theory object to direct realism that for it perception cannot be causal, and misperceiving is impossible ('the argument from illusion'). Direct realists object to the representative theory that they do not experience any interpreting of sensations, and that something not true or false cannot be a basis for something that is.

Representationalists hold that knowledge claims should rest on what cannot be false. The active intellect can be right or wrong in interpreting the sensation, but in sensation itself the mind is a passive recipient of what comes to it from the external world. However, this leaves open whether the external world exists at all (SCEPTICISM). One might reply that the existence of material things is merely a HYPOTHESIS, or move on to PHENOMENALISM (the view that material things are not anything over and above sensations).

One can avoid having to choose between representationalism and direct realism, by denying that only judgments can be true or false. In a visual illusion the look of a thing is non-veridical. In the well-known Müller–Lyer figure, one line looks longer than the other, but is not. This is not a matter of judgment. They still look unequal to someone who, knowing it to be an illusion, judges them to be equal. This provides no foothold for generalised scepticism. One cannot be aware of how something looks without being aware of the thing which looks. See APPEARANCE; ILLUSION, ARGUMENT FROM; SENSE-DATUM.

person, *n.* a term sometimes used in distinguishing a non-dualist from a dualist conception of how body and mind are related (see MIND–BODY PROBLEM). DESCARTES, having in his *Meditations* (1641), and elsewhere, argued for body and mind being distinct SUBSTANCES, wrote to Princess Elizabeth of Bohemia (28 June 1643) contrasting his dualist conception of body and mind with 'that notion of their union which everybody always has in himself without doing philosophy—viz. that there is one single person who has body and consciousness'. In recent philosophy the concept of a person, which Descartes admitted that everybody always has, has been defined by P. F. STRAWSON (*Individuals*,

London, 1959, Ch. 3) as 'the concept of a type of entity such that *both* predicates ascribing states of consciousness *and* predicates ascribing corporeal characteristics, a physical situation, etc., are equally applicable to a single individual of that single type'. Descartes had called the notions of mind, of body, and of the union of body and mind, 'primitive' notions, meaning that each 'is known in a specific way and not by comparison to another kind'. The notion of MIND is known by pure intellect; that of body, by pure intellect aided by imagination; that of the union, neither by the intellect, nor by the imagination, but by the senses. Strawson, like Descartes, calls the concept of a person, as he defines it, 'primitive', but explains this in a non-Cartesian way: 'a necessary condition of states of consciousness being ascribed at all is that they should be ascribed to the *very same things* as certain corporeal characteristics, a certain physical situation, etc'. Descartes would have ascribed them to a mind, an entity that could, in theory, exist apart from a body.

LOCKE defines a person as 'a thinking intelligent being, that has reason and reflection, and can consider itself as itself, the same thinking thing, in different times and places; which it does only by that consciousness which is inseparable from thinking' (*Essay*, II xxvii 9). By 'consciousness' Locke does not mean just the self-consciousness of the moment. Consciousness, he says, 'can be extended backwards to any past action or thought'. A person will be the same person as a person existing at an earlier time, even with a different body, if only he is conscious of that person's actions. That Locke thinks a person can be conscious of the actions of someone with a different body is indicated by his saying that a person, at the resurrection, can have the same consciousness as he has now, 'though in a body not exactly in make or parts the same which he had here'. Strawson, in remarks about resurrection, does not exclude this possibility. However, his point is that if someone survived in a *disembodied* state his concept of himself as a person would become so attenuated as to make survival unattractive.

personal identity, *n*. the term 'identify' has two senses: to pick out, or to recognize. Identification in the first sense may be called 'individuation'; in the second sense it involves the judgment that two individuations are of one and the same person. The philosophical problem is on what basis, in principle, such judgments should be made.

If one held that the mind can exist apart from the body (CARTESIAN

DUALISM), one would not make bodily IDENTITY a NECESSARY condition of personal identity.

There is a difficulty in the way of treating what people claim to remember as a sufficient condition for their being identical with the person whose experiences they seem to remember. It is essential to our concept of MEMORY that we have a means of distinguishing genuine from seeming memory. Without some means of making the distinction, the statement that memory is a sufficient condition of personal identity is not genuinely intelligible.

A problematic case of a different sort is that of someone, X, whose brain is bisected, half being transplanted into another human body, that of Y, the original brain of which has been removed. From the mouth of what was Y's body there now comes an utterance in which a claim is made to be X, only in Y's body. The self-styled X-in-Y claims to remember doing what X, but not Y, did. There is not the same reason to question the statement that the self-styled X-in-Y remembers doing what X did as there is to question the statement that someone remembers doing what someone long since dead did, for there is a physical basis for the memory, the transplanted half-brain. Should we say that the self-styled X-in-Y really does remember doing what only X did, and so really is X, or should we insist that he cannot be X since that would mean that there are two people who are numerically the same person, which is logically impossible? In such a case the competing claims of memory and bodily identity to be the CRITERION of personal identity may seem to be equally valid (or invalid).

Thomas REID objected that to treat memory as the sole criterion of personal identity is inconsistent with saying that someone cannot remember something he did earlier: that requires some other criterion of personal identity than memory. David HUME concluded that 'memory does not so much *produce* as *discover* personal identity, by showing us the relation of cause and effect among our different perceptions' (*Treatise*, I iv 7). However, since causal relations among experiences 'may diminish by insensible degrees, we have no just standard, by which we can decide any dispute concerning the time, when they acquire or lose a title to the name of identity' (*ibid.*).

WITTGENSTEIN remarks that 'our actual use of the phrase "the same person" and of the name of a person is based on the fact that many characteristics which we use as the criteria for identity coincide in the vast majority of cases' (*The Blue and Brown Books*, 1958, p. 61). Situations are imaginable in which the characteristics do not coincide.

Should this be described by saying that our usual concept of personal identity does not apply in such situations, or by saying that they show that our belief that personal identity is an all-or-nothing matter is mistaken?

phenomenalism, *n.* the theory that, as BERKELEY put it, stones, trees, books, and the like, are 'collections of IDEAS', or, as J. S. MILL put it, MATTER is 'a permanent possibility of SENSATION'. In other words, to talk about material things is another way of talking about the EXPERIENCES, or possible experiences, of sentient beings.

Someone who believed the proposition 'All actual and possible experiences are such as to confirm the existence of a table in my study' would have every reason to disbelieve, and no reason to believe, the proposition 'There is not a table in my study'. Phenomenalism goes further and says that the PROPOSITIONS 'All actual and possible experiences are such as to confirm the existence of a table in my study' and 'There is not a table in my study' are logically incompatible.

It is particularly easy for a logical positivist, who understands MEANING in terms of VERIFIABILITY, to slip from the former to the latter. Application of the verifiability principle to propositions about material things has the consequence that they cannot meaningfully be said to exist independently of actual or possible experiences of them.

phenomenology, *n.* literally the 'science of appearances', in modern philosophy the doctrine put forward by HUSSERL. It involves a method which is used to examine the mere being and function of intentions in conscious existence, while setting aside the question whether the OBJECT of our awareness exists independently of us. This process of phenomenological reduction is to leave us with bare consciousness while holding the contents in abeyance *(epoche)*. What we do under such conditions is to intuit 'ESSENCES', which are meant as somehow lying halfway between abstract being and being-of-a-certain-kind, a somewhat obscure business. These phenomena are non-empirical, somewhat in the sense of KANT's synthetic *a priori*, and are to fit into a coherent whole, which is then to underpin experience. A constant motive throughout is to divorce LOGIC from empirical psychology. The use made of this method by existentialists, and others since, rather differs from the views developed by Husserl. The term is also used in a less metaphysical sense, to distinguish appearances from actual things (ontology).

philosophical analysis, *n.* a translation of a statement which is thought to be philosophically unsatisfactory, into others like it in having the same MEANING but regarded as philosophically satisfactory.

Analytic philosophers between the world wars took 'like it in having the same meaning' to refer primarily to truth and falsity. They differed in their reasons for regarding statements as satisfactory, or not. For some a philosophically satisfactory statement directly pictured the atomic facts. That choice is based on the metaphysical theory that the ultimate constituents of the universe are particular entities (with certain qualities) which are 'externally' related (the relations are not reducible to the qualities of the related entities). This was the logical atomism propounded by Bertrand RUSSELL in opposition to the absolute idealism of F. H. BRADLEY in particular. G. E. MOORE, like Russell, was opposed to absolute IDEALISM and practised philosophical analysis, but, unlike Russell, did not justify satisfactory statements in terms of logical ATOMISM. In his attempted analysis of statements about material things into statements about sense-data (see SENSE-DATUM), he regarded the latter as satisfactory because we might at worst misname them.

Analysis as the philosopher's task lost favour for various reasons. Where a metaphysical theory about language and reality was involved, the seeds of doubt were sown in the 1930s. Gilbert RYLE ('Systematically Misleading Expressions', *Proc. Arist. Soc.* 1931–32) queried the meaningfulness of atomic sentences 'picturing' atomic facts on the ground that a fact is not a collection of bits in the way in which a sentence is an arranged collection of noises, and so cannot have a structure to be deemed like, or even unlike, the structure of the sentence. The main attack came from within the movement. Ludwig WITTGENSTEIN in his later philosophy repudiated the logical atomism of his *Tractatus Logico-Philosophicus* (London, 1922), the book which together with the *Principia Mathematica* of Russell and A. N. WHITEHEAD (Cambridge, 1910–13) and Russell's 'Philosophy of Logical Atomism' (*Monist*, 1918), provided the metaphysical backing for analysis. In his posthumously published *Philosophical Investigations* (Oxford, 1953, 23) Wittgenstein remarked, dryly, 'It is interesting to compare the multiplicity of the tools in language and of the ways they are used, the multiplicity of kinds of word and sentence, with what logicians have said about the structure of language. (Including the author of the *Tractatus Logico-Philosophicus*.)' He was disputing the notion that meaning has to be understood in terms of truth-conditions, or that, as he put it (*Zettel*, Oxford, 1967, 331), the rules of grammar are to be justified as one can justify a sentence by pointing to what verifies it. As to that, it would be better to say that the rules of grammar are arbitrary; and, given the prevailing inclination to think of meaning in terms of truth-conditions, it would be better to ask, not for the MEANING of an expression, but for its use. For those influenced by Wittgenstein's later philosophy, the philosopher's task became the perspicuous description of use rather than the analysis of meaning.

philosophy, *n.* The topic of this dictionary. Those who study it disagree to this day on how they should define their field. Whereas mathematicians or biologists have on the whole no doubts about what it is they study, namely the properties of numbers and of living things respectively, philosophers still find the very DEFINITION of their field controversial. The word is Greek and was from ancient times construed in two ways. One is to view it as love of wisdom (from Greek *philos* friend, *sophos* wise). The other is to take it as what occupied the wise friends, these latter being the members of the early Pythagorean brotherhood. The borderline between philosophy and what we now call science (to the Greeks, natural philosophy) is not clear-cut. Fundamental questions concerning features common to all things were treated by ARISTOTLE under the heading of 'first philosophy', later called METAPHYSICS. What survives of this in later terminology is that in philosophy we are dealing with general questions. This is not to say that we may not treat a very specific problem in a philosophical way: this involves assessing how the special features to hand fit into a wider framework of more general ones. In dealing with problems in this way, we do not simply state our case but argue for it; that is, show by argument how it is linked with other things that are already admitted. Here it is easy to misconstrue what a philosopher is at. Clearly, argument as such never establishes that something is the case: in the end, some things must simply be seen as they are, or if this cannot be secured, assumed to be so for the time being (the time, that is, in which argument takes place). To show that something is so we must always start from something else that has already been established. For this reason, much philosophic argument is negative in kind, showing that certain assumptions lead to impossible consequences. General questions of a philosophic kind occur in all fields of systematic study. That is why specialists have something to gain from appreciating the nature of general questions.

physicalism, *n.* originally the theory that first-person utterances like 'I am now excited', while appearing to be about the speaker's mental state, are really about a physical OBJECT, his body, that can be observed by anyone. The first-person seemingly psychological sentence 'has the same content as the physical sentence "My body is now in that condition which, both under my own observation and that of others, exhibits such and such characteristics of excitement"' (R. CARNAP, 'Psychology in Physical Language' in A. J. Ayer, ed., *Logical Positivism*, Glencoe, Illinois, 1959, p. 191). A more recent version of physicalism would identify the excitement not with behaviour but with some process in the brain (J. J. C. Smart, 'Sensations and Brain Processes', *Philosophical Review*, LXVIII, 1959, 141–156). See IDENTITY HYPOTHESIS.

Plato, (*c*.428–*c*.347 BC), born into a rich aristocratic Athenian family, wanted to enter politics when he came of age, but was disillusioned first by the injustices of the oligarchic government in which his relatives Charmides and Critias were involved, and later by the actions of the democracy which succeeded it, particularly the trial and execution of SOCRATES in 399 BC. In his best-known dialogue, *The Republic*, he sought to provide a theoretical foundation for a government that would embody the justice he had found to be lacking in the actual governments of his day. His only active (and unsuccessful) intervention in politics, as an adviser, was in Syracuse, Sicily (see his *Seventh Letter*). Some time before his second visit to Sicily in 367 BC he founded the school known as 'the ACADEMY'. His career as a writer of dialogues may have begun before this. In his early dialogues he memorialized Socrates and his method of philosophising by making him chief participant and questioner. His teaching in the Academy was interrupted for a third visit to Sicily in 361–360 BC when he was nearly 70. He survived an illness caused by the hardships of the journey, and died aged about 81.

Plato's most influential contribution to philosophy is his THEORY OF FORMS. Scholars disagree about the order in which some of the dialogues were written. If the *Timaeus*, in which the theory is defended, is later than *Parmenides*, in which it is criticised, then that is reason for thinking that Plato did not abandon the theory. There is stylistic evidence of the *Timaeus* being later, but G. E. L. Owen (*Classical Quarterly* N.S. 3 (1953) 79 ff.) has argued persuasively for its being earlier. Recognising that the placing of some dialogues (e.g. *Timaeus, Cratylus*) is controversial, Plato's more important dialogues may be grouped as follows:

Early period: *Charmides, Laches, Lysis, Protagoras, Gorgias, Meno, Euthyphro, Apology, Crito, Cratylus*.

PLATO

Middle period: *Phaedo, Symposium, Phaedrus, Republic, Timaeus*.
Late period: *Parmenides, Theaetetus, Sophist, Statesman, Philebus, Laws*.

Among the many aspects of Plato's philosophy that have proved important in the subsequent history of philosophy are: anti-conventionalism in philosophy of language; DUALISM of impression and reflection in the theory of PERCEPTION; dualisms as regards KNOWLEDGE and belief, soul and body; anti-democratic elitism in political philosophy; proof of soul-like prime movers in cosmology. Most of them are related in one way or another to his most important theory, the theory of Forms.

The dialogue *Cratylus* opens with the question whether 'there is any principle of correctness in names other than convention and agreement' (384 d). The alternative view is that names 'are natural and not conventional', so that 'there is a truth or correctness in them which is the same for Hellenes as for barbarians' (383 a). That there is some sort of objective correctness seems to be presupposed in such dialogues as *Charmides* and *Laches*; they are (unsuccessful) attempts to discover, by discussion, supposed real definitions of 'self-control' and 'courage'. So far as the theory of Forms is a theory in the philosophy of language, Plato's FORMS are postulated OBJECTIVE principles of correctness, that is, principles other than those deriving from convention and agreement.

Ordinarily we should not hesitate to say that we can *see* that two things are the same colour, or *feel* that one thing is harder than another. Plato demonstrates, in part of the dialogue *Theaetetus* (184b–186e), how vulnerable our ordinary understanding of perception is to questioning that starts from considerations about sense-organs. We are easily persuaded to distinguish between 'the impressions which penetrate to the mind through the body' and our 'reflections about them'; and to admit that 'knowledge does not reside in the impressions, but in our reflection upon them'. Plato has in mind such reflections as that things are the same or different, or odd or even, or exist or do not exist. The distinction between impression and reflection can be applied throughout perception, to yield the conclusion that strictly speaking we do not even see that something is white or feel that something is hard. Our apprehension of it as white or hard involves an intellectual process of 'interpreting' or 'classifying' a SENSE-IMPRESSION. In terms of the distinction between particular and universal, a sense-impression is a particular, and so having a sense-impression cannot amount to even the most rudimentary knowledge *about* anything. For that, the sense-impression must be brought under a universal, which is an object of thought. This dualism of impression and reflection is a recurrent element in the history of philosophical theorising about perceptual knowledge. In the writings of Bertrand RUSSELL, for example, it corresponds to the distinction between KNOWLEDGE BY ACQUAINTANCE and KNOWLEDGE BY DESCRIPTION.

Ordinarily we do not hesitate about saying that one person knows what another person only believes. Plato admits as much in the *Meno* (97a–98c), with the example of one man who knows the way to Larissa and another who merely judges correctly which is the road. In the *Republic* (475e–480a) he distinguishes between KNOWLEDGE *(episteme)* and belief or opinion *(doxa)* by saying that they are different faculties with different objects, and that 'these admissions do not leave place for the identity of the knowable and the opinable' (478b). Knowledge is the mental state of the man 'whose thought recognises a beauty in itself'; opinion, that of the man 'who believes in beautiful things, but neither believes in BEAUTY itself nor is able to follow when someone tries to guide him to the knowledge of it' (476c). How to distinguish knowledge and belief is a perennial question in philosophy. Some recent philosophers would say that Plato's formulation in terms of mental states is misleading. It led him to say that knowledge and belief have different objects. Some recent philosophers, following J. L. AUSTIN, look instead at the different SPEECH ACTS performed by someone saying 'I know . . .' and 'I believe . . .'. The former is an act of avouching, which attracts reproach if what the speaker said he knew turns out to be false.

For Plato the objects of knowledge and belief are respectively invariable and invisible Forms apprehended by thought, and variable and visible particulars apprehended by the bodily senses. Given that there are these two realms, it seems inevitable that soul is more like the invariable and invisible and body like the variable and visible. Thus the dualism of the objects of knowledge and belief is complemented with a dualism of soul and body such that only the soul is capable of passing 'into the realm of the pure and everlasting and immortal and changeless' (*Phaedo* 78d–79d). Some 2000 years later DESCARTES's mind–body dualism supplanted that of Plato.

In the *Republic* the Socratic search for a definition of a Form finally meets with success. Justice is the requirement 'that each man must perform the social service in the state for which his nature was best adapted' (433a). Combined with the thesis that only philosophers, after a long training, can comprehend the Form of the good, and are therefore fit to rule, this yields the conclusion that 'unless either philosophers become kings in our states or those whom we now call our kings and rulers take to the pursuit of philosophy seriously and adequately, and there is a conjunction of these two things, political power and philosophical intelligence, while the motley horde of the natures who at present pursue either apart from the other are compulsorily excluded, there can be no cessation of troubles' (473d). Recent discussions of Plato's views on the ideal state have centred on Karl POPPER, *The Open Society and its Enemies*, Vol. 1, *The Spell of Plato*.

In part of his last dialogue, the *Laws* (894a–907b), Plato argues that the primary CAUSE of movement must be something that is able to move itself as well as other things. We talk of a self-moving thing as being alive, that is, as having soul in it. It follows that soul is the universal cause of all change and MOTION. We must assume that there are two controlling souls, 'one beneficent, the other capable of the contrary effect'. Revolution being a superior sort of movement, the revolution of the heavenly bodies is caused by one or more beneficent souls. Such souls are worthy to be esteemed gods. Being good, they are 'mindful of us' and 'never to be seduced from the path of right'.

This was Plato's own view, in his last years. It is significant that the view is attributed to 'an Athenian'. Another view, involving the Forms, is given in the *Timaeus*: a divine artificer models likenesses of the Forms in a receptacle, space. Although the *Timaeus* view is described as no more than 'a likely tale', and is put into the mouth not of an Athenian but of someone identified as a Pythagorean, it was the *Timaeus* view that proved more influential, at least among the Neo-Platonists. The view expounded in the *Laws*, however, influenced ARISTOTLE.

Platonism, *n.* The influence of Plato's teaching, both in the published *Dialogues* and oral, was such that many philosophers may be described as Platonists. It is usual to distinguish between the Platonism of the Academy, the NEO-PLATONISM developed by PLOTINUS in the 3rd century AD, and subsequent movements such as that of the CAMBRIDGE PLATONISTS in the 17th century. The term Platonist may be applied more strictly, on the basis of adherence to Plato's central doctrines, and in particular to his THEORY OF FORMS, or more loosely, as in the case of the Cambridge Platonists, on the basis of sympathy with the general moral intent and anti-conventionalist presuppositions of the Socratic dialogues. In the more strict application of the term, two aspects of the Theory of Forms are important: that there is one supreme FORM, the Form of the Good, which has a role in the apprehension of the other Forms comparable to that of the sun in the apprehension of visible things (*Republic* 508b, 509b, 514a–517a), and that the visible world was created by a divine Artificer modelling likenesses of the Forms in a receptacle, space (*Timaeus* 51b–52b). According to ARISTOTLE (*Metaphysics* 987 b 15–988 a 16) Plato's teaching in a lecture on 'The Good' favoured an interpretation of the theory of Forms in mathematical terms, in which the Form of the good becomes 'The One'. The Neo-Platonic version of these aspects of Plato's theory provided some of the material for the philosophy of the Christian religion propounded by St AUGUSTINE.

Plotinus, (*c*.205–270), born at Lykopolis, Upper Egypt. Plotinus was probably a Hellenized Egyptian. He studied philosophy from the age of 28 under Ammonius Saccas, about whom little else is known than that Plotinus held him in high regard. He went to Rome in 244, founded a school of philosophy, and started writing about 10 years later. His works were grouped by his pupil Porphyry into six books, each containing nine chapters; hence the name Enneads. They expound a version of PLATONISM known as NEO-PLATONISM because of modifications he introduced, partly to accommodate certain ideas derived from ARISTOTLE and the Stoics. Neo-Platonism formed a bridge between Platonism and the Christian philosophy of St AUGUSTINE.

Plotinus held that reality comprises several spheres of being, the most important being those of intellect and soul, emanating from 'the One', which is the centre of goodness and is in some sense 'beyond being' (cf. Plato, *Republic* 509 b). The spheres further from the centre are timelessly dependent on those nearer, as an image is dependent on an archetype. The outermost sphere is that of material things, matter being furthest from goodness. There is an outgoing of power from the centre, and this is reciprocated in a loving attitude of the outer parts to the more central (cf. Aristotle, *Metaphysics* 1072 b 3). The One is unknowable. An indescribable mystical union (see MYSTICISM) with it is possible, but rare. Such union is the aim of man's existence.

pluralism, *n*. the view that there is not just one SUBSTANCE ('MONISM'), or two substances ('DUALISM'), but that there are many, a plurality of, substances. SPINOZA was a monist, DESCARTES was a dualist, LEIBNIZ was a pluralist. In political theory, pluralism is the view that there is no single overriding interest, but a range of competing interests.

political philosophy, *n.* the examination of the State and its functions (from Greek *politikos* pertaining to the *polis* city), first figures as a fully fledged enquiry in PLATO's dialogue *The Republic* (in Greek, *Politeia*). He there argues for a certain division of activities, with each group having to stick to what is appropriate to it: the rulers form an elite trained in all the excellences, especially philosophy. Elsewhere, Plato considers a variety of possible constitutions, and finally gives a detailed account of what should legally be enacted. For ARISTOTLE, the city is the proper framework for man to unfold his full abilities and reach his proper development: man is a being of the city, or political animal. Many thinkers throughout the ages have contributed to the examination of political activity, from those who wished to justify a particular AUTHORITY or the division of power between several authorities (e.g. Church and State in the Middle Ages), the description of the practical wielding of power (Machiavelli), the idealist theory of HEGEL and the materialist doctrines of MARX and his followers, the SOCIAL CONTRACT theories of HOBBES and ROUSSEAU, and utilitarian and pragmatic theories of the 19th and 20th centuries. A great philosophical debate is that between the supporters of democracy as against totalitarian views. In recent times attempts have been made in the analytic tradition to examine the language used by politicians and by students of political theory. Some political thinkers have put forward views that hardly seem attainable in practice. For example, anarchist theory, which is one offshoot of Marxism, supposes that social existence could go on without any legal framework at all (anarchy is from Greek *anarchia* absence of rule). If men were other than they are and all of them always respected the interests of others, this might be possible, but since they do not it is not. In fact human societies are arenas of conflict between opposing interests that must marginally take account of each other to make social existence viable. For the rest, the distinction between social theory and political philosophy is vague and perhaps not worth making precise.

Popper, (Sir) Karl Raimund (1902–), studied philosophy in his native Vienna, taught in New Zealand (1937–45) and thereafter at the London School of Economics. His philosophy is in many ways opposed to that of the VIENNA CIRCLE: where they stressed verification, he insisted on FALSIFIABILITY as the basic feature of scientific theory, and the effort of falsifying hypotheses as the principal task of the scientist. Thus he is opposed to the inductivist account of scientific method, as explained in his *Logic of Scientific Discovery* (1934, English translation 1959). Although a realist as regards epistemology, he regards the OBJECT of our KNOWLEDGE as something that through critical examination undergoes a kind of EVOLUTION: knowledge grows in an organic way. In his later thought he recognises three realms: one of material objects, another of mental processes, and a third of organic activity to which belongs the growth of culture. As to social theory, in *The Open Society and its Enemies* (1944) he opposes and criticises what he saw as the totalitarian systems of PLATO, HEGEL and MARX and proposes instead an approach based on scientific method and in tackling specific difficulties.

positivism, *n.* a philosophic doctrine which holds that we must confine ourselves to what is given to us in sense-experience as sources of KNOWLEDGE. Thus positivism rejects all metaphysical speculation and abstract theorising, and even a critical examination of its own presuppositions. The term itself is due to COMTE who first presented a system of positive philosophy. He held that civilisations go through three phases, the first theological, the second metaphysical and the third and last, scientific or positive. This approach was taken up by later 19th century thinkers who were influenced by the great strides in science, notably MACH. Thus the positivist sees his task in finding the general principles of science starting from EXPERIENCE. In this it is related to the generally empirical temper of the sciences as seeking to proceed by observation and experiment. Where positivism as a philosophy was less felicitous was in its later reliance on a somewhat simplistic account of experience itself in terms of sense-data (see SENSE-DATUM). When it is combined with an emphasis on logical ANALYSIS of scientific language, it gives rise to LOGICAL POSITIVISM, an influential doctrine until after the mid-20th century.

potentiality, see ACTUALITY AND POTENTIALITY.

pragmatism, *n.* a philosophy that arose in the United States in the late 19th century and first put forward as such by PEIRCE. The basic principle is that in order to assess the significance or MEANING of what we say we must examine what practical bearings it has on human activities. This philosophy remained predominantly American, being developed mainly by William JAMES and DEWEY. When James introduced a rather different slant by stating that truth is what has fruitful consequences, which as it stands is a CRITERION of truth, Peirce distanced himself from the theory and called his own approach 'pragmaticism'. As a theory of truth, pragmatism fails like any other such theory based on a criterion, but as a sociological policy, it has been highly influential in America, particularly in the educational writings of Dewey. Pragmatism has aims that are not unrelated to those of the utilitarian philosophers in England (see UTILITARIANISM).

predicate, (from Latin *prae* in front, *dicere* to say, literally that which is said in front of)

1. *n.* a term of grammar and LOGIC referring to that which is said about something else, called the SUBJECT. Thus, in the sentence 'the cat is on the mat', what comes before 'is', namely 'the cat', is the subject, while what comes after ('on the mat') is the predicate.

2. *v.* to predicate *P* of *S* is to say that *S* is *P*. The word 'is' is called the *copula*.

pre-established harmony, see MIND–BODY PROBLEM.

Pre-Socratic philosophy. The term 'Pre-Socratic' is used of those philosophers, from about 600–400 BC, whose interests were mainly in COSMOLOGY, the theory of the universe as an ordered system, and in cosmogony, the theory of its generation. This marks them off from the SOPHISTS and SOCRATES, whose main interests were in human affairs— ETHICS and politics. They are marked off from their predecessors by their theories not involving the supposed capricious acts of anthropomorphic gods. Their theorising, however, bears little relation to that of present-day scientists, often being based on the most tenuous of analogies, and rarely being directed towards prediction and control. Even the most modern-sounding of their theories, the ATOMISM of Leucippus and DEMOCRITUS, is better understood in the context of ELEATICISM, a rationalist theory which denied all reality to the sensible world, than as the product of properly scientific theorising and empirical testing of theories.

ARISTOTLE, in his survey of the Pre-Socratic philosophers (*Metaphysics* 983 a 24 ff.) said that most of them sought explanations in terms of what he called the MATERIAL CAUSE, the matter of which things consist. This gives a misleading and inadequate impression of their place in the history of philosophy. A more adequate impression can be gained from a study of PLATO's development, in his THEORY OF FORMS, of ideas derived from PYTHAGORAS (the ideas of a mathematical reality behind the world of the senses, and of the soul as existing before and after its present embodiment), HERACLITUS (the idea of the world of the senses being for ever in a state of change, or 'flux'), and PARMENIDES (the idea of a distinction between the real, unchanging, unitary world that can be understood by the soul, and the illusory, changing, pluralistic world of the non-comprehending senses). See

ANAXAGORAS, ANAXIMANDER, ANAXIMENES, EMPEDOCLES, MILESIAN SCHOOL, THALES, XENOPHANES, ZENO OF ELEA.

primary and secondary qualities. Scientists explain our EXPERIENCES of say, sound and colour, not by saying that physical things really are sonorous or coloured, but by saying that they have certain other qualities that cause our sense-organs to be stimulated so as to produce these experiences in us. For example, violin strings of different lengths or under different tensions vibrate, when plucked, at different speeds; an experienced high note corresponds to a high speed of vibration, a low note to a slow speed. The science-based distinction between primary and secondary qualities is between the qualities regarded as causally efficacious (the speed of vibration of the strings is a primary quality) and those we attribute to OBJECTS only because of our experiences (the sound we say the violin string makes is a secondary quality).

The distinction philosophers make between primary and secondary qualities relates more or less closely to this science-based distinction. The relevance is most obvious in the remark by John LOCKE that '*bodies* produce *ideas* in us . . . manifestly *by impulse*, the only way which we can conceive bodies operate in' (*Essay* II viii 11). It is less obvious in Locke's conclusion that our 'ideas of primary qualities of bodies are resemblances of them' whereas those of secondary qualities are not (*Essay* II viii 15). First, whereas in talk of IDEAS being produced in us by impulse, an 'idea' can be understood as an act of perceiving, in talk of ideas resembling or not resembling qualities of bodies, some other understanding of 'idea', perhaps involving a REPRESENTATIVE THEORY OF PERCEPTION, seems called for. Secondly, the conclusion requires an additional premiss, to the effect that if something is not needed for causal explanation it can safely be assumed not to exist.

In general, philosophers agree about which qualities are primary, which secondary. The exception is when primary qualities are said to be those that are inseparable from, or essential to, bodies. DESCARTES says that hardness is not essential to any body, such as stone, 'because if the stone were liquified or reduced to powder, it would no longer possess hardness, and yet would not cease to be a body' (*Principles* II 11). Locke says that however much you divide a grain of wheat 'each part has still solidity, EXTENSION, figure, and mobility' (*Essay* II viii 9). These quotations suggest that the difference between them, about whether or not hardness or solidity is a primary quality, is an experimental issue, but that is misleading: their disagreement reflects the rationalist and empiricist approaches to the understanding of impenetrability. According to Descartes the concept of the impenetrability of two bodies can be accommodated even if matter is understood as having only the qualities that can be treated mathematically. According to Locke the idea of impenetrability is acquired empirically, either by the sense of touch or by finding that certain actions, such as the bringing together of one's hands when there is an object between them, are impossible.

Prime Mover, see FIRST MOVER.

privacy, *n.* in EPISTEMOLOGY, that of which only one person can be immediately conscious is said to be 'private' to him. Thus, following DESCARTES's DEFINITION of 'thought' as 'a word that covers everything that exists in us in such a way that we are immediately conscious of it', our thoughts are private to us even if others can infer what they are from what we say.

The notion of privacy is important in the philosophy of MIND. One 20th century Cambridge philosopher, G. E. MOORE, said that the characteristic of being directly known by one MIND only might be proposed as a CRITERION of what is mental, though he himself thought that the abnormal phenomena of co-consciousness in a case of split personality might constitute an exception. Another, John Wisdom, explicitly embraced privacy as the defining characteristic of mind: 'The peculiarity of the soul is not that it is visible to none but that it is visible only to one'.

Talk of the soul, or mind, being 'visible' is, of course, metaphorical. It suggests that a person can say what he thinks only by virtue of an inward inspection ('intro-spection'). LOCKE called this 'REFLECTION', and said of it: 'Though it be not sense, as having nothing to do with external OBJECTS, yet it is very like it, and might properly enough be called internal sense' (*Essay* II i 4). Taking an utterance like 'I hope you pass the exam.' as a report of something the speaker has observed in himself is disputed by those who call it an 'AVOWAL'. See INTROSPECTION, OTHER MINDS.

private language, *n.* in his *Philosophical Investigations* (Oxford, 1953) I, 243 WITTGENSTEIN asks whether we could imagine a language the individual words of which 'are to refer to what can only be known to the person speaking; to his immediate private sensations. So another person cannot understand the language'. In subsequent sections he argued that we could not imagine such a 'private language'. The argument involves asking and answering a great many questions, beginning with 'How do words *refer* to sensations?', to which part of Wittgenstein's answer is that 'the verbal expression of pain replaces crying and does not describe it' (244), so that 'my language is not a "private" one' (256). In 258 Wittgenstein asks whether someone could give himself a kind of OSTENSIVE DEFINITION of a sensation-word, and so be able to keep a diary about the recurrence of the sensation. Some commentators have taken this to be the key question, but have differed in their understanding of the significance of Wittgenstein's long treatment of it. If 384 ('You learned the *concept* "pain" when you learned language') is taken as a key remark then the central point of the private language argument may be that there cannot be MEANING without the possibility of telling whether or not the use of a word is correct, and that this possibility cannot exist apart from there being a public use of words, a regular practice by reference to which a word can be said to be used correctly or otherwise. See PRIVACY.

privileged access, *n.* the expression is used pejoratively by philosophers opposed to CARTESIAN DUALISM to characterize what DESCARTES called the 'IMMEDIATE awareness' a person has of his own, and only his own, thoughts. The 20th century British philosopher Gilbert RYLE distinguished two features of privileged access: (a) 'a mind cannot help being constantly aware of all the supposed occupants of its private stage' ('consciousness'), (b) 'it can also deliberately scrutinise by a species of non-sensuous PERCEPTION at least some of its own states and operations' ('introspection'). Some philosophers, e.g. Franz BRENTANO, have held INTROSPECTION to be infallible, and this is sometimes incorporated into the notion of privileged access. See AVOWAL, PRIVACY.

probability theory, *n.* (from Latin *probo* test) is an attempt at finding a FORMAL device for assessing what is likely to happen, given certain information in circumstances where we cannot provide a conclusive demonstration. The subject was first developed in the 17th century, mainly to underpin games of 'chance'. Thus at dice, it seems intuitively reasonable to suppose that an unloaded die of six sides is equally likely to land on one of them (one excludes the possibility that it might be balanced on a corner or edge). In this way one tried to give a numerical account of what might be expected to occur. None of the formal DEFINITIONS of probability that have been worked out has ever been quite satisfactory, and the subject remains rather controversial. A mathematical theory does not itself solve this problem, it merely provides ways of working out complicated cases, once a definition has been stipulated. To take our example, one definition is that the probability is the proportion of cases turning out in a given way if the event is indefinitely repeated: the probability of throwing any given number from 1 to 6 with a true die is 1/6. What, however, is here meant by true? No more than that each side is equally likely to turn up. If we take a physically uniform die and throw it at random many times, every side will turn up roughly in one-sixth of cases. What is meant by 'random'? No more than that the way of throwing does not favour any side. The whole thing becomes circular. What is, indeed, of great practical value is the working out of complicated coincidences of several characteristics given some prior assumption of the numerical proportions. Insofar as such assumptions are in fact more or less accurate in practice, usable results can be obtained. Even so, we must not be overawed if something highly improbable in this sense nevertheless occurs. Strictly speaking, a statistical result obtained by means of probability assumptions does not solve a problem, it poses one. Or at least, if it satisfies some practical demands, it still raises a theoretical problem rather than solves it.

proper name, *n.* a tag given to a specific person or thing. Thus Ben Nevis is the proper name of a Scottish mountain, *Victory* is the proper name of the British flagship at Trafalgar, and Nelson the proper name of the admiral who commanded and died on her. Other quite different items may bear the same proper names. The point is that if we know nothing further about their bearers, such names do not convey anything. On the other hand, we can always define them away in terms of the bearers' characteristics. Thus, the mountain could be specified by its height and geographical co-ordinates, the ship by the dockyard and date of its building, and the admiral in terms of his unique career. When one and the same OBJECT has several different proper names, we must be careful how we handle statements. Thus one and the same star is called Morning Star and Evening Star, but it is wrong to use the former name in the evening and the latter in the morning. This is an instance of proper names that carry some descriptive element. So indeed do many given names of people, usually because when the names first came into use, those who gave the name to a child hoped that it would come to exemplify what the name describes.

proper object, *n.* the proper or special object of a sense, defined by Aristotle as the one kind of object which a sense such as hearing or

234

sight discerns. Aristotle says that sight or hearing 'never errs in reporting that what is before it is colour or sound' (418 a 15).

On the face of it the example of sound being the proper object of hearing seems the clearest. There is only one thing that a bell makes when it is struck which can be heard, and that is a sound. Nobody would err, and say it was a colour or a smell they heard. Still, there is a problem. One can often tell, just by listening, whether a sound is coming from one's right or one's left. Why should there be just one proper object of hearing, the sound, and not two, the sound and where it is coming from? Nobody would err, mistaking the direction from which the sound was coming for something else, like a colour or a smell.

Similarly, in the case of vision, why should not the farness or nearness of a coloured object, as well as its colour, be regarded as a proper object? This question engaged BERKELEY. He held that we know the distance of an object by how much we have to move to be in contact with it (*New Theory of Vision*, 126). In looking at a distant object we have certain SENSATIONS arising from the disposition of our eyes, which suggest to us that we should have to move a little or a lot to be in contact with it. The same sensations would occur in a man born blind who was made to see, but they would not signify distance to him, since the appropriate ASSOCIATION OF IDEAS would not have been built up.

There is experimental evidence that some degree of distance-perception by vision is possible without learning. If having a CONCEPT is primarily a matter of having a capacity to do something (excluding the reflective capacity to talk and think about one's capacity) then there seems no good reason to deny that infants have the concept of distance, or that distance, like colour, is a proper object of vision, even though it is not exclusively an object of vision.

property, *n.* (from Latin *proprius* one's own). In philosophy, a thing's own. ARISTOTLE defines it in the *Topics* (102a, 18–20) as something that does not exhibit a thing's ESSENCE, but belongs to that thing alone and is convertibly predicable of it (for example, a human can learn grammar, and whoever can do that is a human).

proposition, *n.* in philosophy, whatever it may be that we express in using language, more particularly in saying that something is thus and thus. However, this remains highly controversial in that different thinkers take very different views of what propositions are, or whether indeed there are such things at all. Some take a psychological view and hold that propositions are essentially bound up with our beliefs and assertions. Others insist that while what we believe are indeed propositions, these do not somehow depend on our believing them. A rough-and-ready view is that a proposition is what is stated by a categorical sentence (one that states that something is, or is not, so). Those who take the non-psychological view see LOGIC as dealing with propositions and their interrelations. As such, propositions are not assignable to any particular language.

Protagoras, (*c.*490–*c.*420 BC), the most famous of the professional SOPHISTS, the travelling teachers described by Xenophon as 'those who offer wisdom for sale in return for money to all comers'. He was well known in Athens, where he was a friend of Pericles; and he lived for a time in Sicily. One of his books, on *Truth*, began with a pronouncement about man being the measure of all things, the meaning of which is discussed by PLATO (*Theaetetus* 152). When the same wind is blowing, one person may feel chilly, another not. The wind is to each as he perceives it. 'PERCEPTION, then, is always of something that *is*, and, as being KNOWLEDGE, it is infallible'.

With this doctrine Plato contrasts another, a 'secret' doctrine, that is in fact the doctrine of HERACLITUS, but which Plato, with obvious irony, attributes to Protagoras. This is the doctrine 'that nothing is *one* thing just by itself, nor can you rightly call it by some definite name, nor even say it is of any definite sort'. Plato himself made use of this Heraclitean doctrine of opposites in his THEORY OF FORMS (cf. *Republic* VII 523–4).

psychical monism, *n.* the doctrine that there is only one thing, *psyche* mind, and that things that appear to us as material are, in themselves, psychical. See ANIMISM.

psychoanalysis, *n.* a therapeutic method involving the theory that there is a part of the MIND of which we are not conscious but whose contents (unconscious thoughts and desires) determine how we behave and feel. That there can be unconscious desires was evident to the founder of psychoanalysis, Sigmund Freud (1856–1939), from the possibility of post-hypnotic suggestion. A wish to do something can be implanted in someone under hypnosis, and this can make him do it, without knowing why, some time after he has been awakened from hypnosis. In the case of post-hypnotic suggestion the subject does not recall being asked to perform the action because someone else, the hypnotist, told him to forget being asked. According to Freudian theory certain thoughts or fantasies occurring in infancy or childhood are 'repressed' by the person himself. They are repressed because they belong to one part of him (the 'id') whose thoughts, of a predominantly sexual or libidinous character, are unacceptable by another part (the 'superego'). One such fantasy is that of a son killing his father so as to take his place with his mother, a fantasy whose name is taken from the Greek myth of Oedipus. It is held that there is a period (the 'latency period') when this desire is inactive. Then, at puberty, it is again aroused, but the situation can usually be resolved by finding an object for sexual affection outside the family. If the usual psychological development through various stages in childhood had been hindered, so that there was 'fixation' at some stage, then there may be the sort of resolution we characterize as neurotic or psychotic. The primary aim of psychoanalytic therapy is to enable a person to find a resolution he can live with, without too much distress either to himself or to others. It is held that to resolve the situation he must first acknowledge it, not just intellectually as a theory applicable to anyone, but as concretely instantiated in his own mental life. Two ways of achieving this are by the interpretation of dreams (in which the manifest dream content is revealed as the expression of desires which have been 'censored' by the superego), and free association (in which what is said in seemingly random response to stimulus words is used by the analyst as a key to unconscious thoughts). An essential factor in the employment of these techniques is the presence of the analyst, as someone other than the subject's parents, in relating to whom the subject can reorganise his affective life (transference).

Is Freudian theory true? Is it true, for example, that a son unconsciously wants to kill his father and have sexual intercourse with his mother? There are two ways of treating this question, a plain way and a philosophical way. Following the plain way it might be said that while it is eminently plausible that a son has strong feelings towards his mother and father arising from such facts as that, as an infant, he gets nourishment from his mother's breast and that there are occasions when he and his father may seem to him to be in competition for her attention and love, there is little, if any, evidence from outside the psychoanalytic situation to support the Freudian interpretation of these feelings in terms of sexual fantasies and their repression. Freud's assumption that for what happens in infancy and childhood to have an effect on what happens later, including later sexual maladjustments, what happens in infancy and childhood must itself be sexual, remains controversial.

PSYCHOLOGY

Following the philosophical way, attention may be drawn to a feature of our discourse about the mind. WITTGENSTEIN once wrote:

If someone had said 'Napoleon was crowned in 1804', and we asked him 'Did you mean the man who won the battle of Austerlitz?' he might say 'Yes, I meant him'. And the use of the past tense 'meant' might make it appear as though the idea of Napoleon having won the battle of Austerlitz must have been present in the man's mind when he said that Napoleon was crowned in 1804.

The implication of Wittgenstein's remark is that the idea of Napoleon having won the battle of Austerlitz need not have been present in someone's mind at the time he mentioned Napoleon for him to say, truthfully, using 'mean' in the past tense, that when he mentioned Napoleon he meant the man who won the battle of Austerlitz. In other words it is a feature of our use of 'mean' that the CRITERION of the truth of what happened earlier (someone's meaning the man who won the battle of Austerlitz) is what he says later. Similarly, it might be said, in Freudian theory the criterion of the truth of the son, as a child, unconsciously wanting to kill his father, is that, as an adult under psychoanalysis, he can accept that interpretation of his dreams in terms of the Oedipus myth. Freudian theory is true to the extent to which people find it makes sense of their inner life. Many people are prepared to revise their view of themselves in line with it.

While doubts may be expressed about details of psychoanalytic theory, Freud has done more than anyone else to undermine the notion, implicit in Cartesian philosophy of mind, that a person cannot but know how he feels, and the reasons for his feelings as he does. Freud's influence is apparent both in the arts (surrealist painting, the modern novel, films) and in what ordinary people say and do. His influence is out of all proportion to what is scientifically verifiable, in the narrow experimental sense of 'science', in psychoanalysis. See PSYCHOLOGY.

psychology, *n.* was defined as 'the science of mental life' by William JAMES in 1890, and as 'the science of behaviour' by J. B. WATSON in 1914. How does mental life differ from life in general? How does behaviour differ from movement in general?

ARISTOTLE characterised life, at the lowest level, in terms of self-nutrition and growth. Plants have life. At a higher level, animals are, additionally, capable of SENSATIONS and desire, and, some of them, of locomotion. Man has the power of THINKING, a MIND: he can plan how to achieve his ends. Had Aristotle used the term 'mental life' he would have defined it in terms of 'purpose' and 'reason'. To him, the appropriate mode of explanation of such life was teleological (in terms of ends).

Whereas for Aristotle the relation of mind and body was a special case of the form–matter relation, for DESCARTES mind was something to be opposed to body. Mind and MATTER are distinct SUBSTANCES, and a person's mental operations are those about which he cannot be in doubt, of which he is 'immediately conscious' (see IMMEDIATE). Mind and body interact causally in virtue of being somehow united through the pineal gland in the brain. Mind acts on body in voluntary ACTION: a movement of the body is the effect of a VOLITION in the mind. Body acts on mind in PERCEPTION: a sensation or IDEA in the mind is the effect of stimulation of a sense-organ. According to Descartes, LOCKE and others, thinking is the relating of ideas. According to HUME, HARTLEY and JAMES MILL the principles of relationship are those of 'association' (see ASSOCIATION OF IDEAS). There is, in this, the possibility of a mechanism of mental life as deterministic as the mechanism of the material world. The difference is in how we find out about it: we each have PRIVILEGED ACCESS to our own mental life, by INTROSPECTION.

The move to re-define psychology as the science of behaviour was made for negative reasons. It was, at once, a rejection of teleological modes of explanation, and above all a rejection of the introspective method. The concept of behaviour was treated either as though it needed no elucidation, or as though it was that of a simple, or a complicated, response to stimulation. A reflex would be a simple response. The discovery by the Russian physiologist, I. P. Pavlov, that a dog could be 'conditioned' to respond to a substitute stimulus, was welcomed as providing a bridge to the explanation of more complicated behavioural responses. In behaviourist psychology the principles of conditioning came to play a role analogous to that of the principles of the association of ideas in traditional introspectionist psychology. To Pavlov's 'classical' conditioning was added B. F. Skinner's 'operant' conditioning. It was even claimed that 'linguistic behaviour' could be explained in terms of conditioning.

BEHAVIOURISM was not the only reaction to Cartesianism and the way of ideas. The Cartesian identification of the mental with that of which we are immediately conscious was rejected in the theory and practice of PSYCHOANALYSIS. The ATOMISM of the way of ideas, for example in trying to account for perceptual experience in terms of sensations each having a constant relationship with a particular stimulation of the sense-organs, was rejected by the Gestalt psychologists.

Philosophers distinguish between behaviourism as a response to the 'other minds problem', and behaviourism as a methodology of psychology. As a methodology of psychology it is criticised on the grounds that it ignores the distinction between an *event*, such as a reflex response to a stimulus, and an *action*. An event is to be explained in terms of what has made it happen, such as the tap below the knee which makes the knee jerk up. An action, on the other hand, may be explained, to someone acquainted with a social practice of some sort, in terms of its role in that practice. For example, one may explain the action of someone raising his arm by saying that he is voting to go on strike. This serves as an explanation for someone acquainted with such human institutions as organized labour, withdrawal of labour, and so on. If psychologists debar themselves from talking the language of human institutions, it may be because they mistakenly assume that they thereby protect psychology's right to be regarded as a science. The assumption is that only explanations which have a cause–effect, or stimulus–response, pattern are properly scientific.

Fortunately, this debilitating assumption has lost a lot of ground, not so much because of the criticisms of philosophers (though they have played a part), but because of the invention, during and since the Second World War, of machines whose 'behaviour' positively invites description in precisely the mentalistic terms the behaviourists try to avoid. Machines were invented, for example, to track the flight of an enemy aircraft, to store the information obtained by such tracking, to forecast the aircraft's probable position at a future time, to make corrections to that forecast as further information becomes available, and to aim a gun at the position the aircraft is expected to reach, with the purpose of shooting it down. The fact that one could describe the machine's behaviour in terms of information, forecasting, correction, expectation and purpose was seen as being entirely consistent with the machine itself being describable in exclusively physicalistic terms (wires carrying electrical currents, and so on). If mentalistic terms can be used to describe a machine's behaviour without our having to postulate a non-material substance somehow interacting with the machine, why should they not be used, similarly, to describe human behaviour? The difference between men and machines is that men are, to a degree, conscious of what they do, and of why they do it. However, the psychologist, as scientist, is not required to answer philosophical questions about the nature or purpose of CONSCIOUSNESS. It is enough that he should not be deterred, by a false notion of what is scientific, from describing human actions in terms which have meaning in virtue of human concerns. He can, with a good scientific conscience, again define his science as that of mental life. The mind, as one psychologist (G. A. Miller) has put it, has returned to psychology on the back of the machine. See CONDITIONING, GESTALT PSYCHOLOGY.

punishment, theory of, *n.* a group of doctrines that try in various ways to justify a person being punished for the breaking of a law or regulation. Positions in this group vary greatly. Thus punishment may be retributory (the worth of an eye for an eye, to state Exodus 21:24 accurately); reformative, when a transgressor is deprived of his freedom with a view to regenerating him; utilitarian, for the sake of the greatest good for the greatest number, when the common good seems to be served; deterrent, to discourage others from acting in the manner punished; eliminative, when the transgressor is simply removed from society to protect it from his further attentions. The philosophic aspect of these punitive approaches concerns the justification, if any, for inflicting the punishment. This involves the nature of the rules that have been broken and to what extent they deserve the status they have. At this point we have reached a central theme of philosophical enquiry: what is JUSTICE? On this there are various views that remain mutually incompatible. In some respects, most thinkers would indeed agree: there must be some equity, in the sense that like should be treated alike. This at once raises difficulties: like in what respect? Thus, if a rich man's son steals for the thrill of it, is that in the relevant respect the same as the case of one who steals a loaf of bread because he is hungry and destitute? These are difficult issues and require much tact, insight and human sympathy on the part of those who dispense justice and in the course of it decree punishments. In practice, special circumstances are often allowed to count where the bare handing down of a punishment or sanction would be pointlessly harsh. Still, this does leave us with the difficult problem of responsibility: if I commit a punishable offence, is the fault of transgression mine, or is it to be attributed to my social condition? On this, opinions remain radically divided.

Pyrrhonism, *n.* the form of SCEPTICISM named after Pyrrho of Elis

PYRRHONISM

(*c*.365–275 BC). Scepticism in general is opposed to any claim that we know the real nature of things ('dogmatism'), but may take the form either of claiming that we do not know, or of suspending judgment. The former was the scepticism of the ACADEMY under Arcesilaus of Pitane (*c*.315–240 BC) and Carneades of Cyrene (*c*.213–129 BC). (Academic Scepticism was mitigated by the view that we can know certain things to be probable.) The latter is Pyrrhonism. A Pyrrhonist typically suspends judgment, acknowledges his lack of comprehension, refrains from making claims to KNOWLEDGE (including the claim that he does not know), and thereby hopes to attain tranquility of mind. Pyrrhonism may be characterized as much by the recurrence of these notions (*epoché* suspension of judgment; *akatalepsia* lack of comprehension; *aphasia* silence; *ataraxia* mental tranquility) as by the use of any particular kind of argument or by the scepticism being directed towards any particular subject-matter. Pyrrho himself left no writings, and may have been honoured more as the exemplar of how a Pyrrhonist should conduct his life than for his philosophical teachings. According to his foremost pupil, Timon of Phlius (*c*.320–230 BC), he taught that to attain the desired *ataraxia* a philosopher should ask the question 'How are things constituted?' and answer it with the reflection that all we know is how things appear to us; and ask 'What should be our attitude to reality?' and answer it with a decision to suspend judgment.

Pyrrhonism of a more systematic kind developed out of Academic Scepticism, through rejection, as dogmatic, of the Academic distinction between the probable and the improbable. It was put on a systematic footing by Aenesidemus (1st century AD), who was born in Crete, was a student at the Academy and taught in Alexandria. Aenesidemus's philosophy is described in detail by SEXTUS EMPIRICUS (*c*.150–210), whose *Hypotyposes* and *Adversus Mathematicos* (translated as *Outlines of Pyrrhonism* and *Against the Logicians, Physicists, and Ethicists* by R. G. Bury (4 vols, London and Cambridge, Mass., 1933–49)) are the principle sources for knowledge of Greek scepticism. Aenesidemus listed 10 *tropoi*, or modes of sceptical argument, concerning the reliability of the senses, and eight concerning causal reasoning. About the reliability of the senses he argued that different animals experience things differently because of differences in their sense-organs. Sufferers from jaundice declare that objects which seem to us white are yellow, so animals which have yellow eyes probably have different perceptions of colour (Sextus Empiricus, *Outlines*, I

44). Who is to say whose perception is true? What is the CRITERION of truth?

On the question of a criterion, the Stoics (see STOICISM) had held that there is a special kind of SENSE-IMPRESSION, one which 'is eminently perceptive of real OBJECTS and reproduces with artistic precision all their characteristics' (Sextus Empiricus, *Against the Logicians*, I 248). Such an impression is 'apprehensive': it 'grasps' its object, and such a grasping does not permit of being mistaken. The Academic sceptic Carneades attacked the notion of such an impression, holding true impressions to be intrinsically indistinguishable from false ones. What we have, he held, is not a criterion of the truth of a perceptual assertion, but a criterion of our being justified in making a perceptual assertion. This is a matter of the impression being credible, of its being consistent with other impressions, and of its passing tests of reliability. Even if it satisfies this criterion the impression may be false. All we can claim is knowledge of probabilities, not certain knowledge. The Pyrrhonist, on the other hand, suspends judgment even about probabilities.

The writings of Sextus Empiricus, rediscovered in the RENAISSANCE, influenced modern philosophers from MONTAIGNE and GASSENDI onwards. His arguments and examples recur in the work of philosophers such as BERKELEY and HUME.

Pythagoras, (*c*.570–*c*.504 BC), grew up on the island of Samos, about 25 miles north-west of Miletus, the home of the still active MILESIAN SCHOOL of philosophy. He probably visited Egypt and Babylonia. Around 525 BC he left Samos to escape from the tyranny of Polycrates, and settled in Croton in Southern Italy, south of the Gulf of Taranto. There he founded an order that was both religious and philosophical. It became powerful politically; there was a revolt against it in about 500 BC; and Pythagoras took refuge in Metapontum, about 80 miles to the north, where he died.

Members of the order, the Pythagoreans, observed a rule of secrecy. This, together with the practice of crediting the founder of an order with any discoveries made, or doctrines adopted, by its members, makes it difficult to say what elements of Pythagoreanism are due to Pythagoras himself, but it is likely that he is responsible for the discovery of the numerical basis of MUSICAL CONCORDANCES, and for the doctrines of the kinship of all living things and of the transmigration of souls. The alternative possibility is that he brought all these doctrines back from Babylonia. *Philo* (trans. F. H. Colson and G. H.

Whitaker, Vol. IV, p. 235) described the Chaldeans (or Babylonians) as having

> the reputation of having in a degree quite beyond that of other peoples, elaborated astronomy and the casting of nativities. They have set up a harmony between things on earth and things on high, between heavenly things and earthly. Following as it were the laws of musical proportion, they have exhibited the universe as a perfect concord or symphony produced by a sympathetic affinity between its parts, separated indeed in space, but housemates in kinship.

The Pythagoreans probably knew some of the theorems subsequently proved by Euclid in his *Elements*. Of these, Pythagoras himself may have known the theorem that bears his name (that the square on the hypotenuse of a right-angled triangle is equal to the sum of the squares on the sides enclosing the right angle). See PYTHAGOREANISM.

Pythagoreanism, *n.* in spite of the secrecy of the Pythagoreans it is possible to reconstruct, from what PLATO and ARISTOTLE and others wrote, a fairly homogeneous body of doctrine that may be called 'Pythagoreanism'. So reconstructed, it combines a religion offering salvation from repeated incarnations (souls endlessly migrating from one body to another, perhaps even from a human body to a non-human one, such as that of a dog) with the HYLOZOISM of the MILESIAN SCHOOL, and with a theory, supported by a discovery about MUSICAL CONCORDANCES, about the real nature of the first principle and ELEMENT, accounting for what is orderly and unchanging in the universe (for the universe being a *kosmos* i.e. basically orderly and unchanging). The transmigration of souls involves the doctrine that all living beings are akin, perhaps even including some plants, such as beans, among living beings. The doctrine that the better one knows something the more one becomes like it involves all these points.

PYTHAGORAS had discovered that musical concordances correspond to the precise numerical ratios 1:2, 2:3 and 3:4. If a length of string is bridged so that it is divided in one of these ratios then the notes produced by vibrating the pieces on either side of the bridge will be concordant. The Pythagoreans seized on this as providing the key to an understanding of *all* order; musical order was their paradigm for understanding the order of the whole universe. Moreover, they seem to have thought of numbers as substantial, witness ARISTOTLE (*Metaphysics* 1083b 17): 'these thinkers identify numbers with real things; at any rate they apply their propositions to bodies as if they consisted of those numbers'. Whether numbers, so conceived, played the role that had been given to the opposites ('the hot', 'the cold', and so on) in other cosmologies, is doubtful.

ANAXIMANDER had taught that the opposites are in the *apeiron* (the 'boundless' or 'unlimited') and are 'separated off'. The Pythagoreans were able to salvage at least part of this, the 'unlimited'. Just as the whole field of sound is reduced to order by imposing the relevant system of ratios on it, so the mathematical order of the whole universe is produced by the imposition of limit *(peras)* on the unlimited. The Pythagoreans equated the limit and the unlimited with oddness and evenness respectively, and from these generated all the numbers which, as substantial, constitute the reality of everything.

The Pythagoreans differed from Milesian thought in that philosophy for them was a purification, a way of salvation. They thought that by contemplating the intelligible mathematical reality of the divine *kosmos*, their souls would grow to resemble that reality, to partake more and more of its divinity and so, eventually, be released from the grim round of successive incarnations in mortal bodies. Thereby the notion of the soul as distinct from the body, and the carrier of the real identity of the person, was introduced into philosophy.

Alongside the contemplative aspect of their religion there was a practical one, though some of the moral precepts, such as that of abstaining from beans, are hard for us to recognise as moral. According to Cicero *(On Divination)* Pythagoreans were forbidden to eat beans because they have 'a flatulent tendency inimical to the pursuit of mental tranquility', but the true explanation probably involves the kinship doctrine.

The above omits the details of Pythagoreanism, such as the generation of geometrical figures from numbers and the reduction even of abstractions like justice to a number (four; cf. Aristotle, *Nichomachean Ethics* 1131 a 10–20). It includes much of what proved influential in subsequent philosophy, particularly in Plato.

Some of Plato's debts are evident in his dialogues. There is the doctrine of successive reincarnations, employed to explain how learning is really recollection, in the *Meno* (81 b–d); the doctrine of kinship, in the *Gorgias* (508 a); the doctrine that the better one knows something the more one becomes like it, in the *Republic* (500 c–d). The *Phaedo* embodies the Pythagorean notion that philosophy is a preparation for death (64a) and for IMMORTALITY. The *Timaeus* is Plato's version of the Pythagorean account of how the universe is formed by the laws of harmony.

The more metaphysical of Plato's debts are not so accessible. Perhaps Plato thought they should not be communicated in writing. Plato's treatment of Pythagorean number theory and its relation to his own THEORY OF FORMS may have been in an unpublished course of lectures on 'The Good'. Such knowledge as we have of it comes largely from Aristotle.

Q

quantifier, *n.* in LOGIC, an expression like 'for all *x*', 'for some *x*', used in putting sentences of everyday language into a form using symbols.

Quine, Willard Van Orman (1908–   ), American logician and philosopher, professor at Harvard, has contributed greatly to modern LOGIC and has criticised current assumptions of EMPIRICISM. Thus, he questions the sharp distinction between ANALYTIC AND SYNTHETIC. Since, in his view, we must take into account a whole system of findings when we make any statement, we can exercise some freedom in choosing what we regard as analytic (sometimes called the Duhem–Quine thesis). Along with this goes a theory that translation from one language into another is essentially indeterminate, because we have no prior rules to establish how a speaker of a foreign language, which we seek to learn, is taking a particular word. This notion is not satisfactory: at that rate we could never communicate with others who speak our own language, or perhaps even remember what we ourselves meant on a previous occasion. As regards the question of what there is in the world (ontology), Quine holds that to be is to be a value of a variable. To explicate this dictum, we commit ourselves to there being items *Y* in the world if we assert that there is an *X* such that *X* is a *Y*. The *X* is a variable in a language. What we actually thus allow to exist depends on the sort of statements we commonly do make. Ontology then becomes a function of linguistic use. These positions are explained in *From a Logical Point of View* (1953).

R

rationalism, *n.* is the philosophic position that sees all KNOWLEDGE of the world as based on reason (Latin *ratio*) alone. Thus we are supposed to be able to excogitate how things are. From this it is a short step to the view that the world is itself constructed on rational lines; that is, in ways that belong to our reason. Opposed to this is the view that our knowledge must rest on EXPERIENCE, an outlook called EMPIRICISM (from Greek *peira* experience). Rationalist thinkers tend to assume that the MIND and its powers are given all of a piece, so that there seems no genuine room for learning anything. At the same time they take the world to be reducible to simple ELEMENTS, from which everything can be constructed by LOGIC alone. The best field to illustrate this is MATHEMATICS, which is readily organised in this manner. So are highly mathematicised branches of science (one used to speak of 'rational mechanics' when referring to the mathematical theory of mechanics). Insofar as the progress of scientific theory requires a leap of the IMAGINATION ahead of experience, scientific enquiry involves a rationalist feature. However, this cannot function in a context totally bereft of experience. Even mathematics has to be learnt like anything else. Still, that twice two makes four is not quite on a par with grass being green. For one thing, mathematics has the widest scope, being exemplified everywhere, while findings about grass are less general and less abstract.

Rawls, John (1921–), American philosopher known above all for his *Theory of Justice* (1971). He there develops a model of the just society, starting with a SOCIAL CONTRACT notion and applying a principle of fairness that is reminiscent of KANT'S CATEGORICAL IMPERATIVE; one must approve the rules as fair leaving aside how they would affect oneself, given the sort of person one is. This runs against the utilitarian practice (see UTILITARIANISM) of simply putting the general good before individual interest. Nevertheless, some notion of the common good remains in the theory: all must enjoy the greatest measure of freedom compatible with that of others, but inequalities are rationally defensible if the result benefits those who are least well placed.

real essence, see REAL, ESSENCE.

realism, *n.* in MEDIEVAL PHILOSOPHY, is the theory that UNIVERSALS have 'real' (thinglike) existence, as against the opposite view of NOMINALISM, where universals are mere names. In modern philosophy, the term connotes a theory of KNOWLEDGE according to which the world is furnished with independent OBJECTS and that it is these we perceive directly when we train our senses on them. This is opposed to a variety of views according to which we perceive something else: whether appearances, sense-data or some other intermediate entity that stands between us and the world. One reason for such a view is that we sometimes misperceive (the argument from illusion): we seem to see things that are not there, or that appear otherwise than they are; what then is it that we see in such cases? Still, if we conclude that all we ever see is visual sense-data, we make normal seeing depend on the exceptional case of mis-seeing (a word which is unusual but should perhaps be adopted, just as we use 'mis-hear'). In fact it is the other way round: misperceiving is parasitic on normal perceiving. There is a whole range of realist theories of PERCEPTION, from the naive REALISM of the plain man and the scientist in action (whatever he may say he holds) to more or less complicated compromises with non-realist views. Realism and opposing theories have opposite problems: the realist has to give a convincing account of error, his opponents must explain truth. On balance it seems a more hopeful task to tackle the former.

reality, *n.* (from Latin *res* thing) whatever is regarded as having existence as an OBJECTIVE thing, and not merely in appearance, thought, or language. For example, G. E. MOORE says that ethical PROPOSITIONS 'cannot be reduced to any assertion about reality' (*Principia Ethica*, Cambridge, 1903, 114). He evidently thinks of the natural world as the only world that exists objectively, and excludes the truths of ETHICS from it on the ground that 'good' is not a natural property. See NATURALISTIC FALLACY.

reductionism, *n.* the attempt to explain away something that is in some respect puzzling, by reducing it to something else that is, in that respect, not puzzling. Philosophical BEHAVIOURISM is an example. Statements about other people's minds (e.g. 'He is in pain') are puzzling in that they seem to go beyond the evidence for making them (observation of his moaning, etc). How can one justify the inference from painful behaviour to pain? A philosophical behaviourist simply offers a philosophical analysis of statements about other minds in terms of statements about behaviour. He 'reduces' the former to the latter (see MEANING). The term 'reductionism' is used, also, of the attempt to explain away some whole science, such as PSYCHOLOGY, in terms of another, such as physiology. JOHN STUART MILL accused Auguste COMTE of such reductionism (Mill, *System of Logic*, 1843, VI iv 2).

reflection, *n.* THINKING or (LOCKE) the inner observation of mental operations. See INTROSPECTION.

Reformation, *n.* the great split in the Western Church in the 16th century (see CHRISTIANITY), producing a permanent division between Roman Catholicism and Protestantism. Attempts at correcting worldly excesses of the clergy go further back, of course. The Waldensians of southern France in the 12th century were a group who aimed at this, and so were the English Lollards of the 14th and 15th centuries, who had been inspired by Wycliffe. However, the precipitating event was Luther's action in challenging Rome by nailing a list of 95 theses to the church portal at Wittenberg in 1517. The motives were various, and partly nationalistic: one malpractice resented by the Germans was the sale of indulgences (tickets reducing one's stay in purgatory) by Italian clerics for the purpose of building St Peter's at Rome. Luther, an Augustinian monk, did not at first intend to start a new church (no more than did Jesus of Nazareth), but was gradually driven to a complete break with the papacy. While in temporary hiding, he translated the Bible into German, making it accessible to everyone. In Switzerland, Zwingli and Calvin started similar movements, and in England the Church, though retaining some Catholic practices, acquired a new foundation in the 39 Articles which are in essence Protestant-inspired. By the early 17th century, much of Europe had become heavily Protestant, but the Catholic Church regained a good deal of ground through the Counter-Reformation that followed the Council of Trent (1545–1563). What all strands of Protestantism have in common is their belief that GOD speaks directly to human souls. Catholicism, by contrast, relies strongly on the intervention of a priesthood guided by church tradition.

The main effect of the Reformation was to undermine the spirit of obedience to any clerical authority, which paved the way for the development of modern science and philosophy. Thus the humanist efforts of the RENAISSANCE were able to grow into a permanently secular movement of intellectual enquiry, which has lasted ever since.

regress, *n.* (from Latin *regressus* a going back), in LOGIC, the recurrence, after some argument, of the same question with which one began. This may happen indefinitely often, in which case the regress is called infinite, and the initial question remains unanswered. See ARGUMENT FROM DESIGN.

Reid, Thomas (1710–1796), was born near Aberdeen, attended Marischal College and became a Presbyterian minister. In 1751 he was appointed to a regentship at King's College, Aberdeen. In 1764 his *Inquiry into the Human Mind on the Principles of Common-Sense* (hereafter, *Inquiry*) was published. Apart from an introduction and a conclusion it consists of five chapters, one on each of the senses of smelling, tasting, hearing, touch and seeing. In it Reid criticises what he calls the 'theory of ideas' or 'ideal system' of DESCARTES, MALE-BRANCHE, LOCKE, BERKELEY and HUME, the fundamental principle of which is 'that every object of thought must be an impression, or an idea, that is, a faint copy of some preceding impression' (*Inquiry*, Ch. 2, Sect. 6). In its place Reid offers an account of PERCEPTION which he claims to be in accord with the principles of common sense mirrored in our everyday language about what we perceive. In the same year as the *Inquiry* was published, Reid went to Glasgow as Professor of Moral Philosophy. His *Essays on the Intellectual Powers of Man* (hereafter, *Essays*) was published in 1785. In this book, which is long, repetitious, and not as revealing on perception as the *Inquiry*, Reid extends his criticism of the ideal system over a wider field, and argues, about MEMORY for example, that the OBJECT of the mental operation is the actual past event and not a present representation of it, a memory image. In his *Essays on the Active Powers of Man*, 1788, Reid defends a rationalist theory of ETHICS against the analysis, by HUTCHESON and Hume, of moral judgment in terms of sentiments of approbation and disapprobation.

Reid sees the ideal system as leading inevitably to Hume's SCEPTI-CISM. The philosophers who advocate the theory of ideas have offended against everyday language, which expresses the common sense of mankind. Ordinarily understood, to 'have an idea' is simply to think. An IDEA as an object of thought is 'a mere fiction of philosophers' (*Essays*, I, Ch. 1). Similarly, these philosophers have misused the word 'impression'.

There is a figurative meaning of impressions on the mind . . . but this meaning applies only to objects that are interesting. To say that an object which I see with perfect indifference makes an impression upon my mind is not, as I apprehend, good English . . . When I look upon the wall of my room, the wall does not act at all, nor is capable of acting; the perceiving is an act or operation in me. That this is the common apprehension of mankind with regard to perception is evident from the manner of expressing it in all languages (*Essays*, II, 4).

Reid put the blame for much wrong theorising about perception on analogical reasoning from a supposed similitude of MIND to body (*Essays*, I, 4). It is this that leads to philosophers talking of impressions on the mind as if they were thereby explaining the manner of perception (*Essays*, II, 4). The vulgar, Reid implies, are right in not seeking a theory to account for the operations of their minds. They simply say what they are conscious of (*Essays*, II, 9).

Some of Reid's arguments are similar to those employed by ARNAULD, against Malebranche, in his *Treatise on True and False Ideas*, 1683. In the other direction, Reid is a spiritual ancestor of G. E. MOORE in his advocacy of common-sense convictions supposedly expressed in what we ordinarily say. Scottish common sense in the 18th century was a forerunner of Cambridge common sense in the 20th, and of the Oxford philosopher, J. L. AUSTIN, in his *Sense and Sensibilia*, 1962. The rejection of the question 'How do we perceive?', if intended to elicit an answer that modifies our everyday language about what we perceive so as to take account of the physical basis of perception, is echoed in the writings of Gilbert RYLE (*Dilemmas*, 1954, Chapters 5–7).

On some of the central issues Reid paid no more than lip service to everyday language, and embraced uncritically the views of the philosophers he claimed to be hell-bent for scepticism. Locke had held that what we ordinarily call the colour of an external object is really a SENSATION it causes in us, a sensation comparable to the stomach-ache caused by eating something indigestible. Reid recognised how unacceptable this is to the philosophically-unindoctrinated, but sided with Locke against the vulgar: when we look at an object there are sensations in us that are distinct from, and quite unlike, the quality we call 'colour' in the object of vision. He paid lip service to everyday language by advocating that colour-words be used, not of the sensations in us, but of the qualities in external objects that give rise to them, so that we can continue to say, for example, that snow really is white (*Inquiry*, Ch. 6, Sect. 5). He sought to avoid the route to scepticism which consists in interposing a veil of ideas between the mind and the external world by saying that sensations are not *objects* we feel, but mental *acts* we perform (*Essays*, I 1)—acts that immediately 'suggest' a corresponding quality in an external object. Berkeley, in his *New Theory of Vision*, (1709), had written of visible ideas suggesting distance. Reid took over Berkeley's notion of suggestion but altered it so as to allow for there being 'natural and original' suggestions. For example, 'certain sensations of touch, by the constitution of our nature, suggest to us extension, solidity, and motion, which are nowise like to sensations' (*Inquiry*, Ch. 2, Sect. 7). He applies this to colour and shape, but so distorts the usage of the word 'suggest' that it is hard to assess his theory. Why does he say that the shape is suggested to us, instead of simply saying that we see the shape? The question 'Why do you believe in what suggests itself to you when you are not aware of what suggests it?' is conducive to scepticism in a way in which 'Why do you believe in what you see?' is not. As to our belief in the external world, his 'suggestion' account is not very different from Hume's account: in what they say about perception Hume and Reid are equally far removed from common sense.

relativism, *n.* in philosophy, generally means the position that there are no absolute truths or values. The classical expression of relativism is the dictum of PROTAGORAS, that man is the measure of all things. It is of course a commonplace that different people like, or approve of, different things. If now everyone insists on calling what he likes 'good', then there is no absolute MEANING to that term, other than just that whoever uses it refers to things he likes. A more extreme form of relativism applies to categorical statements. Thus, what looks small to a giant looks big to a dwarf, so that it seems impossible to say absolutely that an OBJECT is big or small. In fact, such puzzles arise only if we forget that here one always compares two sizes, namely that of the object with that of one's body. Relativism in the softer sense, that we must consider the bearing of statements in their general setting, is of course straightforward, even if not always properly observed. Thus anthropologists must be careful not to interpret their observations in terms of the presuppositions peculiar to their own background and civilisations. An insidious form of relativism, much favoured by some schools of psychiatry, has it that everyone's feelings are true for him or her. This means no more than that we all tend to be mildly self-satisfied. A thoroughgoing relativism is self-defeating, because it could never be consistently stated.

relativity theory, *n.* a modern account of SPACE AND TIME, going back to the work of Albert EINSTEIN in the early 20th century. Whereas NEWTON held that space and time are absolute, that is independent of anybody observing them, Einstein analysed the way in which we measure space and time and from that analysis built up his theory of relativity. According to this, the spatio–temporal framework of the world is essentially tied to the process of observing it, and this somewhat shakes our traditional intuitions in that area. In particular, while the classical notions of space and time were independent of each other, relativity theory sees them closely linked in a single space–time. This is indeed a new concept and different from the views held on this subject by philosophers from ancient times. The theory of relativity comes in two forms, the special and the general. The special theory considers frameworks in uniform relative motion to each other and turns out to provide an invariant form of the laws of electrodynamics (that is, the mathematical form of these laws is the same in either of the two moving frameworks). The general theory considers frameworks in arbitrary relative motion to each other and enables the law of gravitation to be given in invariant form. Einstein's theory of gravitation is marginally more adequate than Newton's, although Newton is generally adequate, even for getting to the moon.

religion, philosophy of, *n.* an examination of the concepts of religious theory and their function in practice. In particular, it concerns theological themes, the nature and existence of a GOD or gods, and the way in which God is related to the world, whether as creator, organiser, ruler or giver of moral commands. In this wide sense, theology borders on aspects of METAPHYSICS. This is clear from the way PLATO treats the FORM of the Good, and ARISTOTLE sees first philosophy as involving CONCEPTS such as those of a first CAUSE and an unmoved mover. These metaphysical notions greatly influenced Christian thinkers of a later age. Indeed Christian theology might be called Greek philosophy applied to Old Testament ethical ideas and views of God. This is the tradition in which various proofs for the existence of God arose. These in turn have all of them been criticised as invalid. In particular, the Protestant view is that the God of the testaments is not logically establishable but must be revealed through faith. Even Catholic tradition allowed no more than that we can prove that God exists, but not what he is like, which again is a matter of revealed religion. This so-called '*via negativa*' in theology is reminiscent of the Parmenidean One (see PARMENIDES), of which nothing can be asserted except unity. Indeed, this is one of the sources of all subsequent theological theorizing. In modern existentialist theology (see EXISTENTIALISM), the way to God lies through a leap of faith. Much modern theology in any case involves a psychological examination of what is involved in asserting one's belief in a god. More recently still, in the wake of analytical philosophy, some thinkers have examined the structure of religious language and what it aims to achieve. Some forms of modern religious philosophy, the so-called 'god is dead' theology which goes back to NIETZCHE's view to that effect, is a kind of return to Greek views, according to which the gods are remote from human affairs and take no interest in our individual lives. For the rest, it is clear that the pursuit of a moral life does require a divinity to give it external sanction. This much was indeed clear to Plato.

Renaissance, *n.* (*French* rebirth) a period of cultural revival at the end of medieval times, when renewed interest was taken in the ancient civilisations of Greece and Rome. The movement began in the 14th century in Italy, travelled to France in the 15th and to England and Germany in the 16th. This was essentially a return to pre-Christian traditions and gradually undermined clerical supremacy. Scholars began to study in their own right, without allowing anyone to prescribe the intellectual space in which they must move. At the same time as a vigorous effort at editing and publishing ancient texts, there was a rise of national literatures. In the classical spirit, people broke away from excessive concern with the next world in favour of enhancing life in this one. This switch was greatly furthered by the so-called humanist movement (see HUMANISM), the work of thinkers and teachers of what we now call the humanities: philosophy, history, languages. In particular, Scriptures were now studied not from Latin translations, but from the original Hebrew (*Old Testament*) and Greek (*New Testament*). Indeed, the editions of classical texts from this period remained in use until displaced by modern editions in the mid–19th century. The Renaissance did not as such produce a philosophy of its own, but was much given over to Neo-Platonist views (see NEO-PLATONISM). Typical of its outlook was an interest that was unbounded: the aim was to be universally informed and competent. This ideal of the universal man has become increasingly impossible to attain, because of the vast accumulation of specialised knowledge since then. We now know more and more about less and less.

representative theory of perception, see PERCEPTION.

romanticism, *n.* a style of THINKING and looking at the world that dominated 19th century Europe. The term is not very precise and literally goes back to the rise of tales in the Romance language in early medieval times, as against works in classical Latin. Since many of these tales were about courtly love and other sentimental topics, the term later came to be used to refer to an outlook marked by refined and responsive feelings and thus inward looking, subjective, 'sensitive', given to noble dreams. The romantic movement took off as the 19th century ENLIGHTENMENT went past its peak. Still, such generalisations are always too simple. Indeed, the Enlightenment itself had some romantic features, notably the view that man was infinitely improvable by education. More generally, any form of neglecting or ignoring EVIL is a romantic streak. ROUSSEAU's notion of the noble savage is typically romantic. The metaphysical poets in England are romantic in inspiration and so is the *Sturm und Drang* of late 18th century Germany. GOETHE shows both classical and romantic sides. His *Werther* (1774) is a prototype of romantic sentiment. The idealist philosophy of the late 18th and early 19th centuries is essentially romantic, and so is much of the music of the immediate post-classical style. Just as blind optimism is romantic, so is blind pessimism (e.g. SCHOPENHAUER). In political thought, it may be best to distinguish romantic streaks here and there, rather than give various thinkers definite labels. Thus, egalitarianism is a typically romantic notion, while the statement that the price of liberty is eternal vigilance (ultimately due to Curran) is not. In general, the opposite of romanticism is classicism, which is governed by precise measures and an outward looking attitude. Although some people are doubtless predominantly marked by either one or the other, in most there are traces of both.

Rousseau, Jean-Jacques (1712–1778), French-Swiss man of letters and philosopher, was the first major figure in the romantic reaction (see ROMANTICISM) to the 18th century ENLIGHTENMENT and a precursor of the French Revolution. He is best known for his political theory as outlined in *Du Contrat Social* (1762), where he argued that supremacy in the State must remain with the people, who have the right to vote on any legislative proposal (see SOCIAL CONTRACT), This, of course, leaves the minority view ignored. To overcome this objection, he postulated a 'general will' which is somehow always right. This encourages the view that the State is a higher entity than the citizens that live in it, with a will of its own. Many of these topics were discussed by thinkers of the following generation and by apologists of the revolution of 1789. In his didactic novel *Émile* (1762), he put forward his views on education. According to the book on the social contract, he had argued that man is by nature free, while in the civilised state there must be legal sanctions. So now we find that the 'noble savage' is corrupted by culture, so that in education we should preserve the child's natural unspoilt condition as best we can: there should be no compulsion or rote learning, but acquisition of KNOWLEDGE through doing things. At each stage, we must recognise what children need and what they are developed enough to do, in order that they should learn to live satisfying lives as free citizens. The setting should be rural, to avoid the corrupting influence of cities. These views were unusual at that time and have greatly influenced progressive notions in modern education.

Russell, Bertrand Arthur William, 3rd Earl (from 1931) (1872–1970), English philosopher, grew up in the home of his grandfather, Lord John Russell, the Victorian prime minister, and studied MATHEMATICS at Trinity College, Cambridge, where he met WHITEHEAD, with whom he published *Principia Mathematica* (1910–13). He taught philosophy at Trinity from 1910 to 1916 and was then expelled because of pacifist activities that landed him in jail in 1918. Between the wars he did much lecturing at home and abroad, ran a progressive school and published many minor works on a range of social, political and historical topics. During the Second World War he stayed mainly in North America, teaching at various universities but being rejected as a candidate for a professorship at New York (1940) on account of his ATHEISM. Returning to England in 1944, he went on writing and lecturing, received the Order of Merit in 1949, and in his last years took an active part in the Campaign for Nuclear Disarmament, which involved another short stay in prison. He began his career as a mathematician. After an early phase of IDEALISM, which then dominated the universities, he broke away, partly under the influence of G. E. MOORE, and adopted a realist position, which accorded well with his mathematical interests. This point of view prevails in his *Principles of Mathematics* (1903). In *Principia Mathematica*, the foundations of LOGIC and their link with MATHEMATICS are presented in a strictly FORMAL manner, and the theory of types is devised to cope with certain PARADOXES that appeared in the system. In 1911, he published *Problems of Philosophy*, an introduction to these problems which continues to be very readable. In it he introduces the distinction between knowledge by description (the French *savoir*) and knowledge by acquaintance *(connaître)*. All our actual KNOWLEDGE arises from knowing in the second sense: I know directly when I am in the presence of a thing, so that acquaintance guarantees existence; as regards physical OBJECTS, they must be seen as causing sense–data, so that the objects are known by description. At a later stage, he changed his views and regarded physical objects as logically constructed from sense–data, which is a view shared by logical positivists (*Our Knowledge of the External World*, 1914). In formal logic, one of his contributions is the theory of descriptions, a way of eliminating PROPER NAMES and coping with PROPOSITIONS whose subjects belong to empty classes. One aim of *Principia* was to show how mathematics was derivable from logic. However, it has since been found that the outcome of such an attempt depends on whether class membership is regarded as a logical or a mathematical relation. His *Analysis of Mind* (1921) treats mentality as having degrees, and regards what he calls 'mnemic causation' as probably derivable from ordinary physical causation in biological tissue. As a writer and polemicist, Russell has something of a Voltairean waspishness and elegance. In 1952 he received the Nobel prize for literature.

Ryle, Gilbert (1900–1976), Oxford philosopher best known for *The Concept of Mind* (London, 1949) and for his editorship of the philosophy journal *Mind*, 1947–1971.

Ryle's paper 'Systematically Misleading Expressions' (*Proc. Arist. Soc.*, 32, 1931–32) was the first statement of the view that, as WITTGENSTEIN later put it, 'philosophy is a battle against the bewitchment of our understanding through the means of language' (*Philosophical Investigations*, Oxford, 1953, I 109). In this early paper of Ryle's this view of philosophy was allied with the logical atomist doctrine that philosophically satisfactory expressions are ones that directly picture atomic facts. Ryle dropped the logical atomist overtones in later statements of his view about the nature and method of philosophy, such as in the lecture, *Philosophical Arguments* (Oxford, 1945), he gave on being made Wayneflete Professor of Metaphysical Philosophy in Oxford. In this lecture, philosophy was revealed as having not only a negative aim, that of freeing us from conceptual confusions, but also a positive one, that of showing how CONCEPTS are really related to one another.

The two complementary aims are at work in *The Concept of Mind*. The negative aim is that of showing that a certain view about the application of epithets like 'careful', 'stupid', 'logical', 'unobservant', 'ingenious', 'vain', 'methodical', 'credulous', 'witty', and 'self-controlled', is mistaken. The view Ryle holds to be mistaken is that the application of these epithets involves our 'making untestable inferences to ghostly processes occurring in streams of consciousness which we are debarred from visiting'. Ryle's negative aim is thus to show that what he calls 'the dogma of the Ghost in the Machine' is entirely false. His positive aim is 'to rectify the logical geography' of the 'careful', 'stupid', etc. epithets.

Ryle has a further unstated aim exhibited in his use of the term 'mind', namely to promote a use different from that of those who use it in opposition to what is not mind. The aim is exhibited in his calling the 'careful', 'stupid', etc., epithets, *'mental-conduct* epithets', and in his saying that the contrast, the opposition, of mind and matter is illegitimate. (It involves the 'category mistake' of representing differences between the physical and the mental as 'differences inside the common framework of the categories of "thing", "stuff", "attribute", "state", "process", "change", "cause" and "effect"'.) In Ryle's use of the term 'mind', the opposition *is* illegitimate, since to say that somebody did something carefully, etc., is to describe the manner of their doing it; it is not to describe something other than their performance, such as their experiences in performing in this manner. Experiences are not mental, in Ryle's use of the term 'mental', since 'having a sensation is not an exercise of a quality of intellect or character'. 'To use an objectionable phrase', he said, 'there is nothing "mental" about sensations'. This, at the time, was revolutionary. It was an outright rejection of PRIVACY as the CRITERION of the mental, and led, as Ryle suspected it would, to his being described as some sort of behaviourist.

In *Dilemmas* (Cambridge, 1954) Ryle sought to show that philosophical problems, such as the freewill–determinism problem (see FREEWILL AND DETERMINISM), can be solved not by coming down on one horn of the dilemma, but by exhibiting the apparent conflict as a consequence of conceptual confusion. Later works include *Plato's Progress* (Cambridge, 1966) and a collection of papers entitled *On Thinking* (Oxford, 1979).

S

Sartre, Jean-Paul (1905–1980), French writer and philosopher, was an atheist existentialist (see EXISTENTIALISM), although he repudiated the label, and in his account of freedom is perhaps better regarded as a follower of FICHTE. In his plays and novels he shows man as the architect of his own life and character. That is somewhat reminiscent of ARISTOTLE, for whom the good man becomes so through becoming used to performing good actions. In Sartre, the basic feature is freedom to decide for oneself. His literary work is full of acute insights into human behaviour and motivation. He is pessimistic in outlook, somewhat inclined towards SOLIPSISM, and regards hell as 'other people'. Politically, he supported the French Communist Party, but broke with it after the Hungarian invasion of 1956. His main purely philosophic treatise, *Being and Nothingness* (1943), is much influenced by HEIDEGGER and contains an account of consciousness as an ontological fact, and a conception of the negative as not just denial but some sort of entity in the manner of the German philosopher. During the war, Sartre had joined the Resistance, and afterwards, in 1945, founded the literary journal *Les Temps Modernes*, concentrating thenceforth on literary activity. A treatise on man as an ethical agent, promised at the end of *Being and Nothingness*, never appeared.

scepticism, *n.* (from Greek *skepsis* doubt) the view that our claims to know various things, such as that there are physical OBJECTS that exist independently of our perceiving them, or that there are other minds, cannot be accepted without justification; that there is no adequate justification for such KNOWLEDGE claims; and hence that we ought either to deny that we know these things, or to suspend judgment about them. The former was the dogmatic scepticism of the Middle Academy under Arcesilaus of Pitane (*c.*315–240 BC) and Carneades of Cyrene (*c.*213–129 BC), the latter the Pyrrhonian scepticism (after Pyrrho of Elis, *c.*365–275 BC) of Aenesidemas (1st century AD) (see PYRRHONISM). An issue between the Stoics (see STOICISM) and the Sceptics was whether there is a means of judging, a 'CRITERION', to distinguish veridical sense-impressions from others. The Stoics held there is, the Sceptics either that there is not or that what we have is at best a criterion for being justified in making a perceptual assertion, even if it is in fact false. This was discussed in the writings of SEXTUS EMPIRICUS (c.150–210), rediscovered in the RENAISSANCE. They influenced both theologians, such as Luther, and philosophers, including MONTAIGNE, GASSENDI, DESCARTES, MALEBRANCHE, BAYLE and BERKELEY.

Having systematically doubted everything he could, Descartes sought a basis for justifying some of our ordinary knowledge claims in the indubitability of *cogito ergo sum* ('I think therefore I am'), (see COGITO) and the reflection that all that assures anyone of its truth is that it is clearly and distinctly conceived. This new philosophy, with its DUALISM of mind and body and PRIMARY AND SECONDARY QUALITIES, served only to channel scepticism into new forms, calling forth yet more paradoxical ways of opposing it. The most paradoxical was the IMMATERIALISM or IDEALISM of Bishop BERKELEY: one cannot be sceptical about the existence of material things, because really they are no more than collections of the things of which we are immediately aware, namely 'ideas'. To Thomas REID it seemed preferable to question the basic assumption of idealism, the 'way of ideas' of Descartes and LOCKE. KANT'S TRANSCENDENTAL idealism combined scepticism about knowing things in themselves with an explanation of how we experience an objective world subject to universal causation.

Some present-day philosophers distinguish between a question *in* a language and a question *about* the language. The question *about* the physical object language is whether we are justified in using it. A philosophical realist takes this to mean 'Are there entities of the kind referred to in the language, that is, entities which can exist unperceived?' This cannot be answered in terms of the criteria with which we operate *in* the language, and there are no others. Thus justification, interpreted in a realist fashion, is illegitimate. Consider an analogy. European settlers in a land traditionally inhabited by nomadic tribesmen may talk of 'staking claims' to areas of land, and of 'owning' such land. They erect boundary fences with warning signs. To the nomadic tribesmen all this is incomprehensible. How can anyone own *land*! All one can say is that some people use the ownership language, about land, and others do not. The difference between the physical object language and the land-ownership language is that everyone uses the former language. See EPISTEMOLOGY, ILLUSION, ARGUMENT FROM, KNOWLEDGE, OTHER MINDS PROBLEM, PERCEPTION.

Schlick, Moritz (1882–1936), German philosopher, from 1922 professor at Vienna, founded the VIENNA CIRCLE and was one of the leading logical positivists of his time. He rejected the Neo-Kantian tendencies (see KANT) and the PHENOMENOLOGY of HUSSERL, practising instead the sort of critical analysis of PERCEPTION found in MACH. He accepted the strong verification principle, which, however, excluded not only speculative METAPHYSICS but theoretical science as well, and even his own early 'critical realism'. Still, this did not disturb him, since he felt that what mattered was sticking to the rules of the language adopted in scientific work. In the light of this he held that ethical talk expressed attitudes rather than facts (see FACTS AND VALUES). He died before his time, assassinated by a student.

scholastic, *adj.* (from Latin *schola* school) the philosophy taught in the schools in monasteries and abbeys in the Middle Ages, and, by derivation, a method of disputation pioneered by Peter ABELARD (1079–1142). 'Scholastic' is sometimes used as a term of abuse by those who think the method lends itself to the making of endless and fruitless distinctions. The 'Golden Age' of scholasticism was the 13th century, and the most famous scholastic philosopher was St Thomas AQUINAS.

Schopenhauer, Arthur (1788–1860), German philosopher who developed a theory in which the ultimate driving force of reality was the will. Although an atheist, he was influenced by Buddhist (see BUDDHISM) and Vedantic thought. In *The World as Will and Idea* (1819), he develops the view that the evil and pain in the world result from the exercise of the will. By extension, he recognised a cosmic will operating in the world, a blind force that produces strife and must be overcome if one is to achieve some escape from the troubles that beset life. This generally pessimistic theory carried considerable romantic appeal in the early 19th century (see ROMANTICISM). In some details, he foreshadowed modern depth-psychology, in that he regarded the will as sometimes preventing our becoming aware of our true motives: much mental activity occurs at an unconscious level. As a writer he was scornful of the pompous output of academic philosophers of his time and adopted a much more elegant style. His *oeuvre* is not extensive and he himself said that he was an 'oligographer' (a writer of little).

science, philosophy of, *n.* the study of various general problems particularly important in scientific activity, and an examination of the nature and function of scientific theory itself. In modern times those who have contributed to this field have often been scientists rather than philosophers, but at the very beginning there is PLATO, who in his *Phaedo* first put forward the method of HYPOTHESIS and DEDUCTION. What a scientific theory must do is to 'save the appearances', an expression used at first of the apparent motions of the heavenly bodies in astronomy, but later extended to all 'phenomena' (appearances). The scientific method has never been better stated, and it remains more or less a correct account of what scientists in fact do, whatever they might say they do. As regards our apprehension of facts through PERCEPTION, scientists have from time to time taken various philosophical views not so much after having examined them but because they seem somehow easy to work with. By and large, some form of sense-data theory is accepted by most scientists. As to theory, there is a variety of views. Some regard the language of theory mainly as a matter of convention (Poincaré), which is adopted on pragmatic grounds because of its useful results. The pragmatic view has come to the fore in certain areas of modern science (e.g. quantum theory), where we no longer seem to be able to follow the course of events in detail but merely notice initial conditions and final outcome. As against the classical view of science yielding definite conclusions, certain modern developments are said to favour the notion of the statistical or probabilistic nature of results (see PROBABILITY THEORY). Here, too, the working scientist is often better than the speculators about the nature of science: one who works in a laboratory is of necessity a naive realist, or else he could not read his instruments. On the question of how theories are set up, philosophers have again taken various views. Some regard the process of scientific work as one of INDUCTION (HUME, MILL), going from particulars to universals in terms of more or less probable inferences. PEIRCE was the first to reinstate the method of hypothesis and deduction, pointing out that INDUCTION has to do with the testing of hypotheses, not with their setting up. In our own time, POPPER has strongly opposed inductivism and favours the putting forward of daring hypotheses (because they are more exposed to falsification). A further question is whether we can criticise a theory piecemeal, or whether we must take it as a whole. Clearly, a theory of some scope will not be given up because of some local blemish that can somehow be patched up. This points to an organic feature in scientific theories and is most readily appreciated by biological scientists. There remains the question of what makes a theory acceptable: in practice it is often the majority view or consensus amongst scientists. Nevertheless, they could all be wrong. It is this logical circumstance that has misled some thinkers into regarding truth, in science and elsewhere, as something relative to a given setting. On the contrary: we must simply allow that we are extremely liable to error.

secondary qualities, *n.* see PRIMARY AND SECONDARY QUALITIES.

semantics, *n.* (from Greek *sema* sign) the theory of how words have MEANING, is a concern both of students of language and of logicians and philosophers. On the practical side, it is a descriptive account of any actual (natural) language. On the theoretical side, it considers the constructions of systems of meaning-rules. Thus what we study here are interpreted signs (signs with their meanings specified), in contrast with SYNTAX where we leave the signs uninterpreted. One problem that belongs to semantics is whether, and if so how, there come to be semantic shifts (drifts of meaning). Another is to examine how the surface semantics of a language might be derived from a deeper level of signification. Some of these problems shade off into psychological enquiry. By sign here we refer to a mark (not necessarily physical) with a meaning or signification. See LANGUAGE, PHILOSOPHY OF, and CHOMSKY.

sensation, *n.* a feeling in some part of one's body, such as a pain in one's hand; or a sensation of something one is touching, such as a sensation of the furriness and warmth of a cat; or, controversially, a sensation of whiteness on seeing snow, or a sensation of screeching on hearing an owl.

DESCARTES said that nature had taught him, by his bodily sensations, that he was not present in his body merely as a pilot is present in a ship, but 'as it were mixed up with' his body, so that he and it formed a unity *(Sixth Meditation)*. By his MIND being 'mixed up with' his body he did not mean that his mind was in the parts of his body in which he had sensations. 'Pain in the hand is not felt by the mind inasmuch as it is in the hand, but as it is in the brain' *(Principles*, IV cxcvi). That is, for a pain caused by the hand being squeezed to be felt in the hand a nervous impulse must reach the brain, with which the mind has connections via the pineal gland.

According to the 'Local Sign' theory of Hermann Lotze (1817–1881) a person can say whether a pain is in his right hand or his left by virtue of some additional quality of the pain which serves as a sign to him of the location of the cause of the pain. Oswald Külpe (1862–1915) held that the experienced difference between a pain in one's right hand and one in one's left can be simply one of the place in which it is felt, just as the experienced difference between a sound heard as coming from one's right and one heard as coming from one's left can be simply one of the direction from which the sound is heard as coming. Like the explanation of the locating of sound-sources, the explanation of the locating of bodily sensations can be purely physiological. Külpe called the assumption that the locating must involve 'local signs', and conscious inference, a 'metaphysical prepossession'.

One can talk of having a sensation of something one is touching, such as a sensation of the furriness and warmth of a cat. Some philosophers say that this involves having bodily sensations, in one's fingers, which give one's sensations their character. Normally one attends to the qualities of the OBJECT, but one can attend to the sensations in one's fingers: one infers that the cat is furry and warm from one's fingers feeling furry and warm when one touches it. This seems more plausible in the case of the warmth than in the case of the furriness, since warmth is a recognised bodily sensation. There is a difference of category between feeling the warmth of something with one's fingers, and one's fingers feeling warm, witness the use of the words 'of' and 'with' in the former, but not in the latter. One's fingers feeling warm is not a matter of feeling the warmth of one's fingers with something (or if it is, we are not talking about a bodily sensation).

The use of words like 'warm' to refer both to qualities of objects and to bodily sensations was exploited by BERKELEY in an argument for our not being justified in calling objects warm *(First Dialogue)*: being sentient, we can feel warm; to be justified in calling objects warm we should have to be justified in ascribing to objects something like what we feel when we feel warm; but objects are non-sentient; so there is no basis for the ascription of warmth to objects.

Does one have a sensation of whiteness on seeing something white? Thomas REID remarked: 'Though all philosophers agree that in seeing colour there is sensation, it is not easy to persuade the vulgar that in seeing a coloured body, when the light is not too strong nor the eye inflamed, they have any sensation or feeling at all' *(Essays*, II 18).

The difficulty of persuading 'the vulgar' that they have sensations of colour could be avoided, whilst retaining the possibility of questioning whether things are as they seem, by talking, not of 'sensations', but of 'appearances'. This alternative terminology is employed by Berkeley *(New Theory of Vision*, 44) and by HUME *(Enquiry*, 12 I 118) in an argument for our not seeing what we would ordinarily be said to see. In Berkeley's version, the argument goes: from a mile away a tree presents an 'obscure, small and faint' appearance; close up, the appearance is 'clear, large and vigorous'; but the tree does not change; since what I see changes, and the tree does not change, what I see is not the tree. Thomas Reid rejects this as absurd, on the grounds that if it is a real tree I see (I am not hallucinating) then its appearance *should* alter as I approach it (*Essays* II 14).

Sensation is sometimes said to be an ELEMENT in perception that is interpreted to yield a judgment. A person cannot be said to be right or wrong in having a sensation, but can be said to be right or wrong in making a judgment. Those who distinguish in this way sometimes accuse 'the vulgar' of mistaking a judgment for a sensation, particularly as regards the distance and three-dimensionality of objects. Descartes says that the size, shape and distance of a staff 'clearly depend upon the understanding alone', but 'are vulgarly assigned to sense' because 'custom makes us reason and judge so quickly' that 'we fail to distinguish the difference between these operations and a simple sense perception' (*Reply to Objections*, VI 9). Locke gives much the same explanation of our thinking we actually perceive a globe as convex, when really the IDEA we receive from the globe is only a plane variously coloured (*Essay*, II ix 8–9). Berkeley holds that the only things we sense by vision are the 'PROPER OBJECTS' of vision, which do not include distance and three-dimensionality. That we do not sense what, following MALEBRANCHE, he calls the 'outness' of objects, enables him to deal with an obvious objection to his IDEALISM, namely 'that we see things actually without or at a distance from us, and which consequently do not exist in the mind' (*Principles* I 42). See APPEARANCE, IDEA, KNOWLEDGE.

sensationalism, *n.* the theory that KNOWLEDGE is derived from sensations. The concept of SENSATION used in this rests on two questionable assumptions: that we have not only bodily sensations and sensations of touch, but also sensations from the functioning of all of our senses, including the most important, vision; and that a sensation is an ELEMENT in PERCEPTION of which the perceiver is conscious and which is interpreted to yield a judgment, the perceiver being passive and neither right nor wrong in respect of sensation, but active and either right or wrong in respect of judgment. On this view nothing is both sensory and veridical (or non-veridical) independently of what judgments the perceiver makes. There can be no visual illusion (sensory and non-veridical) that the perceiver may rightly judge to be non-veridical.

Were the two assumptions justified, sensationalism would be important as a doctrine of the validity of ideas (if IDEAS are identified with sensations, or regarded as being derived by a legitimate process from sensations), and as a doctrine of the nature of the world in so far as it is an OBJECT of perception. The first doctrine is EMPIRICISM (which involves the denial that any ideas are innate). The second is PHENOMENALISM.

The process whereby sensations are supposed to be built up into knowledge is called 'the ASSOCIATION OF IDEAS'; and the process whereby general ideas are supposed to be derived from sensations is called 'ABSTRACTION'.

In modern philosophy, HOBBES, LOCKE, CONDILLAC and HUME are sensationalists. BERKELEY held sensations to have a spiritual cause, GOD. This qualification was removed in Ernst MACH's thoroughly sensationalistic philosophy of science.

sense-datum, *n.* what is 'given' in sense-perception, according to philosophical theories of perception propounded by RUSSELL, MOORE, and others in the early part of the 20th century.

Like the term 'SENSATION' in the REPRESENTATIVE THEORY OF PERCEPTION, it is often introduced along with a distinction between mediated awareness of OBJECTS in the external world and immediate awareness of the SENSATION or SENSE-DATUM. Whereas a sensation is by definition mental, a sense-datum might be mind-independent. The first users of the term seem to have wanted it to be neutral as between the representative theory and other theories. Moore, for example, sought to introduce it by a sort of OSTENSIVE DEFINITION, a 'picking out' of an element in one's experience of an object, an element that might continue to exist after the EXPERIENCE.

One objection to this notion of 'sense-datum' was that Moore represented as resolvable, by further discussion, questions he should have answered in introducing the term, so as to make it clear whether he was talking about physical objects, or optical appearances, or what. See APPEARANCE.

sense-impression, *n.* the impression, or IDEA, said to be imprinted on the MIND as a result of the sense-organ being stimulated. If no idea is imprinted on the mind, LOCKE says, 'there follows no sensation' (*Essay*, II ix 4). REID commented:

It is evident, from the manner in which this phrase ('impression') is used by modern philosophers, that they mean, not barely to express by it my perceiving an object, but to explain the manner of perception. They think that the object perceived acts upon the mind in some way similar to that in which one body acts upon another, by making an impression upon it. (*Essays on the Intellectual Powers of Man*, Essay II, Ch. 4).

If Reid is right then Locke held a representative theory of PERCEPTION: ideas are things that represent external OBJECTS to us. However, this way of reading Locke has recently been questioned. See EXPERIENCE.

sensible, *n.* **1.** that which makes sense, as opposed to nonsense.

2. that which can be perceived by the senses (touch, sight, hearing, etc.). In the philosophy of PLATO, the sensible in the second sense is opposed to the INTELLIGIBLE (see FORM).

Sextus Empiricus, (2nd century AD, sceptic philosopher whose extant works are *Hypotyposes* and *Adversus Mathematicos (Outlines of Pyrrhonism* and *Against the Logicians, Physicists, and Ethicists),* trans. R. G. Bury, 4 vols, London and Cambridge, Mass., 1933–1949). See PYRRHONISM.

Sidgwick, Henry (1838–1900), English philosopher, studied at Cambridge and became professor there. In his *Methods of Ethics* (1874) he puts forward a hedonistic principle of a universalised kind: we must further the good of others as much as our own (see HEDONISM). This principle of benevolence is in line with his utilitarian position, which in his view was what common sense dictates.

Smith, Adam (1723–1790), Scottish moral philosopher, professor at Glasgow and friend of DAVID HUME, is perhaps best known for his pioneering treatise on economics, *The Wealth of Nations* (1776). In this work, he frequently uses notions from his *Theory of Moral Sentiments* (1759). The central notion here is that of sympathy, also important for Hume, according to which it is from a fellow feeling amongst human beings that we derive our moral judgments, which are thus not dominated by our own advantage but have a quite impartial status.

social contract, *n.* a notion of POLITICAL PHILOSOPHY, according to which societies arise from individuals who agree to abandon their 'state of nature', in which everyone is out for himself alone, and come together in communities, giving up certain individual habits (such as indiscriminate killing) for the good of the whole. This is a theory about the origin of society and assumes that the individual is prior to the group, a rationalist assumption that has been abandoned in the light of anthropological enquiry. Traces of this view go back a long way, but explicit social contract theories start in the wake of the RE-FORMATION, with HOBBES's *Leviathan* (1651) and LOCKE's *Two Treatises of Civil Government* (1689). A different form of the theory figures in ROUSSEAU's *Du contrat social* (1762), where the coming together depends on the operation of a 'general will', a somewhat elusive entity. These now abandoned social contract views must not be confused with the various contracts that are made in societies that already function, where clearly many agreements are made, and undone, from time to time.

Socrates, (470–399 BC), Athenian philosopher immortalized in PLATO's early and middle dialogues. Socrates himself left no written works, and there is a 'Socratic problem', as to how far the Platonic Socrates corresponds to the historical one. Other sources mentioned are the works of Xenophon; a comedy, *The Clouds*, by Aristophanes; and ARISTOTLE's 'historical' survey of earlier philosophers in his *Metaphysics*.

Xenophon adds nothing of philosophical significance to the Platonic picture, but in his account of Socrates's trial and last days confirms the profound impression made by Socrates on those who knew him well. The Socrates of Aristophanes' *Clouds* appears to be little more than a caricature of a typical Sophist (see SOPHISTS), dubbed 'Socrates', and given a mask that made the actor look as fascinatingly ugly as the real Socrates. One implication of *The Clouds*, that the real Socrates initially shared some of the cosmological interests (see COSMOLOGY) of the pre-Socratic philosophers (see PRE-SOCRATIC PHILOSOPHY), can probably be accepted. The same is said by Plato's Socrates (*Phaedo* 96 a), although Aristotle described him as 'busying himself about ethical matters and neglecting the world of nature as a whole'. Plato, Xenophon and Aristotle agree that his main concern was with the ETHICS of human conduct. Plato puts the THEORY OF FORMS into Socrates's mouth, but on Aristotle's evidence (*Metaphysics* 987 b 1, 1078 b 30) it was Plato's own theory. It probably seemed to Plato, who accepted what HERACLITUS had said about SENSIBLE things always changing, to be presupposed by the Socratic search for stable definitions.

Socrates's method was to ask people series of questions with the aim of discovering in what justice or courage or piety or temperance or friendship or the like really consists. He would pretend ignorance, and ask, not for examples of justice, courage, and the rest, but for an account, a *logos*, of what the examples have in common which makes them all instances of the thing in question. That is, he would ask for an informative, universally valid, DEFINITION. The procedure was inductive—a movement from the many particular instances of justice, to the one thing, justice itself, which they exemplify. When someone was bold enough to proffer a definition Socrates would subject him to a cross-examination eliciting a number of PROPOSITIONS which, together, usually showed the proffered definition to be inadequate. Even if the procedure produced no result the participants were wiser at the end, in that they were now aware of their ignorance.

What lay behind this method? First, that the words 'justice', 'courage', are <u>not</u> mere conveniences of discourse, corresponding to nothing natural or real. Second, that to know in what some virtue consists is to recognise that one cannot be truly happy without possessing it; no one would knowingly do wrong. Third, that what matters above all else is the care of the soul: the man who knowingly acts rightly cannot be unhappy even in the face of death.

The first of these presuppositions has been questioned by those who say that the MEANING of a word is fixed by how we actually use it, and that we can use the word 'courageous', for example, as we do, without being able to say, or knowing, what courageous acts have in common other than that they are courageous. The second has been questioned by those, such as Aristotle (*Nicomachean Ethics* 1145 b 27), who say it 'plainly contradicts the observed facts': people do sometimes act against what they know to be the better course.

Socrates's fame rests not on these questionable presuppositions of his philosophical method, but on the method itself—and on his personal testimony to the third presupposition. In 399 BC he was tried for 'not worshipping the gods whom the State worships, but introducing new and unfamiliar religious practices; and, further, of corrupting the young', charges which reflect more on the accusers than on the accused. He was sentenced to death by drinking hemlock. The sentence had to be postponed for some time during which his friends visited, and talked with him, in prison. Plato's *Phaedo* is a moving account of these last days in Socrates's life. Evidently Socrates exhibited surprising calmness in the face of death. Plato attributes to Socrates a belief in the soul's IMMORTALITY, and much of the conversation in the dialogue is concerned with the arguments for immortality. Whether the real Socrates believed in immortality may be doubted.

The dialogue *Phaedo* concludes: 'Such was the end of our comrade, who was, we may fairly say, of all those whom we knew in our time, the bravest and also the wisest and most upright man'.

solipsism (from Latin *solus* alone and *ipse* self). Originally used (e.g. by KANT) as a term for practical egoism, 'solipsism' came to be used in the late 19th century for the theoretical view that only I and my EX-PERIENCES exist. As stated by a critic of solipsism, the argument for it is: 'I cannot transcend experience, and experience must be *my* experience. From this it follows that nothing beyond my self exists, for what is experience is its (the self's) states' (F. H. BRADLEY, *Appearance and Reality*, London, 1893, p. 218).

As the premiss of this argument suggests, the roots of solipsism lie in the 17th century saying that all one is immediately aware of, in PER-CEPTION, is one's own 'SENSATIONS' or 'ideas'. Because the term 'IDEA' was used to mean not only a 'sensation' but also what gives a word its MEANING, the statement of solipsism seemed to be meaningful; and the theory, however incredible, seemed to some to be necessarily true. When logical ATOMISM took the place of SENSATIONALISM in the philo-sophy of language, things changed in one respect. WITTGENSTEIN, in his logical atomist *Tractatus Logico-Philosophicus* (London, 1922) said that 'what solipsism *means*, is quite correct, only it cannot be *said*, but it shows itself' (5.62). Finally, with the rejection of both the saying that perceiving is having 'sensations', and of both sensationalism and logical atomism in the philosophy of language, solipsism came to be seen as signifying no more than the possibility 'of turning all statements into sentences beginning "I think" or "I believe" (and thus, as it were, into descriptions of *my* inner life)' (Wittgenstein, *Philosophical Investigations*, Oxford, 1953, I 24 cf. 402–3). See PRIVATE LANGUAGE.

Sophists, *n*. so called from a word meaning 'to become wise or learned', were itinerant Greek teachers of the 5th century BC. They taught many things, but are best known, through PLATO's criticisms of them, as teachers of how to win moral and political arguments without much regard for the truth of what was being argued for. Probably what Plato most disliked about them was that they reacted against ELEATICISM not as he did, with a theory of two worlds, an INTELLIGIBLE world of Being and a SENSIBLE world of Becoming, but by trying to explain things in ways that did not require a super-sensible reality. Whereas Plato would say that the coming into being of anything is 'by participation in the reality peculiar to its appropriate universal', they would 'have no concern or care whatever for such an object' and

271

explained BEAUTY, for example, by reference to 'a gorgeous colour or shape' (*Phaedo* 100 b–101 e). Although the superiority of Plato's explanation (his 'THEORY OF FORMS') is not now regarded as evident, his assessment of the Sophists has tended to stick; the term 'sophism', for instance, means 'a specious but fallacious argument'.

In HEGEL's history of philosophy the Sophists figure as subjective idealists. The truth behind this characterisation of them relates to the antithesis between nature or reality *(physis)* and what is believed in, practised or held to be right *(nomos)*. The Sophists raised such questions as 'Do the gods exist by *physis*—in reality—or only by *nomos*?', 'Is the State something which arises naturally, or does it require some sort of SOCIAL CONTRACT?' and 'Is virtue *(areté)* a natural or divine gift, or can it be taught?' Whereas the philosophy of the Pre-Socratics had tended to be a philosophy of *physis*, the philosophy of the Sophists tended to be one of *nomos*. See PRE-SOCRATIC PHILOSOPHY, PROTAGORAS.

soul, *n.* we usually distinguish 'soul' and 'MIND', but no longer in the way ARISTOTLE did. He defined soul *(psyche)* as 'the first grade of actuality (that is, the possession, not the exercise) of the capacity which any natural (as distinct from artificial) body has, within itself, to initiate changes in itself and in other things'. Only a body that is alive has this capacity. Therefore the soul is inseparable from a live body (*De Anima*, 413 a 4) and thus is not immortal. But there is one capacity, the capacity for thought, that does not involve a body. Aristotle calls the thinking soul 'the mind' *(nous)*, and says 'The mind seems to be an independent substance implanted within the soul and to be incapable of being destroyed' (*ibid.*, 408 b 18). This is what he later calls 'the mind as active' (*ibid.*, 430 a 15), not 'the mind as passive'.

DESCARTES defined 'mind' as a SUBSTANCE distinct from MATTER, and therefore capable of immortality. He said 'I use the term "mind" rather than "soul" since the word "soul" is ambiguous and is often applied to something corporeal' (*Arguments proving the existence of God, etc.*, Definition VI). This ambiguity of 'soul' was ignored by later philosophers and the term came to be used widely in a non-Aristotelian sense, especially by religious philosophers who want to prove that there is something in us that is immortal. See IMMORTALITY.

space and time, the general framework in which everything in the world goes on, of interest to both scientists and philosophers. Thus some physicists have regarded them as absolute (NEWTON) and others as in various ways relative, either that they are relational (consist of relations), or somehow relative to the observer and his way of measuring them (EINSTEIN). For KANT they are respectively the outer and inner sense for the coherence of EXPERIENCE. Some have distinguished the space and time of physics and those of psychological experience (what is a short time by a clock may feel long to one who experiences it, as for example in dreams but also in some wakeful events). Various questions have exercised thinkers' minds about the nature of space and time: do they exist by themselves, or must there be things 'in them'? The atomists held that space was empty, ARISTOTLE that it must be full. By the RENAISSANCE the concept of space as empty re-emerged but modern science has returned to Aristotle's view, although what is in 'empty' space are 'fields', defined mathematically and observed in action. Are space and time finite or infinite? Various opposing views have been held. Are space and time bounded or unbounded? About this, too, opinions have differed. For Newton, space was infinite and unbounded, for Einstein it is finite and unbounded (in the sense in which a spherical surface is). Related to this is the question whether space is Euclidean (obeys the principles of Euclidean geometry) or not. According to Einstein's theory, space–time is non-Euclidean. Some of these questions have not been entirely resolved yet. Scientifically, their main importance concerns COSMOLOGY, the study of the history of the universe as a whole. See RELATIVITY, THEORY OF.

speech act, *n.* doing something in saying something. For example, in saying 'I promise to return your umbrella' I am making a promise; I am not simply saying that something is the case. See AUSTIN.

Spinoza, Benedict (Baruch), 1632–1677, Jewish-Dutch philosopher who made his living by grinding and polishing lenses. He had a rabbinical education and founded the 'higher criticism' of the Bible, but was excommunicated from the Sephardic synagogue in Amsterdam in 1656. The Elector Palatine offered him the chair of philosophy at Heidelberg University in 1673, but he declined. In his lifetime he published a geometrical version of DESCARTES's *Principles of Philosophy* (Amsterdam, 1663) and a *Treatise on Theology and Politics* (Amsterdam 1670), a defence of the liberty of thought and speech, but the work for which he is famous as a rationalist metaphysician, his *Ethics*, was not published until after his death (1677).

The main metaphysical idea behind Spinoza's *Ethics* is that Descartes was right about mind and body being distinct, but wrong about the nature of SUBSTANCE, and hence wrong in describing the distinctness of mind and body as the distinctness of two substances. Really they are two distinct attributes of one substance, which has an infinity of attributes, mind and body being the only two we apprehend. This follows, by various moves, from substance being 'that which is in itself' (i.e. whose existence is independent) 'and is conceived through itself' (*Ethics*, I, Definitions, 3).

What follows from this being the real definition of substance is that all explanations of a certain kind, namely those that explain what happens by reference to someone's, or something's, *activity*, are wrong. This kind of explanation had taken various forms. ARISTOTLE had implied that a man is active in moving his hand, is immediately responsible for its MOTION (*Physics*, 256a). Descartes held a man's activity to be confined to that of moving a small gland in his brain (*Passions of the Soul*, 34) or, on second thoughts, that of performing an 'action of the soul', a VOLITION, which makes the small gland move by virtue of soul and body being somehow united (*ibid.*, 41). MALE-BRANCHE explained the union of soul and body in terms of GOD making a bodily event occur on the occasion of a mental event, and vice versa (*Search after Truth*, Bk. 6, Pt. 2, Ch. 3). Spinoza propounded a necessary connection between the essential nature of substance, identified with 'God', and the modifications of the attributes of the substance, identified with 'Nature', comparable to necessary connections in geometry. He was led by his substance-MONISM to reject the activity view of causation in favour of the God/Nature entailment view, while leaving the entailment mysterious. 'God', for Spinoza, is 'free', and necessarily so, but only in the sense that substance is not limited by anything outside itself. Moreover, he had to reject the account we ordinarily give of someone having done something freely (namely, that he could have not done it). Specifically, he had to reject the account Descartes had given of human error, since it involved the notion that a person is free to believe what he does not perceive clearly and distinctly. Spinoza provided alternative accounts, in terms of our consciously participating in the 'freedom' of the substance of which we are, in some sense, parts. To the extent to which we are aware of this participation, our IDEAS are 'adequate'.

In spite of being expressed in the technical philosophical vocabulary of 'substance', 'attributes', 'modes', 'adequate ideas', and so forth, some of Spinoza's thoughts have had a profound influence, and have circulated extensively in a simplified form. One such is the thought that what happens in the mind and what happens in the brain are the same happenings, only apprehended differently (the DOUBLE-ASPECT THEORY). Another is the thought that we can avoid debilitating passions, such as hatred, by coming to see what happens as part of the necessary order of things. This is our intellectual way of escape from the 'bondage' of the passions. From the outset Spinoza's metaphysics had been at the service of ETHICS. In an early work, the *Treatise on the Improvement of the Understanding*, he declared his aim to be to find out 'whether, in fact, there might be anything of which the discovery and attainment would enable me to enjoy continuous, supreme, and unending happiness'. He never represented the attainment as easy. What has to be attained is the conscious realisation of oneself as part of the infinite substance, God, and there are powerful forces that bind men to the blindness of their EMOTIONS.

Stoicism, *n.* named after the *Stoa Poikile* (Painted Colonnade) in Athens, where its founder, Zeno of Citium, Cyprus (*c.*336–*c.*264 BC) lectured (see ZENO THE STOIC). His doctrines were systematically expounded and defended by the third head of the Stoa, Chrysippus of Soli, Cilicia (*c.*280–*c.*207 BC), sometimes called 'the second founder'. The movement spread from Athens to Rome, and lasted some 500 years. Early Stoicism taught that the end of man is 'to live in harmony with nature', but such was the Stoic conception of nature, and of the means of understanding it, that Stoic ETHICS is in fact inseparable from Stoic physics and LOGIC.

By 'nature' may be meant either the nature of man alone, or the nature of man as a part of the universe. The central doctrine of early Stoicism relates to the latter. The nature of man alone is such that he instinctively values certain things, such as self-preservation, but when his place in the wider context is considered an action such as suicide may be seen to be the only fit and proper one. The values arising from man's nature alone are merely relative; absolute value is to be found elsewhere.

Like HERACLITUS, the early Stoics saw the world as ordered by a divine reason, pervading it in the form of an active fiery substance. The wise man learns the order and willingly accepts his place in it. Logic, being concerned with the criteria for particular truth claims and with the truth-functional connections between PROPOSITIONS, is involved in the learning process. Virtue is an attitude of mind, the cheerful acceptance, based on KNOWLEDGE, of what has providentially been ordained.

Although the Stoics regarded the order of nature as deterministic (see

DETERMINISM), Chrysippus held a subtle view on freedom and determinism being compatible. A man is fated by nature to do what he does, but he himself contributes to that fate since he is part of nature *(confatalia)*. Character determines action, but character is not irredeemably fixed at birth by external forces.

Stoic influences are evident in CHRISTIANITY and, in modern philosophy, in Spinozism. It shares with the former the problem of evil, and with the latter the problem of giving an account of freedom which makes it compatible with determinism. Whether a person's character is entirely determined for him or, to some extent, by him, goes on exercising 19th and 20th century philosophers (e.g. JOHN STUART MILL, *System of Logic*, 1843, VI, 2). See SPINOZA.

Strawson, Peter Frederick (1919–   ), English philosopher, professor at Oxford, was one of the main figures of the 'ordinary language' thinkers of the mid-20th century, and criticised Russell's theory of descriptions as confusing reference with description (see DESCRIPTION, THEORY OF). Later, he became interested in what he called descriptive METAPHYSICS, in studying the problem of how to define individuals (*Individuals*, 1959). In his work on LOGIC he defends the view that in making statements we presuppose the existence of the subject class, as ARISTOTLE had done. As regards truth, he rejects the correspondence theory, since statements, when true, do not so much correspond to facts, but rather state them (see TRUTH, THEORIES OF).

structuralism, *n.* an approach to various philosophical and sociological problems in terms of the general pattern that they seem to exhibit. The notion stems from MATHEMATICS, more particularly from the study of groups (in the technical sense) that began in the mid-19th century. Since then the structuralist outlook has been manifest in a variety of fields: the social analyses of MARX, the psychological ones of Freud, the linguistic ones of Saussure, the anthropological ones of LEVI-STRAUSS. As a general way of tackling issues, it was particularly widespread in France in the mid-20th century, where it extends into the literary arts as well. The tenets of structuralism are often not very explicit but rather elusive. In a sense, it reminds one somewhat of the Aristotelian notion of FORM, as against content (see ARISTOTLE); however, it would be more appropriate here to speak of the study of formed contents, showing how they are connected and resemble each other in different fields.

subject, *n.* **1**. as opposed to OBJECT. Whenever we see, hear, smell, taste, remember, imagine, think, etc. 'there is always a distinction between that *of* which we are conscious and our consciousness of it' (G. E. Moore, 'The subject-matter of Psychology', *Proc. Arist. Soc.*, 1909–10). 'That of which we are conscious' is the object; we are the subject.

2. as opposed to PREDICATE. In the sentence 'The cat is on the mat', what comes before 'is', namely 'the cat', is the subject, while what comes after, namely 'on the mat', is the predicate.

subjective, *n.* existing only for a SUBJECT, as opposed to OBJECTIVE.

substance, *n.* (from Latin *sub* under, *stare* stand) 'substance' means what 'stands under' other things, and what we know when we 'under-stand' (i.e. grasp the nature of) things. These correspond to ARISTOTLE'S 'primary' and 'secondary' substance. Aristotle called individual things, such as an individual man, 'primary substances'; for him, individual things underlie everything else: 'Everything except primary substances is either predicated of primary substances, or is present in them, and if these last did not exist, it would be impossible for anything else to exist' (2 b 4).

How are individual things understood? This, for Aristotle, is a matter of how they are defined: by stating the species and genera to which they belong. Species and genera may be called 'secondary substances'.

To say of a man that he is white, that he runs, and so on, is irrelevant to the DEFINITION (2 b 35), for the definition expresses the nature of a thing, namely the facts of generation and growth. If you fell a tree and make a bed from the wood, the 'nature' of what you make is wood, not a bed. For if you bury the bed in earth, and the rotting wood acquires the power of sending up a shoot, what comes up will not be a little bed, but a little tree (193 a 12). An individual man has human offspring in virtue of being a man, not in virtue of being a runner. That he runs is accidental (see ACCIDENT), it is not essential (see ESSENCE) to his nature. We grasp the essential nature of an individual thing in knowing that it belongs to the species man, but not in knowing that it runs. Hence running, unlike being a man, is not a substance, not even a secondary one.

Distinguishing between substance-PREDICATES, such as 'is a man', and non-substance-predicates, such as 'runs' and 'walks', Aristotle can explain change. By changing, the same primary substance (e.g. an individual man) can have contrary non-substance-predicates ('runs' and 'walks'), at different times.

Aristotle, in calling everyday objects like men and horses 'primary substances', was reacting against PLATO'S THEORY OF FORMS, in which visible beautiful things are subordinated to something that is not visible but intelligible, BEAUTY itself. These FORMS 'exist apart' from the visible things (1078 b 31). Aristotle rejected Plato's other-worldly Forms. They could not explain either the BEING or the becoming of things: not the being because 'they are not *in* the individuals which share in them' (1079 b 17); not the becoming: 'though the Forms exist, still things do not come into being, unless there is something to originate movement' (1080 a 3). To explain a man's coming into being we must know some biology.

Later philosophers used the term 'substance' in reacting to Aristotle's views, rejecting explanations of the becoming of the things in terms of their belonging to this or that natural kind of things (species), and of their developing as they do because that is their 'end'. Natural kinds were rejected for CORPUSCLES of MATTER, and FINAL CAUSATION for EFFICIENT CAUSATION. DESCARTES wrote to Plempius (3 October 1637): 'Like a mathematician I took account of nothing but sizes, shapes and motions, and so I cut myself off from all the subterfuges of philosophers', namely from natural kinds and FINAL CAUSES.

Descartes came to use the term 'substance' through his method of doubt and the attendant conclusion that minds and matter can exist separately. Neither 'stands under' the other, and so they are substances, though not in an absolute sense since they both depend on GOD (*Princ. Phil.* I 51–2). Being substances, they have ESSENCES: that of MIND is THINKING, that of matter is EXTENSION. The existence of mental substance then seems assured by reflecting that if a thinker (a mental substance) did not exist there could be no thinking, yet thinking undoubtedly exists. Because he recognises two created substances, mind and matter, Descartes is called a DUALIST.

How can mind and body interact, if they are substances that share nothing save being created by God? Descartes said mind and body interact by being united. MALEBRANCHE, SPINOZA, and others, saw that this merely raises the new question what is meant by the 'union' of distinct substances.

SPINOZA, rejecting Descartes' view of substance, supplied a definition combining features of both of Aristotle's senses. 'By substance I mean that which is, in itself; and is conceived through itself' (*Ethics* I Def. 3). By 'is, in itself' he meant that substance is self-sufficient, able to exist independently of anything else. By 'conceived through itself' he meant that we can think of a substance without thinking of anything else. This definition, together with other definitions and AXIOMS, enabled him to prove to his own satisfaction that just one substance exists, which he called God or nature; it is absolutely infinite, having infinite attributes. Of these we know two, thought and extension. The essences of Descartes' two substances re-emerge as two attributes of Spinoza's one substance. Descartes's 'union' of a person's mind and body is explained as each being the same mode of the one substance, but expressed in different attributes: mind and body are two aspects of the same reality.

Spinoza thought that his notion of substance was useful for philosophy. LOCKE was sceptical about 'the very great clearness there is in the doctrine of substance and accidents' and about the doctrine being useful in deciding questions in philosophy (*Essay*, II xiii 20). Nevertheless he did use the term 'substance': '. . . not imagining how simple ideas can subsist by themselves, we accustom ourselves to suppose some substratum wherein they do subsist, and from which they do result; which therefore we call substance' (*Essay*, II xxiii 1–2). Locke's careless use of the term 'IDEAS' when he meant qualities, led BERKELEY to say that there is a 'manifest contradiction' in the notion of ideas existing in an unperceiving thing (*Princ.* I , 7) and hence that 'the very notion of what is called matter or corporeal substance involves a contradiction in it' (*Princ.* I , 9). Locke's conjoining 'wherein they do subsist' and 'from which they do result' made it unclear which he meant: the first suggests the logical point that PREDICATES must have a SUBJECT. LEIBNIZ commented: 'In distinguishing two things in [any] substance, the attributes or predicates, and the common subject of these predicates, it is no wonder that we can conceive nothing particular in the subject. It must be so, indeed, since we have already separated from it all the attributes in which we could conceive any detail' (*New Essays*, II xxiii 2).

The phrase 'from which they do result' suggests the scientific point that the sensible qualities of things depend on their corpuscular structure. Why then speak of 'substance'? Locke's puzzling use of the term 'substance' shows that we must distinguish between logical and scientific points.

sufficient reason, principle of, *n.* the statement that nothing exists or happens without a reason that accounts for its BEING or happening. The most complete formulation of it is due to LEIBNIZ. It is on this basis that he regards our world as the best possible, since if it were not, GOD would not have created it. This really involves another sense of reason with ethical overtones. Furthermore, one can take the principle in a FORMAL, logical sense, that in a valid argument, the premises are sufficient reason for the conclusion, and conversely, one may try to find sufficient reasons to justify a given statement. The principle is related to, though not quite the same as, that of causality, at any rate for LEIBNIZ. A causal nexus may indeed be a reason why something happens, but a reason might not be causal. The distinction seems likely for a rationalist, but less than clear for an empiricist. At all events, Leibniz regarded the principle of sufficient reason along with that of CONTRADICTION as the cornerstones of reasoning. The scope of this would, however, no longer be taken as wide as Leibniz thought: one can give no reason why there is anything at all, rather than nothing; this is not the sort of thing for which there are reasons.

syllogism, *n*. (from Greek *syn* with, *logismos* argument) a type of FORMAL argument in which one goes from two premises to a conclusion, each of the three PROPOSITIONS being of the SUBJECT-PREDICATE form. For example: all M are P, all S are M, therefore all S are P, is a syllogism. The first is the major premiss and contains the predicate, P, of the conclusion. The second, or minor, premiss contains the subject, S, of the conclusion. M is called the middle term, which links the premises but does not appear in the conclusion. The first systematic account of syllogistic reasoning was given by ARISTOTLE in his *Prior Analytics*. In each syllogism there are exactly three terms. The propositions can be either universal or particular (concerning 'all', or only 'some' S), affirmative or negative (asserting that S 'is', or 'is not' described by P). By varying the position of the terms and the forms of the proposition, we obtain 256 possible patterns in four figures. Of these syllogisms only 19 are valid, namely those that fulfil certain conditions on terms and forms. In medieval times, the valid syllogisms were summarised in a Latin mnemonic in which each of them was given a name. The example given above belongs to the first figure and is called 'barbara'. Syllogisms that contain only categorical propositions are called categorical. They form the starting point of Aristotle's LOGIC. If a syllogism contains modal propositions, for example, 'X must be Y', it is called modal. Syllogistic argument remained central in the study of logic until the early 19th century.

synthetic, see ANALYTIC.

T

Taoism, *n.* a Chinese philosophic doctrine that goes back to the 3rd century BC. The central concept of this philosophy is that of *tao* the way, and hence the proper conduct of man, a notion found throughout CHINESE PHILOSOPHY. It is also the basic concept from which the world itself is derived. As such it has always existed, even before there was a world. As a philosophy, Taoism was first expounded in the book called the *Taote ching*, a compilation from about 300 BC. It introduces a basically naturalistic view of the world and advocates a simple life close to nature. In some ways it is reminiscent of Stoic doctrines that arose in Greece about the same time. Taoism later declined in influence, being displaced by neo-Confucian thought since about the 9th century AD. Religious Taoism is thoroughly polytheistic and has taken on many aspects of BUDDHISM. Moreover, it has a multiplicity of sects. On the whole, it concentrates on promoting a satisfying earthly life within an ethical framework.

Tarski, Alfred (1902–1983), Polish logician, taught at Warsaw (1926–1939) and then went to the United States where he taught at Berkeley. His most important work in philosophy is in the field of SEMANTICS (the theory of MEANING), where he evolved the so-called semantic theory of truth, worked out for a formalised language, which treats 'is true' and 'is false' as part of a METALANGUAGE (i.e. one in which we talk about the given language). He has contributed to various aspects of modern LOGIC, and to studies on the foundations of MATHEMATICS.

tautology, *n.* (from Greek *tautos* the same, *logos* that which is said) a repetition of, or saying the same as, something already said. In propositional LOGIC (concerned with the connections between PROPOSITIONS), a tautology is any formula that comes out true for any distribution of truth-values for its constituents. Thus '*p* or *not-p*' is a tautology, since it is true whether *p* be true or false.

teleology, *n.* (from Greek *telos* end, *logos* discourse or doctrine) the study of ends or FINAL CAUSES, especially as related to the evidences of design or purpose in nature. FINAL CAUSES are opposed to EFFICIENT CAUSES. ARISTOTLE gave priority to teleological explanation, unlike modern philosophers and scientists from the time of GALILEO, GASSENDI and DESCARTES.

Thales, (*c*.624–*c*.546 BC), a citizen of Miletus, the richest and most powerful Greek city on the coast of Asia Minor, destroyed *c*.494 BC. He was traditionally counted as being one of the Seven Wise Men, and was credited with being able to put his mathematical and astronomical knowledge to good use. He is said to have predicted, though at best only from knowledge of the regular occurrence of eclipses every 18 years, an eclipse of the sun that occurred in 585 BC. That it occurred at the time and place of a battle, and was nearly total, served to make the prediction memorable. A story to illustrate his practical acumen is reported by ARISTOTLE (*Politics* 1259 a 9). He is said to have been able to tell, from his study of the heavenly bodies, that there would be a large olive crop. So he paid in advance to hire, at olive-pressing time, all the olive presses in Miletus on the island of Khios to the north. Then, when there was a sudden rush of requests for their use, he hired them out on his own terms, thus showing that 'philosophers can easily be rich if they like'. To balance this, a story with a less happy ending is told by PLATO (*Theaetetus* 174a). Thales was so intent on his star-gazing that a well at his feet escaped his notice, he fell into it, and was mocked by 'a witty and attractive Thracian serving-girl'. Possibly both stories were made up to illustrate the worldliness or otherwise of the philosophical life; that they were told at all is evidence that Thales had quite a reputation as a sage. The best evidence of this is the phrase 'The man's a Thales' in Aristophanes's play, *The Birds* (1009). Apart, possibly, from a nautical star-guide, Thales probably left nothing in writing. His fame as a philosopher is due almost entirely to Aristotle (*Metaphysics* 983 a 24–983 b 27), who credited him with being the originator of philosophical enquiry into the first principle and ELEMENT of existing things, namely something that may appear to have various qualities at different times but in fact preserves its own nature throughout these phenomenal changes.

Thales's originality lay in the novelty of looking for an explanation of natural things within nature itself. It was a radical departure from explanation in terms of the caprices of anthropomorphic gods. That Thales took the first principle and element to be water is, by comparison, unimportant. We do not know why he took it to be water (or even whether Aristotle's understanding of what he meant by water being the first principle and element is correct). Aristotle conjectured that it was 'from seeing the nurture of all things to be moist'. See ANAXIMANDER, AXAXIMENES, MILESIAN SCHOOL.

theism, *n.* (from Greek *theos* god) is the view that there is such a thing as GOD. Depending on how many of them one takes there to be, we have monotheism (one god), polytheism (many gods) and appropriate compound terms for numbers in between. Theistic views may be based either on simple faith, or on attempts at accounting for what happens in the world. For the latter case, a whole range of arguments for the existence of god has been considered by philosophers over the ages. All of these proofs have been rejected by some philosophers, but the question remains controversial in that some others may accept them. Much here depends on what the god in question is taken to be like, and what his existence must account for: some regard god as the creator of the universe, as a giver of moral laws, as a source of universal benevolence, as an ultimate judge, or as several of these at once. Whether the proofs carry weight depends on whether one accepts the premisses. Where the only ground for admitting the existence of a god is unexamined belief, argument is of course ineffective either way. Some arguments have been conclusively refuted. Thus, the notion that there could be no morality without a god has been quite undermined by PLATO in the *Euthyphro*. That the thought of a powerful being who can put things to right offers comfort to many, is indubitable. VOLTAIRE, with tongue in cheek, says that if God did not exist, one would have to invent him.

theory of Forms, Plato's, see FORM.

theory of Ideas, Plato's, see FORM.

thinking, *n.* called by HOBBES (*Leviathan*, 1651, Ch. IV) 'mental discourse' to distinguish it from verbal discourse (i.e. what one says in words, either inwardly or out loud). LOCKE, similarly, distinguished between 'mental propositions' and 'verbal propositions', and explained why it is not generally recognised that there are both: '. . . it is very difficult to treat of them asunder. Because it is unavoidable, in treating of mental propositions, to make use of words; and then the instances given of mental propositions cease immediately to be barely mental, and become verbal' (*Essay*, IV v 3). Thinking, or entertaining mental propositions, is, according to Locke, a matter of being employed about 'objects of the understanding' which each thinker is conscious of in himself, and which Locke thinks are best called 'ideas' (*Essay*, I i 8). IDEAS, the materials of thinking, come from EXPERIENCE, which is either of external SENSIBLE OBJECTS (SENSATION) or of the internal operations of our MINDS (REFLECTION) (*Essay*, II i 1–5). Words have MEANING by signifying ideas (*Essay*, III ii 1–3). Words are necessary because, as a later writer put it, 'mind cannot work upon mind directly' (G. S. Bower, *Hartley and James Mill*, London, 1881, p. 46). If, by telepathy, one person could be directly aware of the mental PROPOSITIONS of another person then there would be no need for language.

To some philosophers this theory of thinking seems so obviously correct as not to be a theory at all. There is a non-technical sense of 'idea' which makes 'Thinking is having ideas' a truism, and it is easy to forget that Locke's use of the term is not this non-technical one. In Locke's use there is a problem as to what it can mean to say that two people have the same idea and so mean the same by some word. Presumably 'same idea', for Locke, means 'similar ideas', but how can ideas, if they are internal objects, be compared to see if they are, or are not, similar?

This has led to a reconsideration of thinking, and its relation to speaking. Instead of speech being verbalised and uttered thinking, is thinking inward speech? If it is then the problem of how there can be common meanings if ideas are private does not arise. The CRITERION of whether a language-learner is using a word in its common meaning will be public: a matter of whether his use of the word conforms to the rules implicit in the linguistic practice of the community. In this respect it is better to say that thinking is inward speech than that speech is verbalised and uttered thinking.

In another respect it is wrong to say that thinking is inward speech. 'I think it is going to rain' does not function as 'The words "It is going to rain" are passing through my mind' functions. If inward speech is the sort of thing we mean by a 'mental process' then thinking is not a mental process, nor yet behaviour. This is stressed by WITTGENSTEIN in his later philosophy (e.g. *Philosophical Investigations*, Oxford, 1953, esp. I , 308, but see also I , 150–5, 316–49, 361–3; II xi, pp. 211, 218).

Thomism, *n.* the philosophy of St Thomas AQUINAS.

transcendental, *n.* (from Latin *transcendo* climb beyond) a term coined by the SCHOLASTICS to refer to terms that could not be predicated under a single Aristotelian category (see CATEGORIES) but cut across these (for example, the terms 'BEING', 'unity' and the like). KANT has given the term a new meaning of his own: for him an enquiry is called transcendental if it concerns the *a priori* preconditions of any EXPERIENCES. Such an enquiry is undertaken in his First Critique, where the scope of pure reason is examined. Various deductions there given are called transcendental because they come before experience. The term must not be confused with one that looks very similar, namely, 'transcendent', which indeed has the same etymology. It is used to refer, both in scholasticism and later, to what lies totally beyond experience and our cognitive power. At best, this might be granted by revelation.

Trotsky, Leon (Lev Davydovich Bronstein) (1879–1940), Russian Jewish revolutionary and colleague of LENIN, created the Red Army after the revolution of October 1917, but later fell out with the Party and was exiled, and eventually murdered by a Stalinist agent in Mexico. In political philosophy, he figures as the defender of violence for the sake of attaining political goals. Besides, he thought that to be effective, the revolution that had taken place in Russia must be at once spread to Europe as a whole, whereas Lenin was more interested in consolidating it at home. Trotsky eventually came to hold that the October Revolution had been betrayed.

truth, theories of, *n. phr.* a set of different accounts aiming at defining truth by some CRITERION or other. Perhaps the most widespread view is the so-called correspondence theory, according to which a statement is true if it corresponds with the facts. The source for this is usually given as PLATO's *Sophist* (263b). However, Plato does not really speak of correspondence: he merely says that a statement is true if it states things as they are. Another common view is the coherence theory: a statement is true if it hangs together with a whole system of other truths. This commends itself to mathematicians, because a mathematical statement must certainly fit in with the rest of the subject. There has been a redundancy theory put forward by F. P. Ramsey that to say p is true is no more than stating p. The semantic theory of truth (TARSKI) concerns the notion of truth in formalised language and somewhat reminds one of Plato. It states that '"p" is true in L if p', which is a statement in a METALANGUAGE. STRAWSON's performative theory of truth denies that 'true' says anything about a statement, or adds anything to what a statement declares. A famous theory of truth, due to William JAMES, is called the pragmatic theory: according to this, a statement is true if it has useful consequences. In the end, it seems that we cannot do better than Plato. Indeed, any theory that makes truth depend on some CRITERION, C, is self-defeating. For suppose we ask whether such a theory is true, then that question must be answered yes or no without the intervention of the criterion. Thus, the ordinary sense of true cannot be tied to any criterion. Looking for one is just not the sort of thing one can sensibly do about truth.

truth-value, *n*. the truth (or falsity) of a PROPOSITION. See LOGIC, MEANING.

types, theory of, a device invented by RUSSELL to cope with the PARADOX about classes that goes by his name. We observe that classes and their members are on a different level. If we fail to observe this distinction, we can generate silly questions; thus we can ask whether the members of a club have paid their annual subscription, but not whether the club itself has. With this kind of proviso, Russell's paradox disappears: a class is of higher type than its members. However, this did not help with linguistic paradoxes such as the Liar. Russell therefore developed a more complicated, 'ramified' theory in which each level has infinitely many types. This, however, causes trouble with the foundations of MATHEMATICS, so that an AXIOM of reducibility was invented that allowed one to get back to the bottom level. The ramification move was not a success. Various developments in the theory of types have been proposed by logicians to cope with set theory.

U

universals, *n*. the term has its place in 'linguistic realism', the notion that correct use of a word is not just conforming to the implicit rules for it, but that the linguistic practice itself conforms to something. A linguistic realist holds that the rules of grammar require justification rather as one justifies a sentence by pointing to what verifies it. WITT-GENSTEIN opposed the notion, saying that 'the use of language is in a certain sense autonomous' (*Zettel* 320, 331). Hermogenes, in PLATO's dialogue *Cratylus* (384d), was opposing linguistic REALISM in Plato's THEORY OF FORMS, when he said that he could not convince himself 'that there is any principle of correctness in names other than convention and agreement'.

To believe in universals is to believe that large things are properly called 'large' because, over and above our criteria for this, they have largeness in common. It is this extra-linguistic item (that is not just a matter of satisfying our linguistic criteria for being large) that is the 'universal', largeness.

Plato's version of linguistic realism, his theory of Forms, has been described as a theory of universals, but this is misleading. The extra-linguistic reality, for Plato, was not the largeness which sensibly large things have, but largeness in itself. What led him to distinguish between largeness in itself, the object of intelligence, and large things, the object of SENSATION, was the REFLECTION that in SENSIBLE things largeness is confounded with its opposite, smallness. 'For the clarification of this', he said, 'the intelligence is compelled to contemplate the great and the small, not thus confounded but as distinct entities, in the opposite way from sensation' (*Republic* VII, 524C). The FORM of largeness is largeness in itself, not thus confounded with its opposite, smallness, but separate. The many sensibly large things, Plato says, are copies of the Form in a receptacle. There can be many of them because the receptacle is extended; it is space (*Timaeus*, 52b).

ARISTOTLE, on the other hand, actually used a word translatable as 'universal', and spoke of them in the language of 'things': 'Some things

287

are universal, others individual. By the term "universal" I mean that which is of such a nature as to be predicated of many subjects, by "individual" that which is not thus predicated. Thus "man" is a universal, "Callias" an individual' (*On Interpretation*, 17a 39).

Another linguistic realism is the theory that what justifies our linguistic practice with the word 'large' is not large things having the universal, largeness, in common, but their resembling one another (in respect of largeness). LOCKE, when he says that 'nature, in the production of things, makes several of them alike' and that general ideas 'have their foundation in the similitude of things' (*Essay*, III iii 13) held this theory. By 'nature' he meant what exists independently of human observers. Not so JOHN STUART MILL, who said that 'resemblance is evidently a feeling; a state of consciousness of the observer' and that 'feelings of resemblance, and of its opposite dissimilarity, are parts of our nature' (*System of Logic*, I iii 11).

Opposed to these is the theory of NOMINALISM, that what large things have in common is their being called 'large', or that their being called 'large' is the respect in which large things resemble one another. Nominalism goes to the opposite extreme to the theories of universals and resemblances. They purport to justify the rules implicit in our linguistic practices. An extreme nominalist talks as if there were no rules. Whether anyone actually is a nominalist in this extreme sense may be questioned. Most so-called nominalists seem to formulate their theory in such a way as to allow for a term's application in a particular case being justified by accepted practice.

It is difficult to defend the theory of universals against that of resemblances, and vice versa. In what sense do large things have largeness 'in common'? Numerically the same object, a salt cellar, may have been on the dinner table as is now on the breakfast tray. The table, the night before, and the tray, the morning after, had that object in common.That is not the sense in which large things are said to have largeness 'in common'. The salt cellar exists in its own right, so to speak. Largeness, as Aristotle recognised in spite of calling universals 'things', does not. The difference between the theories seems largely verbal, but someone committed to universals could say, as some philosophers have, that resemblance itself is a universal, the most general of universals.

Moreover, both common features and resemblances seem consequential: two things have largeness in common if they are both large, rather than vice versa; they resemble one another in respect of largeness if they are both large, rather than vice versa. What is their both being large other than their both satisfying our criteria for being large? See CONCEPT.

utilitarianism, *n.* is the theory of ETHICS on which we must judge actions in terms of their consequences: if these are good, so are the actions: if not, not. Goodness in turn is to be judged in terms of the amount of happiness that an action produces. According to HUME, this is how people actually make ethical judgments. The term utilitarian is applied to BENTHAM and his followers, particularly JOHN STUART MILL. The theory has some ancient antecedents, particularly in Epicureanism. As a modern doctrine it is often applied as a CRITERION for legislation. The theory can be taken in various ways: descriptive, as what does happen, or normative, as what should be done. Some utilitarians take into account only amount of pleasure, others distinguish quality as well, which somewhat weakens the principle. A further distinction lies between judging the consequences of particular actions and assessing what follows from acting according to certain rules (e.g. abiding by the Ten Commandments). This introduces a further complication: rules are in force to secure orderly social existence, which therefore must itself be regarded as good. This likewise is not simply and strictly a utilitarian consideration.

utopianism, *n.* (from Greek *ou* no or *eu* well, *topos* place) from Thomas More's *Utopia* (1516) denotes an outlook that envisages perfect conditions of human life that are nowhere realised, or indeed realisable. Thus any imaginative account of such conditions, or any theory that sees heaven on earth as a possible outcome (e.g. MARX's withering away of the State), or theories that view human progress as inevitable, may be described as utopian. So are views that man will in due course become thoroughly improved and morally transformed, or indeed eventually saved. Utopian literature and theorising point to conditions that might at least be partially pursued, even if they are unattainable. Doctors quite sensibly pursue medical research although men do not become immortal.

V

validity, *n.* in LOGIC, the feature of those arguments in which certain premisses correctly lead to the conclusion. For example, if *a*, *b*, *c* are real numbers, then the argument from '*a* is greater than *b*' and '*b* is greater than *c*' (the premisses) to '*a* is greater than *c*' (the conclusion) is valid. The fact that an argument is valid says nothing about the truth or falsehood of any of its component PROPOSITIONS. However, if a valid argument has true premisses, then it will have a true conclusion. The validity concerns the form of an argument, while truth and falsehood concern the contents of its constituents. From valid argument alone, we cannot establish that anything is the case. For that, we need true premisses: to find any of these is rather more difficult than to argue validly. Hence FORMAL logic is relatively the lesser part of philosophical investigation. Still, the fallacies (see FALLACY) committed when we argue invalidly must be recognized as such. A general classification of such fallacies is difficult, but some of the more common ones are well understood and have been given names (e.g. 'begging the question', when one assumes a conclusion, instead of proving it).

verifiability, *n.* the feature of a PROPOSITION that enables us to check that it is true. Thus, the proposition that water expands on freezing can be checked by exposing a bottle, full of water and securely sealed, to sub-zero temperatures: after a while, the glass will shatter. Clearly, a false proposition cannot be verified. Neither can what some call analytic truths, namely propositions that are regarded as true by virtue of their structure alone (some regard mathematical propositions as of this kind). A verifiable proposition has to be contingent, so that its truth is not a foregone conclusion. Logical positivists (see LOGICAL POSITIVISM) have raised verifiability to a principle of MEANING: whatever fails to admit of verification (analytic truths excepted) is meaningless. In this way they have ruled out traditional METAPHYSICS, but strictly speaking much theoretical science as well. A further point is that the amassing of instances in which a particular event has been verified will not ensure that a universal proposition stating that all such events will occur is established as true. Successful checking of this kind at best makes it more likely that the universal is true. This general difficulty, sometimes called the problem of INDUCTION, cannot be solved. If we do not perceive universal characteristics in the particular instance, no multiplication of instances will establish the universal.

Vico, Giambattista (1668–1744), Italian philosopher, developed an original theory of history completely at odds with the ENLIGHTENMENT then in vogue in France, England and Germany. In *Scienza Nuova (The New Science)*, finally revised in 1744, he rejected the Cartesian approach to history via clear and distinct IDEAS. His own principle he stated as '*verum factum*', that is, truth is what is done, and the converse. Thus, CERTAINTY attaches to what we ourselves have made. It is because we have constructed mathematical systems that MATHEMATICS are certain. It is to the extent that we intervene by experiment that we are certain of physical facts. Moreover, what human beings construct (or perhaps contrive) above all is their own history: hence the primacy of historical knowledge and insight. To understand history, we must grasp how our language has grown from its roots in the mythological past. In this way we can come to see the total pattern of historical development at any given stage. These views have greatly influenced historians and social theorists ever since.

Vienna Circle, *n.* a group of thinkers who gathered round M. SCHLICK from the early 1920s onwards. They shared a science-based outlook in the spirit of E. MACH and were hostile to old-style METAPHYSICS (even if their own assumptions had metaphysical features). Their general doctrine is called LOGICAL POSITIVISM. As a group they ceased to function when the members were scattered abroad under the impact of the Nazi regime after 1938. Schlick himself was murdered by a student in 1936.

volition, *n.* mind–body dualists (see DUALISM) explain a voluntary movement as a bodily MOTION caused by an ACTION of the mind called a 'volition' or 'act of will'. DESCARTES, for example, says that the mind 'simply by willing, makes the small gland to which it is closely united move in the way requisite for producing the effect aimed at in the volition' (*Passions of the Soul*, 41). The 'effect aimed at in the volition' is a bodily motion (say of the left or right hand).

Does a volition have a character of its own, independent of the 'effect aimed at'? If it has, then we find out at what a certain volition must have been 'aimed' from the EFFECT it has, and we learn what volitions to perform to produce the effects we desire. If it has not (if its 'aim' is what characterises a volition), then the connection between a volition and its effect is internal. On this interpretation, prior to EXPERIENCE of certain volitions regularly being followed by certain bodily motions we can tell, simply from the character of the volition, what effect it should have. We can 'see' the connection, instead of merely having to accept it as a brute fact.

The difference between the two interpretations is significant for empiricists, who seek to identify some EXPERIENCE as the source of each of their IDEAS. One such idea is that of power, or necessary connection between CAUSE and effect. An empiricist who thinks of an act of will as having an internal connection with a bodily movement is likely to identify the alleged experience of causing a bodily motion by willing it as the source of his idea of power. Only in such an experience does it seem to him that he has an inside view of power being effective. As John LOCKE expressed it, 'the idea of the beginning of motion we have only from reflection on what passes in ourselves, where we find by experience, that, barely by willing it, barely by a thought of the mind, we can move the parts of our bodies which were before at rest' (*Essay*, II xxi 4).

If all knowledge of causal connections is based on the experience of constant conjunctions of events, then the connection between a volition and a bodily motion must seem either not to be causal, or to be as external as any other causal connection. It was on these lines that David HUME criticised Locke: 'So far from perceiving the connection betwixt an act of volition, and a motion of the body, 'tis allowed that no effect is more inexplicable from the powers and essence of thought and matter' (*Treatise*, I iii 14, appendix insertion).

Some see the difference between a voluntary movement and an involuntary one (such as a reflex) simply in that we can properly ask about the former some questions that do not arise about the latter. We can ask, of the person who performed a voluntary movement, why he did it, expecting an answer in terms of his reasons. One who holds this view will regard the volition theory as a dualist abberration. See FREEWILL AND DETERMINISM.

Voltaire, (François Marie Arouet) (1694–1778), French philosopher and man of letters, was one of the *philosophes* and a typical ENLIGHTENMENT figure. Educated by Jesuits, he became virulently anti-clerical and favoured the religious tolerance central to the Enlightenment as a whole. This attitude was strongly influenced by his exile in England

(1726–1729), where he absorbed the views of LOCKE and NEWTON, as appears in his *Lettres philosophiques sur les Anglais* (1733). In it he satirised conditions in France and had once more to flee. From 1750 to 1753 he was at the court of Frederick II (the Great) of Prussia in Berlin, and in 1755 settled in Geneva, returning to his native Paris only shortly before he died. In 1759 he published the satirical tale *Candide*, perhaps the best known of his many works. This is a fierce demolition of philosophical optimism of the kind familiar from LEIBNIZ (who thought that ours was the best of possible worlds). The earthquake that had destroyed Lisbon in 1755 led him to conclude that there can be no all-powerful and all-benevolent deity. His views of religion and of ETHICS were based on principles of natural law, and while he had been influenced by English DEISM, he rejected all dogmatic religion. His defence of the wrongly executed Calas for alleged impiety (1762) marks open hostility towards the Catholic establishment in France *('écrasez l'infâme!')*. He had contributed many entries to the *Encyclopédie*, and when this was officially suppressed, he put the censors to merciless ridicule. It is largely through his efforts that a spirit of toleration became widespread in Western Europe, even if it suffered great setbacks in our own time.

W

Watson, J. B. (1878–1958), the first self-styled psychological behaviourist. He held that man's behaviour should be explained in terms of 'stimulus' and 'response'. The psychologist can himself provide the stimulus: he is in the business not only of predicting, but also of controlling, human activity. See BEHAVIOURISM.

Whitehead, Alfred North (1861–1947), English mathematician and philosopher, studied MATHEMATICS at Trinity College, Cambridge, where he later taught, and collaborated with Bertrand RUSSELL on *Principia Mathematica* (1910–13). From 1910–14 he taught at Imperial College, London, and in 1924 became professor of philosophy at Harvard. His early interest in mathematical form (*Treatise on Universal Algebra*, 1903; *Mathematical Concepts of the Material World*, 1905) later gave way to a philosophy of nature that was to cover the total findings of modern science. Characteristic of his position is that he departs from the traditional approach in terms of simple OBJECTS with their various courses, and rather sees everything as events that flow into each other, a view directly influenced by modern field theories of physics and by the notion of energy flow in electrodynamics (in some ways, this reminds one of HERACLITUS). Thus he describes PERCEPTION not in terms of sense-data, but recognises the fact that we take in whole situations in a way that is not very precise at the fringes: we notice that something is happening. These views were elaborated into a system of first philosophy, notably in *Science and the Modern World*, 1926, *Process and Reality*, 1929, and *Adventures of Ideas*, 1933. His interests were unusually wide and extended to education and natural theology as an underpinning of our general sense of value. His philosophy has been called organicist (in contrast to the 'mechanicist' approach of Newtonian science), in that it views the world as an organic structure functioning organically.

Wittgenstein, Ludwig (1889–1951), an Austrian who spent much of his life in England, being Professor of Philosophy at Cambridge from 1939 to 1947. He wrote two very influential philosophical classics, the second being a rejection of the first. The first was the *Tractatus Logico-Philosophicus* (London, 1922) ('the *Tractatus*'). The second, published posthumously, was the *Philosophical Investigations* (Oxford, 1953) ('the *Investigations*'). Between the two there was a period in which he deserted philosophy, being 'of the opinion that the problems have in essentials been finally solved' (*Tractatus*, p. 29).

In both his earlier and his later philosophy Wittgenstein was concerned with problems of language, thought and reality. In a notebook used in the preparation of the *Tractatus* he wrote 'My whole task consists in explaining the nature of the proposition' (*Notebooks 1914–1916*, Oxford, 1961, p. 39). The first of two preliminary studies for the *Investigations* begins with the question 'What is the meaning of a word?' (*The Blue and Brown Books*, Oxford, 1958, p. 1). The later philosophy is a conscious rejection of the earlier. A key section of the *Investigations* (I 23) ends: 'It is interesting to compare the multiplicity of the tools in language and of the ways they are used, the multiplicity of kinds of word and sentence, with what logicians have said about the structure of language. (Including the author of the *Tractatus Logico-Philosophicus*.)'

Is there one way in which all words have meaning? Do the words 'hope', 'red', 'promise', 'here', 'sorry' and 'good', for example, all have MEANING in the same way? Three possible answers are (a) that the use of all of them is 'to stand as outward marks of our internal ideas' (LOCKE, *Essay*, II xi 9), (b) that they are all used in sentences to state what is the case, (c) that they are used in a variety of ways, even the same word being used in different ways in different utterances; for example, 'I *hope* you'll come' is used to urge someone to come, whereas 'I *hoped* you'd come' is used to report the speaker's past state of mind. Of these three answers the third comes closest to that given by Wittgenstein in the *Investigations*. The second answer comes closest to that given in the *Tractatus*, and rejected in the *Investigations*. It is a version of 'the idea that language always functions in one way, always serves the same purpose' (*Investigations*, I 304). However, this understates the radical difference between the two. The *Tractatus* embodies the metaphysical doctrine that besides the reality that justifies us in saying something there is a reality that justifies the very language in which we say it. Wittgenstein nowhere in the *Tractatus* implies that the conformity of language and reality is to be explained causally. Unlike Russell, whose version of logical ATOMISM is in the tradition of HUME and MILL, Wittgenstein has no empiricist theory of meaning. He thought that for a PROPOSITION to say something it must be 'a picture of reality' (*Tractatus* 4.01). Were it not a picture then a man would not be able to understand a proposition he had not previously encountered. Regardless of its truth or falsity, a proposition is a picture of reality; it has, and shows, the same logical FORM as that reality. That, for the early Wittgenstein, is what has to be accepted, the given, which he rejects in the *Investigations*, where he says that 'what has to be accepted, the given, is—so one could say—*forms of life*' (II xi p. 226).

The *Tractatus* distinguishes between the propositions of our natural language, which need to be analyzed for us to realise that they are pictures of reality, and 'elementary' propositions, the ones into which they are analysed, the analysis being a matter of showing the former to be 'truth-functions' of the latter. The elements of an elementary proposition are names, the things named by them being what they mean, simple objects which 'make up the substance of the world' (*Tractatus* 2.021), substance being 'what exists independently of what is the case' (2.024); substance is 'the fixed, the existent', as opposed to the configuration of simple objects, which is 'the changing, the variable' (2.0271). There is a limit to what can be said. The form of representation of reality that is common to all pictures of reality shows itself in them, but what is shown cannot be said. As he puts it in the *Notebooks*, 'What can be said can only be said by means of a proposition, and so nothing that is necessary for the understanding of *all* propositions can be said' (*Notebooks*, p. 25). The *Tractatus* ends with the remark 'Whereof one cannot speak, thereof one must be silent' (7).

Wittgenstein gives no examples of analysis into elementary propositions, and no examples of 'simple objects'. His reason for assuming them is a corollary of the picture theory: propositions, being pictures, must have a sense that is definite. What is pictured cannot be indefinite. 'The demand for a simple thing *is* the demand for definiteness of sense' (*Notebooks*, p. 63, cf. *Tractatus* 3.23). In the *Investigations* he rejects the notion that there cannot be sense without definiteness of sense (I 91–115 esp. 99), and with it the metaphysical realism of the *Tractatus*.

It is their 'performing their office' that gives words and sentences their 'life', distinguishing them from the senseless utterances of a parrot. Wittgenstein introduces the concept of a 'LANGUAGE-GAME' to stress that the speaking of language is part of life's activities (*Investigations* I 23), and 'as much a part of our natural history as walking, eating, drinking, playing' (I 25); just as there are any number of games so there are any number of uses of signs, and just as games do not have to have anything in common properly to be called 'games' (I 67) so the uses of signs do not have to have anything in common; just as there are rules of games so there are rules of language (I 31ff). A language with no rules, no possibility of saying that a person is using an expression correctly or incorrectly, a PRIVATE LANGUAGE, would be no language at all. People agree in the language they use, just as they agree in their forms of life. The agreement between people is the result of their having had the same training (I 206), whereby they mastered the system of language within which the sign has life. People with a different natural history, a different training, would have different concepts. By a 'form of life' Wittgenstein does not mean anything very esoteric.

Wittgenstein's later philosophy has implications for the treatment of many of the traditional problems of philosophy, particularly those in the philosophy of MIND that have their source in DESCARTES'S mind–body DUALISM and LOCKE'S empiricist doctrine that words signify ideas, and ideas come from SENSATION or REFLECTION (introspection). Given dualism and empiricism it seems that words like 'hope', 'pain' and 'understand' must have meaning either by signifying private states or processes, or by signifying kinds of behaviour. When the OTHER MINDS PROBLEM is raised, the choice seems to be between SCEPTICISM, an implausible argument from analogy, and a counter-intuitive BE-HAVIOURISM. Wittgenstein tackles the problem at its source. In response to the question 'How does a human being learn the meaning of the word "pain"?', he writes: 'Here is one possibility: words are connected with the primitive, the natural, expressions of the sensation and used in their place. A child has hurt himself and he cries; and then adults talk to him and teach him exclamations and, later, sentences. They teach the child new pain-behaviour' (*Investigations*, I 244). Given this account of how a human being learns the meaning of the word 'pain' there is no more an 'Other Minds' problem than there is a philosophical problem about people having a form of life that involves crying when they are hurt and responding as they do to others who cry. A pain may be said to be in a person's mind, but 'the concept of pain is characterized by its particular function in our life' (*Zettel*, Oxford, 1967, 532). See AUSTIN, J. L., AVOWAL, CONCEPT, CRITERION, DEFINITION, PSYCHOANALYSIS, SOLIPSISM, THINKING, UNIVERSALS.

X

Xenophanes, (*c.*570–*c.*475 BC), a poet-philosopher born in the Ionian city of Colophon, a few miles north-west of Ephesus, spent much of his long life in Sicily at Zancle (now Messina) and Catania. He was critical of THALES and PYTHAGORAS, ridiculing the latter's doctrine of the transmigration of souls with a poem in which Pythagoras said to a man beating a dog, 'Stop, do not beat him; it is the soul of a friend, I recognize his voice'. In his turn he was one of those about whom HERACLITUS remarked, 'Much learning does not teach insight'; and ARISTOTLE (*Metaphysics* 986 b 26) described him as 'a little too naive'. Some say that he founded the Eleatic School of Philosophy: in fact he influenced its true founder, PARMENIDES.

Xenophanes's most notable contributions to philosophy concern GOD, and KNOWLEDGE. About God, he said that he is one (as opposed to the many gods of Greek mythology), that he is in no way like mortals either in body or in mind (again, unlike the gods of mythology), and that 'he remains in the same place, moving not at all, but without toil shapes all things by the thought of his mind'.

Xenophanes distinguished between knowledge and opinion, saying that even if a man should fully succeed in saying what is true he could not be certain; it would only be opinion, not knowledge. The distinction between opinion and knowledge, APPEARANCE and REALITY, was implicit in the speculations of the Milesian philosophers about the first principle and ELEMENT of things, but Xenophanes made it explicit, and in so doing prepared the way for Parmenides and the Eleatic School. See MILESIAN SCHOOL.

Z

Zeno of Elea, (*fl.* *c.*464 BC), pupil of PARMENIDES who sought to defend Parmenides's view that what exists must be one and motionless, and what appears to our senses is illusory. He attacked the common sense view that there are many things some of which move, by trying to show that common sense is wrong. In Plato's dialogue *Parmenides* (128 d), Zeno, on a visit to Athens with Parmenides, tells Socrates that his book is a defence of Parmenides's argument against its detractors, in which Zeno 'pays them back in the same coin with something to spare' by arguing that 'their own supposition that there is a plurality leads to even more absurd consequences than the [Parmenidean] hypothesis of the one'.

Zeno's arguments are reported by ARISTOTLE and involve the CONCEPT of infinity. The best known are on bisection and on Achilles and the tortoise. The bisection argument 'asserts that there is no motion because that which moves must arrive at the half-way stage before it arrives at the goal' (Aristotle, *Physics* 239 b 11–13). Before going *any* distance one must first go half of it (and half of that, and so on). So one can never start.

Aristotle objects that Zeno confuses 'two senses in which length and time and generally anything continuous are called "infinite"' (*Physics* 233 a 21–31). The term 'infinite' may mean 'quantitatively infinite', or 'infinite in respect of divisibility'. Paradoxes arise if we ignore this difference as, for example, in the statement that the *infinitely* many parts into which a finite length can be successively divided must add up to an *infinite* length. In Zeno's arguments about MOTION, time complicates the solution: we must relate the divisible only to the divisible, or the quantitative only to the quantitative. Doing one thing before or after another belongs to the quantitative (in time), length being bisectable belongs to the divisible (in space). The bisection argument relates the quantitative in time to the divisible in space.

The Achilles argument (Aristotle, *Physics* 239 b 15–18) involves the same ambiguity, but is complicated still further. Fleet-footed Achilles and a slow tortoise run a race. The tortoise is given a start, and we expect that Achilles will quickly overtake it. However, on reaching the tortoise's starting point Achilles finds that the tortoise has moved and thus gained a new start; the same situation as before, and so on indefinitely. See ELEATICISM.

Zeno the Stoic, (*c*.330–*c*.260 BC), born at Citium in Cyprus, was the founder of STOICISM, so called after the painted colonnade *(stoa)* in Athens, where he taught. He had studied in the ACADEMY and under the Cynic philosopher Crates (see CYNICS). Only fragments of his works survive, but he seems to have laid down the general principles later followed by the Stoic school.